When Peace Is Not Enough

When Peace Is Not Enough

How the Israeli Peace Camp Thinks about
Religion, Nationalism, and Justice

ATALIA OMER

The University of Chicago Press
Chicago and London

Atalia Omer is assistant professor of religion, conflict, and peace studies at the Kroc Institute for International Peace Studies and the Department of Sociology at the University of Notre Dame. She is also a faculty fellow at the Notre Dame Center of Religion and Society.

The University of Chicago Press, Chicago 60637
The University of Chicago Press, Ltd., London
© 2013 by The University of Chicago
All rights reserved. Published 2013.
Printed in the United States of America

22 21 20 19 18 17 16 15 14 13   1 2 3 4 5

ISBN-13: 978-0-226-00807-3 (cloth)
ISBN-13: 978-0-226-00810-3 (paper)
ISBN-13: 978-0-226-00824-0 (e-book)

Library of Congress Cataloging-in-Publication Data

Omer, Atalia, author.
  When peace is not enough : how the Israeli peace camp thinks about religion, nationalism, and justice / Atalia Omer.
      pages cm
  Includes bibliographical references and index.
ISBN 978-0-226-00807-3 (cloth : alkaline paper) — ISBN 978-0-226-00810-3 (paperback : alkaline paper) — ISBN 978-0-226-00824-0 (e-book)   1. Arab-Israeli conflict—1993—Peace. 2. Peace movements—Israel. 3. Arab-Israeli conflict—Social aspects. 4. Group identity—Israel.   I. Title.
  DS119.76.O46   2013
  956.05'4—dc23
                                                          2012044799

♾ This paper meets the requirements of ANSI/NISO Z39.48-1992 (Permanence of Paper).

For

Dan Omer

(1940–84)

and

Oscar Mareni (Herlinger)

(1906–2011)

CONTENTS

ACKNOWLEDGMENTS

My late father, a journalist, a poet, and a social critic, lived a short and brave life on the radical margins of Israeli society. I am profoundly indebted to him for his legacy. This book is grounded in my memories of his struggle against religious and political coercion, against the occupation of Palestinian territories, and for social justice and equality.

As much as my father was a principled critic of Israel's ethos, my late grandfather was a stone in its foundation—Zionist Congress delegate, celebrated veteran of Britain's Jewish Brigade during World War II, resistance fighter against the British Mandate in Palestine, and the first post–Israeli independence treasurer of the municipality of Jerusalem. My earliest memories are of their frequently fierce opposition to one another, unyielding, but loyal. I carry this dual legacy with me today; out of a deep sense of gratitude and love I grapple with it across the pages of this book.

I have been involved with the Israeli peace movement my entire life, and I remain committed to the overarching vision of the movement. Yet it is with a desire to assess and transform the premises of peace activism in Israel that I write, realizing potential implications of this case for questions of peace and justice in other zones of conflict. Only after I completed my military service and moved away from Israel to pursue my higher education in the United States did I begin to systematically question what had consistently puzzled me earlier: What is the meaning of a Jewish national identity? How might it be reconciled with secularity? How might rethinking Jewish-Israeli nationality relate to the "peace process" with the Palestinians? This line of questioning led me to explore the case of Israel with the intention to think more acutely about religion, nationalism, and the transformation of conflicts largely defined by identity claims. It has been an odyssey that required developing fluency in diverse theoretical and disciplinary terrains. I am deeply grateful to the many mentors and intellectual guides I had along the way. I spent the early years of my training in Islamic and Near Eastern Studies at the University of California, Santa Barbara. There I benefited especially from the guidance of Richard Hecht, who has remained a mentor and a friend throughout my academic development. I am grateful to other teachers who shaped my thinking during my Santa Barbara years, including Manoutchehr Eskandari, Stephen Humphreys, Juan Campo, and Barbara Holdrege.

As a graduate student at Harvard University, I was fortunate to cross paths with brilliant conversation partners, teachers, and mentors. I am particularly thankful for the conversations and classes I had with Harvey Cox, Robert Orsi, Asher Biemann, Lawrence Sullivan, Herbert Kelman, Peter Gordon, David Carrasco, Diana Eck, Luis Girón Negrón, and Francis Fiorenza. At Harvard I also encountered Professor David Little. Little's work on religion, ethnoreligious national conflict, and peace became pivotal for this book. Most important, Little has been an interlocutor, a mentor, a colleague whose intellectual rigor, generosity, and persistence pushed me beyond what I imagined at the time. He insisted on a kind of conceptual clarity that obliged me to reach conclusions I was not able to anticipate when I began my research. It was during one of our long conversations that Little's insistence upon a constructive approach to religion, conflict, and peace led me to shift from a focus on the "obvious" to the "nonobvious." The obstacle for reframing the discussion of justice in Israel/Palestine was not only the standard conception of "religious radicalism" but also the model of which I understood myself to be an example—a peace-seeking Israeli who operated with certain discursive presuppositions (although Little would refuse to use the concept of "discourse"). This insight grounds this book. Professor Little continues to be a mentor and a friend. He read and reread the manuscript multiple times and offered invaluable feedback. I am also thankful to Ronald Thiemann (of blessed memory) and Stanley Hofmann at Harvard and Yehouda Shenhav at Tel Aviv University, Israel. I am indebted to my colleagues at the Kroc Institute for International Peace Studies at the University of Notre Dame who so generously read through my manuscript and offered critiques and suggestions, including John Paul Lederach, Daniel Philpott, and R. Scott Appleby. Appleby, especially, mentored me through the process of revising and editing the book manuscript. I am equally grateful for Scott's capacious vision for what peace studies can (and should) be. Christian Smith, my colleague in the Department of Sociology at Notre Dame, also provided incisive feedback on the manuscript as well as guidance and support in the publication process.

I received major institutional and other support along the way. I am thankful for the generous fellowships from Harvard's Center for the Study of World Religions, the Weatherhead Center for International Affairs at Harvard University, and the Charlotte W. Newcombe Doctoral Dissertation Fellowship. I am also thankful to the Notre Dame Institute for Advanced Studies where, as a fellow in the fall of 2011, I put the finishing touches on the book. I also had the opportunity to present various portions of this book to challenging and energizing audiences. I especially want to thank John Kelsay, Martin Kavka, Aline Kalbian, and Sumner B. Twiss for inviting me to present segments of this manuscript to the Religion, Ethics, and Philosophy Colloquium at Florida State University, and to Notre Dame's Center for the Study of Religion and Society for providing another stimulating platform from which to present my work on several occasions. Far from least, the Kroc Institute for International Peace Studies itself has afforded support by providing a context of remarkable collegiality and interdisciplinarity and by embodying the vision of peace and justice shared by Joan B. Kroc and Father Theodore Hesburgh.

I owe gratitude to a whole cast of characters for the friendship and support without which writing this book would have been an endeavor much more solitary and much less edifying. Intellectual friends who have become colleagues and co-conspirators, and fellow travelers who have become family: Yael Kravitz, Myriam Arazi-Guy, Sarah-lé and Shabtai Gershon (Z"l), Aviva and Zelig Segal, Deena Lipkies, Elena Jimenez, Paula Gray, Carla and Martine Singer, Eva and Yoel Haller, Ceila and Yoseph Marcus (Z"l), Alyson Dickson, Z Kermani, Charlotte Harrison and Mark Schuster (of blessed memory), Ann McClenahan, Andy Friedman, Patrick Charbonneau, Erez Naaman, Vikram Khurana and Chee Yeun Chung, David Kim, Christian Rice, Priscilla Little, Katherine Marshall, Mary Ellen O'Connell, Gayle and David Hachen, Peter Chulak, Asher Kaufman, Slavica Jakelić, and Barbara Lockwood. I am grateful to my editors, Douglas Mitchell and Tim McGovern, and to Emily Gravett for editorial support. I am also grateful for the challenging feedback from the anonymous reviewers.

Most important, I owe thanks to my mother, Nurit Manne Adizes, who has been an endless source of support and strength. I am also grateful for the encouragement and understanding from my stepfather, Ichak Adizes, my siblings Nimi and Cnaan Omer and Topaz, Shoham, and Sasa Adizes, and my parents- and grandparents-in-law Kathy and Lance Springs and

Alois and Jim Lewis. I conclude the list with thanks to Jason Springs—my partner, colleague, and soul mate—for countless conversations that enriched and fine-tuned the arguments that unfold in this book, and to our little babies born during the writing: Yehonathan Daniele and Pnei'el Alois Omer-Springs, the loves of my life.

University of Notre Dame
December 15, 2012

Earlier versions of chapters 1, 2, and 3 appeared in three distinct journal articles. I explore some conceptual limits of the Israeli peace camp in "Religion versus Peace: A False Dichotomy," *Studies in Ethnicity and Nationalism* 7, no. 3 (December 2007): 109–31. An earlier articulation of my theoretical approach appears as "The Hermeneutics of Citizenship as a Peacebuilding Process: A Multiperspectival Approach to Justice," *Journal of Political Theology* 11, no. 5 (October 2010): 650–73, and as "Can a Critic Be a Caretaker Too? Religion, Conflict, and Conflict Transformation," *Journal of the American Academy of Religion* 79, no. 2 (June 2011): 459–96.

Memories

I grew up in Jerusalem as a second-generation Jewish Israeli. My paternal grandfather came to Palestine in the early phases of the Nazi rise to power. His decision to uproot from Austria was ideologically motivated and a source of dismay to his German-assimilated family. With the exception of his young nephew, who was put on the *Kindertransport* and sent to Sweden, and a brother who fought with the British army, all of my grandfather's close relatives vanished in gas chambers and crowded ghettoes during World War II. He survived and established his new life in Palestine and later in the Israeli Jewish state. My grandmother's family had also come to Palestine before the war. Propelled by the burning desire to educate a new Hebrew generation in Zion, her relatives were among the founders of the first Hebrew gymnasium in Palestine. My late father—a writer, journalist, and cultural critic—was raised, like many of his generation, in a home haunted by the ghosts of those who had died in the Holocaust. This was a home that during the daily *schlafstunde* was filled with the music of Mozart, Beethoven, and occasionally even Wagner. This was a home that saw the Zionist project as a remedy to (the perceived inevitability of) reoccurring catastrophe. Zionism promised the possibility of a safe haven and was redemptive in the sense that it embodied the self-making of a new Jew or Hebrew who was normal, heroic, and finally "at home," rather than sickly, passive, and dislocated. It was also a home that exemplified a fundamental yet (increasingly) ambiguous break between Judaism and Zionism, on the one hand, and between Israel and the diaspora, on the other. My grandmother's central childhood memory was the harassment she endured in the Polish city of Lódz as a child who attended Hebrew kindergarten. The harassment came from Orthodox Jews who viewed Zionism as a profound violation of the religious injunction against human-initiated return to the land of Zion and who resisted Zionist-Hebraic initiatives that relocated Hebrew into the realm of the mundane. My grandfather eagerly followed the general trend of the early prestate years and shed his German name, embracing a Hebraic one.

By the time I was born, the Holocaust ethos had intensified and become central to processes of socialization within the Israeli state as well as, more broadly, the Jewish diasporas. I participated in the almost mandatory trip to Poland, visited ghettoes and death camps, and carried the Israeli flag proudly across the Polish streets. Shortly after my trip, I was drafted into compulsory service in the Israeli military (the IDF) as were the other kids in my cohort. We were socialized in a certain way that overlooked the tragic connections between the Holocaust and the displacement of the Palestinians. Likewise, challenging the legitimacy of the Zionist enterprise as the vessel of redemption for all Jews was taboo; the myth allowed one to question only its territorially minimalist or maximalist executions. But from my childhood to my time in the IDF, I had probed what it might mean to be Jewish, Israeli, and a secularist at the same time. Why was every soldier in the IDF given a copy of the Tanakh upon completion of basic training? What precisely was the Jewish meaning of the Israeli state, considering how many people in my milieu viewed themselves as simultaneously atheist and Jewish? What might be the implications of deeply debating these questions?

I was also the daughter of a critic of Israeli culture and religious coercion in the Jewish nation-state. My father, who died too young at the age of forty-four, publicly questioned the legitimacy of the occupation of the 1967 territories even before the euphoric celebrations were over in June of that year. His position, unpopular at the time, pushed him to the margins of Israeli society. Years later, I am proud of his consistently prophetic voice that emerged out of a profound moral outrage. My intellectual exploration of the topic of ethnoreligious nationalism, and my focus on the relevance of perceptions of citizenship and belonging to issues of peace and justice, are grounded in my recognition that the precise Jewish significance of the Israeli state still needs to be debated. Even a secularized interpretation of Judaism as mere "ethnicity" or "nationality" is not fixed or self-evident. But these concerns are also grounded in my father's outrage and foresight concerning the corrupting nature of military occupation.

This book explores the conceptual blinders of the Israeli peace camp. By focusing on the perceptions of marginalized groups within the Israeli and Jewish contexts, I highlight how hybrid identities may provide creative resources for peacebuilding, especially in ethnoreligious national conflicts where political agendas are informed by particularistic conceptions of identity. The study highlights three such groups: the Mizrahim or "Arab Jews" (Israeli Jews who trace their ancestry to Arab and/or Islamic countries of origin), Palestinian Israelis (Palestinians who remained within the 1948 borders), and non-Israeli Jewish thinkers and activists from various diasporas whose voices have also been marginalized by the dominant discourse of Zionism. This dominant discourse has tended to privilege Ashkenazi, or European, Jewish identity and history. The ethos of Zionism has focused on the plight of European Jews while silencing Mizrahi histories from the Middle East and North Africa. This discourse has also silenced diasporic Jewish communities by assuming that Israel represents Jews everywhere and by glossing over millennia of Jewish learning and flourishing outside the biblical landscape. Likewise, the privileging of Ashkenazi conceptions of identity has enabled the cultivation of a self-perception of Israel as a part of the "West" despite its geographical location in the "East." It has rendered the hyphenated identities of "Arab Jews" and "Palestinian Israelis" seemingly oxymoronic. Similarly, the "diasporic Jew" is construed as somewhat inauthentic since authenticity is tied to physical rootedness in the land. My focus on these hybrid identities illuminates how a radical critique exposes the conceptual and ideological constraints of the Israeli peace camp. It also gestures toward why undertaking a shift from critique to a constructive reframing of questions of identity is pivotal for processes of peacebuilding and radical change. This reframing is, in turn, highly hermeneutical, deeply embedded in symbolic vocabularies and cultural and religious imaginations.

Identity, Conflict, and Peace

In ethnonational conflicts, questions of peace and justice entail negotiations not only over resources, territory, and power but also over identity, symbols, and memory. In his definitive study of the Sudan, Francis Deng interprets the conflict between the north and the south as a contestation between competing conceptions of Sudanese identity. He consequently underscores the connections between religion, culture, and ethnicity and the definition of national identity. Accordingly, if the nation is defined through an exclusionary reliance on markers such as race, ethnicity, and religion, it is inherently discriminatory and thus fundamentally unjust:

> In situations where the nation or the country is defined with reference to the racial, ethnic, cultural, or religious identity of a dominant group, whether a majority or a ruling minority . . . these factors do become bases for discrimination. And although constitutional provisions and other legal instruments

might prohibit discrimination, as long as the framework is defined in terms that exclude, subordinate, or marginalize those who do not fit the definition of the nation, discrimination becomes inherent. How the country or the nation is defined or conceived is therefore critical to the status of the citizens. The way to guarantee equality among citizens is either to exclude from the definition of the national framework those factors of identity that provide bases for discrimination or to define identity in terms that are inclusive.[1]

This quotation suggests that in order to rectify a discriminatory framework, the "nation" ought to be redefined in inclusionary terms. Similarly, in his discussion of the civil war in Sri Lanka (1983–2009) between Sinhala and Tamil conceptions of nationalism, Rohan Edrisinha highlights constitutionalism as a framework for conflict management and transformation: "the creation of a plural democracy in which the various communities can live with dignity and justice must depend on a supreme constitution which upholds values and principles and acts as a bulwark against majoritarianism."[2]

In both the Sudan and Sri Lanka, the conflict is defined as a "civil war," a configuration that implies (but by no means necessitates) unifying and integrative rather than secessionist or separationist impulses (the Sudanese civil war, in fact, led to the creation of an independent South Sudan). In view of that, both Deng and Edrisinha, in their respective contexts, articulate justice by reframing or redefining the parameters of the nation. In contrast, the case of Israel/Palestine is perceived by participants and observers alike as a conflict between two distinct nationalisms rather than two competing visions of the same nation. As a result, the separationist impulse purportedly dominates as the most appropriate logic of peacemaking.

Indeed, the Israeli historian Ilan Pappé has suggested that despite pretenses to the contrary, Israeli peace efforts, most notably in the signing of the Oslo Accords[3] and its aftermath, have been beholden to what Israeli political geographer Oren Yiftachel referred to as the "ethnocratic logic of Israeli infrastructures."[4] Accordingly, the principles for the allocation of rights and resources are based on ethnic conceptions of citizenship (*jus sanguinis*) rather than territorial definitions (*jus soli*),[5] precipitating a system of "creeping apartheid"[6] and contributing to what the Israeli sociologist Baruch Kimmerling read as the gradual yet systematic "politicide" of the Palestinian people.[7] In this context, the motivation for peacemaking often revolves around demographic concerns. Rather than challenging it, the Oslo configuration contributed to the general reinforcement of a Zionist consensus because not once did it involve a reevaluation of the idea of a Jewish state.[8] Nor did it involve a consideration of the status of the Arab citizens of

Israel in a future realignment.[9] In the parlance of peace studies, this line of questioning that goes beyond a view of peace as the cessation of direct or explicit violence falls under the purview of *peacebuilding*. Unlike peacemaking, it is a comprehensive approach that attempts to confront and transform root causes of a conflict and also to envision peace as a process designed to tackle systemic or structural violence.[10]

In fact, in her comparative study of peace agreements in South Africa, Northern Ireland, Bosnia-Herzegovina, and Israel-Palestine, Christine Bell ranks the Oslo Accords as the least successful because they failed to address the basic questions of human rights and because they were premised on the principle of separation rather than integration. She writes:

> In both their text and their implementation the Israeli/Palestinian peace agreements demonstrate an almost complete divorce between the concept of peace and the concept of justice. The concept of peace embodied in the agreements is a concept of managed separation, whose contours are shaped by Israeli security concerns. The negotiating dynamics between the parties mean that it was always unlikely that the agreements between them would include human rights constraints on Palestinian autonomy. However, it would have been possible for the entire process to have been subject to overarching international law constraints, although imagining this is difficult, and involves reimagining the entire process and international context.[11]

Clearly, the reinforcement of the status quo in the Oslo configurations was not merely inadvertent but rather deliberate at the most or sublimated at the least. Hence, neither Deng's emphasis on how the nation is defined or perceived vis-à-vis religion, culture, and ethnicity nor Edrisinha's insistence on constitutionalism as a way of mediating individual rights and collective identities and grievances seems relevant to transforming the Palestinian-Israeli conflict. In evaluating the Israeli peace camp, this book explores the assumptions that inform the separationist impulse underlying the Zionist peace camp. A key to this effort will amount to linking peace platforms directly to questions of justice.

This undertaking involves an exposition of the boundaries of Israeli liberalism with the intention that such scrutiny might propel a constructive reevaluation of questions of peace and justice in Israel/Palestine. My argument is that while the Zionist Israeli peace camp identifies itself as "liberal" in its self-perception and self-representation, the peace platforms it advances betray a commitment to illiberal conceptions of nationhood. This underlying illiberality, however, is frequently sublimated, thereby legitimating the continuous maintenance of an axiomatic claim for Jewish hegemony within the Green Line or the 1949 armistice agreements. This is clearly illustrated by the insistence on the so-called two-state solution guiding the Oslo Accords because it entails a persistent cultivation of ethnorepublican identity and practices.

The designation "ethnorepublicanism" underscores that Israel maintains an interrelated commitment to an ethnocentric Jewish national identity and to a particularly Eurocentric and orientalist interpretation of this national identity. Hence, the lines of exclusion are drawn internally and externally, thereby discriminating against and marginalizing non-Jews and non-Ashkenazi Jews.[12] Whether it interprets the Jewishness of Israel in terms of "culture," "history," or "religion," the Zionist commitment to a Jewish nation-state means—even in its most liberal forms—an underlying institutional mechanism that facilitates the privileged position of Jewish Israelis. This commitment manifests itself especially in constraining the sphere of collective rights granted to the Palestinian citizens of Israel. Further, the normative adherence to a Eurocentric conception of Israeliness results in the systemic discrimination against the Mizrahim.

This ethnorepublican commitment has informed the interpretations of peace and justice pertaining to the Palestinian-Israeli conflict. The challenge here is not to show that those explicitly chauvinistic voices within Israeli society hinder the possibility of transforming the conflict (this is quite obvious), but rather to expose how the illiberal aspects of self-identified "liberal" voices within Israel truncate, however inadvertently, the possibilities for integrating peace and justice. This task highlights how internal questions of social justice relate to broader, external considerations of peace with the Palestinians.

The overwhelming inclination of Israeli liberalism to differentiate between the question of the occupation of Palestinian territories and the question of social justice became evident with the emergence of the so-called Tents Revolution in the summer of 2011 (and again in the summer of 2012). This social protest was spearheaded by young Israeli activists who became fed up with the rising cost of living and thus set up tents in the midst of the most lavish boulevards in Tel Aviv. This act of protest captivated a diverse slice of Israeli society who became disillusioned and frustrated with neoliberal socioeconomic policies and their predatory consequences. After decades in which political divides were marked by positions vis-à-vis territorial maximalism or minimalism (with maximalism associated with the "right" and minimalism with the "left"), the protest movement of 2011 advanced a nascent articulation of a sociopolitical "left." However, in an op-ed piece in the *New York Times*, Dimi Reider and Aziz abu Sarah were correct to notice that "there is one issue conspicuously missing from the protest: Israel's 44-year occupation of the Palestinian territories."[13] The outrageous cost of living in Tel Aviv and broad, deepening inequalities are not unrelated to decades of military occupation and disproportionate spending on militarism and settlement construction. The matter is one not only of reallocating resources but also of probing into the meanings of membership in the Israeli nation-state. Many protesters recognize the connections between neoliberalism, the settlement movement, and the infrastructure of the occupation,[14] but they do not put them on their banner in the effort to cultivate the broadest possible social consensus and maintain the momentum of the movement. However, the conceptual distinction between domestic social justice and the occupation (despite acknowledging connections) contributes to legitimizing precisely what needs to be debated and interrogated, namely, the ethnorepublican ethos and its undergirding institutional mechanisms.

Consequently, I highlight in this book the deeply flawed form of Israeli liberalism by illustrating its continuous and rather unreflective reliance on an ethnorepublican conception of nationhood. This exposition also sheds light on the conceptual tensions inherent in the liberal framework itself. Additionally, the book explores internal resources that could enable reimagining a less flawed, more inclusivist form of nationalism. These resources include the counterhegemonic experiences of Mizrahi and Palestinian Israelis and alternative Jewish ethical traditions. It is important that the reader notes that I am not proposing simply abandoning the politics of identity (a point I revisit throughout the book). It is crucial to keep in mind that my sustained critique, reframing and reimagining the available possibilities, does not relinquish liberal norms and democratic practices (human rights, rule of law, etc.). In fact, in a certain sense, these norms and practices remain indispensable. The objective, rather, is to employ critique in ways that expand upon and conceptually enrich the capacity of such norms and practices to successfully intervene in a relational and historical context of conflict so deeply entangled with and perpetuated and exacerbated by forms of structural and cultural violence. The point is not to supersede liberal norms and practices but to historicize and conceptualize their implementation as a self-correcting enterprise that is, as such, intrinsically hermeneutical and entails multidirectional and multiperspectival conception of justice and peace. This requires a symbiotic relationship between liberal norms and practices and critique. This book aims to strike a balance between the equally indispensable constructive and critical dimensions for grappling with questions of justice and peace in any context of conflict. Critique is necessary not simply to illuminate and contest Israeli liberalism but as a tool for persistently challenging the blind spots to which liberalism itself is prone. In fact, one reason the case of Israel is particularly instructive is in exemplifying the limitations of liberalism as a set of tools for the purposes of peacebuilding.

A Multidisciplinary Lens

This book contributes to a range of disciplines and fields of study. The intended audience of this work includes those who are interested in the Israeli-Palestinian conflict and the Israeli peace movement specifically, as well as readers in cultural sociology, religious studies, political science, and cultural theory more generally. I purposely venture to bridge these academic disciplines and put them in direct conversation with questions of peace, justice, and conflict transformation that have preoccupied peace studies. I demonstrate that the Israeli-Palestinian case illuminates both the contributions and the limitations of each of these disciplines in providing resources and conceptual frameworks for transformation.

The field of peace studies has focused on the analysis of conflicts and the study of the practices of peacebuilding, including human rights advocacy and specialization, humanitarian assistance, international law, peacekeeping efforts, NGO management, negotiation and mediation efforts, and conflict analysis. I contend that these need to be further enriched by conversations with the field of normative political theory. Normative political theory, and especially the literature that explores questions of multiculturalism, has focused on ethnocultural justice. Therefore, political theory, in its preoccupation with justice, identity, and mediation among competing conceptions of the good within the political framework, needs to become an interlocutor with peace studies. Likewise, religious studies, and the critical analytic tools that recent challenges to a simplistic secularism paradigm have brought to the fore, could bring nuance to the enduring reliance of peace studies on rigid analytic distinctions between identity indices such as ethnicity, nationality, culture, and religion. Additionally, the focus of cultural theory on the relationship between power and conceptions of identity could help peace studies with the analysis and transformation of structural and direct manifestations of violence.

Bridging cultural theory, religious studies, and peace studies would also embolden existing works and approaches already subsumed under the subgenre of "religious peacebuilding." Whereas this subgenre has studied the potential contribution religion could make to conflict transformation, it has not sufficiently theorized how religion could contribute to reframing and reimagining national narratives or how, even in their secular varieties, these narratives draw on selective interpretations of antecedent ethnic, cultural, and religious resources.[15]

At the heart of my discussion is the assumption that how people understand their identity is open to interpretation and challenges from within and without the boundaries of the community. In fact, it is precisely those boundaries that are subject to investigation and redescription in light of the demands of peace and justice (demands that are likewise open to scrutiny and contestation). In this regard, the book resonates with and contributes to the study of boundaries (and a related focus on borders) in cultural sociology.[16]

Sociologists Michèle Lamont and Virág Molnár's distinction between symbolic and social boundaries is especially helpful to the kind of analyses I undertake in this book. These authors view "symbolic boundaries" as constituting the "conceptual distinctions made by social actors to categorize objects, people, practices, and even time and space." In contrast, "social boundaries," the authors continue, "are objectified forms of social differences manifested in unequal access to and unequal distribution of resources (material and nonmaterial) and social opportunities."[17]

Significantly, "symbolic boundaries" are located on "the intersubjective level," whereas "social boundaries" manifest in actual patterns of social interactions and group classifications.[18] Lamont and Molnár underscore the importance of analyzing the relationship between symbolic and social boundaries, arguing that it is only when symbolic boundaries are widely accepted that they can inform the actual patterns of social interactions. Hence, they call for further development in the study of how the *content* of symbolic boundaries informs the construction and reproduction of social boundaries.[19]

But simply because symbolic boundaries are accepted does not mean they are just and/or justifiable, although they may appear to be so through a variety of social and cultural mechanisms. My study of the Israeli peace camp and its conceptual blinders (born out of a sustained commitment to an ethnorepublican conception of citizenship) illuminates what French sociologist Pierre Bourdieu meant by "symbolic violence."[20] This concept denotes that social structures are often unself-consciously violent in that they enable, normalize, and inhabit discriminatory and dominating practices.[21]

"Symbolic violence" is usually not even acknowledged by those captivated within it as constituting "violence." Instead, it remains unnoticed, misrecognized, and inculcated in the practices of daily life: through what Bourdieu terms *habitus*, or internalized cultural dispositions, the effects of symbolic violence translate into social (class) boundaries.[22] The analysis of the Israeli peace camp I offer in this work exposes how the symbolic violence inherent in the ethnorepublican ideological orientation of Israel delimits the possibilities of imagining justice vis-à-vis the Palestinians. I also suggest resources for challenging and deconstructing symbolic forms of violence that inform and naturalize social boundaries, making them seem "natural" and "legitimate." The process of denaturalizing and reimagining such boundaries is highly interpretive and therefore may necessitate calling upon marginalized and eclipsed historical, cultural, and religious resources, as well as upon those groups and individuals that occupy spaces of hybridity, which challenge rigid conceptions of social boundaries as fixed and impermeable.

This focus on change that calls upon the retrieval, appropriation, and empowerment of marginalized perspectives suggests the link between symbolic and social boundaries. This line of research necessitates an exploration of the substantive meanings of symbolic boundaries and how they emerged into a position of acceptability and legitimacy, in addition to a recognition of symbolic boundaries as spaces that can challenge the seeming rigidity and permanence of social (national) boundaries. Actual physical border zones have long been recognized as spaces of "hybridity," "liminality," and "creolization."[23] My study will show how hybrid identities within and without Israel—those identities that challenge the bifurcated construal of "Arab vs. Jew" and "Palestinian vs. Israeli," along with those (primarily diasporic) voices that challenge the conflation of "Israeli" and "Jew"—could potentially confront the symbolic boundaries that constrict the visions of justice put forward by the Israeli peace camp.

The bridging of otherwise disparate disciplinary conversations in peace studies, religious studies, cultural and political theory, and cultural sociology, therefore, enables a descriptively thick analysis of conflict that includes a substantive exposition of symbolic (or in the terminology of peace studies, "structural" and "cultural") violence as well as a constructive imagining and reimagining of social and political boundaries. This constructive reframing of boundaries is normatively oriented and challenged by a multiperspectival approach to justice, one that calls upon and centralizes the voices of oppressed and marginalized groups as resources for deconstructing and reconstructing social and symbolic boundaries.[24] This book pushes beyond an analysis of symbolic violence to an interpretive or reinterpretive engagement with the seemingly axiomatic hold of certain conceptions of identity, which subsequently informs conceptions of peace and justice as they pertain to the Israeli-Palestinian conflict.

Plan of the Book

This book is divided into three sections. Each section addresses central theoretical points as well as specific sectors of the peace movement. The first section explicates the theoretical framework and introduces a history of the Zionist peace movement. In chapter 1, I outline how the liberal self-perception of the secular Israeli left restricts discussions of peace and justice to the interrelated formulas of "land for peace" and "the two-state solution." This chapter focuses on the Peace Now (PN) movement because it has come to represent most widely the Israeli secularist consensus on peacemaking. Despite its energetic, colorful, and (formerly) wide appeal, PN, I argue, traveled across a rather limited ideological landscape. It affirmed the construal of Israel's Jewish character along ethnic or national rather than religious lines, highlighting the demographic imperative for striking a peace agreement and downplaying alternative modes of imagining Judaism vis-à-vis Zionism. In fact, the possibility of imagining alternative Zionisms was never even contemplated.

An axiomatic and narrow interpretation of Israeli Jewish identity has guided PN's conception of peace and justice. Since its birth on the eve of the Camp David Accords, PN has reaffirmed rather than challenged the conceptual reinterpretation of the Palestinian territories occupied in 1967 as *reclaimed* rather than *conquered* land. This maneuver, chapter 1 explains, is consistent with the ambiguities inherent in secular Zionism and its choice to "return" to Palestine—a choice that entailed violent repercussions for the indigenous Palestinian population as well as clashing with particular interpretations of the resources of Judaism. Secular Zionism also puts forward an ahistorical argument in support of peacemaking. Indeed, the eventual adoption of the two-state formula indicated a growing awareness of the devastating effects of the occupation as well as a recognition that the ongoing de facto annexation of East Jerusalem and large areas of the West Bank and the Gaza Strip threatened the integrity of Israeli democracy. But this realization did not catalyze a substantial reorientation or new formulas for thinking about peace as a comprehensive process that entails the transformation of underlying structures, ideologies, and relational patterns. Turning the discussion to a more theoretical level, chapter 2 focuses on the aforementioned importance of bridging gaps among the various disciplines and fields of political science, religious studies, and peace studies in an effort to think constructively and strategically about the transformation of ethnoreligious national conflicts.

In chapter 3, I develop the notion of the *hermeneutics of citizenship* as a method of understanding the challenges to building peace. This method shows how religion fits into the invisible lines of identity formations and how it may inform an ethnonational agenda. Hence, the hermeneutics of citizenship focuses on the experiences, resources, and writings of myriad marginalized voices as a way of analyzing conflict and peace. This approach pushes the conversation beyond the bounds of one group's narrative toward a multiperspectival approach to justice. Such an approach deeply challenges one group's narrative of victimhood and perception of injustice in light of the narratives of other affected groups.

Hence, this approach is thoroughly contextual without being relativist. To contribute to processes of conflict transformation, such an inquiry needs a creative reimagining of identities. In the Israeli case and other areas where ethnoreligious nationalism is rife, such a reimagining cannot bracket religion as an auxiliary factor or as a mere repository of symbolic resources but rather needs to negotiate the underlying mythology of the nation and how it appropriates religious motifs.[25] The cases of the Palestinian Israelis and the Mizrahim, by virtue of occupying hybrid locations, provide potential resources for renegotiation. The hyphenated groups of the "Arab Jews" and "Palestinian Israelis" challenge the dominant construal of Israeli Jewish identity as antithetical to Arab and Palestinian identities. The retrieval of nonnationalistic Jewish ethical traditions[26] also challenges what may constitute an axiomatic reduction of Judaism to Zionism. Broadening the conversation in such a way situates the analysis of justice in a thick hermeneutical questioning of subjective perceptions of identity—a questioning that may result in redrawing the thresholds of inclusion and exclusion. Hence, denaturalizing the perceived connections between religion and national identity through a focus on marginalized narratives could expand the (re)interpretive possibilities available for religious peacebuilding in zones defined by ethnoreligious national claims.

Acknowledging the ramifications of debates over citizenship for the conflict with the Palestinians does not preclude recognition of and sustained engagement with the legacy of Jewish persecution, displacement, and extermination, most recently during the Holocaust, or with the profound fear of extermination by the hostile countries bordering the Israeli state. Rather, the hermeneutics of citizenship captures the tragic interlocking narratives of Palestinian and Jewish uprootedness and sufferings and demonstrates how those narratives are embodied in the authentic experiences and perceptions of both Jews and Palestinians. The "security argument" so often pronounced by Israeli and non-Israeli Jews regarding their commitment to the ethnocratic project—namely, that Israel is a place of Jewish refuge and self-determination—is born out of genuine experiences of existential threats.

Chapter 3 then explains how the hermeneutics of citizenship expands on existing theories of religion and peacebuilding and extends important conversations in the academic study of religion that center on power analysis as a means of critiquing decontextualized modes of studying religion.[27] A primary constructive approach that already defines the study of religion, conflict, and conflict transformation[28] highlights, as I reread it, not only how religion may relate to chauvinistic interpretations of nationhood but also how religion's internal plurality could be related to reimagining ideological formations and reified identities. I expand on this constructive approach by pointing to its continuous privileging of liberal conceptions of religion as an interiorized mode of being and as relating to the ultimate or the sacred. This orientation permeates the practical dimensions of the field of religious peacebuilding. I argue that a framework for conflict transformation needs to engage alternative conceptions of the place of religion in public life.

The second section of the book studies the explicitly religious Zionist peace camp and examines issues of pluralism and synagogue-state relations in Israel. In chapter 4, I map the conceptual contours of the religious Zionist camp, situating it within the broader spectrum of explicitly religious responses to Zionism and Israel. I then highlight the positions of prominent thinkers and activists, such as Yeshayahu Leibowitz, David Hartman, and Aviezer Ravitzky, who represent alternative articulations of the relationship between religion and nation. In doing so, they underscore the irreducibility of religion to the formulation of the nation. The chapter also links this discussion of religious thinkers to a broader conversation concerning state-synagogue relations in Israel. Specifically, I examine a document titled "A Comprehensive Proposal for Dealing with Issues of Religion and State in Israel." Drafted by Israeli professor of law Ruth Gavison and Rabbi Yaakov Medan, the "Gavison-Medan Covenant," as it came to be known, constitutes a collaborative attempt by a religious leader and a secularist jurist to recognize internal pluralities within the Jewish public and to reflect on the implications of such plurality for questions of religion and state. For example, the Covenant expands the definition of a "Jew" to include those who converted within the context of Reform Judaism. This entails a direct challenge to the monopoly of the rabbinate in Israel and the halakhic definition of a Jew as the child of a Jewish mother or a person converted through Orthodox Judaism. Although the Gavison-Medan Covenant represents an attempt to renegotiate the meanings of Jewish life in Israel, its vision of pluralism is limited by an axiomatic commitment to Jewish hegemony. Thus, I show how the Gavison-Medan document, with its focus on internal Jewish pluralism, is abstracted from a consideration of the relevance of this discussion to broader intergroup questions of justice. In doing so, I hope to illustrate the conceptual limitations of the liberal discourse of multiculturalism.

In chapter 5, I anchor the analysis using the case of Rabbis for Human Rights (RHR). This rabbinical organization (founded in 1988) grounds its human rights advocacy and protest in the humanistic Jewish tradition and the Universal Declaration of Human Rights. I examine RHR not only because, as a religious organization, it offers the most systematic challenge to the "land theology" of the messianic settlers but also because it contests some of the defining dimensions of the Zionist paradigm of citizenship.[29] In particular, RHR legitimates pluralistic interpretations of Jewish identity in the contemporary world and thus rejects the monopoly of the rabbinate in the Zionist secular nation-state. Similar to Gavison and Medan's rationale, RHR also presents an important case for examining the efficacy of liberalism as a framework for articulating questions of peace and justice in ethnoreligious national contexts and for reviewing the relevance of polycentric critiques of the liberal thread of multicultural theories of citizenship.[30] This is due to what I identify as RHR's basic affinity with American revised liberalism, specifically its explicit reliance on Jewish American liberal thinking and orientation.

But, unlike the Gavison-Medan Covenant, RHR substantially engages the meanings of "return" as an opportunity for rethinking Judaism, the nature of covenantal relations, and the promise of the land. A contextualized analysis of Jewish return (one that is attentive to marginalized and repressed voices and histories) would challenge and redefine the deployment of a messianic and metahistorical concept in light of human and historical realities. Accordingly, the notion of Jewish chosenness and divine election would be conditioned entirely on just practices.

While RHR has indeed exemplified liberal interpretations of Israeli nationalism or Zionism, this is an insufficient tactic for peacebuilding because the very inability to question Zionism as Israel's theory of political legitimacy constitutes a root cause of the conflict with the Palestinians. Drawing on the prophetic Jewish tradition, advocating religious humanism, and performing radical acts of solidarity with the victims of Israeli political practices, while indispensable, fall short of challenging the basic Zionist frame that perpetuates the conflict. Peacebuilding requires confronting the history of modern political Zionism and its victims (including Zionism's Jewish victims) as well as a substantive rather than a cosmetic reconfiguration of the Jewish meanings of Israeli citizenship. I therefore highlight the case of RHR in chapter 5 to develop a focused discussion of both the theoretical and the practical aspects of religious peacebuilding. Outlining the conceptual and ideological limitations of RHR clarifies the strategic effectiveness of the hermeneutics of citizenship and of the religious peacebuilder, in addition to the scholar of religion, as a critical caretaker of tradition, challenging the interrelation between power, national identity, and religion.

Broadening the discussion concerning the interrelation between Judaism, the Jewish people, and Israel entails integrating alternative nonnationalistic Jewish voices and ethical-philosophical traditions into the conversation concerning the Jewish meanings of Israel. Here I focus on the reflections of Jewish thinkers and activists, such as the philosopher Judith Butler who retrieves the thoughts of the Jewish German philosophers Hannah Arendt and Walter Benjamin, among others, to argue that the condition of liminality and nonbelonging is more "Jewish" than land ownership. While Arendt and Benjamin are now widely read by political philosophers and religious ethicists, their voices do need to be retrieved in the context of the discussion of Jewish nationalism. Butler underscores Benjamin's indebtedness to a particular interpretation of the Jewish kabbalistic tradition. On this basis, she highlights a different Jewish orientation that gestures toward the possibility of a multiperspectival approach to justice—one that cannot tell the Jewish narrative without recognizing its inherent connections to a Palestinian one—and the possibility of coexistence in Palestine/Israel. Arendt's condemnation of the Zionist construal of the "Jewish people" as unitary and homogenous further enables Butler's critique and revalorization of the category of "diaspora." At the same time that her appealing to nonbelonging or alterity retrieves Jewish resources, Butler's imagining of questions of justice as the reframing of ethical relations to non-Jews is thoroughly relational (or what I call multiperspectival). Her notion of relationality coheres with Palestinian cultural critic Edward Said's recognition, toward the end of his life, of the ethical potentialities enfolded in connecting Palestinian and Jewish experiences of dispersal and dispossession. Relinquishing relationality as the foundation for imagining ethical cohabitation in Palestine/Israel, Butler underscores, would merely reaffirm the "exclusive cultural framework of Jewishness."[31] Certainly, I concur that relationality is a condition for reimagining justice. However, I argue that Butler's "proviso" that "coexistence projects can only begin with the dismantling of political Zionism"[32] may posit the goal as a precondition and thus counter the creative potentialities of the relational model. In chapter 5, I further examine the indispensable innovations and conceptual and practical limitations of this model of ethical cohabitation.

Chapter 5 also presents other diasporic voices that offer a critique of Israeli policies and signal countercultural currents that celebrate Jewish diasporic life. This trend is "countercultural" because it illuminates a break from a teleological Zionist construal of Jewish history wherein diasporic Judaisms and millennia of Jewish diasporic cultures and languages are devalued vis-à-vis life within the Zionist-Hebraic framework. Hence, chapter 5 argues that a focus on the occluded other as a key for thinking about peace-building and conflict transformation must go beyond a focus on Zionism's direct victims (Palestinians, Mizrahim) to entail a consideration of marginalized Jewish diasporic voices as well as the resituating of religious Zionism within the broader spectrum of Jewish responses to modernity.

The third section of the book is dedicated to a study of why hybrid identities born out of the dynamics of conflict may help to creatively reframe the question of membership in Israel and subsequently expand the discussion concerning peace and justice vis-à-vis the Palestinians. Chapter 6 focuses on "The Future Vision of the Palestinian Arabs in Israel"—a pivotal document put forward by a wide consensus of Palestinian Israelis in 2006. In distinction from the Zionist groups, the Palestinian citizens of Israel who signed this document favor a conception of justice anchored in their experiences of injustice due to their indigenous and minority status as citizens within Israel.[33] Their experiences enable Palestinian Israelis to shed light on the systemic or root causes of the broader conflict with the Palestinian people in a way that challenges the premises of the Zionist peace camp. Thus, justice, as envisioned by this subaltern group, amounts to an effort to redefine the character and ethos of the Israeli nation-state in a way that would recognize and include them as full citizens. In turn, such a redefinition of Israeli ethnocracy might facilitate a reconceptualization of the broader conflict with the Palestinian people and a reinterpretation of what may constitute a just peace.

The Palestinian citizens of Israel hence occupy a "third space," which cultural theorist Homi Bhabha describes as a discursive site that demonstrates the fluidity, elasticity, and historicity of identities.[34] While their history of occupation and discrimination confronts Zionist presuppositions and practices and exposes central inconsistencies inherent in the definition of Israel as Jewish and democratic, their hybrid position as non-Jewish Palestinian citizens of Israel provides them with lived resources to renegotiate and reconstruct an interpretation of Israeliness. The Vision document does just that. It conveys a clear attempt to renegotiate Israeli identity by recognizing how the hybrid position and the history of Palestinians in Israel contests Zionist perceptions of peace and justice. Indeed, the Vision focuses exclusively on the particular case of the Palestinian citizens of Israel, but its proposals bear important implications for conceptualizing justice in the broader context of the Palestinian-Israeli conflict. The Vision and similar formulations by Palestinian Israelis are laden with possibilities for denaturalizing or dispossessing the meanings of belonging to Israel in order to reconceptualize the justness of relations among Palestinian, Jewish, and non-Jewish Israelis and non-Israeli Jews.

While the Vision precludes a substantive mention of the broader Palestinian problem, as many of its critics have pointed out, its formulations are grounded not only in an appeal to human rights conventions and international norms but also in a self-assessment of the relation of Palestinian Israelis to both Israel and Palestine. In its insistence on the fundamental centrality of the events of 1948 and on the recognition of the systemic discrimination against the Palestinian citizens of Israel, the Vision is also consistent with a demand for truth-telling and acknowledgment of past injustices as a critical step in the substantive transformation of conflicts. It is further consistent with an emphasis on thinking comprehensively about peace because measuring how the status of Palestinians in Israel figures into peace agreements may shed light on their underlying conceptions of justice.

Chapter 7 discusses the new Mizrahi discourse that articulates a radical alternative to the hegemonic Ashkenazi ethos. Such an alternative necessitates a conscious effort to reveal the basic dichotomies inherent in how Zionism, which the Mizrahi interlocutors perceive as Eurocentric and orientalist, has viewed and treated non-European Jews in Israel. It also calls for reclaiming Mizrahi interpretations of Jewish identity and history. This chapter illuminates the link between Mizrahi and Palestinian histories and the important connections between "domestic" struggles for social justice and broader concerns with Israeli-Palestinian peace. The chapter concludes that Mizrahi histories potentially provide ample resources for a localized and contextualized renegotiation of Jewish Israeli identity. This conversation, however, is situated within a broader debate loosely defined as "post-Zionism."

The label of "post-Zionism" is confusing because, just like Zionism, it encompasses a wide variety of theoretical positions and political implications.[35] Since the 1990s, the theorists associated with the post-Zionist moment in Israel—the new historians,[36] the critical sociologists,[37] and the poststructuralist, feminist, and postcolonial critics[38]—have mounted offensives against what they view as the hegemony of Zionist historiography, sociology, and discursive practices, respectively. One central political inference of this intellectual turn involves a recognition of the imperative to move away from the ethnocentric institutional framework of the Israeli state by cultivating liberal, democratic apparatuses and a corollary civic Israeli identity or by developing a polycentric, multicultural, democratic system.[39]

Post-Zionists have indeed highlighted the question of citizenship in Palestine/Israel as the central locus for thinking constructively about a peace that is also just. The polycentric thread has made the most significant strides in this direction. It stresses the need for deconstructing monocultural conceptions of nationhood and even radically rethinking the logic undergirding power structures. This approach to multiculturalism confronts (and deconstructs) the attributes of political liberalism, neoliberalism, and neorepublicanism. The polycentric model of multiculturalism is deployed as a framework for thinking through issues of recognition and redistribution intrinsic to the Palestinian-Israeli complexities in a way that would avoid majoritarian, assimilationist, and hegemonic inclinations.[40]

However, post-Zionists of those varieties still do not recognize the persistent relevance of religion to rethinking the domains of Israeli citizenship and secularity. Chapter 7 demonstrates that neither the call for a culturally and religiously neutral definition of citizenship, as in various postnationalist options,[41] nor the post-Zionist polycentric framework of multiculturalism inspired by the postcolonial critique of political liberalism, develops a thick and culturally specific conception of a reimagined or reinterpreted Israeli Jewish identity.

In sum, the study of the radical Mizrahi discourse in chapter 7 shows that while recognizing the centrality of citizenship debates to questions of peace and justice, the post-Zionist turn has underestimated the intricate and profound interplay between the role of symbolic, cultural, and religious vocabularies in the formation of political identities and legitimizing myths, on the one hand, and the demands of statecraft, on the other. Unlike the assimilationist and incorporationist positions characteristic of neoliberals and neorepublicans, Israeli polycentrism views multiculturalism and heterogeneity as a normative political and moral principle that should guide the organization of the society.[42] Hence, as a theory of justice, polycentric multiculturalism may potentially offer a framework to articulate and synthesize questions of peace and justice. Multiculturalism, thus construed, enables thinking about justice vis-à-vis the main schisms identified in the Israel/Palestine contexts. It entails airing the systemic causes of injustice and division in order to transform them. This process would involve an introspective look at the ethnorepublican logic of the Israeli nation-state, including its sublimated manifestation in the Zionist (liberal) peace camp. Yet this polycentric proposal does not articulate what cultural substance or common thread would hold the differentiated groups together in one polity because the structures of the "state" always have to be legitimated through a certain construal of the "nation."

The conceptual framework developed in this book suggests that the restructuring of the political system and the rearrangement of power configurations need to be accompanied by a reimagining of the "ties that bind" and vice versa.[43] The process involves both a deconstructive critique of power and a constructive hermeneutics of cultural and historical resources. Hence, an attempt to propose a counterhegemonic rearrangement needs to take into consideration not only how to deconstruct the Zionist status quo in order to facilitate a polycentric polity but also how to *imagine* alternative interpretations of Jewish Israeli identity (as well as other identities that may partake in the polity). Just as RHR's activism demonstrates that a scrutiny of Jewish resources needs to be supplemented with a structural systemic critique of power, the specific case of radical Mizrahi activism shows that the analysis of power needs to be accompanied by a scrutiny of cultural, historical, and religious resources in order to imagine the transformation of a context defined by ethnoreligious national claims.

Indeed, the exclusive nationalism that defines the settlement movement and its sympathizers and political and financial enablers constitutes an obvious obstacle for peace and justice. However, one contribution of this book resides in "exposing" how the less obviously exclusive liberal and secular interpretations of Zionism and Israeli identity have likewise normalized and contributed to enduring systemic forms of violence. Subsequently, they too block possibilities for imaginative reframing of questions of peace and justice. Liberal discourse enables delinking the discussion of Judaism as "belief" from the framing of Jewish identity as "ethnicity," "nationality," and "history." Because these identity constructs reside at the root of the Israeli-Palestinian conflict, evading the challenges offered by the hermeneutics of citizenship precludes the possibility of a substantive transformation of the Palestinian-Israeli conflict. The hermeneutics of citizenship as a multiperspectival and polycentric method for thinking about justice, therefore, marks the other main contribution of this book. It broadens the imaginative vistas of questions of peace and justice by contextually exploring counterhegemonic perspectives from within the margins of Israeli society as well as wider Jewish conversations about the meanings of modern Jewish identities and experiences.

A pivotal question animating the book, hence, concerns what kind of transformative changes need to take place in order to articulate more just conceptions of peace. Indeed, nationalism constitutes a dynamic construct and reality. Zionism, in its varieties, has changed over time too. A political scientist, Nadav Shelef, argues that change in national ideologies can be explained neither as a function of rational adaptation to external trauma nor merely as the product of elite manipulation and imposition. Instead, he deploys the theoretical framework of evolutionary change to explain sub-stantive ideological and fundamental transformations.[44] Here he includes the gradual ideological acceptance by ultranationalist territorial maximal-ists of a partition of the land, the acceptance of religion's role in public life on the part of both Labor (left) and Likud (right) secular political move-ments, and the gradual desacralization by religious Zionists (in the post-2005 "disengagement" from Gaza) of the Israeli state and its instruments, such as the IDF.

Ideological and definitional changes occur in part as the unintentional by-products of day-to-day political, domestic, and mundane intra- and in-terparty engagements, even if the two other paradigms of change in national ideology remain operative as well. It may be the case that an evolutionary paradigm that removes the supposed necessity of identifying intentionality in the analysis of change can explain the ideological shift of the right-wing ultranationalist Israeli political parties toward recognizing the right of Pal-estinian statehood and the related need to withdraw from at least some of the occupied territories. While this change resonates with a "peace agenda," it denotes a merely cosmetic rather than a substantive ideological shift. The evolution of views of the scope of the territory and the permissible role of religion in public life has not transformed the ethnocentric definition of membership in the Israeli nation-state.

This book illustrates that the lack of substantive change on this front is due to secular nationalism's axiomatic acceptance of religious symbols, im-ageries, and justifications. This explains why religious Zionists may "evolve" out of their instrumental reliance on, and theological dialectic with, secular Zionists. Secular Zionism is intricately tied to religious and theological mo-tifs, even if those motifs are secularized and ethnicized. Glossing over this definitional question limits the scope of peace and justice. The question is not whether conceptions of national movements can change (or evolve) over time. Certainly, this is where one's optimism can reside. Instead, the issue is why one cannot submit to processes of political and ideological "natural selection" and retroactive analysis but rather needs to probe *intentionally* the fundamental question of who "we" are as a "nation." This kind of probing does not carry the same kind of normative cynicism that a reliance on evolutionary dynamics may entail. The "peace" that may be the outcome of pragmatic adaptability or evolving contraction of expansive nationalist schema (an unintended by-product of mundane political exchanges) is not enough, as the title of this book suggests, because it does not tackle the fundamental question of membership and how it relates to broader issues of justice. Even more benevolent motivations—such as a sense of inconsistency between one's "enlightened" values and the reality of occupation, as in the case of the Israeli peace camp—are not sufficient. Therefore, the questions that guide my inquiry are: What notions of "peace" and "justice" have the movements associated with the Israeli peace camp advanced? What conceptions of Israeli nationalism (and/or Zionism) have they affirmed or debated? Have these conceptions determined their understandings of peace in this particular ethnonationalist context? Have they critically linked domestic questions of social justice with their interpretations of the Palestinian-Israeli conflict? Finally, how do these movements view religion in relation to nationality? To these questions I now turn.

ONE

Peace, Justice, and the Zionist Consensus: Peace Now and the Blind Spots of Peacemaking

Introduction

One of my first memories was the moment the Israeli peace movement was born in the 1970s. My father carried me on his shoulders through the streets of Jerusalem to join thousands of other protesters exerting pressure on Prime Minister Menachem Begin to negotiate a peace agreement with Egypt. I was too young to understand this momentous event, but it made a powerful and lasting impression on me. A few years later, my father again took me to light a candle at the makeshift memorial for peace activist Emile Gruenzweig, who was murdered by a radical, ultranationalist religious supporter of Rabbi Meir Kahane. This murder—shocking to many peace activists—marked "religion" as the primary obstacle for peace. Secular Israelis spoke enlightened words of reason while religious settlers and other extremists were thought to jeopardize every possibility for peace.

This is a familiar thesis that took the burden away from secular Jewish Israelis to scrutinize their own understandings of the Jewish significance of Israel and the violent implications of their commitment to Jewish democracy. For years my understanding of peace was framed by this standpoint. I heard my friends talk about how "the people on the hills" (i.e., the settlers) corrupt and destroy the Israeli experiment. If it were not for them, we could have negotiated something rationally. This argument is echoed in the scholarship of that era as well.[1]

While there are countless peace organizations working in Israel/Palestine, this chapter focuses on Peace Now (henceforth PN) because the movement has come to represent the Israeli consensus with respect to the logic of peacemaking.[2] Classified, in what follows, as the "consensus," therefore, are those peace groups and organizations that do not challenge in a systematic and principled manner how the official Zionist presumption of Israel's character as Jewish and democratic may be integral to questions of peace and justice for Palestine.[3] Nevertheless, this "consensus" category includes a variety of interest groups, such as the religious peace organizations, which have deliberately sought to rethink the meaning of Israeli citizenship as articulated by PN and Meretz—the political party with which the secular Zionist peace camp has come to associate most closely since the formation of this party in the early 1990s. Still, the conceptions of peace and justice that these groups articulate do not deviate in any substantial way from the bounds of what came to be considered legitimate and permissible Zionist debates during the years leading up to the establishment of the state.

This chapter, consequently, argues that the secularist and liberal self-perception of the loyal or Zionist left constrains its ability to hermeneutically engage the political theology that delimits the moral imagination of the peace consensus. The Israeli sociologist and cultural critic Yehouda Shenhav is therefore correct in his evaluation of the Israeli left and its reluctance to view the events of 1948 and 1967 as composing a continuum, representing two phases of one process of conquest and population displacement.[4] The reification of the Green Line as a firm border, he argues, facilitated a false moral distinction between the legitimacy of Israel Proper and the illegitimacy of the occupation.

Shenhav further claims that the so-called Israeli left is not only detached from the demands and experiences of the Palestinians but also disconnected from ultra-Orthodox settlers, Mizrahi Shas supporters (Shas being a Mizrahi Haredi party running on a platform of social justice), and the immigrants from the former Soviet Union who rally behind the ultranationalist agenda. He contends that the ascendance of an ultranationalist agenda is not a departure from an Israeli ethos but rather entirely consistent with its ideological formation. The mainstream is also resistant to recognizing that Israel is located in the Middle East, in an Arab context. Hence, the "nostalgia" many of those self-described as "left-leaning" Israelis experience toward the pre-1967 "good old Israel" also translates into a desire to remain "guests" in the region: a European Western outpost. The settlers become important for Shenhav because the Israeli left usually treats them as a homogeneous group, overlooking not only important internal divergences but also how the settlements constitute the last bastion of a social welfare state, now dissolved as a result of neoliberal policies.

Notably, the drive for privatization and liberalization precipitated the reframing of peace in economic terms. This reframing came from the most privileged and primary beneficiaries of the neoliberal socioeconomic framework. The early republican Zionist ethos (with all its democratic-socialist proclivities) has indeed diminished in significance as a result of profound socioeconomic, political, and cultural transformations, accompanying the rise of global trade. Ironically the same group of people who had comprised the founding elite of Israel now embraces a post-Zionist and neoliberal ethos of privatization. In short, the kibbutznik of yore, once embodying the Israeli ideal, has become the high-tech cosmopolitan capitalist of today. Both "characters" are mere caricatures, but ones that gesture toward the actual prevalence of broad socioeconomic and cultural values. Israel, in the aftermath of neoliberal privatization, is now a society marked by profound inequalities between the rich and the poor. Shenhav strives to connect supposedly "domestic" social justice concerns with a broader consideration of the Palestinian-Israeli conflict. Unifying the normative discussion in such a way, therefore, does not associate peace with evacuating settlers from their homes. Instead, dissolving the spatial and normative differentiation between 1948 and 1967 leads Shenhav to imagine a radical reconfiguration of the geopolitical space along religious and communal lines, loosely arranged under a democratic consociational federation.

Certainly, an analysis that focuses on 1948 and 1967 and beyond within a unitary spatial and normative frame exposes the conceptual blinders of the Israeli left with great precision. But more is needed to understand why the state established within the 1949 armistice lines has endured as an authentic representation of Israeliness. Beyond the critique that identifies the Eurocentric nationalism of the peace camp and its inclination to normalize the pre-1967 acts of conquest and displacement, the process of conflict transformation will have to reimagine Jewish Israeli identity as local (of the Middle East) and as a nonhegemonic presence in the region. This constructive move cannot simply translate into the geopolitical reconfiguration of Israel/Palestine because that could amount to a dismissal of what is experienced as authentic and real. Simply invoking the reconfiguration of Israel as a state of all its citizens, for instance, could be interpreted as diminishment or eradication of the authenticity of Jewish Israeliness, with its very real existential meanings. Likewise, simply reimagining the geopolitical space as a consociational arrangement does not provide substantive sociocultural resources that might enable the cultivation of commitment to such an overarching but loosely connected arrangement. Instead, one needs to explore why the ahistorical interpretation of Jewish settlement as an act of "return" to Palestine has not only typified the messianic settlers but also reverberated in the Israeli peace camp. One needs to interrogate how it has prevented diverse groups within this camp from imagining peace and justice beyond the ideological confines of Jewish majoritarianism. As we will see, the re-imagining of questions of peace and justice, for this reason, must move beyond a deconstructive critique of underlying power structures and ideological formations toward a constructive rethinking of questions of identity. In these discussions, the interface between religion and nation needs to be made explicit and debated.[5]

Because the peace movement is not a fixed phenomenon but rather a dynamic one, the chapter is structured somewhat chronologically, proceeding from the early prestate programs for binationalism advanced by Brit Shalom and Ihud to the more recent Gush Shalom and its critique of the Oslo Accords and PN. Part 1 introduces the binational platforms and the alternative Zionisms advanced by Martin Buber, Judah Magnes, and other prominent individuals prior to the establishment of the Israeli state. It shows that binationalism, at this time, was a legitimate Zionist option. Part 2 highlights the historical bias integral to any official and extraparliamentary attempts to think about peace in the aftermath of the 1967 war. By historical bias, I mean that the territories occupied in 1967 were described as if they were *reclaimed* rather than conquered. This historical/mythological bias, not inconsistent with the Zionist venture in Palestine more generally, leads to the articulation of the "land for peace" formula. Part 3 turns to the story of PN, its emergence on the eve of an opportunity of peace negotiations with Egypt in the late 1970s, its conceptual transformations as a result of the First Lebanon War in 1982, and the eruption of the First Intifada in 1987. Finally, part 4 discusses the parliamentary dimension of the secular Zionist peace camp and how the Oslo Process reflected the culmination of profound economic, social, and political transformations dating back to the 1980s. The chapter concludes with the story of Gush Shalom, along with its critique of the consensus peace camp and its interpretation of the Oslo Accords and their eventual failure. Gush Shalom exposes some of the fundamental problems with PN. Yet it too, I contend, is tied to an incoherent and reductive secularist version of Zionism.

I. Contextualization: The Biltmore Program and *Wirklichkeitszionismus*

With the end of World War II still far off, and the news of the dire predicament of European Jewry unequivocal, delegates from a variety of Zionist organizations convened in the Biltmore Hotel in New York City to discuss the direction and strategy of the Zionist movement.[6] Official Zionist policy was codified in the Biltmore Program of 1942 under the leadership of David Ben-Gurion, who was at the time the chairman of the Palestine Executive of the Jewish Agency. On this occasion, it became clear that the intention of the Zionist leadership was to establish a Jewish demographic majority in the land. In particular, the conference was convened in response to the British White Paper of 1939.[7]

The White Paper imposed significant restrictions on Jewish immigration to Palestine and land purchases and thus signaled to the Zionist leadership a departure of the British government from earlier promises issued by British foreign secretary Arthur James Balfour and Lloyd George.[8] The Biltmore Program demanded unlimited immigration in order to change rapidly the demographic makeup of Palestine and facilitate the establishment of a Jewish majority. While the Biltmore Conference was not the first context in which the Zionist leadership had invoked such a demand, the establishment of a Jewish majority now became intimately tied to the moral obligation to save the Jews of Europe.[9] This interlinking imperative became foundational to the Zionist ethos that ensued.

Hence, in these particular circumstances, the Zionist movement saw a substantial narrowing of what could be considered acceptable interpretations of Jewish national revival in Palestine. While unpopular and politically inchoate, binationalism had, in effect, constituted a debatable option in Zionist parlors prior to the 1940s. The empirical reality that unfolded in Palestine precipitated a lively and intriguing debate over the meaning of Zionism as it came to be indivisibly linked to the question of Jewish-Arab relations in the land. Already in the prestate or "Yishuv" period, faced with an undeniable Arab indigenous opposition to Jewish settlement programs, Zionist thinkers such as Buber, Yitzhak Epstein, Haim Kalwariski, Magnes, Hans Kohn, and Ahad Ha'am had recognized the futility and fallacy undergirding the familiar Zionist slogan: "A land without people for a people without a land."[10]

While not denying the legitimacy of Jewish claims to Palestine, these Zionist thinkers and activists endeavored to reconcile such claims with the rights and well-being of the natives.[11] It was this reconciliatory impulse and recognition of the plight of the indigenous population that motivated them to curtail Zionist territorial and political aspirations. The same attitude also put this group at odds early on with the official Zionist framework, which had begun to assert itself increasingly forcefully and systematically. In his address to the Seventh Zionist Congress (1905), Epstein, for instance, emphasized how early Zionist practices of land purchases had contributed to an unjust expropriation of land. He argued instead for Jewish-Arab rap-prochement and for turning the Arabs into the beneficiaries, rather than the victims, of Zionism—an argument that is quite consistent with the view of benevolent colonialism.[12]

Like Epstein, Magnes, an American Reform rabbi and the first chancellor of the Hebrew University of Jerusalem, highlighted the need for rapproche-ment.[13] Influenced by Ahad Ha'am's "cultural Zionism" (1856–1927)[14]—which rejected the tactics and priorities of political Zionism by arguing for the need to cultivate Zion as a cultural/moral center, to be measured not by physical demographic dominance but rather by cultural flourish-ing[15]—Magnes advanced the imperative to limit the political ambition of the Zionist movement to facilitate the creation of Palestine as a home of two nations.[16] He was thus profoundly wary of the potential long-term ramifi-cations of the Balfour Declaration issued in October of 1917, a promise granted by a British lord to establish a Jewish national home in the land of Palestine.

After the 1929 anti-Zionist riots in Hebron and Safed, Magnes advocated the reorientation of Zionist policy along pacifist lines. He subsequently un-derscored his readiness to relinquish the demand for establishing a Jewish majority and a Jewish state in Palestine and instead advocated the promo-tion of the three Zionist tenets of immigration, settlement, and Hebrew cul-ture while ensuring Arab consent.[17] Magnes's peace platform thus included Zionist notions of cultural revival in Palestine but rejected the imperative to secure a demographic majority. While his peace proposal digressed from the lines of official Zionism, Magnes cannot be classified, by any account, as anti-Zionist—a label later deployed against proposals of a similar kind.[18]

The founding in 1925 of Brit Shalom (translated variously as Covenant of Peace or Peace Alliance), the first peace group in Palestine, was consistent with this call for promoting Arab-Jewish cooperation.[19] Unlike the official leadership of the Zionist movement, the members of Brit Shalom (promi-nent intellectuals like Gershom Scholem and Arthur Ruppin)[20] highlighted the critical centrality of the so-called Arab question. They also stressed the moral rather than the geopolitical dimensions of this question and their rel-evance to the entirety of the Zionist undertaking in Palestine.[21] As I discuss below, the logic of Jewish political autonomy and territoriality had to be constrained by the demands of ethical conduct and the empirical realities of the land.

The group, formed primarily to study Arab-Jewish relations, intended to advance what Buber[22] referred to as *Wirklichkeitszionismus*—a pragmatic Zi-onism attentive to the demographic realities and constraints of Palestine.[23]

Subsequently, Brit Shalom articulated its aim as follows: "to arrive at an understanding between Jews and Arabs as to the form of their mutual social relations in Palestine on the basis of absolute political equality of two culturally autonomous peoples, and to determine the lines of their co-operation for the development of the country."[24] Henrietta Szold, another prominent Jewish affiliate of Brit Shalom, underscored the imperative to transform the Zionist project in Palestine into a morally consistent and broadly acceptable enterprise. Szold famously wrote (in 1942):

> If we do not give every member of the public the opportunity of considering the Jewish-Arab question, we will be committing, I think, an unpardonable sin. Why do I think so? . . . It was Judaism, which brought me to Zionism and I cannot but believe that Judaism, Religion as I understand it, is our moral code; and Judaism bids us to find a way in common with the Arabs living in this country . . . The more I return to this matter, the more do I become convinced that politically as well as morally, the Jewish-Arab question is the decisive question.[25]

To this end, Brit Shalom advocated the need to establish a binational state with a legislative council based on Jewish-Arab parity regardless of their relative size in the population.[26] This framework, the group insisted, was not only the most moral but also the most pragmatically feasible one. Magnes agreed that the marginalization of "Arab-Jewish cooperation" within Zionist discussions constituted "a great sin of omission."[27]

The platform of Brit Shalom was harshly criticized by the contemporary Zionist establishment as at best naïve. The members of Brit Shalom were ridiculed as "deep down assimilationists" and as devoid of "Jewish national feeling."[28] Their proposal was rejected by the Arab side as well. As the majority, the latter had no compelling reason to consent to a parity model.[29]

Brit Shalom ceased to exist in 1933. The group never numbered more than one hundred members of a similar socioeconomic milieu and had not been able to translate its principles into a concrete political platform with a mass base of support and mobilization. The group nonetheless was succeeded by other ideologically similar groups, such as the League of Jewish-Arab Rapprochement and the Ihud Association (Union).[30] The latter, headed by Buber and Magnes (among others), was inaugurated with the knowledge of the catastrophes of World War II. The group still advocated binationalism as the only conceivable option for Jews in Palestine as well as for European Jews who had fled Hitler. By persistently advocating the binational model, Ihud situated itself in opposition to official Zionist venues, for which only varying plans of partition remained within the realm of debatable political options.[31]

A critique of the principles undergirding the idea of partition also came from Hashomer Hatzair (Young Watchman), a left-wing revolutionary socialist movement. The group predicted that partition would precipitate and perpetuate conflict, augmenting rather than eliminating its causes.[32] Thus aligning itself with Hashomer Hatzair's argumentation against partition, Ihud elaborated on the parity-based model already articulated by Brit Shalom before the outbreak of the war. The following excerpt from the platform of the Ihud group, composed by Buber, Magnes, and Robert Weltsch in the summer of 1942, presents the cardinal points of the group and a counterargument to the Biltmore Program:

> The Association Union . . . regards a Union between the Jewish and Arab peoples as essential for the upbuilding of Palestine and for cooperation between the Jewish world and the Arab world in all branches of life—social, economic, cultural, political . . . The main political aims of the Association Union are as follows: A. Government in Palestine based upon equal political rights for the two peoples. B. The agreement of the steadily growing Yishuv and of the whole Jewish people to a Federative Union of Palestine and neighboring countries. This Federative Union is to guarantee the national rights of all people within it. C. A Covenant between this Federative Union and an Anglo-American Union which is to be part of the future Union of the free peoples.[33]

On a theoretical level, the binational platform advanced by both Brit Shalom and Ihud indicated a modernist-secularist assumption concerning the possibility of differentiating the political and cultural realms into clearly separable compartments. This assumption is indicative of their interpretation of citizenship as a neutral category of identity, constituting mere legal status. Hence, even while rendering the federative political constellation of Palestine devoid of specific cultural formulations, the authors of the binational program did not explain why the disparate groups would want to be linked within a single political framework. This proved to be a significant shortcoming. The proposal was premature; there was as yet no Arab Palestinian incentive to partake in such an experiment.

The binational proposal articulated by Brit Shalom and Ihud was and remains problematic in that it did not respond to intracommunal human rights dilemmas and it essentialized or fossilized the two cultures in their autonomous settings. It neglected to address the rights and status of individuals who do not affiliate with either community. It is susceptible to the same kind of critique leveled against the model of conflict management central to liberal multiculturalism, which frequently glosses over the internal plurality of communities and thus reinforces rather than challenges power configurations and normative interpretations of membership. (I unpack this criticism in detail in chapter 2.) Upon closer examination, this binational proposal also contains an ironic bias toward an interior and personal conception of religion, one that overlooks the interface between religion and communal identities. This bias is "ironic" because the binationalism of the proto–peace movement in the prestate era is firmly grounded in a collectivist interpretation of Judaism and Jewish history.[34] Yet religion as viewed by the thinkers of Ihud and Brit Shalom is conceived as contained without remainder in the sphere of the private and personal. This irony animates my critique of the secularist presuppositions ingrained in the secular peace consensus.

Nonetheless, on a more particular level of intra-Jewish conversations in the prestate era, both Brit Shalom and Ihud presciently focused on the question of Arab-Jewish rapprochement and emphasized the imperative to curb Zionist chauvinist impulses (including the possibility of partition). Yet they indisputably operated within the Zionist framework. They did not question the rights of Jews to immigrate to Palestine, settle its land, and revive the Hebrew culture therein. In fact, they reaffirmed a particular Eurocentric Ashkenazi Zionist historiography that posited Zionism as both the center and the telos of Jewish life and destiny. This subsumed all Jewish communities—including non-European centers of Jewish life—under a universalizing historiography. A critique of this unidirectional and teleological interpretation of Jewish history provides a key to understanding why subaltern narratives (and particularly diasporic challenges and Mizrahi experiences, discussed in chapters 5 and 7, respectively) provide underutilized resources for reframing the interrelations between Judaism and Zionism.

While Buber et al. were not in a position to recognize the pervasiveness of the Ashkenazi orientalist discourse, they did question the reliance of official Zionism on the structures of colonialism and the ethical implications of engaging in such activities without the consent of the indigenous Arab population. Of course, such consent was hard to attain, and the presumption that it could have been attained is itself loaded with colonial presumptions.[35] On the other hand, the binational option as articulated by these intellectuals constituted an alternative Zionism. Already in the 1920s, it identified the injustices inherent in what would become in the 1990s the primary formula for peacemaking—namely, the two-state solution.

But already at the critical time of the Biltmore Conference, binationalism was no longer an acceptable topic for debate. The codification of the official

Zionist policy in the Biltmore Program overwhelmed the relentless attempts by Magnes, Buber, and other veterans of the binational model. Magnes, for example, was severely lambasted by the official Zionist leadership for persistently advancing the binational proposal before the Anglo-American Enquiry Commission in 1946 and before the Special United Nations Commission the following year.[36]

With the establishment of the state, the principles articulated in the Biltmore Conference achieved a sacrosanct status. Challenging them became a national taboo. These circumstances further diminished the credibility of alternative proposals, such as the binational platforms advanced by Brit Shalom and Ihud. The Zionist debate became intricately tied to the Holocaust and the imperative to create a Jewish majority in the land of Palestine. Any departure from the basic axiomatic assumptions of official Zionism has since been rendered anti-Zionist and "self-hating." Yet this calumny constituted a divergence from the more flexible and conducive atmosphere characteristic of the Yishuv period prior to World War II.

In sum, despite its radicalism and lack of popularity, the binationalism envisioned by Buber and Magnes had been received as a critique offered from within the parameters of legitimate Zionist conversation. With all of its conceptual problems, the theory of justice guiding Brit Shalom and Ihud (as in the case of future religious peace organizations like Rabbis for Human Rights) was based on the recognition of the equal humanity of the indigenous population and of Judaism as constituting a moral as well as a national imperative. Because Palestine was *not* empty, despite what the famous Zionist maxim claimed, Zionism needed to restrain its messianic vision of return and focus instead on rapprochement as well as cultural development. Out of this orientation, these prototypical groups formulated their notion of "peace" as a program for a binational existence. Directed by secularist-modernist inclinations, the prominent thinkers affiliated with this prestate peace camp thought that the parity model would facilitate peaceful coexistence.

The establishment of the state, however, only solidified the view that the binational option fell outside the permissible bounds of Zionist debate. This narrowing may be attributed to the profound experience of near extermination of European Jewry and the subsequent vindication of political Zionism's assertion that only a Jewish state where Jews constituted the majority of the population could secure the survival of the Jewish people.

This defining narrative that perceives Jewish destiny as perpetually on the verge of extinction has been further vindicated by repeated wars and confrontations with the Arab neighbors of the Israeli state, including the

Palestinians (who were internally distinguished from the broader so-called Arab problem only at a later stage). The basic refusal of Arab and Muslim states to recognize Israel, and the cycles of bloodshed that have characterized modern Middle Eastern and Israeli histories, have enabled the perpetuation of the central notion of Jewish and Israeli struggle for survival in the midst of a hostile world. It is no wonder that out of this worldview and experience, the "recognition of Israel as Jewish" and the maintenance of "Israeli security" emerged as the refrain of Israeli administrations, right, left, or center.

II. Reframing the Occupation

The Peace Formulas: Claimed or Reclaimed?

Laurence Silberstein, one of the most important analysts of Zionisms, underscores that two interrelated binaries were central for the imagining of Zionism as a national movement: homeland/exile and exile/redemption. The act of return subsequently implies the dual processes of deterritorialization, or the "negation of exile," and reterritorialization and the imagining of a new Hebrew who rejects the diasporic Jewish life while reconnecting with the biblical landscape of origin and destination or redemption. He writes:

> Zionists, like all nationalists, presume a natural, isomorphic relationship between the nation, its culture, and the space it represents as its homeland. Only in the homeland do conditions exist that are necessary for the growth and flourishing of the nation and its culture. Conversely, spaces outside the homeland, referred to as "exile," are represented as inimical to such growth and dangerous to the health of the nation. Thus, zionist discourse positions its subjects to accept as true the claim that the "return" of the nation to its homeland is essential to the survival of the nation and the renewal of its culture . . . In zionist discourse, the departure of a sizable part of the Jewish community from the land of Israel, voluntarily or coerced, is represented as the nation going into exile. On the other hand, the migration of a significant part of the nation to the land, such as occurred in the twentieth century, is represented as a return, a redemptive process.[37]

Accordingly, Zionism, like many other *volkist* nineteenth-century nationalist movements, cultivated an organic concept of the relationship between the "people," or the idea of the nation, and the homeland. The application of this concept betrays a projection of a metahistorical Jewish narrative onto historical settings because the physical return to Zion and the establishment of a Jewish nation-state is deemed a redemptive enterprise. Zion thus comes to signify the locus for the physical and historical redemption of the Jewish people. While the diaspora represented "anti-Semitism and persecution, social fragmentation, cultural assimilation, cultural deterioration, suppression of individual creativity," the act of return to the land entailed "safety and physical security, the unification of the nation, protection from external cultural influences, the renewal of Jewish culture, individual creativity, agricultural labor, and spiritual renewal."[38]

In addition to imagining a universal (yet distinctly Eurocentric) Jewish experience and a teleological progression of Jewish history,[39] the homeland/diaspora dichotomy has taken for granted the legitimacy of the Jewish claim to the land of Palestine. This legitimacy is grounded in the biblical narratives and in the idea of the return to Zion that has occupied the Jewish imagination for millennia. Transposing the divine metahistorical event of redemption in Zion (understood as a utopia, a destination outside of ordinary time and space) onto a human-initiated historical act of return to the land of Palestine delegitimizes or overlooks the historical claims of the indigenous inhabitants of the land. This perception is reflective of what I refer to below as "the metahistorical bias of Zionism": its use of the binaries of exile/redemption and exile/homeland and its reliance on a religious messianic narrative elides the historical and physical realities of Palestine. This bias, which views the act of return as unproblematic, is one conceptual blinder that blinkers the ability of the Israeli peace camp to reimagine the parameters of peace and justice.

However, before discussing the implications of this metahistorical bias for the modes in which the settlement of the Palestinian predicament is envisioned, it is necessary to examine the motifs central to the Zionist imagining of the nation. Indeed, the exile/homeland and exile/redemption binaries have been basic to the construction and reconstruction of Zionism. As outlined in *Myths in Israeli Culture: Captives of a Dream*, a work by the Israeli scholar of literature and film Nurith Gertz, one of the defining myths in Israeli culture is the narrative of the few against the many, an ethos that conveys the seemingly impossible task and heroism of the Zionist struggle to establish and defend a Jewish homeland. This narrative has been supplemented by other themes that point, as I will demonstrate, to the Eurocentric and orientalist underpinnings of the Zionist project and to the selective retrieval of Jewish or Hebraic motifs in the construction and reconstruction of the "nation."

Gertz refers to one such theme as "East versus West." Emergent during the War of 1948, this motif has had an enduring legacy; it presents the Israeli as a foot soldier fighting on behalf of Western values against the East. While in earlier Zionist accounts the Arab inhabitant of Palestine was portrayed in an orientalist fashion as "the embodiment of authenticity, youthful vigour and strength"[40]—the antithesis of the passive diasporic Jew and decadent European culture—the War of 1948 marked the inversion of this dichotomy. After this inversion, "an abstract, rootless and ancient Arab civilisation is portrayed as the culture of the desert, and is contrasted with that of Europe, now depicted as a culture of building and planting that embodies human values and strength."[41] In fact, the new Israeli Jew came to be construed as an enlightened European, a representative or an outpost of the Western world.

The narrative of East vs. West also entailed a projection of the attributes of the "passive" and "rootless" diasporic Jew onto the native Arab.[42] This rhetorical inversion and representation of the Arab as rootless is congruent with how the Jewish return to the land of Palestine has been legitimated in Zionist accounts. While the theme of return was justified as a historical right, the history and claims of the indigenous inhabitants of the land were dismissed as nonbinding and inconsequential. The history of modern Israel and the return to the land, in particular, was construed as a direct and uninterrupted continuation of the biblical Joshua's conquest and settlement of the land and the stories of the Maccabees and Masada.[43] This Zionist mythological construal of an uninterrupted Hebraic or Israelite history, laced with the related theme of the "negation of exile," underscores the indispensability of the "land" in the nation's aspiration for rebirth and redemption (understood in terms of physical return or restoration).[44]

In short, a scrutiny of the narration and construction of Zionist and Israeli national identity points to an underlying indebtedness to an orientalist discourse and to a related secularist discourse whereby Israel represents the enlightened and secular "West." This is regardless of a particular conception of Jewish destiny and Jewish or Hebraic narratives that legitimize Zionist claims to the land of Palestine, per se.

On the one hand, the axiomatic Zionist binaries of exile/redemption and exile/return have factored into the themes of the few against the many, the Zionist as an agent of Western values, and the negation of exile through the elevation of Hebraism (the biblical narratives of promise, conquest, and sovereignty) over Judaism (oral tradition, diaspora life, and the lack of political sovereignty). At the same time, they have also inflected the underlying framework of discussions concerning peace and justice. The mainstream peace camp in Israel has operated under the presupposition that Israel's identity as a Jewish state is axiomatic and central to any attempt to think about peace and justice.

This presumption demonstrates how symbolic boundaries, which "separate people into groups and generate feelings of similarity and group membership,"[45] relate to the logic and mechanisms of social relationships. Scrutinizing the symbolic boundaries, in the case of the Israeli peace camp, also illuminates broader geopolitical implications. That is, because such an analysis exposes why a particular view of "group membership" (i.e., the discourse of citizenship and identity) constrains possibilities for conflict transformation, it therefore points to how, beyond territories and the allocation of resources, what needs to be negotiated are the symbolic boundaries of identities, especially if those boundaries are exposed as the root causes of injustice.

The axiomatic character of Israel as a Jewish democracy, moreover, is situated at the heart of the two primary peace formulas promoted by the Israeli secular peace camp and its counterparts in the political establishment: "territory for peace" and the two-state solution. The former formula provided the earliest conceptual basis of peacemaking, dating back to the immediate aftermath of the 1967 War all the way until the First Intifada (1987–93). At this point, the centrality of the Palestinian predicament to the Arab-Israeli conflict finally achieved mainstream recognition. Identifying the Palestinian Liberation Organization (PLO) as the main Palestinian interlocutor of Israeli officials paved the way for the introduction of the two-state solution as increasingly the only viable option.

In both peace formulas, the conception of a "just peace" (which, we will see, is importantly different from *justpeace*) is based on a particularistic sense of Jewish entitlement. The "territory for peace" principle assumes ultimate (and metahistorical) Jewish ownership of the land, despite the more recent historical claims (and physical presence) of Palestinians. Any kind of territorial concession is thus construed as an act of discretion for the sake of neighborly tranquility and recognition of Israel's historical or religious right to self-determination in Palestine. In other words, the principle of "territory for peace" is grounded in a metahistorical bias. Similarly, the two-state platform indicates the right of the Jewish people to cultivate an exclusively Jewish nation-state, which would guarantee the potential citizenship of all Jews throughout the world.

These two interrelated formulas of peacemaking mean that the status of the territories occupied in June 1967 was reinterpreted as *reclaimed* rather than *conquered* land to be returned upon the promise of peace and security. This reinterpretation, which led to the "territory for peace" agenda, was validated by an ambiguous appeal to Israel's historical and/or religious right to the land. Such an appeal was "ambiguous" because of the difficulty of reconciling the antireligiosity of secular Zionisms with their "obvious" reliance on religious justifications. The impetus for the two-state program derived from the demographic argument. Accordingly, the only way to preserve a Jewish demographic majority was to assume a territorially minimalist position. Both arguments are, in effect, conceptually consistent with the secular Zionism of the Ben-Gurion and Ze'ev Jabotinsky varieties. This suggests a diminishing and ever-narrowing ideological distance between the Likud Party on the supposed "right" and the Labor Party on the "left." These political currents finally fused in the 1990s with the aforementioned institutionalization of neoliberal reforms.

It was only after the War of 1967, but especially after the War of 1973, that the prospect of peace became a topic of conversation, featuring initially the "territory for peace" formula and later the two-state solution. These two formulas swerved from the principles undergirding the prestate binational programs of Brit Shalom and Ihud. While the latter programs similarly subscribed to the "myth of return," they also recognized how the realities of Palestine should have limited the project of Jewish political revival in a manner respectful of the rights of the Arab inhabitants. These Palestinian realities, as indicated above, were invalidated or glossed over by the Biltmore formula. The later "territory for peace" and two-state formulas similarly invalidated pre-1967 Palestinian claims and experiences of displacement and have been likewise motivated by the demographic imperative to maintain a Jewish advantage without degenerating into an apartheid-like state. In other words, a just peace is measured in a self-reflexive, particularistic manner—peace is considered just only if it enables the continuous cultivation of Israel as an ethnodemocracy with a *jus sanguinis* principle of citizenship. It is this particularistic orientation that distinguishes the idea of "just peace" from the neologism of *justpeace*, which denotes a nonrelativistic, multiperspectival approach to peace and justice, lacking predetermined endpoints.

Anticipating Peace Now: Possibilities for Peace before Sadat

I return now to the point of departure of this chapter. On November 9, 1977, President Anwar Sadat of Egypt expressed his readiness to visit the Knesset in order to discuss peaceful alternatives to the state of belligerence raging since the establishment of the modern Israeli nation-state in 1948. Begin, the Israeli prime minister, reciprocated by extending a formal invitation to Sadat to come to Jerusalem and address the Knesset. A series of meetings and negotiations, overseen by U.S. officials, ensued with great enthusiasm.

The euphoria, however, proved ephemeral when it became clear that Begin refused Sadat's demands to highlight the Palestinian question as central to the prospective peace with Egypt, and to commit Israel to comprehensive territorial concessions. Moreover, when Sadat discovered that the Israeli housing minister, Ariel Sharon, had authorized further settlement projects in the Sinai area, he abruptly discontinued the talks.[46] The languishing hope of peace constituted the context for the emergence of PN, the largest Israeli peace movement, as a critical and, at times, massive nongovernmental lobby with strong parliamentary connections.

The formation of PN, in effect, culminated a rather intense process dating back to the aftermath of the 1967 war and the consolidation of the Israeli military occupation over the territories it gained. The Khartoum summit meeting of Arab leaders, which convened approximately three months after the war, and its declaration of the "three nos"—no peace with Israel, no recognition of Israel, and no negotiation with the Jewish state—provided the pretext for hardening the line of Levi Eshkol's Labor-dominated government of national unity. While initially there was a sense of diplomatic flexibility, Eshkol's coalition—which included expansionists (those influenced by Jabotinsky's Revisionist Zionism, such as Begin) and Labor hardliners, like Moshe Dayan and Yigal Allon—was now determined to resist pressure, particularly from the UN, to withdraw unilaterally from the territories.[47] This government of national unity chose to interpret UN Resolution 242, passed on November 22, 1967, as permission to hang onto the newly occupied territories for as long as the Arab states rejected Israeli national sovereignty.[48]

The "three nos" vindicated the alleged inevitability of the continuous military occupation of the territories. UN Resolution 242 established the illegality of "the acquisition of territory by war." Yet it conditioned the imperative to withdraw upon the "termination of all claims or states of belligerency and respect for the acknowledgement of the sovereignty, territorial integrity and political independence of every State in the area and their right to live in peace within secure and recognized boundaries free of threats or acts of force." By underscoring Arab rejectionism, and thus the imperative to cling to the territories until Israel's sovereignty was fully accepted, Eshkol's government of national unity "decided not to decide." This policy enabled the survival of Eshkol's fragile coalition and the onset of the settlement project outside the Green Line.[49] However, it also meant that no serious attempt to initiate peace negotiations was made by the Labor-led governments between the War of 1967 and the Yom Kippur War of 1973.[50]

The formula of "land for peace" was ambiguously born out of this national consensus.[51] Shortly after the conclusion of the War of 1967, Allon advanced the prospect of a pending territorial compromise. However, he suggested that, rather than a compliance with the logic of Resolution 242, such a compromise entailed a willingness on the part of the Jewish people to give up their right to hold onto the territories—a willingness to mitigate their historical claims to the land for the sake of peace.[52] In July of 1967, Allon proposed a plan to annex strategically certain territories (including East Jerusalem) for a massive settlement undertaking while giving up other territories for the potential establishment of an "Autonomous Arab Region." Subsequently, what came to be known as the "Allon Plan" provided a blueprint for settlement activity from 1967 to 1973.

The Allon Plan reflects how the democratically elected Labor-led coalition interpreted the meaning of peace and justice in the first few years after 1967. So conceived, a just peace entailed full recognition of the sovereignty of Israel on the part of the neighboring Arab countries. In return, Israel was willing to give up some of the territories acquired by conquest, territories to which it has corroborated historical claims through archeological findings and the broader ethos of return to the land where the Hebraic fathers had dwelled (the Tanakh was read as a book of history). Golda Meir, who succeeded Eshkol after his death in 1969, reinforced this formula of "land for peace." On one occasion she commented, "The price [for withdrawal] would be peace, permanent peace, peace by treaty based on agreed and secure borders."[53]

The upshot of this formula under Meir's tenure was the lack of any peace initiative whatsoever. The perception of justice central to the "land for peace" formula therefore suggests a clear departure from the rapprochement model earlier articulated by Buber and Magnes and their cohort. Instead of curtailing the sense of national entitlement in accordance with the realities of the land, the consolidation of power in the Israeli nation-state and the legacy of Jewish persecutions in Europe enabled the unfolding of a myopic outlook that concealed and normalized Palestinian histories of displacement and colonization. What came to be known as the "peace process" resonated most clearly with the concept of "negative peace"—a cessation of direct violence and a sense of security in return for territorial concessions.[54]

Prior to the Yom Kippur trauma, the majority of the Jewish citizens of Israel were content with the logic underpinning the "land for peace" formula as advanced in the Allon Plan. This is evidenced by the lack of a coherent mobilization challenging the implications of this formula. Concurrent archeological discoveries reinforced the idea of the land as reclaimed property.[55] However, a few individuals still attempted to challenge this logic, confronting but not deviating from the acceptable outline of the Zionist conversation. For instance, Arieh (Lova) Eliav, a prominent figure in the Labor Party, articulated a position that put him somewhat at odds with the consensus view on the Arab-Israeli conflict.[56] His innovation, though, was more rhetorical than substantial. He argued for the need to recognize the Palestinians as a national group and to relinquish most of the West Bank and the Gaza Strip in order to create a sovereign Palestinian state on both banks of the Jordan River. Like Allon, however, he invoked the idea that any Israeli withdrawal would amount to a sacrifice of a historical rightful claim rather than a return of the spoils of war. Eliav wrote: "There is room in the land of the Twelve Tribes for the State of Israel and a Palestinian-Jordanian state. In exchange for a full and permanent peace we will waive implementing part of our historical rights in this Arab state."[57]

Clearly, already in the early 1970s, Eliav's rationale and vision of peace diverged from the contemporaneous official line of his Labor Party, in that he advocated the distinct nationhood of the Palestinians (distinguishing them from the wider so-called "Arab problem"). It is only with the events of the First Intifada that such recognition became mainstream practice. Eliav's digression from official formulations, however, did not amount to a transformational shift because his introduction or, in effect, reintroduction of plans for partition, reframed as the two-state solution, still reinforced the premises of the "land for peace" formula. Eliav explicitly reframed the intention to withdraw as an act of peaceful and neighborly generosity, entailing the modest Israeli desire to be recognized in return.

Drawing on biblical warrants, such a conceptual reframing is clearly blind to the perception and experience of Israeli occupation as an act of colonialist aggression. It is similarly blind to the relevance of the pre-1967 history of settlement, expulsion, and conquest as well as the moralistic conjoining of the Zionist policy of Hebraizing Palestine and the Holocaust of European Jews. Hence, unlike the visions of Buber and his associates, Eliav's vision of peace is characterized by an ahistorical interpretation of the reality of Israeli occupation, unconstrained by *Wirklichkeitszionismus*.

The invocation of biblical proofs of ancient physical presence in the land, and the national fascination with biblical archeology in general, attest to the reliance of secular Zionists on a sublimated theology. Yet the secularist orientation of people like Allon and Eliav enables them to think of these sources as mere historical documents. It involves a selective form of literalism (granted that every case of literalism is selective by definition), where certain portions of the Tanakh are read as historical data and others are framed as "legends" or "customs of the time." This approach resonates with my memories from elementary and secondary schools: as a product of the secular education system in Israel, I was taught that the Tanakh was a historical document that relates to contemporary events and contains a land-centric narrative about the beginning of my nation. Indeed the literalist reading of the Tanakh ironically provided for a curious convergence between, on the one hand, extreme secularists like the Canaanites who wished to sever ties from Judaism through a reclaiming of pre-Jewish Hebraic identities and, on the other, religious Zionists who deployed the Tanakh as a title deed to the land, enabling the fulfillment of a Jewish redemption. The mainline Zionist ideology fluctuated ambiguously between the two poles, eventually foregrounding the Holocaust and Jewish martyrology as the core of the Israeli ethos.[58] The reading of the Tanakh (and the Holocaust), in socializing a particular historical Jewish Israeli consciousness, normalized and vindicated Jewish presence in Palestine. Therefore, it obscured the possibility of recognizing how the narratives of Palestinian displacement and uprootedness might challenge the perceptions of peace and justice as imagined within the Zionist vista.

Peace activism in the 1970s was not exempt from the broader ethos. There was no sign of a conceptual move from critiquing the occupation born out of 1967 to scrutinizing the presumed normalcy of the state within the 1948 borders. That was the case even with the most critical and innovative voices. For example, the Charter of the Israel-Palestine Council for Peace (established in December 1975 by Eliav, along with Uri Avnery, Simcha Flapan, and other peace activists) was considered radical because it reaffirmed Eliav's recognition of the necessity and inevitability of the two-state solution.[59] At that time, the Labor Party still held the "Jordanian option" (which called for the absorption of some Palestinian-populated regions into Jordan) as its official position, unwilling to recognize the legitimacy of distinctly Palestinian claims.

The charter, however, makes no attempt to define and explain the meanings or implications of maintaining Jewish political sovereignty. Nor does it challenge the validity of the historic (or rather ahistoric) argument so central to the "land for peace" formula, much less what I have identified as the "metahistorical bias" of that historical argument. It merely identifies the "equal" legitimacy of the Palestinian argument, thereby validating the legitimacy of the Jewish ethnorepublican project. Further, it perceives domestic questions of social justice as distinguishable from, and irrelevant to, the broader conflict with the Palestinians. Consequently, their proposal reinforces the spatial and normative differentiation supposedly denoted by the Green Line. This differentiation betrayed a particularistic rather than a multiperspectival conception of justice, one that could take into account a multiplicity of narratives and experiences, as the story of Jewish "return" cannot be told without the story of Palestinian displacement.

In 1977, Avnery and Eliav established Sheli (an acronym meaning "Peace for Israel"), a political party whose platform was largely consistent with the council's effort to centralize the question of Palestinian self-determination. Grounding the call to self-determination in an appeal to universal rights rhetorically resulted, once again, in a myopic lens that, in putting Palestinian and Israeli claims to nation-statehood on an equal footing, ahistoricized those claims. The council, and later Sheli, were depicted as radical by some analysts. In fact, many Israelis branded them as treacherous.[60] And yet, however radical their validation of an equal Palestinian claim for self-determination may have seemed at the time, they too did not diverge, in either their parliamentary or their extraparliamentary form, from the bounds of legitimate Zionist discourse.

The same way the binational plans devised by Brit Shalom and Ihud enabled bypassing internal questioning of the entitlement to settle Palestine and cultivate a Jewish/Hebraic culture therein, the positioning of Israeli and Palestinian nationalisms as equally entitled to national self-determination eclipses the importance of confronting the root cause of the conflict—the colonial displacement of Palestinians in the first place. In both Sheli and Brit Shalom, the language of equality limited and even obscured the complexities of the situation and the structural inequalities inscribed in its historical particularities. The language also obscured the processes of cultural reframing that may be necessary to imagine a just peace that would address the colonial act of population displacement. Recognizing this defining historical development illuminates the blind spots of the parity model of Buber's binationalism and the two-state formula. The presumption of equality in both instances normalizes the core narrative, which is one of injustice.

While Sheli and the Council for Israel-Palestine Peace represented the emergence of a radical Zionist left, the aftermath of June 1967 also witnessed the emergence of the Movement for Greater Israel.[61] In an attempt to confront this expansionist tide, a few academics, including Yehoshua Arieli, formed the Movement for Peace and Security in July of 1968. Its charter clearly articulated an anti-annexationist stance.[62] Peace and Security challenged the national unity government's decision "not to decide," recognizing that this indecision amounted to an active settlement project in the territories occupied in 1967. While consenting to the "land for peace" logic, and thus holding onto the territories as bargaining chips in the meantime, the movement insisted that no civilian settlement of the newly occupied territories should be authorized. It also demanded that the government declare its intention to refrain from territorial annexation and initiate and facilitate programs for resolving the problem of Palestinian refugees.

Peace and Security, which consciously represented itself as a loyal mainstream Zionist group, failed to generate mass support. This failure may be attributed to what was perceived as the persistent belligerence of the Arab countries as well as to the three-year-long war of attrition along the Suez Canal (1967–70).[63] While the Movement for Greater Israel gathered momentum only by March 1974, when Allon supported Rabbi Moshe Levinger's intention to establish a Jewish settlement in Hebron (1968), the 150 signatures of prominent academics that opposed this turn of events were disregarded. Shortly after Allon gave his tacit approval to Levinger's settlement project, the Israeli cabinet under Meir refused to authorize Nahum Goldmann (the president, at the time, of the World Zionist Organization and the World Jewish Congress) to accept an invitation extended to him by President Gamal Abdel Nasser of Egypt.[64] Nasser had invited Goldmann to come to Egypt to present his position on the possibility of reconciliation between Israel and Egypt. Nasser's condition, however, constituted a demand for the official consent of the Israeli government. The argument against authorizing Goldmann's trip to Egypt was that Nasser's invitation attempted to circumvent Israel's insistence on direct negotiations. Peace and Security mobilized public protests against the government's decision but was unable, once again, to reverse the tide.

That tide amounted to the launching of systematic settlement policies. This development did not cohere with the peace agenda and the willingness to relinquish territories. Still, the peace camp at the time was confined to a very limited ideological frame. The Council for Israel-Palestine Peace, the Sheli political party, and Peace and Security all demonstrated a general acceptance of the official "land for peace" formula. As I have argued, complicity with this formula entailed a metahistorical bias whereby the occupied territories of 1967 were construed as the regained (or even liberated) biblical land and thus as a bargaining chip in the process of overcoming Arab rejection of the existence of Israel.

The council, Sheli, and Peace and Security further connected this formula of "land for peace" to a strong, anti-annexationist stance and eventually (in the case of Sheli and the council) to the inevitable recognition of a two-state solution. While the logic for the two-state formulation derives from a recognition of the universal right to self-determination, its driving force is a particularistic concern with the character of Israel as Jewish and democratic. Because these groups, like PN and Gush Shalom later, perceived themselves to be secularist, liberal, and enlightened, none attempted to complicate the Biltmore formula that equated Judaism with Zionism. Nor did they examine how the conceptual problems inherent in the construct of a Jewish democracy might bear on the unfolding conflict with the Palestinians. Their circumventing of such questions is an indication of how these earlier predecessors of PN reinforced the secular Zionist consensus.

As noted at the outset of this chapter, this myopic prism permitted a conceptual differentiation between the territories occupied in 1948 and those occupied in 1967. This differentiation facilitated the deployment of binaries, depicting the religious settlers in the West Bank and the Gaza Strip as categorically of a different kind than the secular mainstream Israelis within the Green Line. This construal came under scrutiny in scholarly works that illuminated the relations of ideological continuity between secular and religious Zionists as well as the spatial continuities between Israel proper and the settlement project.[65] It is the ideological continuity that enabled the complicity of successive governments (both right and left) with the settlement project in the occupied territories.[66] It is this ideological continuity that also delimited the interpretation of peace and justice in the Israeli-Palestinian conflict. The mainstream secular Zionist peace camp, hence, operated with an axiomatic conception of Israeli Jewish identity. This is typified in the story of PN.

III. Peace Now and the Zionist Peace Camp

The Principles of Disillusioned Patriots

At the beginning of this chapter I recalled my memory of the inception of the PN movement. Its emergence can be attributed to a letter signed initially by 348 reserve officers and noncommissioned officers (and eventually by 250,000 Israelis), an esteemed echelon of the population that could not have been accused of disloyalty or lack of patriotism.[67] The letter, which questioned "the justice of our cause," was addressed to Prime Minister Begin on the eve of one of his several visits to Washington, D.C., in order to assuage President Jimmy Carter's dismay at Israel's handling of the negotiations with Egypt.[68] The prestige of the officers and the substantial and unprecedented public support of their position allegedly led Prime Minister

Begin to Camp David to concede to eventual withdrawal of Israeli presence from the Sinai Peninsula as part of a peace agreement with Egypt.

Henceforth, PN functioned as the most widely supported and influential peace organization in Israel. However, its influence was always limited, and increasingly so with the decline of the Israeli peace movement in general in the aftermath of the signing of the Oslo Accords in 1993 and its significantly diminished ability to exert political and social influence following the assassination of Prime Minister Yitzhak Rabin (1995). This process was compounded by the failure of the Camp David Summit of July 2000, the subsequent eruption of the violent Second Intifada (September 2000), the building of a barrier fence under the leadership of Sharon, the unilateral disengagement from Gaza (summer 2005), and the democratic election of Hamas in 2006, as well as the failure of successive attempts at bilateral negotiations. These events, an Israeli researcher of the peace movement, Tamar Hermann, argues, "led to a complete halt of peace activism in Israel."[69] This halt is represented in the slogan "There is no partner for peace." This slogan presupposes that negotiations failed because "the other side" was persistently "irrational."[70] This slogan is fraught with orientalist motifs as well.

Despite the "death" of the Israeli peace camp, analyzing PN as it dynamically changed over the years provides a glimpse into how this group came to represent a consensus position (eventually embodied in the Rabin administration of 1993) and why this consensus glossed over the underlying meta-injustices informing the Israeli-Palestinian conflict. While smaller groups located left of the movement challenged its consensus platform during different critical intersections like the First Lebanon War and the Intifada, they too had to subscribe to the two-state peace formula, increasingly within the scope of Zionist acceptability, in order to generate any popular momentum on the streets of Israel.

The officers' letter that led to the emergence of PN expressed a general anxiety that a rare opportunity for peace might be sacrificed on the altar of expansionist settlement ideology. The officers, whose defining military experience had been the trauma of the Yom Kippur War,[71] wrote accordingly:

> A government that prefers the establishment of the State of Israel in the borders of a Greater Israel above the establishment of peace through good neighborly relations, instills in us many doubts. A government that prefers the establishment of settlements beyond the "Green Line" to the elimination of the historical quarrel and the establishment of normal relations in our region, will awaken in us questions as to the justice of our cause. A government policy which will continue the domination over millions of Arabs may damage

the democratic and Jewish character of the state and make it difficult for us to
identify with the path taken by the State of Israel.

Already this initial letter reflects the basic and perhaps axiomatic principles that would guide the PN movement for years to come, from its role in
the Camp David Accords through its positions on the First Lebanon War,
the First Intifada, the Oslo Accords, the Second Intifada and the failure of
Oslo, and, finally, the Second Lebanon War and beyond. The letter shows
that the primary target of the officers' critique was the specific expansionist
ideology of the Likud Party and the settlement movement. Their concern is
centered on how the occupation of the Arab territories conquered in 1967
would contradict the identity of Israel as Jewish, democratic, enlightened,
and "Western."

Thus, the letter did not depart in any significant way from the Zionist
tenets already laid out in the Biltmore Program. In fact, the letter defined PN
as a consensus Zionist movement. Like the Allon Plan, it did not question
the legitimacy of the pre-1967 borders. Nor did it challenge the metahistorical underpinnings of the "land for peace" formula and the imperative
to cultivate Israel's character as both "democratic and Jewish," an imperative critically challenged by the reality of its domination over millions of
non-Jewish Arabs. But the letter, like the Charter of the Council for Israel-
Palestine Peace earlier, did not articulate what precisely such a constellation entailed outside of a rather narrow demographic argument. Indeed,
the leaders of the movement intentionally allowed for broad ideological
flexibility in order to maintain a wide base of popular support.[72]

In its subsequent 1978 position paper, PN highlighted that "Israel and
Zionism cannot be based on the domination and suppression of another
nation." It added: "The occupation corrupts the occupier."[73] This formulation substantiates my charge that the Israeli peace camp is afflicted with
historical amnesia enabled by a metahistorical outlook. PN chose to draw a
distinction between Israel proper and the territories occupied in 1967 and
to delimit its discussion of the occupation and its implications accordingly.
Thus, it focused its efforts initially on advancing peace negotiations with
Egypt. After the Camp David Accords, the movement chose to concentrate
its efforts on protesting the settlement policy in the occupied territories.
Notably, while discussing the corrupting effects of the occupation on the
occupier, the position paper makes no reference to the particular predicaments of the occupied. Only later, in the months leading up to the Lebanon
war, would the brutality of the occupation come into sharper relief.

Fighting in a War of Choice?

Launched in 1982, the First Lebanon War provided the next landmark moment in the history of PN. The reluctance of the movement to protest promptly what was quickly considered a war of choice signaled, in the eyes of more radical activists, its moral decline. I sample such positions below. Because of PN's investment in projecting a patriotic image, the group was a latecomer to the antiwar protest, spearheaded by the Committee Against the War in Lebanon (CAWL), an organization composed in part by some of the members of an early and marginalized communist party by the name of Siah (the Israeli New Left).[74] The CAWL emerged out of a group that had been formed the previous year, the Committee for Solidarity with Bir Zeit University (CSBZU). The latter group—comprising Jewish peace activists, such as physics professor Daniel Amit from the Hebrew University, a coalition of left-wing groups, and a number of instructors from the Palestinian Bir Zeit University—protested the creation of the Civilian Administration of the occupied territories in November 1981. The establishment of this administrative body had been correctly interpreted as an attempt to normalize the occupation.[75]

Transformed into its new role as the CAWL, the CSBZU instantly mobilized against the war. Conversely, the leadership of PN had initially avoided openly criticizing this expansionist "war of choice" owing to their fear of being depicted as unpatriotic. But two weeks into the fighting, PN finally questioned in an advertisement: "Why are we killing and being killed in Lebanon?"[76] Indeed, it rapidly became clear that the invasion, which was construed as a brief military operation to "restore peace to the Galilee," intended to destroy the infrastructure of the PLO in Lebanon and to intervene in the Lebanese civil war on behalf of the Christian Falangist forces. This calculated but fatal decision of Sharon (then the minister of defense) to catalyze a "regime change" in Lebanon led to a massacre (1982) in the Sabra and Shatilla refugee camp instead. The CAWL interpreted Sharon's support of the Falangists as an indication of his ultimate intention to reshape Lebanon under a Falangist government, which would, in turn, repress the PLO in Lebanon and thus enable Israeli annexation of the Palestinian occupied territories.[77]

When Sharon's "secret agenda" was eventually communicated by the CAWL (and soldiers returning from the field), a host of other antiwar groups sprang forth. For example, Yesh Gvul (There Is a Limit/Border) decided to actively refuse service in Lebanon.[78] Similarly, Parents Against Silence (PAS) demanded the immediate return of their children from Lebanon.[79] PN and the CAWL flooded the streets of Israel in protest, especially after the complicity of the IDF in the Sabra and Shatilla massacre was made known in September 1982.[80] It was in this heated and polarized context that Emile Gruenzweig, a PN activist, was killed by a hand grenade thrown at a PN demonstration in Jerusalem on February 10, 1983.

Informed observers of the Israeli peace movement noted that Gruenzweig's murder precipitated a sense of a loss of innocence in PN.[81] Because the grenade was thrown by a Mizrahi Israeli Jew, the traumatic murder of a peace activist aroused an acute interethnic tension, filled with anti-Mizrahi rhetoric. As a result, the Mizrahi East for Peace Movement was formed.[82] East for Peace was able to link, to a certain degree, the question of social justice in Israel proper to the peace program and structures of occupation and domination of the Palestinians—an oversight on the part of PN, a privileged and economically comfortable elite. In addition to the metahistorical bias that had construed the question of return to and settlement in Palestine as an axiomatic entitlement, East for Peace thus exposes another spatial and conceptual bias: a differentiation between the so-called ethnic and "internal" problem with the Mizrahim, as well as the Palestinian citizens of Israel, and the "external" conflict with the Palestinians. This conceptual bias is informed by the spatial bias that distinguishes qualitatively between the territories occupied in 1967 and Israel proper within the Green Line. As I illustrate in subsequent chapters, emphasizing the counternarratives of the "domestic other" might "denaturalize" those distinctions, permitting reimagining, and critical reframing, of the question of peace and justice in the broader context of the Israeli-Palestinian conflict.

Indeed, after the murder of Gruenzweig, PN turned its focus briefly inward to reflect on the rising tide of atavistic support of the explicitly racist rhetoric and platform advanced by the American-born Rabbi Meir Kahane. A campaign was launched, calling for legislation against racism. While the intention was to delegitimize Kahane's participation in the Knesset, the upshot of the antiracist legislation was the official and mainstreaming delegitimization not only of explicitly racist propaganda but also of the non-Zionist Israeli left.[83] For example, section 7A (1) of the Basic Law (the skeleton frame of Israel's constitutional law turned into an uncodified constitution) reads: "The Knesset excludes candidates for election to the Knesset if those candidates explicitly or implicitly suggest the denial of the existence of the State of Israel as a Jewish and democratic state."[84]

Hence, although Kahane's rhetoric offended the sensibilities of most Israelis, the mainstream Zionist consensus nonetheless secured the ethnoreligiocentric definition of the Israeli state. Even from within the ranks of the judicial system—a bastion of liberal secularism—Chief Justice Aharon Barak elucidated what was meant by the imperative to maintain the identity of Israel as Jewish:

> What, then, are the central characteristics shaping the minimum definition of the State of Israel as a Jewish State? These characteristics come from the aspects of both Zionism and heritage. At their center stands the right of every Jew to immigrate to the State of Israel, where the Jews will constitute a majority. Hebrew is the official and principal language of the State and most of its feasts and symbols reflect the national revival of the Jewish People.[85]

The second right-wing government of Benjamin Netanyahu (formed in 2009) accelerated Israel's chauvinistic impulse. Under the sponsorship of the Russian-born ultranationalist minister of foreign affairs Avigdor Lieberman, the Knesset considered legislation that profoundly threatened the future of the Palestinian citizens of Israel. The legislation included a bill that called for outlawing the commemoration of the Naqba (the Palestinian catastrophe of 1948). Another bill conditioned citizenship on the willingness to take an "oath of loyalty" to Israel as a "Jewish, Zionist, and democratic state." An additional bill rendered criminal the public denial of Israel's right to exist as a Jewish state.[86] This trend constitutes a slippery slope with further attempts by Netanyahu's right-wing coalition in 2011 to criminalize dissent by outlawing Israeli support of the Boycott, Divestment, and Sanction (BDS) campaign against the occupation. Likewise, the Knesset passed bills limiting the amount of funds that Israeli human rights organizations and NGOs could receive from foreign contributors. Consistent with such legislative development, the Israeli Supreme Court and other judicial checks increasingly turned into enablers rather than resisters of the ethnocentric logic and institutional framework. For instance, in July 2012, former Supreme Court Justice Edmond Levi released the report of a panel appointed by Prime Minister Netanyahu tasked with the interrogation of the legality or illegality of the occupation. This report concluded that the Fourth Geneva Convention's prohibition against transferring of civilian population by an occupying force does not apply to the case of Israel's settlement of the West Bank because there had not been an antecedent recognition of any country in that territory. The committee headed by Levi, therefore, reached the "legal" conclusion that there is no such thing as an Israeli occupation, a legal maneuver (or a variation of it) that has, in the past, enabled the de facto annexation of Jerusalem.[87]

The Occupation Makes Us Look Bad!

The eruption of the First Intifada in December 1987 signified another watershed moment in the life of the Zionist peace camp. Already in the months leading to the Intifada, a new informal group named Dai La'Kibush (Enough of the Occupation) emerged, calling for the unambiguous and immediate termination of the occupation and for negotiations with the PLO concerning a two-state solution.[88] This group, in the tradition of PN, allowed for broad ideological participation. It conducted frequent vigils and organized visits to the territories, hospitals, and refugee camps in order to "bring back home" news about the brutality of the Israeli occupation.[89] To this extent, Dai La'Kibush further reinforced and deepened the activists' exposure to the human stories of the occupied. The group represented the Intifada as a legitimate struggle and as a means of liberating Israel from the morally detrimental burden of oppression.[90]

The first year of the Intifada marked also the twenty-first year of Israeli occupation outside the Green Line. That year a new group, aptly named "the Twenty-First Year," was formed. The group issued a manifesto titled the *Covenant Against Occupation*. Composed by Israeli academics (primarily Adi Ophir and Hanan Hever), the *Covenant* stresses how the continuous occupation demolished the democratic fabric of Israel, turning Israeli democracy into a mere façade. It reads: "Israel is losing its democratic character. The continued existence of the parliamentary regime within the 'Green Line' cannot disguise the fact that Israel rules over a population . . . which is deprived of all democratic rights." The *Covenant* further accentuated the corrupting and insidious dimensions of the occupation: "The 'nice' Israeli expresses his or her anguish, remonstrates and demonstrates, but by accepting the terms and norms of political conduct set by the regime implicitly collaborates with the occupation."[91]

The *Covenant* constituted a direct attack on PN and its strategy of "nice," civilized, sporadic, and situational political protest against the occupation by individuals who would later execute repressive orders as reservists in the IDF—complying with the morally cleansing "shooting and crying" Israeli syndrome, which afflicts the economically and socially privileged strata in particular.[92] This syndrome is symptomatic of how the occupation of the 1967 territories naturalized and reinforced the identity of Israel as Jewish and democratic. It is morally cleansing in that agonizing over the illegality and illegitimacy of the occupation absolves one from introspection about how it is related to the realities at home, within the bounds of Israel proper, and how it may truncate a substantive peace agenda. Certainly, PN has tended to acquiesce to the metahistorical and conceptual/spatial biases inherent in the Israeli ethos.

By contrast, the *Covenant* called for a total refusal of any form of complicity with the occupation: "Refusal is the only morally and politically sound form of participation in Israeli society during the occupation. Refusal is a way out, a source of hope for our moral integrity as Israelis."[93] In sum, the *Covenant* of the Twenty-First Year highlighted the totality of the occupation and the dire threat it posed to the semblance of democracy in Israel proper, the general complicity of Israelis (including the Zionist peace camp) with structures of domination and oppression, and the need for a moral struggle against every aspect of the occupation.[94]

The picture depicted by the Twenty-First Year illuminated the centrality of the occupation to Israeli society. However, despite the *Covenant's* call for radical action, the mobilization and protest strategies of the group did not significantly diverge from the underlying commitment of the liberal contingent of the peace camp. Israeli critic and peace activist Reuven Kaminer points out that when the Intifada was a year old, for example, the group organized a "camp-out" outside of a detention center. In order to attract crowds, the organizers were careful to reduce the scope of their protest to acceptable parameters. While they did not condone holding the detainees in Ansar Prison, they nevertheless limited their protest exclusively to the poor treatment of the Palestinian prisoners. Thus, the revolutionary implications of the *Covenant* were abandoned for the sake of consensus yet again.[95]

By construing the "occupation" as the primary threat to Israeli democracy, the *Covenant*, in effect, overlooked the question of the problematic identity of Israel as a Jewish democracy. The *Covenant* did not link the treatment of the Palestinian minorities in Israel proper with the predicament of the Palestinians outside of the Green Line. Nor did it draw a connection between the occupation and the socioeconomic dynamics in Israel. Its point of departure, like that of the consensus peace camp, was June 1967. Its critique of the occupation was profound but did not radically depart from the central premises undergirding PN.[96] Thus, when the possibility of negotiations with the PLO became dimly attainable in 1989, the Twenty-First Year reverted to a traditional Zionist demand for explicit recognition of Israel by the Palestinians and a complete neglect of terrorism.[97]

Hence, the group also reinforced the "peace with security" slogan of the conventional peace camp. This slogan is consistent with the usual demands implied by the notion of "negative peace" (which entails the absence of open war and direct violence but does not redress the root causes of conflict). Engaging the concept and possibility of "positive peace"—one that focuses on the transformation of undergirding relational patterns—however, can come about only through questioning of structural and cultural violence and recognizing the interconnections between membership in Israel, social justice, and the occupation of Palestinian territories and people.

Nevertheless, the Twenty-First Year identified the systemic problems of the occupation and their ramifications for Israeli society very lucidly.[98] Along with Yesh Gvul, it generated an important debate within the peace camp about questions of conscience and the limits of state authority. The case of the complicity of SS soldiers with the Nazi regime was cited frequently as a relevant example. The refusal of the activists of Yesh Gvul to serve in the occupied territories on moral grounds significantly diverged from "acceptable" protest practices.[99] Because the PN leadership identified the strength of the movement with its patriotic obedience to the law, it wished to contain any form of protest within the legal framework. Hence, their activists would shoot first and cry later, as the cliché had it. They had to follow orders as Israeli citizens and soldiers in the IDF while crying over their complicity with an illegal occupation.

Groups such as Enough of the Occupation, Yesh Gvul, Women in Black, and the Twenty-First Year immediately recognized how the Intifada ultimately accentuated the moral and political imperative to negotiate with the PLO in order to establish a Palestinian state. Conversely, in the early phases of this uprising, PN was still reluctant to shift to the two-state formula, away from the more careful "land for peace" framework. Thus, it focused its protests on a more cautious argument against Israel's contribution to the diplomatic impasse.[100] As has been its practice since the late 1970s, the primary target of its critique was the Likud Party, now under the leadership of Yitzhak Shamir. (The movement tended to be dormant during the Labor-led coalitions in the Knesset.) A decade or so after the officers' famous letter to Begin, PN mobilized its constituency in order to encourage Prime Minister Shamir to collaborate with U.S. secretary of state George Shultz's initiative in 1988, modeled on the Camp David autonomy principle.[101]

The collapse of the Shultz initiative, aided by a confluence of events, led the PN movement to realize the infeasibility of the so-called Jordanian option. These events included the inauguration of yet another Shamir-led coalition in 1988, the Basam Abu Sharif document that indicated a willingness among some segments within the PLO to think of a two-state option, the Jordanian King Hussein's renunciation of any claim to the West Bank in July of 1988, the decision of the November 1988 Palestine National Council meeting in Algiers to accept the previously rejected 1947 UN Resolution 181 calling for the partition of Palestine, and Yasser Arafat's official denunciation of terror in the subsequent month. The upshot of departing from the Jordanian option was the recognition of the PLO as the representative agency of the Palestinian people and, finally, the cautious embrace of the possibility of a two-state platform.[102]

This reorientation, however, was not revolutionary but rather consistent with a concurrent shift in the Labor Party's approach to peace. Rabin and Shimon Peres announced publicly that with the failure of the Jordanian option, Israel would need to contend directly with the Palestinians, who would be required to elect their own representatives by means of a democratic election in the territories. Consistent with the Camp David Accords, an interim period of autonomy would precede full-fledged negotiations of a final arrangement between Israel and the Palestinians.[103] Nonetheless, the departure from the initial position of the PN movement precipitated an intense period of pressuring the Shamir-led government to negotiate with the PLO as well as launching intense Palestinian-Israeli dialogues across the Green Line.[104] The movement's eventual cooptation of the two-state program led to the disintegration of the smaller Enough of the Occupation and the Twenty-First Year groups in 1989.[105]

Stronger and reinvigorated, PN devoted considerable resources to monitoring the construction of settlements outside the Green Line and developing channels of communication with the Palestinians. However, the months leading up to the First Gulf War and the war itself presented significant difficulties to the peace camp because Arafat opted to support Saddam Hussein of Iraq. In spite of this, the peace movement decided to continue the informal talks, criticizing the closures frequently imposed on the territories as unwarranted. After the Gulf crisis had subsided, the movement exerted pressure on the Shamir coalition to collaborate with the new initiative by George H. W. Bush and U.S. secretary of state James Baker to convene an international conference and bilateral talks.[106] When Shamir finally gave in to the Baker initiative, what came to be remembered as the Madrid Conference took place in October of 1991. The processes, which began in Madrid, eventually led to Oslo.

PN, as I mentioned, emerged out of the profound disillusionment caused by the 1973 war compounded by the political revolution of 1977 and the prospect of a missed opportunity for peace with Egypt. Nonetheless, like the earlier Peace and Security group, PN, in its approximately thirty years of existence, has tried to package itself as a patriotic Zionist movement for peace. In this effort, the movement has capitalized on the military prestige of its founders in order to validate its critique of specific Israeli policies. Consequently, the movement reached a point of crisis as a result of the diminishing value of the military in the 1990s, the emergence of a new business sector to prominent position, and the concomitant culture of neoliberalism that permeated the Israeli landscape.

While remaining an independent extraparliamentary movement, PN also held strong ties to the Knesset. In particular, the movement affiliated itself ideologically with the Citizens Rights Movement (CRM), Shinui, Mapam, and certain elements within the Labor Party.[107] While these political parties are all conventionally considered synonymous with the "left" and an integral part of the peace camp, they differ from one another in significant ways on socioeconomic issues.[108] In fact, the classification of the "peace camp" as occupying the "left" of the political spectrum often constitutes a misnomer. In what follows, I discuss the parliamentary dimensions of the loyal peace camp.

IV. The Peace Contingency in the Knesset

It is worth exploring in some detail the platform of Meretz—the political party most closely associated with the Zionist peace camp. By looking at Meretz's platform, which has tied its vision of peace to at times antireligious militancy, one may further discern the ambiguities and internal contradictions of the Israeli Zionist secularist left.

This political party came into being out of an alliance of the three political parties most closely associated with the Zionist peace camp—CRM, Mapam, and Shinui. Mapam, the Labor Party, represented remnants of the old socialist Zionism.[109] The CRM and Shinui parties emerged decades after Mapam in the early 1970s. The former parties focused primarily on questions of civil rights and the need for economic and political liberalization—an approach that put them in tension with the socialist Mapam. Mapam embodied the old Zionist state-centered legacy of economic and social organization.

Shinui and CRM generally supported the liberalization and transformation of the Israeli economy and concurrently propelled the so-called "constitutional revolution" of the 1990s.[110] Implementing a local interpretation of the Thatcher-Reagan framework, the liberalization and privatization of the Israeli economy involved a set of interrelated transformations on judicial and political levels.[111] Despite their neoliberal economic orientation, Shinui and CRM came to represent the Israeli "left" owing to their peace platforms. This representation is a misnomer, however, because their neoliberal stance prevented them from recognizing the interconnections between questions of poverty and marginalization of certain strata within

Israel and the conflict with the Palestinians. When one attempts to think holistically about peacebuilding, however, those connections become clear and important.[112]

An examination of Meretz's platform indicates that, by and large, the party replicates Zionist themes without problematizing their premises or reflecting on their implications for the conflict. For example, Meretz's stated principles reaffirm the commitment of secular political Zionism to the concept of a Jewish democracy. Its platform declares: "The principle of freedom of religion or freedom from religion requires the separation of religion and state." It also, however, stresses that "Israel is a Jewish and democratic state; a state of all its citizens—Jews and Arabs alike."[113] These statements point to the party's identity as a champion of individual rights and liberties. Yet the affirmation of Israel's identity as a Jewish democracy, while championing the cause of religious freedoms, is obviously problematic because it points to the deep ambiguity underlying secular Zionism—an ambiguity that, while situated at the heart of the conflict, is not explicated, analyzed, or debated by the party's faithful. To this extent, Meretz echoes Israel's Declaration of Independence with its ahistoric allusion to the story of exile and return.

Certainly, in its discussion of peace with the Palestinians, Meretz draws a distinction between Israel proper and its minorities, on the one hand, and the inhabitants of the territories occupied in 1967, on the other. The assumption seems to be that the recognition of legitimate Palestinian claims for nation-statehood outside the Green Line absolves Meretz from confronting the practices of land confiscation, annexation, and discrimination committed within the borders of 1948. This disconnect has inhibited the development of a self-critical left.[114] Indeed, the impetus of Oslo, in the words of Israeli cultural critic Amnon Raz-Krakotzkin, was a desire for "the return to a homogeneous Jewish society. The idea was to get rid of the occupation in order to get rid of the Palestinians, in order to recover the Israeli self-image as innocent and progressive."[115] Such an attitude is reflective of the familiar cry of the peace movement that the occupation corrupts the occupier. Meretz is no different. The party replicated rather than problematized central Zionist themes: the centrality of Israel vis-à-vis the Jewish diasporas and the automatic right of Jewish return to the land of Israel. Even the choice to apply the concept of "return" to the immigration issue underscores that Meretz's interpretation of the interconnectedness between religion, nationalism, and the question of citizenship inadequately addresses the complexities, affinities, and overlaps of those identity markers as well as the question of how religion contributes to drawing ethnic and cultural boundaries. Even in the explicit attempt of Yossi Beilin, a prominent leader of the Israeli secular left, to conceptualize the precise relation between religion and state, the truisms of secular Zionism reverberate:

> There is a growing realization that a new path must be charted in regards to the relationship between religion and state. This new path would aim to fulfill Israel's role as a Jewish and democratic state, while taking into consideration Israel's special conditions and circumstances: as the state of the Jewish people, as a Jewish and democratic state with a considerable non-Jewish minority population, as a state whose Jewish citizens are religious, traditional and secular and as a state with a feeling of responsibility and significance for the Jewish people in the Diaspora.[116]

Beilin's statement underscores the assumption that Israel's commitment to its democratic tradition is to be constrained by its central location vis-à-vis Jewish communities around the world. This formulation, however, does not solve the inherent contradictions and undemocratic implications of the cultivation of a Jewish democracy. Beilin's desired political framework would ostensibly accommodate "religious, traditional and secular" Israeli citizens. Characteristic of an unreconstructed secularist orientation, his articulation does not take into account how Judaism as a cultural, national, and/or ethnic identity constrains the scope of democracy in Israel and what the implications of this blind spot may be for the conceptualization of peace and justice vis-à-vis the Palestinians. In the fashion of the secularist discourse, Beilin neutralizes the important connections between the ethnocentric underpinnings of Israel and the Palestinian-Israeli conflict by compartmentalizing religion as an issue solely of faith.

This kind of approach bypasses the importance of negotiating and reframing religion qua national identity as a key location for conflict transformation and peacebuilding. As mentioned above, Beilin's normalization of the ethnocentric identity of Israel is also reflected in his critique of the growing preoccupation with the concept of just or positive peace. In an essay that addresses this issue, he replicates the dominant storyline concerning the emergence of Zionism in a Europe plagued by modern forms of anti-Semitism:

> Educated and secular Jews were becoming increasingly sure that they could no longer live in Europe and realize their potential as people. They then proposed the idea of Zionism which advocated establishing a state, in which the citizens would be mostly Jewish, in the land of Israel where a Jewish state

existed 2000 years earlier. This was a land that had been the object of yearning for the Jewish people since they were exiled from it. It was also a land where Jews, albeit in small numbers, lived throughout an exile that lasted thousands of years.[117]

Beilin also chronicles how a series of rejections of pragmatic settlements contributed to the perpetuation of the Palestinian-Israeli conflict, thereby underscoring that the application of the concept of just peace is not only redundant but also dangerous because it presupposes the validity of the counterconcept of "unjust peace." The latter, Beilin concludes, can be used rhetorically to reject settlements that, if accepted, would have brought the cessation of violence. For instance, in reflecting on the missed opportunity of UN Resolution 181, which called for the partition of Palestine in November 1947, Beilin writes:

> In hindsight, it is clear how "just" this peace might have been. On the one hand, it provided a partial solution to the terrible distress of the European Jews, having made it clear to all that their lives could have been saved had they been permitted to immigrate to Israel. On the other hand, the war in 1948, and its many dead, could have been avoided. This war witnessed the burial of Holocaust survivors who lived through the camps, came to Israel, found themselves forced to bear arms and fight the Arab armies, and were killed. Israel buried 1 per cent of its population during the war in 1948–9. Thousands of Palestinians were killed, and 700,000 became refugees; some for fear, some due to their leaders' propaganda, and some were deported by the Jews who felt that nothing they would do could measure up to the dire conditions their people had to endure during the war. The Palestinian feeling that this was an "unjust peace" in 1947 stood in their way of getting a greater measure of justice for themselves and for the Israelis alike.[118]

Even with the supposed acknowledgment by Palestinian president Mahmood Abbas that the rejection of the UN partition plan constituted a mistake in hindsight, Beilin's telling of this missed opportunity glosses over the suffering and loss experienced historically by the Palestinians, for instance, the loss of their land and houses due to Zionist settlement in the prestate era. The focus on the Jewish narrative of persecution, extermination, and settlement in a land of refuge is exclusivist, overlooking a multiperspectival consideration of the ramifications of return for the indigenous inhabitants of the land.

Indeed, Beilin circumvents this moral dilemma by focusing only on the continuous physical Jewish presence in the land of Palestine since the time of the biblical exiles, thereby avoiding any attention to the land's other inhabitants. Beilin's account also neglects an analysis of Zionism's indebtedness to the colonial framework and discourse that enabled much of the early Zionist undertaking. He outlines the various documents granted to the Jews by the British mandate as yet other missed opportunities. He discusses the proposal by Lord William Peel, which envisioned the establishment of the Jewish state on less than 20 percent of the land. Beilin retorts: "Had both sides agreed to the Peel proposal, two states would have been established two years before the Second World War, and eleven years before the British mandate expired."[119]

Beilin's approach to and perception of Jewish history and the Palestinian-Israeli conflict are those of a liberal secularist thinker and political leader and testify to the central ambiguities of the Zionist secular peace camp. While Beilin avoids the undemocratic implications of the continuous cultivation of a Jewish democracy (one that indeed allows for a variety of modes of being Jewish, including that of a Jewish atheist), the Israeli historian Ilan Pappé explains that this commitment to the Jewish-democratic construct constitutes a root cause of the Palestinian tragedy because it systematically entails the working assumption that "every means is fair to ensure that there will be a Jewish majority, because without a Jewish majority we will not be a democracy."[120] The Israeli ethos and experience also connect the majoritarian commitment to the physical survival of the Jewish people. That this commitment to majoritarianism is the "root cause" of the conflict was not confronted by the liberal Zionist camp because such a confrontation would involve negotiating what may be perceived as nonnegotiable cores of the Jewish Israeli ethos as articulated in the Declaration of Independence and replicated in the Meretz platform. Rather than challenging it, the Oslo Accords and later the Geneva Initiative—both configurations made possible by Meretz—contributed to the general reinforcement of the Zionist consensus.[121]

V. Religion, Ethnicity, and the Secular Israeli Peace Camp

Undeniably, Meretz directed much of its effort to combat religious coercion and to challenge and reform what is commonly referred to as the "status quo" of religion and state in Israel. Accordingly, the party fought to expand the definition of conversion, liberalize family law, and draft yeshiva students for compulsory military service—to name only a few pieces of legislation (associated with the so-called constitutional revolution of the 1990s). But because its position on the Palestinian issue derived from a separationist impulse, the party interprets Israel's Jewish character primarily in demographic and cultural terms, presupposing the possibility of clear relegation of Judaism qua religion to the private sphere. This presumption betrays a clear secularist bias that cannot be sustained in contexts where the threshold for citizenship is defined by blood.

While Meretz's efforts to pluralize Israeli Judaism are indeed consistent with its commitment to individual liberties, its vision of a just peace is based on the two-state solution, which assumes an ethnocentric definition of citizenship in Israel. Further, the legitimacy of the Israeli state, even when articulated in terms of Jewish history and culture rather than religion, can never be entirely divorced from religious markers of identity. That the messianic dimensions of secular Zionism are sublimated does not mean that they do not exist or do not exercise a powerful hold on how Meretz envisions justice vis-à-vis the Palestinian predicament.

The nongovernmental Zionist peace camp, as exemplified in the chronicles of PN, also eluded a thorough confrontation of the underlying religious motifs of secular Zionism, manifested in the reduction of Judaism to Zionism and the reframing of "Jewish" as a "historical," "cultural," and/or "national" marker of identity. It did not examine how the conceptual problems inherent in the construct of a Jewish democracy might relate to the conflict with the Palestinians. It also failed to link apparently "domestic" questions of social justice to the conflict with the Palestinians.

PN indeed defined itself as a consensus Zionist movement. Despite its wide appeal, however, the movement traveled across a rather limited ideological landscape. Accordingly, the movement did not question the legitimacy of the pre-1967 borders. Nor did it challenge the ahistorical logic of the "land for peace" formula and the imperative to cultivate Israel's character as "democratic and Jewish." It also alienated the Mizrahim, rendering questions of social justice irrelevant and "domestic."[122]

Focusing on the territories conquered and occupied in 1967 enabled the predominantly Ashkenazi Israeli liberal left to maintain a conceptual differentiation between its view of the ethnic rift between Ashkenazim and Mizrahim and the divide between Jews and Palestinians. This differentiation only reinforced the orientalist, colonialist, and modernist underpinnings of secular Ashkenazi liberalism. Indeed, the eventual adoption of the two-state formula indicated a growing awareness of the devastating effects of the occupation as well as a recognition that the ongoing, de facto annexation of East Jerusalem and large areas of the West Bank and the Gaza Strip threatened the integrity of Israeli democracy. But this introspection did not catalyze substantial reorientation of, or new formulas for, thinking about peace and justice. That the mainstream peace camp did not tackle the root causes of the conflict can be attributed to the conceptual blinders of the secularist discourse and their enabling of an unproblematic acceptance of nationality and Judaism qua ethnicity as fixed categories of identity.

VI. Gush Shalom

Under the leadership of veteran peace activist Uri Avnery, Gush Shalom (GS) challenged some of the premises inherent in PN and its parliamentary counterpart Meretz.[123] GS formulated its protest program in accordance with the following principles:

> Putting an end to the occupation; Accepting the right of the Palestinian people to establish an independent and sovereign State of Palestine in all the territories occupied by Israel in 1967; Reinstating the pre-1967 "Green Line" as the border between the State of Israel and the State of Palestine (with possible minor exchanges of territories agreed between the parties); the border will be open for the free movement of people and goods, subject to mutual agreement. Establishing Jerusalem as the capital of the two states, with East Jerusalem (including the Haram al-Sharif) serving as the capital of Palestine and West Jerusalem (including the Western Wall) serving as the capital of Israel. The city is to be united on the physical and municipal level, based on mutual agreement. Recognizing in principle the Right of Return of the Palestinian refugees, allowing each refugee to choose freely between compensation and repatriation to Palestine and Israel, and fixing by mutual agreement the number of refugees who will be able to return to Israel in annual quotas, without undermining the foundations of Israel. Safeguarding the security of both Israel and Palestine by mutual agreement and guarantees. Striving for overall peace between Israel and all Arab countries and the creation of a regional union.[124]

From the excerpt above, it is clear that GS (established in 1993) is fraught with the same kinds of contradictions characteristic of Meretz and PN. It conceptualizes East Jerusalem as the capital of the Palestinian state, a central issue of contention. But it treats the fundamental question of the right of return of the Palestinian refugees in an ambiguous manner indicative of the movement's commitment to ensuring the Jewish character of Israel. Its declaration of principles (as in the case of the Geneva Initiative) grants the need for a *theoretical* concession on the refugee issue while imposing a *practical* "negotiated quota" in order to leave "the foundations of Israel" intact.

This ambiguous stance is further reiterated in one of Avnery's position papers in which he calls for a truth commission to explicitly highlight Israel's historical culpability in creating the refugee problem. Avnery, however, repeats the demand for imposing a quota for the sake of preserving the Jewish identity of the Israeli state:

> The historic compromise between Israel and Palestine is based on the principle of "Two States for Two Peoples." The State of Israel is designed to embody the historic personality of the Israeli-Jewish people, with the Arab citizens of Israel, who constitute a fifth of all Israeli citizens, being full partners in the state. It is clear that the return of millions of Palestinian refugees to the State of Israel would completely change the character of the state, contrary to the intentions of its founders and most of its citizens. It would abolish the principles of Two States for Two Peoples, on which the demand for a Palestinian state is based. All this leads to the conclusion that most of the refugees who opt for return will find their place in the State of Palestine.[125]

Avnery's analysis of the necessity to impose limitations on the right of return is based on a strict interpretation of the two-state formula. The imperative of return ought to be curtailed by the objective of maintaining two separate states, distinguished from one another by what he essentializes as their distinct "historic personality." This formulation prioritizes the particular Zionist imperative to maintain a Jewish demographic majority in Israel proper over the recognition of the legitimacy of the right of return for Palestinian refugees. Certainly, the GS platform challenged the parameters of acceptable Zionist debate, but it did not question the debate's basic premises. Overlooking the underlying causes of the conflict also limited GS's ability to confront conventional Israeli interpretations of just peace.

Before turning to my critique, I should note that the movement pushed the bounds of acceptability on a number of fronts. As mentioned, Avnery's suggestion of a truth commission in order to provide an integrated historical account of the ethnic cleansing of 1948 (and 1967) constitutes a dramatic, myth-shattering, and revolutionary step for a Zionist peace group. Also, in contrast to the "metahistorical bias" so central to PN, Avnery argued that the War of 1967 and the settlement movement constituted a direct continuation of rather than a radical break from the pre-1967 geopolitical configurations:

> Many Israelis believe that "The Six Day War" was the root of all evil and it was only then that the peace-loving and progressive Israel turned into a conqueror

and an occupier. This conviction allows them to maintain the absolute purity of Zionism and the State of Israel up to that point in history and preserve their old myths. There is no truth in this legend. The war of 1967 was yet another phase of the old struggle between the two national movements. It did not change the essence; it only changed the circumstances.[126]

Indeed, GS mounted an intense offensive aimed at the complicity, complacency, and naïveté of the secularist Israeli Zionist peace camp as exemplified by PN, its most audible and visible exemplar. In the process, the movement exposed some of the blind spots of the secularist-liberal left: its metahistorical bias, its delusional interpretation of the Oslo Accords as a "breakthrough," and its self-righteousness in response to the al-Aqsa Intifada that erupted in September 2000 and declined in intensity by 2005.[127]

Nonetheless, by positing the two-state formula as his point of departure in thinking about justice for the Palestinian refugees, Avnery revealed his own blind spot. He is reluctant to explicate what he means by "the historic personality of the Israeli-Jewish people" cultivating "Israel's historic character," apart from guaranteeing a demographic majority and a vague romantic *volkist* notion of authentic self-realization. While recognizing the need to address publicly the memory of past injustices, the GS platform, owing to its secularist orientation, overlooks the importance of reimagining or reframing the discourse of Israeli citizenship, an undertaking that necessitates a hermeneutical engagement with the question of religion qua national identity.

GS, like PN, focuses its critique almost exclusively on the occupation and its detrimental, corrupting effects, implying the irrelevance of debating Israel's Jewish character as part and parcel of developing a democratic framework for thinking about peace and justice in a substantive way. Particularly, the movement does not address how the significance attributed to Israel as a Jewish nation-state by world Jewry influences the conflict with the Palestinians. Nor does it concern itself with the relevance of the Arab minorities in Israel or with the discrimination and marginalization of the Mizrahim to the larger peace framework. The struggle for "minority rights" is categorized as a "domestic" matter. These interrelated oversights indicate how the unchallenged acceptance of the tradition and premises of Ashkenazi secular Zionism avoids redressing and acknowledging the root causes of injustice or the question of structural and cultural violence. Hence, the movement fails to identify the centrality of the Mizrahi condition, the deep theological compass of Israeliness, and the relevance of questions of social justice to peace.

GS nonetheless remains a courageous agent of peace that challenges some of the central taboos of the Israeli ethos and perceptions of the conflict with the Palestinians. Other such voices exist. One powerful example is that of the "refuseniks"—high school students who refuse their drafting into the IDF and reservists who refuse to serve in the occupied territories. Many of them have proved their heroism and patriotic commitment to the security of the Israeli state but have come to the realization that business as usual cannot continue. The words of Yonatan Shapira, a refusenik protesting the draft surrounding the Gaza war of 2009–10, capture this sentiment:

> I was an operational pilot and captain of Blackhawks. About 5 years ago, we wrote The Combatants Letter in which we refused to participate in the air force's and IDF's war crimes in the occupied territories. People tell me things like: "empathy and compassion is a civilian word that I leave at home before I go on active duty" and this is how they can bomb a school in Gaza. I suddenly realize how all kind of horrible things happened throughout history to our people, to other people. Nice and good individuals turn into war criminals of an incredible measure. It isn't possible to bomb and kill civilians in quantities and expect that everything will go on as usual and we will go on talking to our friends and families; be somewhat leftist and somewhat rightist . . . put the girl to sleep. It won't just go forever.[128]

Shapira's epiphany echoes the radical critique articulated in the *Covenant Against Occupation* years before. They are important and brave voices of protest and possible change. However, the analysis of the secular Israeli peace movement in this chapter suggests that the question of the occupation of the 1967 territories is deeply connected to addressing the internal fissures within Israel proper, including a substantial conversation concerning the Jewish meanings of membership in the Israeli state. Shapira and many other secular critics of the occupation overlook this link between social justice concerns and the broader story of the Palestinian-Israeli conflict.

Conclusion

While PN (and the Zionist peace camp more generally) directed its activity in opposition to the Likud Party and the settlement movement, it never disputed the Zionist taboos as outlined in the Biltmore Program. Despite an increased moral revulsion about the Israeli occupation of Palestinian territories, the story of the secular Zionist peace camp in Israel betrays a general lack of reflexion about how Judaism and Ashkenazi Eurocentrism (orientalism) play into its mode of imagining the social and political boundaries of Israel.

Nonetheless, before proceeding with a critique of the Zionist paradigm and historiography, it is important to underscore how the genuine fear of extinction embodied in the experience and memory of the Holocaust influenced the psyche of Jews and Israelis around the world and how it also contributed to delimiting the perceptions of justice vis-à-vis Palestine. Growing up an Israeli Jew instills a deep sense of existential threat. This existential insecurity assimilates memories from the ghettoes and death camps in Europe with memories from the many wars since Israeli independence and the fear of being overwhelmed by surrounding Arab nations. While the memory and commemoration of the Holocaust may have been used instrumentally in processes of nation building and socialization in Israel,[129] and in generating a strong pro-Israel lobby (especially in the United States) that fed into a broader landscape of Holocaust piety, this does not detract from the authenticity of the fear of extinction and of a recurrent Holocaust ingrained in the minds of Israeli and non-Israeli Jews.

As I mentioned, I belong to a generation of Israelis who grew up with grandparents with numbers tattooed on their arms and memories of homes and relatives that are now gone. The formidable centrality of this memory in the formation of Israeliness and contemporary Jewish identity needs to be recognized as urgently as the catastrophes of the Palestinians and the "domestic" Jewish victims of a Euro-Zionist agenda. The transformation of the Israeli-Palestinian conflict will require redressing those sites of memories in tandem with one another.

Accordingly, the next two chapters turn to a multidisciplinary discussion of the conceptual frameworks available for the analysis and transformation of these conflicts, with a particular emphasis on how religious and subaltern resources can inform peacebuilding processes.

TWO

Bridging Disciplines and Reimagining "Who We Are"

The analysis of conflicts that involve identity claims necessitates drawing on the insights of diverse disciplinary approaches. Therefore, this chapter highlights the need to connect peace research, religious studies, and political theory. A multidisciplinary approach, I contend, will enrich the theory and practice of conflict transformation as a process that involves reimagining the boundaries of "who we are"—boundaries that are neither fixed nor predetermined. Such a reframing of the symbolic (intersubjective) boundaries of identity will bring to light and transform structural and symbolic forms of violence, which often lie at the heart of violent conflicts.

The concept of reimagining the nation with due attention to the role of religion in the national ethos, understood as a peacebuilding practice, plays on Benedict Anderson's familiar analysis of the "nation" as an "imagined community."[1] On Anderson's account, the modern nation is *imagined* out of its religious and cultural roots.[2] This observation points to one central paradox of modern nationalism: its concurrent modernity and antiquity.[3] Postcolonial theorists, however, have pointed out that analyses of how the nation has been imagined must always be attentive to the power structures and to whoever is left out of the normative definition of the nation.[4] It follows that the act of reimagining the "nation" vis-à-vis its cultural and religious resources entails a reconfiguration of the power structures as well.

In the case of Israel/Palestine, any substantial challenge to the consensus separationist logic of peace would require deploying postcolonial *deconstructive* analytic tools grounded in political theory as well as *reconstructive* engagement with the resources of the tradition that has been selectively retrieved for the legitimization of national claims. The reconstructive lens draws and expands on insights from peace studies, especially the subgenre of religion and peacebuilding. Attentiveness to the dynamics of deconstructing and reconstructing the national ethos shows that an analysis of power is integral to envisioning the transformation of ethnoreligious-national conflicts in accordance with the imperatives of human rights conventions. This transformation involves a view of the "nation" as a highly interpretive and elastic construct.

The need to transcend violence through a process of (inter)subjective reframing animates what Mennonite peace practitioner and scholar John Paul Lederach calls the "moral imagination." Lederach explains that the "moral imagination" entails the cultivation of "the capacity to imagine ourselves in a *web* of relationships that includes our enemies; the ability to sustain a paradoxical curiosity that embraces complexity without reliance on dualistic polarity; the fundamental belief in and pursuit of the creative act; and the acceptance of the inherent risk of stepping into the mystery of the unknown that lies beyond the far too familiar landscape of violence."[5] This spiritual intuition informs Lederach's approach to peacebuilding as a process striving for constructive social change. He argues that deploying the metaphor of the "web" could open up new venues for the reflective "peace practitioner" to engage creatively in the transformation of violent relational patterns. Lederach highlights the importance of cultivating in the peace practitioner (beyond the "skill sets" of mediation and conflict analysis) creativity and intuitive proclivity for "knowing things kinetically, visually, metaphorically, and artistically."[6] This mode of training, he suggests, cultivates the "moral imagination" of the on-the-ground peacebuilder and her ability to capitalize on serendipity or unexpected moments that could lead to transcending the underlying logic of violence and injustice.

The multidisciplinary approach I develop in this chapter shows that such broadening of the imagination would *also* necessitate analytic creativity. It would require drawing on the deconstructive insights of cultural theory, the conceptual frameworks of political theory, and conversations in the study of religion and neighboring fields, all of which problematize conventional modes of thinking about international relations and the role of religion in conflict and conflict transformation. This multidisciplinary lens enriches and broadens the analysis of conflict and facilitates creative modes of (re)thinking peace and justice. My approach does not supersede the "moral imagination" but rather complements it.

I. Peace Studies: Justpeace and Strategic Peacebuilding

The interrelated concepts of conflict transformation and peacebuilding denote a rather recent focus in peace research on holistic frameworks and processes for engaging the dynamics of conflict and peace.[7] The term "conflict transformation" emerged out of a concern that the idiom of "conflict resolution" did not engage, in the words of Lederach, "the deeper structural, cultural, and long-term relational aspects of conflict."[8] The academic field and practice of conflict resolution concentrates its resources on devising immediate solutions to immediate problems. The concept of conflict transformation, on the other hand, offers a more holistic approach that views conflict as symptomatic of underlying structures and relationships. The transformation of conflict, therefore, entails a diagnosis of these core conditions, a capacity for "moral imagination," and a long-term plan for reconfiguring the underpinning patterns that have given rise to violent conflict.[9]

Such diagnostic and introspective work constitutes a form of cultural therapy and may require practitioners in the field of conflict transformation to facilitate trauma healing and to devise mechanisms for instituting programs of restorative and transitional justice. The process of conflict transformation requires a complex and multidimensional approach to conflict. It includes creating a framework interlinking the immediate situation and the deeper relational patterns and contexts. This conceptual framework could explain the dynamics of the conflict as well as suggest the type of changes needed to reframe the deeper roots of the conflict.[10] This understanding of conflict transformation resonates with the analysis of the Israeli peace camp presented in this book. Indeed, elevating subaltern narratives and visions of justice to center stage as I do exposes the political theology of Israel (in its secular and religious variations) as the epicenter of conflict and suggests a fertile ground for a constructive transformation of the conflict with the Palestinians. The path to conflict transformation, in other words, travels critically and constructively through a reexamination of "who we are" as a nation and a society.

The phrase "conflict transformation" thus came to denote a sustained theoretical emphasis on implications for peace practitioners who engage in long-term processes of bringing about systemic change.[11] The concept of peacebuilding similarly points to the multiple dimensions and spheres integral for transforming conflict situations. This holistic approach to peacebuilding reflects an increased focus in peace studies on the relevance of justice to analyses of conflict and peace. Indeed, concern with systemic injustices, scrutiny of the root causes of conflicts, and questions of structural or indirect violence have been a preoccupation of peace studies at least since Johan Galtung (often called the "father of peace studies") articulated the interrelated concepts of structural violence in the late 1960s and cultural violence in the late 1980s and 1990s.[12]

The notion of transformation indicates that "positive peace" is more than the mere absence of war and explicit (or direct) violence.[13] Galtung clearly links his analysis of structural violence to the concept of "positive peace," which involves the transformation of underlying systemic violence. Hence "positive peace" entails (but cannot be simply reduced to) social justice. This turn away from "negative peace" toward "positive peace" paves the way for a more substantive and contextual discussion of justice.

Galtung's contribution notwithstanding, his approach still carries a rigidity symptomatic of the disciplinary disconnect between peace studies and cultural theory and discursive critique. This deficiency and lack of self-reflexivity could grotesquely implicate the peace scholar or practitioner, despite their best intentions, in forms of cultural and discursive violence. Thus Galtung alluded to and retrieved the motifs of the "Protocols of the Elders of Zion" to explain the global financial crisis of the 2000s, and in a formal lecture at the University of Oslo, he (hypothetically) attributed the brutal murder of scores of Norwegian youth by Anders Behring Breivik, a Norwegian Islamophobe, in the summer of 2011 to the Israeli Mossad. These comments implicate Galtung in an insidious form of cultural violence, in anti-Semitism.[14] Despite his interlaced commitment to conceptions of "positive peace" and thus to overcoming cultural modalities of violence, the anti-Semitic connotations of his remarks are violent in their implications and are to be rejected.[15] This dissonance is not untypical of the language deployed by the largely Western and urban pro-Palestine solidarity movement: On the one hand they tend to dissociate the critique of Israel from the charge of anti-Semitism. On the other, they trivialize and dismiss the historical, cultural, and religious Jewish meanings of Israel. This dismissal, not accountable to the violence it reproduces, inhibits the effectiveness of these organizations as agents of peacebuilding,[16] if only because it invites potential interlocutors to stop listening. A critique and self-reflexivity, therefore, need to become integral components of peacebuilding. Of course, the self-reflexivity available in poststructuralist social theory degenerates into endless critique, in need of the kind of constructive objectives of peace studies.

Certainly, the more recent preoccupation with questions of conflict transformation on the part of peace studies signals a movement away from its original concentration in political science to fields of humanistic inquiry and the social sciences, including disciplines such as psychology, theology, and anthropology. Such a multidisciplinary orientation emboldened the analysis of structural and cultural violence and enriched specific strategies for conflict transformation in particular contexts. This became especially important with the recognition that related to the problem of a misdistribution of resources are particular vindicating cultural perceptions of entitlement constitutive of "cultural violence."[17]

This expansive insight in peace research animates the recently coined concept of "strategic peacebuilding"—a term that gained prominence as a result of extended scholarly conversations at the Kroc Institute for International Peace Studies at the University of Notre Dame.[18] The rationale behind "strategic peacebuilding" is that conflict transformation entails "strategizing" and "collaboration" across multiple disciplines and spheres of activity. In a co-authored essay, Lederach and R. Scott Appleby explain that "strategic peacebuilders must embrace complexity and find within any given situation or issue practical approaches that stitch together key people and initiatives to reduce violence, change destructive patterns, and build healthy relationships and structures."[19]

Lederach and Appleby further highlight that strategies of peacebuilding need to be oriented by the concept of *justpeace*, which they view as "a dynamic state of affairs in which the reduction and management of violence and the achievement of social and economic justice are undertaken as mutual, reinforcing dimensions of constructive change."[20] The concept of justpeace entails "the redress of legitimate grievances and the establishment of new relations characterized by equality and fairness according to the dictates of human dignity and the common good."[21] The neologism "justpeace" is therefore distinguished from what the two words "just peace" may denote: rather than presuming a *static* or formulaic conception of justice, it emphasizes a *process* that encompasses a multiplicity of perspectives; and instead of a unified conception of justice, it presents a contested conception that, while dependent on the idiosyncrasy of each context, does not betray a relativistic stance.

In their collaborative work, Pierre Allan, a scholar of international relations, and Alexis Keller, a human rights expert, also develop an approach to "just peace" (they do not use the neologism of justpeace but approximate its elastic connotations) that illuminates the importance of broadening the discussion of justice beyond particularistic and identity-based arguments to an analysis of the web of relationships that encompasses one's enemies as well as one's friends. Accordingly, they articulate the notion of "thick recognition," which, going beyond "thin recognition" (entailing the kind of tolerance implied by a negative conception of peace), reimagines identities without neutralizing and equalizing the memories and practices of the old. Processes of reconciliation, for this reason, may necessitate a reframing of "who we are" rather than a restoration of a preconceived idea concerning the boundaries of a group identity.[22]

Not unlike the notable Harvard social psychologist Herbert Kelman's notion of "reconciliation as identity change,"[23] the process of thick recognition entails the cultivation of mutual empathy, the development of an intersubjective consensus, and the interrogation of one's own identity. The process of thick recognition, however, challenges Kelman's insistence on holding onto perceived "cores" of the identities in question as a precondition to undergoing reconciliatory revisions.[24] Hence, while thick recognition of the "other" is of critical consequence, a process of introspection is just as important for moving toward a "just peace"—a reevaluation of *who we are* may lead us to reevaluate the type of concessions we are willing to make.[25]

The constructive lens afforded by justpeace contests the presumed fixity of the liberal peace, without relinquishing a commitment to democratic practices and institutions associated with the tradition of liberal political theory. While the insights of cultural and critical theories are beyond the usual scope of peace studies, the elasticity justpeace gestures toward could productively and synergistically accommodate deconstructive critique, pivotal for the processes of interrogating and reimagining *who we are*.[26] As a peace studies concept, it offers a challenge to the liberal peace tradition and its frequent obscuring of cultural and systemic violence. Further, peacebuilding as a synergetic concept that could be expanded to integrate critique becomes also a self-reflexive enterprise, one that, unlike Galtung's application of this concept, is conscious of its own complicity with cultural forms of violence.

The emphasis on justpeace is indeed very effective in normatively orienting my analysis. In the context of Israel/Palestine, the exploration of the claims of ethnoreligious national ideologies would have to recognize the perceived authenticity of such claims but would also need to push beyond particularistic perceptions of victimhood and justice. This comprehensive and holistic approach to peacebuilding illuminates the importance of attitudinal change as one aspect of the multidimensional process.[27]

Highlighting the grievances and demands of subaltern communities within Israel amplifies the ethnorepublican ethos and its overarching structures as underlying the Palestinian-Israeli conflict. The focus, in chapters 6 and 7, on the Palestinian Israelis and the Arab Jews and on redressing structural violence, cultivating a culture of human rights, and devising a transformative framework for thinking about restorative justice is consistent with the long-term objectives encompassed by the concept of "strategic peacebuilding."[28] This approach subsequently deduces that redressing injustices within Israel proper would transform the modes in which a justpeace for the Palestinian-Israeli conflict may be imagined. Having stressed the intricate relations between domestic and international affairs, I proceed with a discussion of the utility and limitations of normative political theory's conceptions of political justice.

II. Normative Political Theory and the Question of Justice

While preoccupied with questions of justice, conventional political theory has not extended itself very frequently beyond the conceptual bounds of liberal Western democracies. Yet two recent exceptions may suggest a potentially creative departure from this conceptual trap that presupposes the naturalness of nations and states and subsequently delimits the scope of justice within these geopolitical bounds. The work of liberal theorist of multiculturalism Will Kymlicka exemplifies one scholarly current. The other is found in the work of pragmatist political theorist Nancy Fraser. There is also a third relevant trend that is subsumed under the subgenre of reconciliation or transitional justice literature and is typified especially in the work of political scientist Daniel Philpott's efforts to theorize compatibility between theories of political liberalism and conceptions of reconciliation that focus on the "restoration of wounded individuals and relationships."[29] Still, I argue that justpeace in the context of Israel-Palestine resonates with a certain current in peacebuilding literature and practice that views reconciliation as a transformative process rather than a return to an antecedent "harmony."

Multicultural Odysseys

In his *Multicultural Odysseys: Navigating the New International Politics of Diversity*, Kymlicka engages the limitations of and problems with the global diffusion of liberal multiculturalism, understood both as a political discourse and as a set of legal norms.[30] While promoting a view of multiculturalism that is persistently consistent with liberal values, Kymlicka nonetheless offers a critique of the general inclination to approach various instances of group-rights violations with a generic or "thin" framework of minority rights. This restrictive framework may enable the perpetuation of unjust political arrangements, bypassing internal debates concerning power sharing, self-government, and cultural rights.[31]

Kymlicka's scholarship, therefore, signals a move beyond the conceptual confines of political theory and the debates about multiculturalism in European and North American contexts to a critical engagement with liberal multicultural conceptions of justice and citizenship as a framework for conflict transformation. He attempts to bridge two seemingly disparate debates: the one related to "the politics of difference" or "identity politics" and the other to the "politics of reconciliation" or "transitional justice." While the politics of reconciliation is a central topic in contexts transitioning away from direct violence, the politics of identity focuses on the contestation of structural violence in already established Western democracies.

In an introduction to an edited volume, *The Politics of Reconciliation in Multicultural Societies*, Kymlicka and co-author Bashir Bashir explain the relevance of linking the two sets of conversations in a way that could embolden the theoretical underpinnings of peace research. "At the philosophical level," their argument goes, "the normative and conceptual premises invoked by theories of reconciliation in divided societies relate to those invoked by theories of inclusive citizenship in diverse societies." "At the empirical level," the authors continue, "the actual practice of reconciliation and reparations affects the deliberative and agonistic character of politics, or the pursuit of a more multicultural conception of citizenship."[32]

By the "agonistic character of politics," the authors refer to the agonistic approach to democracy[33] that highlights the vocalization of excluded and marginalized groups and a conception of the "political" as an open arena defined by moral pluralism and cultural diversity.[34] The agonistic framework enables one to upset a proposed link—characteristic of many reparations movements around the globe—between democracy and the intent of a society to redress past injustices. Agonistic theories question the naturalness of the "we" or the group that is supposedly in need of repair. Therefore, the agonistic model suggests that the veneer of equality as a framework of healing may actually become an effective silencing technique.[35]

When grounded in the insights of agonistic democratic theory, reconciliation might mean transformation and creative innovation rather than restoration of an elusive preexisting "we"—a new conception of both the self and the other that focuses on how to transform mortal enemies into adversaries who engage civically with one another.[36] This approach offers a potentially creative analytic tool for thinking imaginatively about contexts delineated by seemingly rigid boundaries of identities, as in Israel/Palestine (though it does not yet translate into a design for conflict transformation processes).[37] It resonates with the contention above that reforming the boundaries of justice or reinterpreting the meanings of justpeace would depend on reimagining the "we." In the case of Israel, recognizing Israel proper as guilty of the same moral corruption that the loyal peace camp attributes to the military occupation of the territories conquered in 1967 necessitates a rethinking of Israel's communal identity. This reimagining cannot take place without exploring substantively how religion relates to the narration of national history.

The agonistic angle, therefore, is helpful in stressing the fluidity of national identities, regardless of their self-projection as "natural" and "self-evident." Kymlicka and Bashir, however, identify the multicultural conception of citizenship as a corrective to what they deem the limitations of the agonistic model. They concur with the agonistic critique of the supposed cultural neutrality of aggregative and deliberative approaches to democratic practice, highlighting their obvious biases toward the dominant cultural groups—presupposing the majority-minority configurations as a "given" rather than as the (always contestable) historically situated outcome of the interfaces between symbolic boundaries and sociopolitical practices. But Kymlicka and Bashir expand the agonistic theoretical focus on the "universality of moral pluralism" by also locating this discussion of inclusive citizenship in the modern ideology of the nation-state and its monocultural presumption. This presumption or methodological nationalism—often bracketed in political theory—undergirds the histories of exclusion, marginalization, and discrimination that animate the "politics of identity." Therefore, Kymlicka and Bashir underscore that "the only way to build truly inclusive democracies" is to move beyond monocultural conceptions of nationhood and to institute multicultural frameworks of citizenship.[38] They subsequently conclude that connecting conversations concerning transitional justice with democratic theory could prove effective as a peace-building tool (although they do not deploy the specific concept of peace-building).[39]

Still, moving or diffusing the discussion of multiculturalism beyond the confines of established constitutional democracies in the "West" exposes some of the conceptual and practical limitations of this approach. Those limits, as critics of political liberalism are quick to identify, revolve around the question of legitimacy. They ask whether abstracted principles can ground political cohesion and coherence. While the agonistic approach overlooks the centrality of nationalism to the conceptualization of reconciliation as social transformation, the liberal multicultural framework cannot bracket religion merely as a question of human, civic, and political rights because it is often interlaced with the question of national legitimacy and the coherency of the political body.[40]

Liberal Nationalism: A Framework for Conflict Transformation?

Kymlicka's maneuvering of normative political theory in the global arena resonates with the work of David Little, a comparative ethicist and scholar of religion and ethnonational conflict. In order to highlight the utility of the human rights perspective for the analysis and possible transformation of conflicts, Little superimposes an adjusted interpretation of political theorist John Rawls's idea of "public reason" on a human rights foundation.[41] Little concludes that Rawls's idea of "public reason" as the appropriate vehicle for ensuring equal citizenship in a constitutional democracy is in accord with prescriptions outlined in the UN's Universal Declaration of Human Rights (UDHR).[42]

This claim in favor of what is often called "liberal nationalism" is normative because it presupposes the human rights framework as the most optimal for offering and managing a set of guidelines for transforming intergroup conflict of an ethnoreligious character. However, lines of exclusivity are unavoidable because boundaries are exclusive by definition. Even the most inclusivist forms of nationalisms specify thresholds and barriers, including obvious linguistic ones. The choice of the official language in each national context immediately excludes those who are not fluent in that tongue. The case of Israel illuminates the critical ramifications (for questions of peace and justice vis-à-vis the Palestinians) of challenging and rethinking where the lines of exclusion may run. But as the rising waves of xenophobia in Europe and the United States suggest,[43] this conversation is not irrelevant to other, more inclusivist democratic contexts. They too have particularistic and normative narratives and attitudes that are based in specific but always contested conceptions of nationhood. This is why debating nationalism may become central to thinking about the process of conflict transformation.

In peace studies, an overreliance on human rights conventions suggests a rather restrictive theory of change, one that may benevolently gloss over deeper misframings of the questions of justice. The agonistic emphasis on contesting the "we" as part of healing and conflict transformation coheres with the general inclination of strategic peacebuilding to expand on more restrictive theories of change. Kymlicka already intuits that an overreliance on human rights discourses provides an example of such restrictive engagement with change, one that thinkers and practitioners who assume the more comprehensive and holistic framework of strategic peacebuilding challenge.[44]

A human rights orientation adopts a "thin" approach to the role of national governments. This approach is "thin" because it is designed to safeguard individual liberties and freedoms against doctrinaire regimes and because it underscores the need for political systems that would maximize economic, cultural, religious, and social self-determination.[45] The "thin" or "liberal" form of nationalism and its clear link to peace and stability are contrasted with "thick" or "illiberal" interpretations of national identities and their practices of discrimination and violent repression, both militaristic and cultural.[46]

Whereas the liberal form of nationalism exemplifies a certain degree of adherence to modern legal-rational universalistic norms and demonstrates a principled commitment to democratic apparatuses and human rights conventions, the illiberal type exhibits an inclination toward discriminatory political and cultural practices. In contrast to the *volkist* German model that is "particularist, organic, differentialist, and Volk-centered," the civic French model of nationhood is purportedly "universalist, rationalist, assimilationist, and state-centered."[47] However, this set of dichotomies that marks the civic-ethnic characterization of national phenomena has come under scrutiny as being, in effect, misleading.[48] The civic or liberal form of nationalism is not abstracted from its religious, cultural, ethnic, and historical contexts and presuppositions. In fact, the "nation" is a thoroughly interpretive and elastic construct that is deeply cultural and contextually embodied and cannot be fully grasped by reducing it to a set of constitutional principles.

On Nationalism

Little's own discussion of the "nation" and the "state" as the two terms that make up the hyphenated construct of the "nation-state" underscores the highly interpretive and dynamic properties of this construct. Following Max Weber's definition of nationalism as consisting of "a belief in a subjective descent," and in conjunction with Weber's view of social authority as involving "a 'belief' in the existence of a valid or justified political order," Little contends that state authority is justified by a set of national beliefs and is perpetuated by the imperative to express these beliefs in the infrastructure of the state.[49] This understanding is echoed by theorist of nationalism Anthony Marx, who recognizes the important interrelation between the "state" as an infrastructure of power and the "nation" that lends it popular legitimacy.[50]

While Marx's analysis is "state"-centric, the analysis of another theorist of nationalism, Anthony Smith, is "nation"-centric. The latter's ethnosymbolist approach to the study of nationalism[51] focuses almost exclusively on the "subjective elements of memory, value, sentiment, myth and symbol."[52] Smith defines the "nation" as "a named human population occupying a historic territory and sharing common myths and memories, a public culture, and common laws and customs for all members."[53] What a "national identity" might mean is, according to Smith, a matter for "periodic redefinition."[54] In his formulation, "the cult of authenticity" or "the quest for the true self" constitutes a central facet of nationalist movements. Recognizing the centrality of the "cult of authenticity" to the redemptive pretenses of national movements exposes, in Smith's view, the sacred dimensions of the modern nation.[55]

Based on a synthesis between Smith's and Marx's respective definitions of nationalism and statehood, my central contention is that the coercive power of the "state" is legitimated (or delegitimated) by a particular affirmation of collective identity, the "nation." This affirmation constitutes a form of "belief." It is also, however, embodied in social, political, and cultural practices.[56] A radical change of political structures, therefore, necessitates a radical transformation of a belief system and its constitutive practices and vice versa. By recognizing the highly interpretive nature of nationalisms, one is also able to construct a typology that suggests correlations between various modes of interpretations of one's ethnicity, nationality, and religion and how they may relate to political structures and practices.

Nationalism, Religion, and Violent Conflicts: A Typology

The "thin" human rights approach informs a helpful yet limited typology that correlates illiberal interpretations of religion and/or secularity with exclusive social orders and political attitudes and, subsequently, with the likelihood of the eruption of direct forms of violence. On this account, on the other hand, liberal interpretations of religion as well as inclusivist secularism tends to be correlated with liberal or civic forms of nationalism, designed to mitigate conflicts nonviolently.[57]

In an important work titled *Religious Politics and Secular States*, political scientist Scott Hibbard explicates this framework by locating it in a broader discussion concerning secularism generally and secular nationalism more specifically. The location of a society along a spectrum from liberal to illiberal nationalism depends on "how a given religion (or an official secularism) is interpreted," he writes.[58] As Hibbard has it, liberal interpretations of religion can perform a "priestly" function, thus facilitating inclusive and even pluralistic conceptions of the social order. They can also function "prophetically," helping to resist nonviolently sociopolitical structures that are exclusivist. Likewise, illiberal or communal interpretations of religion can lend themselves to priestly functions, legitimating and promoting exclusivist state practices. However, communal interpretations of religion can also function prophetically. They might, for instance, oppose state mechanisms and social injustices while nonetheless advancing exclusivist conceptions of the political and social order. This may arguably be the case with certain "fundamentalist" movements that offer pertinent critiques of hegemonic interpretations of secular modernity, even though they might advance exclusivist social and political agendas.[59]

Indeed, this typology corrects some of the problems in theories of multicultural citizenship because, while underscoring the importance of differentiating religion from government, it recognizes the continuous role of religion and culture in shaping conceptions of national identity. Unlike the conceptual frameworks of multiculturalism, "religion" is not articulated merely as a "rights" issue (even when it is debated in the context of "identity politics"). Framing religion as a "rights issue" in the contexts of the multiculturalism debates means that it is attended to as a component of a broader discussion of freedom of conscience and of the rights of minorities to practice their beliefs. In many instances of conflict, however, religion is also an issue at the heart of debates over national identity. On this point, this typology is conducive to a constructive approach to religion and peacebuilding in that it focuses on reinterpreting resources from the reservoirs of religions and cultures to fit more consistently into more inclusivist and liberal political arrangements and deeper notions of pluralism than explicitly exclusivist and chauvinistic motifs of chosenness and exceptionalism, which obviously correlate with illiberal political ideologies and practices.[60]

The analysis of the Israeli landscape challenges the typology articulated above. It shows that even the liberal, inclusivist interpretations of national and religious identities put forward by Rabbis for Human Rights (RHR), emblematic of their prophetic role, still participate (however inadvertently) in an underlying Zionist, axiomatic, teleological reading of Jewish history and identity. As I explicate in chapter 5, while the vision of RHR strives to be pluralistic and inclusivist, with respect both to their interpretation of Zionism and to their religiosity, this vision, nonetheless, does not problematize the ethos of "return to" the land. In fact, RHR often grounds its support of Palestinian rights in the Jewish imperative to treat the "stranger in our midst" with the utmost respect and with a recognition of her humanity. And yet the Palestinian is no stranger to the land. In fact, so deployed, this rabbinic conception of "stranger" ultimately affirms forms of exclusion that it aims to overcome. The case of RHR, therefore, illustrates that exhibiting the characteristics of liberal nationalism and inclusive religion could, in effect, enable and reify cultural and systemic forms of violence. This is despite RHR's often heroic commitment to social justice and the end of the occupation.

Beyond the Typology

The strict analytic distinction between civic and ethnic forms of nationalism is, despite its many critics, central to modernist theories of nationalism,[61] as well as to liberal political theory. I indicated that the "civic" model is frequently abstracted from the particular discussions of nationalism and thus becomes a subject for political theorists rather than theorists of nationalism. And, in fact, theorists of nationalism typically focus their study on the mechanisms and forces involved in the construction of boundaries (geopolitical and cultural). Political theorists, meanwhile, tend to presume the "nation," a term they frequently use interchangeably with "society" or "state," as a fixed, closed, axiomatic category, irrelevant to the analysis of the logic and principles undergirding the operation of political systems.[62] It is, however, critically important to reconnect the two sites of inquiry, especially in order to understand the dynamics of ethnoreligious national contestations. At the heart of my effort to reconnect the disciplinary sites of study is the necessity of grappling with nationalism as a theory of political legitimacy.[63]

What I offer here in my analysis of the Israeli peace camp and the types of challenges articulated from the margins of Israeli and Jewish societies is not a rejection of the ideal type of liberal nationalism and its emphasis on inclusivity. I offer, rather, an argument about the ineffectiveness of this model as well as other variations of it (e.g., theories of multiculturalism) when it is deployed as the sole account of change for ethnoreligious national conflicts and in abstraction from the full range of normative and hermeneutical resources for constructive intervention. In other words, my aim is to expand upon critically and hereby enrich the liberal approach by (1) introducing insights from cultural theory that enable deconstructing certain premises about conceptions of identity and (2) stressing the need to concede that contextual variations could dictate departures from the liberal model, which is, as noted, itself highly contextual.

The conception of justice articulated in the human rights approach (above) illuminates the need to correct the Israeli peace camp's flawed liberalism (flawed in that it naturalizes its fundamental illiberality and exclusionary character) through a confrontation of Israel's "domestic" history and human rights violations. Such a confrontation may profoundly erode the logic of the two-state solution as championed by the Israeli peace camp.[64]

Scrutinizing the assumptions of this flawed liberalism necessitates testing the ethnorepublican practices and agendas of the Israeli state against the counterhegemonic narratives of Israel's victims. This is a discursive maneuver in that it aims to unsettle and deconstruct the prevailing hegemonic frames. By introducing subaltern voices, who, themselves, often appeal to universal norms in order to articulate their own claims and experiences of injustice, such a multiperspectival analysis shows that Zionism's sense of injustice is, itself, quite particularistic . This contextualization amounts to the deconstruction of the ethnorepublican ethos propelling the two-state solution. However, this process by itself provides insufficient means by which to transform the conflict. Constructive change requires reimagining the relationship between Judaism and Israeliness and between Jews and Israel.

Hence, while the human rights approach may provide certain parameters for thinking about peace and justice as they translate into a "thin" interpretation of the role of government vis-à-vis cultures, religions, and ethnicities, it cannot be prescribed without a transformative, embedded, and therapeutic confrontation with the underlying causes of conflict. The Zionist Israeli peace camp explored in this book evades such confrontation, subsequently tying its notion of peace to a particularistic and group-oriented conception of justice.

But the issue is not simply that the Israeli peace camp exhibits a "flawed liberalism," that is, one that is blind to its own underlying illiberality. My analysis of the proposals and visions advanced by Palestinian Israelis and the Mizrahim illustrates that even their corrected formulations of liberalism carry some limitations. The problem I identify in their reliance on the human rights framework relates to a distinction I wish to draw between *goal* (or ideal type) and *process*. As construed in the human rights documents, international and universal norms are able to provide a principled basis both for identifying instances of injustice and for envisioning arrangements for redressing those injustices. And yet they do not furnish sufficient tools for the *process* necessary to transform a conflict and approximate this *goal*. The case of the Palestinian Israelis provides a lucid articulation of the destination—a constitutional nation-state that ensures conditions of full and meaningful equal citizenship for all. However, while recognizing Zionism as the root cause of the Palestinian experiences of injustice, the platforms of the Palestinian Israeli sector overlook the importance of religion in the *process* of reimagining Israeli nationalism.

Similarly, non-Israeli Jewish critics who discursively challenge the hegemonic hold of Zionist historiography offer but a narrow constructive prism for transformation insofar as they precondition visions for ethical cohabitation on the "dismantling of political Zionism."[65] Likewise, while the Mizrahim offer penetrating embedded social criticism of the Zionist nation-state and its ideology, they too bypass the process of reconfiguring the role of religion in the interpretation of Israel's national identity. Reimagining the interrelation between religion, nation, and ethnicity is crucial for questions of peace and justice in contexts of ethnoreligious national conflict. This is because exclusivist definitions of national membership (those that invoke religious and ethnic markers of identity) are positively correlated with violent conflicts and clearly present structural and cultural modalities of violence. Such identity indices, however, are also open for interpretation and critical reinterpretation. In fact, this insight is the central premise of my argument for what I call a *hermeneutics of citizenship*. Accordingly, the analysis of peace platforms cannot rely only on the system of human rights or on the sense of particularistic justice voiced by the parties locked in conflict (even the most liberal and presumably peace-oriented ones).[66]

My study suggests that rather than being simply flawed liberalism, Israeli liberalism accentuates the flaws already inherent in the model of liberal nationalism. In other words, the flaw of the ideal type of "liberal nationalism" as an orienting concept (intimately linked to the human rights approach) in peacebuilding and conflict transformation is that it limits itself to a "thin" interpretation of political belonging. Moreover, any effort to reinterpret "religion," "culture," and "ethnicity" must conform to its own modernist and secularist framework of analysis. By this I mean that the secularism enabling the construction of a "thin" conception of the political sphere is itself a culturally, ethnically, and historically specific construct. It is born out of a particular moment in European and North American histories and out of a particular (primarily Christian) religious point of reference. It is crucial to note at this point that my approach to "liberal nationalism" is both historicist and integrationist. It denies neither the indispensability nor the universal applicability of the principles and practices it represents (i.e., constitutionalism, equality, freedom of conscience and religion, democratic forms of engagement, and so forth). However, it does point to the limitations of this "ideal type" as a framework for conflict transformation and constructive change. Especially where the root causes of a conflict are nourished by ethnoreligious definitions of nationhood, the liberal nationalist tendency to relegate "religion" to unobtrusive and undoctrinaire public roles amounts to an inorganic, unconstructive, and perhaps even ham-fisted imposition of its own context-specific conception of the proper interrelation between the "religious" and the "political."

Polycentric Multiculturalism

The polycentric approach to multiculturalism confronts (and deconstructs) some of the critiques of liberal multiculturalism by deploying postcolonial theoretical insights. This orientation positions the liberal view of differentiated citizenship as the mere cooptation of minority groups without rearranging any of the structures of power.[67] Hence, polycentric multiculturalism confronts the existing power equation by challenging its fundamental economic and social structures while still redressing problems arising from misrecognition.[68] However, as historian Dipesh Chakrabarty contends, the "provincialization" of Europe implied in such counterhegemonic, polycentric projects does not need to entail letting go of a basic adherence to universal human rights and conceptions of social justice.[69]

In broadening her discussion to include questions of representation as a key dimension of a triangular theory of justice, Nancy Fraser facilitates a confrontation with what she calls "meta-political injustices" that, unlike "ordinary-political injustices," "arise when the division of political space into bounded polities works to misframe first-order questions of distribution, recognition, and representation."[70] Preoccupation with the "who" of justice challenges the territorial-juridical presuppositions of conventional political theory and illuminates the critical importance of identifying who may be affected by certain policies and practices, regardless of territorial location.

This notion of "misframing" subsequently opens up the discourse of justice beyond the Westphalian framework of bounded territorial nation-states, reveals transnational and transterritorial considerations that cannot be bracketed, and invites critical-theoretical engagement. This resonates with a transformation of the "we" in the agonistic sense. It also goes back to why my friends who flooded the streets of Tel Aviv, Jerusalem, and other urban centers, demanding "social justice," as they did in the summer of 2011, may have assumed an elusive strategy: one that intentionally (for the sake of cohesion) differentiated questions of meta-injustice from other, "ordinary" social justice concerns. Yet despite its effective sensitivity to "meta-injustices," the polycentric approach is also insufficient as a transformative framework.

Political Reconciliation as a Metareframing

The discussion above shows that the later works by Kymlicka and Fraser suggest a distinct trajectory in political theory. Kymlicka recognizes the ethnocentric limits of the liberal discourse yet still wishes to think through the possibility of its global applicability as a framework of conflict transformation. Fraser's analysis, on the other hand, complicates the enduring reliance of justice discourses on the Westphalian paradigm as well as paves the way for outlining meta-injustices through the recovery and articulation of subaltern narratives and voices. The underlying logic of the Westphalian framework, and unrevised liberalism, has defined the terms of the conversation in both political theory and peace research and has lent itself to an occasional *misframing* of the question of justice.

Philpott's work on political reconciliation attempts to show that liberal political theories cannot accommodate conceptions of justice as the restoration of relationships and as the healing of wounds, and that therefore programs of reconciliation need to be grounded in other sources (most likely theological).[71] Yet Philpott does not reject the possibility of expanding the liberal framework to overcome its bias toward public and explicit religious arguments in an effort to think creatively about reconciliation.[72]

In Philpott's work, we begin to see an effort to think about the role of religion in conflict transformation and productively relate those insights to conversations in political theory. Likewise, Kymlicka and Bashir's point about the relevance of the ideology of nationalism to an analysis of ethnocultural justice exposes the presence of a methodological nationalism characteristic of Western democratic theory. Neither Kymlicka nor Philpott addresses the role of religion in transforming and reimagining national identities, however. The agonistic model with its emphasis on the fluidity and historicity of the "we," as well as on the power dynamics undergirding a particular conception of groupness, opens up such possibility. However, while various agonistic models recognize the necessity of engaging dimensions of religion and culture, they do not acknowledge that along with a focus on subaltern voices, the contestation of the "we" necessitates a deeply and persistently hermeneutical engagement with and creative reimagining of the resources of religion and culture. This is especially so when the "we" is explicitly defined along religious and ethnic lines. As noted above, the "nation," constituting a form of belief system, cannot simply cease to exist when its moral deficiencies or unjust claims are exposed. The radical reimagining of symbolic boundaries cannot be achieved simply through a cognitive decree or through an exposition of the artificiality of geopolitical demarcations. For instance, Israeli sociologist Yehouda Shenhav exposes the false territorial and political categories that have dominated approaches to the Israeli-Palestinian conflict. He argues that the moral and spatial distinctions between the borders of 1948 and 1967 constitute a deep and ideological misframing that constrains the possibility of a substantive change and redress of injustice. As Shenhav has it, pivotal to this rethinking of the justice discourse is also the inevitable task of identifying the interconnections between internal and external sites of injustice.[73] Challenging the hold of Westphalian presumptions as they play out in this conflict (instituting seemingly clear boundaries for national projects of self-determination) certainly can enable reframing the boundaries of "who we are." In Shenhav's account, the poor settlers (who ended up residing in settlements out of socioeconomic necessity and who, if only they resided within Israel proper, might have been supporters of an authentic economic left agenda), along with the Mizrahim, and the Palestinians, all could become allies if rigid spatial categories were removed and Israel/Palestine were considered a contiguous space. The upshot of this respatialization, for Shenhav, is the eventual implementation of a loosely connected democratic confederation of small cantons.

However, for any respatializing of geopolitical boundaries to be successful, it will require a more fundamental reimagining of subjective and symbolic boundaries of belonging. These processes of reimagining the "who" (in this case, as a Middle Eastern, nonhegemonic identity) will necessitate an intra-Jewish contestation of the Jewish meanings of Israel. The reimagining of the Jewish identity of Israel and the place that Israel occupies in contemporary Jewish life would drastically transform the parameters of justice vis-à-vis the Palestinians. Without such a translocal scrutiny, encompassing non-Israeli and Israeli Jews, a radical restructuring as proposed by advocates of polycentrism will lack cultural authorization. Even a loosely connected network of consociational cantons needs to be invested with a substantive meaning that will generate commitment for its continuous cultivation. Additionally, there is the challenge (familiar to critics of multicultural and multinational citizenship discourses) of how to ensure that each autonomous politicocultural unit is itself nonhegemonic and nonoppressive to individual members. These points substantiate my claim that a synthetic conversation that highlights the connection between peace studies, theories of justice, and subaltern critical expositions of meta-injustices cannot ignore the question of religion, especially as it relates to conceptions of ethnic and national membership.

The problem of misframing the discourse of justice must be a central concern for the analysis of ethnoreligious national contestations. It is the task of cultural theory to reveal how such a misframing relates to "metapolitical injustices" and to rethink the "who" to whom justice applies. This mode of analysis therefore complements strategic peacebuilding by illuminating the interpretive, contextual, and contested characteristics of justpeace, and by subsequently imagining possibilities for reframing ideological and identity-based perceptions.

Indeed, these important developments in political theory, especially the refocusing of the questions of justice that Kymlicka and Fraser share (albeit from distinctly different philosophical orientations), bring to the fore the relevance of justice discourses to thinking contextually about specific problems. However, with the exception of transitional-justice literature and praxis, this kind of work is only tangentially recognized as relevant to peace studies. Thus, one objective of this book is to illuminate the fruitful connections between peace studies and critical and self-reflexive political theory, with its emphases on multicultural and post-Westphalian justice discourses. Another objective is to bring both cultural theory and a deconstructive lens to bear on the presuppositions underlying Fraser's and Kymlicka's approaches to justice. In short, cultural theory needs to become an important interlocutor in conversations in the field of peace studies.

Such a critical turn is necessary because the liberal framework of multiculturalism does not enable probing into underlying misframing or meta-injustices. The inclination to categorize the question of justice under the problem of "minority rights" could be misleading and gloss over the root causes of conflict and injustice.[74] In the case of the Palestinian citizens of Israel, for example, while the meta-injustice relates to the experience of displacement, the framing of the question of their status in Israel is comfortably subsumed under the heading of "minority rights." The conceptual and ideological blinders that allow us to see only a particular interpretation of the Jewish identity of Israel, in turn, also limit the scope and parameters of justice vis-à-vis the Palestinians in the territories occupied in 1967, the refugee camps, and the various diasporas.

Indeed, the polycentric challenges to the liberal framework of multiculturalism effectively identify the multiplicity of justice discourses and the importance of denaturalizing the boundaries of those discourses. However, as we saw in the intervention above, the polycentric lens merely problematizes the "where" while leaving the boundaries of the "who" intact (even while deterritorialized). Fraser underscores the artificiality of limiting questions of justice to geopolitical boundaries when obviously individuals and groups who are not citizens of a given nation-state may nevertheless be affected by certain policies of the nation-state. Her approach, however, does not offer resources for denaturalizing the subjective boundaries of the "who" that is or may be affected by the discourses of justice.[75]

The analysis above shows that neither the liberal nor the polycentric framework provides space for problematizing or reimagining the question of religion as a marker of political, national, and ethnic identity, however. As I argue in chapters 6 and 7, this oversight is also reflected in the proposals advanced by the Mizrahim and Palestinian Israeli citizens. This is why this trajectory of normative political theory needs to directly engage not only with peace studies and context-specific discussions about conflict transformation but also with the study of political structures and discourses that underpin the interfacing between religion and the ethnocultural imagination. An important step in this direction is to overcome the disjunction between political theory and the study of nationalism. This point invites engagement with the discussion of religion and secularism because, as I suggested above, a "thin" conception of government carries certain presuppositions about the place of religion in political exchanges and in framing the principles of belonging to a "nation."

A Critical Probe: The Discourses of Secularism

The increased multidisciplinarity of peace research and the broadening scope of normative political theory notwithstanding, peace studies has not yet integrated critical-cultural studies and postcolonial theoretical insights as sites of discussion with potential repercussions for strategic peacebuilding. Feminist theorists who study questions of women, agency, and conflict provide a pronounced exception to the mainstream of scholarship in peace studies. While peace studies has, for the most part, presupposed the naturalness of identities as articulated by the spokespersons of national and/or subnational groups, feminist theorists have long connected questions of gender to structural and cultural forms of violence, highlighting the gendered discourses of nationalism and war.[76] A nascent thread of scholarship has begun to focus on questions of gender, problematizing reigning paradigms in conflict and peace studies, but also offering constructive and imaginative modes for rethinking questions of women, agency, and conflict transformation.[77]

Indeed, a gendered perspective highlights the critical-constructive role that women may play in conflict zones as embodying counterhegemonic and subaltern experiences and social spaces. This site of conversation needs to theorize the intersections between women, religion, and questions of agency more vigorously. This question is not resolved by merely analyzing religion as a locus for creative, empowering potentialities found in daily and interiorized religious practices. After all, it does not sufficiently theorize the relevance of religion qua political identity to broader discussions of women and agency in zones of conflict defined by rigid, subjective boundaries. Instead, the study of women and agency often analyzes religion as a repository of symbolic resources that enables women to cope with their dire situations or subvert official accounts of religion.[78] Recent theoretical efforts to challenge a conventional feminist account of female agency as an explicit rejection of patriarchal hegemony successfully rescue the analysis of agency from immediate political reductionism while nonetheless opening the door to cultural relativism and possible valorization of unjust customs and traditions.[79]

Although it is important to explore how and why certain religious practices intensify during times of urgent conflict, it is also critical to interrogate how religion may be implicated and entrenched in the underlying structures of injustice that give rise to direct violence, and to imagine ways of conceptualizing the connections between those two sets of inquiries. Such a conceptual shift entails looking at the selective overlaps between identity markers. This analysis seeks to capture the interconnections between religion and national culture (or "civil religion") and to link this discussion to broader concerns of peace and justice.

In short, my multidisciplinary approach to the question of religion and peacebuilding resonates with the kind of critical engagement with structural and cultural violence undertaken by feminist research. However, I argue that this form of subaltern critique needs to be supplemented by a sustained conversation concerning the interrelation between religion and the modes in which collective identity markers are envisioned and naturalized. Such a conversation necessitates moving away from a persistent conceptual reliance in peace studies on otherwise debunked and problematized modernist and secularist discourses, which reinforce particular historicist interpretations and normative presuppositions concerning the place of religion in public life. The frameworks of feminist theory, in addition to normative political theory and the study of questions of peace and justice in particular zones of conflict, need to account also for the conceptual insights of religious studies, and especially genealogical analyses that expose the meanings of the "religious" and the "secular" in light of particular histories of colonial domination and orientalist discourses.

III. Religious Studies

The theologian William Cavanaugh refers to the conventional treatment of "religious violence" as amounting to the perpetuation of a "myth" and sees the framing of the issue in popular culture, international relations theory, and the academic study of religion as a rhetorical move that enables the cultivation of Western superiority and a further bifurcation of "us" versus "them," continuously perpetuating acts of aggression under the pretense of humanitarianism.[80] A similar bifurcation dominates the analysis of secular versus religious forms of Zionism, rendering religious Zionism an obstacle for peace and glossing over the forms of cultural and military violence authorized by secular and "peace-seeking" sectors.

The scholarship that is the subject of Cavanaugh's critique presupposes the validity of a secularist historiography concerning the displacement of religion from public/political life.[81] This presupposition undergirds an understanding of the modern "nation" as either neutral with respect to religion or—in a Durkheimian fashion—a surrogate religion. But the analysis of ethnoreligious national conflicts, advanced in the present work, depends on theorizing more pivotally how the decentralization of religion relates to the interpretation of religion and culture in the processes of imagining and reimagining a nation. This research program is especially heightened where it is clear that the thresholds of membership in the nation are exclusively ethno- and religiocentric, even if such conceptions of citizenship do not necessarily translate into a theocratic agenda.

One current of scholarship in religious studies that does engage with the publicity of religion and religion's relevance to public debates is associated with the works of José Casanova, Ronald Thiemann, Jeffrey Stout, and Nicholas Wolterstorff, among other influential thinkers.[82] While insightful in explicating modes of interface between the political and the religious/cultural and in revising secularist paradigms, they are thoroughly and self-consciously embedded in Anglo-Saxon, Christian, and mostly North American traditions of political liberalism and (liberal) multicultural interpretations of citizenship.[83] The question remains, however, how a focus on a rich tradition of democratic practices and conversations concerning the publicity of religion can be extended beyond the particularities of liberal and civic conceptions of membership (even if the Christian undertones are not diminished) and whether it can offer a framework for thinking about conflict transformation in zones of ethnoreligious national conflicts. How can the conversations about democratic practices and virtues that allow for explicit religious reasoning unfold in other contexts that do not view the "religious" and the "national" as differentiable facets of one's identity? And how might religious reasoning challenge and perhaps denaturalize axiomatic conceptions of identity, thereby potentially transforming ethnoreligious interpretations of nationhood and moral justifications for engaging in war and

other forms of aggression? A study of the political agenda of Serb nationalism, Hindutva in India, Sinhala Buddhism in Sri Lanka, and Zionism, to
cite only a few examples, attests to this point: any attempt to think about
justice in those situations must involve interrogating and reimagining the
connections between "religion" and "nationality."[84] A creative reimagining
would depend on challenging the rigid boundaries of secularist-modernist
categories of analysis.

In recent years, political theorists have begun to recognize the analytically limiting effects of the secularist-modernist explanatory paradigms.
Elizabeth Shakman Hurd's *The Politics of Secularism in International Relations* effectively engages ongoing conversations in the study of religion
by recognizing, along with Charles Taylor, the historical locations of laic
and Judeo-Christian notions of the "secular." Echoing critics like William
Connolly and Talal Asad, she outlines the categories of the "secular" and
the "religious" as thoroughly constructed modes for authorizing political
arrangements.[85]

Hurd's work exemplifies an attempt to reflect critically on how secularist ontologies and epistemologies have affected and limited the analytic
compass of international relations theories.[86] Accordingly, the failure of
these theories to recognize the socially constructed and fluid nature of the
"secular" and the "religious," as well as the multiple forms secularism has
assumed in different contexts, has significantly constrained their ability to
analyze and formulate responses to how religion transpires in international
affairs.[87] Instead, Hurd suggests deconstructing the premises of the field
of international relations in order to introduce different kinds of research
questions like why and how the boundaries of the secular are refashioned
in particular contexts.[88] The self-reflexivity she advocates, through a careful
consideration of works in religious studies, goes a long way in historicizing
the analysis of the so-called resurgence of religion, locating this discussion
in colonial and oriental discourses and enabling a reconsideration of the
assumptions inherent in "secular" conceptions of identity.[89] This kind of
scrutiny is advantageous also to reimagining Israeli secularism.

Conclusion

Indeed, a human rights orientation could be an integral component in un-
masking unjust practices and structures. For instance, while Israel frames
the erecting of a wall of separation as an act of self-defense (and Israeli and
Jewish perceptions of an existential threat must indeed be taken seriously),
the voices of the people separated from their properties as a result of this

construction project complicate and challenge Israel's myopic position. Are both sides right? Are both wrong? How can and should one adjudicate between their claims? The responses to this line of questioning demand recognizing the claims of peoples caught in the dynamics of conflict on their own terms and in their own contexts, but also an external orientation or theory of justice that provides a compass for determining whose claim/grievance has greater moral currency, urgency, and validity.

This analytic mode is crucial for diagnosing conflicts and for designing strategies of holistic peacebuilding that envision both horizontal (societal, cultural) and vertical (institutional, systemic) processes of healing and restructuring. But whatever diagnosis emerges does not necessarily constitute the final verdict on the matter at hand. The human rights framework, construed as a dynamic international/transnational and cross-cultural tradition rather than as an imperial Western project,[90] thus provides an orientation for a constructive and embedded engagement with traditions, marshaling intra- as well as extragroup resources for redressing the conditions and memories of injustice. But the human rights orientation advances a view of nationalism that, while containing critical insights and normative commitments, is too constraining, and ultimately insufficient, as a program for change.

"Rights," as Michael Ignatieff has argued, "are not the universal credo of a global society, not a secular religion, but something much more limited and yet just as valuable: the shared vocabulary from which our arguments can begin, and the bare human minimum from which differing ideas of human flourishing can take root."[91] This process is especially necessary in zones where denaturalizing the most basic perceptions of "who we are as a group" provides the key for devising frameworks for transforming underlying relationships.

Therefore, the human rights approach, as I view it, affords an important diagnostic lens that can illuminate the underlying causes of conflict. Of course, the Palestinians do not need the UDHR to know that Israel's policy of land confiscation hurts them. But the human rights framework nonetheless provides a vindicating vocabulary that is broadly comparative, drawing analogies to cases of injustice elsewhere. This comparative dimension of the discussion reveals that recognition of injustice endured is not necessarily intuitive and instinctual. Rather, it is grounded in the internalization and awareness of a tradition of human rights that clearly resents injustice and violence perpetrated on the basis of a self-serving agenda.

But my discussion of nationalism, identity, and the limits of multicultural designs of ethnocultural justice suggests that—beyond the diagnostic and inspirational effectiveness of a human rights approach—there lies the task of reimagining "who we are" through an exposition of the conceptual misframing of the discourse of justice. In this context, liberal nationalism, as well as liberal religion, can be found complicit (often despite its own self-perceptions) with the structures of systemic and cultural violence. Liberal nationalism, consequently, provides only a limited framework for conflict transformation.

My approach is consistent, up to a point, with the typology of religion, nationalism, and violence outlined above. It is especially consonant with its insistence on the dynamic, fluctuating, and thoroughly interpretive character of "nationalism," along with its normative commitment to a relatively "thin" view of political membership as a desired remedy and goal for conflicts defined by ethnoreligious national claims. However, the challenge is that a "thin" or "liberal" conception of the "nation" entails certain assumptions about "religion" that are thoroughly context-specific and therefore cannot sufficiently explain why, for instance, framing religion as a matter of private faith (even if it functions prophetically, on occasion) and interpreting one's Jewish identity as merely "ethnic" or "national," as many liberal Israelis do, enable complicity with meta-injustices. I depart from the typology and its assumptions only in pushing it to recognize how its historical blind spots and conceptual limitations can misdiagnose or insufficiently address the roots of conflict, especially by overlooking how and why liberal sectors contribute to and reify undergirding forms of injustice. A key to peacebuilding and conflict transformation, therefore, is to identify not only the obvious obstacles to peace (explicitly violent and chauvinistic segments of the population such as the Jewish settlers in the occupied territories) but also the nonobvious voices of post-Zionist peace-seeking and pluralistic activists.

Certainly, it is important to integrate into one's analysis the discursive critique of secularism that attempts to break away from the liberal conceptual framework with its precise demarcation of the "political" and the "religious." It is likewise necessary to integrate the works of critics of liberalism, such as Iris Marion Young and Michael Walzer, who locate the standards of justice in the particularistic interpretive frameworks of specific societies—an approach that coheres with Ignatieff's thesis about human rights as a starting point from which many forms of human flourishing could emerge. Likewise, the local interpretative process could revise the meanings of universal standards of justice in the kind of a dialectical and cross-cultural manner that marked the drafting of the UDHR. It is crucial, however, to safeguard against a wholesale rejection of everything "liberal," including some of the presumptions about democratic values and practices inherent in human rights conventions on cultural, political, and civic rights. Thus understood, the human rights perspective opens the way for contextual engagements with the particular meanings these principles could assume in particular instances.[92] This multidirectional process does not take identity claims at face value or treat competing claims solely on the level of "rights talk."

Therefore, the method of the hermeneutics of citizenship I develop in chapter 3 not only recognizes cultural and national claims but also denaturalizes them in order to transform the relations of power and to reconfigure the most just political arrangements. This approach cannot circumscribe the "religious" merely under the headings of "rights" because it recognizes the need for a substantive interpretive process that would rethink the definitional interrelationship between religious, ethnic, and national markers of identity.

The study of the Israeli peace camp sheds light on the need to clarify the interrelation between religion, ethnicity, and nationalism through an analysis of power as well as constructive hermeneutics or (re)interpretations of the boundaries of identity and justpeace. The thick analysis of the Israeli peace camp I outline in chapters 4 to 7, accentuated by a focus on counterhegemonic voices as a resource for reimagining questions of peace and justice, constitutes an important dimension in the multifaceted process of peacebuilding. It involves the recognition of the authentic claims and perceptions of ethnoreligious national groups, but it also illuminates the possible implications for a nondeterminist reading of these claims.

Even if we recognize that the use of the Holocaust to vindicate the Zionist project precipitated profound sufferings and injustices for other people, dismissing the authenticity and relevance of the question of the survival of Jewish people would block the possibility of healing and conflict transformation. The eminent Palestinian cultural critic Edward Said concurs. Said's envisioning of a just peace[93] for Palestine is grounded in the secular principle of equality; nonetheless, he introduces intricate and thick historical sensitivities into this model. "Neither Palestinian nor Israeli history at this point is a thing in itself, without the other," he observes. "In so doing we will necessarily come up against the basic irreconcilability between the Zionist claim and Palestinian dispossession. The injustice done to the Palestinians is constitutive of these two histories, as is also the crucial effect of Western anti-Semitism and the Holocaust."[94]

Said's recognition of the profound relational dynamics underlying Israeli and Palestinian identities is insightful as a method for conceptualizing justpeace as involving the renarration of history as fundamentally relational.[95] This method illuminates how identities are constituted by power dynamics but understands the possibility of transformation as one embedded in reconstituting and also remembering these dynamics and the particular memories and experiences of injustice they produce and embody.

While diverging from my approach by insisting on an unreconstructed secularism as a means of liberation from the atavistic inclinations of particularistic conceptions of identity, Said's method of thinking about justpeace coheres with my multidisciplinary approach to the analysis of ethnoreligious nationalism. This approach pushes beyond Lederach's focus on cultivating the "moral imagination" of the peacebuilder to include a sustained and systemic discursive analysis. Such an analysis is neither intuitive nor straightforward. It calls for more than the cultivation of the "moral imagination" of peace professionals. My approach insists on the indispensability of deploying the theoretical insights found in cultural and political theory and religious studies in any attempt to analyze conflicts involving identity claims. Such an analytic preparation could greatly broaden the vistas of the "moral imagination."

THREE

Critical Caretakers: The Hermeneutics of Citizenship and the Question of Justice

Introduction

In this chapter, I develop the concept of the *hermeneutics of citizenship* as a method for thinking about peacebuilding and conflict transformation in conflicts that are explicitly defined by ethnoreligious national narratives and claims. This approach is grounded in a multidisciplinary orientation to the study of conflict and peace—one that, in pursuing justpeace, illuminates the importance of engaging and transforming structural as well as direct manifestations of violence. My point of departure synthesizes the agonistic insight concerning the elasticity and contestatory character of the "we" with the view of nationalism as a theory of political legitimacy that draws selectively on cultural, religious, and ethnic resources.[1] Despite its methodological nationalism, the agonistic view can be read in ways that cohere with an understanding of reconciliation as a process of transforming the boundaries of the community. Any attempt at transformation, however, calls upon a hermeneutics of how religious motifs and particularistic cultural claims and entitlements unfold in the narration of a national ethos and vindicate individual acts of aggression as well as systemic forms of violence. The preceding analysis of the secular Zionist Israeli peace camp illustrated this point.

In chapter 1, I demonstrated that the secular Israeli peace camp is insufficiently reflective about the underlying religious and theological motifs that legitimated the settlement program of the Zionist Congress and the establishment of the State of Israel. Secularist leaders and activists, I demonstrated, hold ambiguous and, at times, paradoxical interpretations of the Jewish meaning of the Israeli state. With a focus on terminating the occupation of the territories of 1967, the secularist peace camp generally endorses the need to cultivate Israel as a Jewish democracy within the borders of 1948.

In this context, "Jewish" has a primarily demographic meaning, implying a commitment to maintaining a state with a Jewish majority, but it also
denotes "culture," "ethnicity," and a national identity defined in part by
its history of persecutions and pogroms. Yet, even this purportedly secular
interpretation of Jewish history and identity amounts to a form of *political
theology* that leads to spatial and metahistorical biases, significantly limiting
the analysis of conflict and the possibility of imagining a comprehensive
approach to peacebuilding.

As we saw in chapter 1, in fact, religious and even theological motifs
pervade the claims and commitments of the self-proclaimed secular Israeli
peace camp, despite the reframing of its "Jewishness" as an ethnic, cultural,
and national identity. Such motifs include the "return to the land" and the
"ingathering of the exiles" (as well as the reading of the Tanakh as a history
book), which are integral to the explicitly messianic moment of redemption. Failure to interrogate the political teleological implications of these
motifs, among others, limits the peace camp's visions of peace and justice.
Secularist and nonreligious leaders and activists view those motifs as pivotal
to any peace agreement with the Palestinians: Israel with minimalist borders needs to retain its Jewish character, which entails an automatic "right of
return" and/or critical quotas imposed on the return of Palestinian refugees
as part of a peace settlement and a truth and reconciliation commission (as
articulated by Gush Shalom and other left-leaning groups, for example).

Justpeace in this context would necessitate challenging the Zionist interpretations of Judaism and Jewish history and, subsequently, reimagining
Jewish meanings of the Israeli state in a way that is more consistent with
a multiperspectival approach to justice—one that, in the words of Edward
Said, recognizes that "neither Palestinian nor Israeli history at this point is a
thing in itself, without the other." The Holocaust and the Naqba (the Palestinian disaster of 1948 or the "War of Independence," as it is called in Israel)
are, by now, inextricably interwoven. Further, a multiperspectival approach
also looks inward to marginalized and silenced voices within the community, in order to trace the power dynamics and probe the interstices of identities inscribed in the construction and reconstruction of social and symbolic
boundaries. This focus on the margins may also highlight resources for creatively reframing those boundaries. In subsequent chapters, I draw on those
voices and explore the challenges and resources they bring to the modes in
which peace and justice are imagined in the Israeli context. The focus on
margins and silences is not only for the purpose of critique but also for the
constructive rethinking of the subjective boundaries of the community.[2]

I. The Hermeneutics of Citizenship

While the polycentric approach to multiculturalism is correct to identify a connection between the misframing of boundaries and meta-injustices, it does not theorize whether certain interpretations of religion qua political identity may themselves be implicated in meta-injustices. It follows that reframing the discourses of justice requires reinterpreting the interface between religion and political identity. The hermeneutics of citizenship is predicated upon the necessity of contesting the boundaries of the "who" to whom justice applies as well as the inextricability of religion, history, and culture in this question. It therefore significantly expands upon conventional approaches to religion and peacebuilding. The hermeneutics of citizenship also challenges the liberal approach to multicultural justice because the liberal frame does not necessarily enable rethinking the boundaries of identities. Nor does it sufficiently account for historical memories of injustice. The hermeneutics of citizenship, by contrast, requires the examination of the internal pluralities of tradition and history as well as the recognition of the predicaments of others. So resituated, the justice question, by default, pushes the conversation beyond the bounds of one tradition and/or the narrative of one group and demands a multifaceted, pluralistic, contextualized, and multiperspectival articulation.

Such an articulation of justice may reveal meta-injustices or the very problem of the "misframing of the discourses of justice."[3] But the case of Israel suggests that the post-Westphalian critique of conventional, territorially based justice discourses needs not only to ask *who* may be affected by decision making but also to probe the complexities in the conception of the *who* to whom justice applies. To contribute to peacebuilding and conflict transformation, such an interrogation needs not only identifying points of misframing but also a creative engagement with reframing or reimagining identities. In the case of Israel, as well as other instances of ethnoreligious nationalism, such a reimagining cannot bracket religion as an auxiliary or epiphenomenal factor or as a mere repository of symbolic resources. Nor can religion be treated simply as a matter of civil liberties (as the Meretz Party does), or as a subset of a broader myopic "rights talk" (freedom of conscience and expression). Instead, such reimagining must bring to light, debate, and negotiate the prevailing political theology and mythology of the nation. So in the same way that Fraser challenges the territorial geography of justice, the hermeneutics of citizenship challenges its subjective parameters.

Both polycentric and liberal approaches to multiculturalism provide a limited scope for conflict transformation because they fail to grapple with the relevance (and at times indispensability) of a multivalent conception of religion for reframing questions of justice. In Israel, the reframing of the justice discourse will necessitate intra-Jewish conversations concerning the interrelationship between Judaism and Israel. The process of reframing would also entail reconfiguring and interrogating the role Palestine has come to play in the Islamist and Arab popular imaginations. The hermeneutics of citizenship is an alternative process of reframing through a necessary analysis of the interrelation between religion and conceptions of identity.

The hermeneutics of citizenship challenges the presumption that secularity might entail governmental neutrality. This presumption is tied to a modernist interpretation of secularity as the absence, negation, or subjugation of religion and its relegation to the so-called private sphere where it poses no threat or obstacle to progress, modernity, rationality, and liberality. As mentioned in chapter 2, this presumption has affected the modes in which questions about religion, conflict, and peacebuilding are commonly framed. It is in this connection that resources drawn from critical, cultural, and postcolonial theories may offer pivotal insights.

Common to these theoretical turns is a critical appraisal of the Enlightenment's universalism and rationalism and the development of nonessentialist conceptual frameworks for deconstructing the teleology of modernity. The teleology of modernity under critique includes the diminishing significance of religion in public life and religion's withdrawal to the nonpolitical, interiorized, and individualized realm of the "private." The related analytical currents in postcolonial studies similarly strive to deconstruct hegemonies by disentangling and denaturalizing the interconnections between "power" and conceptions of identity.

In developing a mode of agonistic democratic engagement, political theorist Chantal Mouffe's scrutiny of the dynamics underlying "social objectivity" captures this interconnection between power and perceptions of identity. In articulating her notion of *hegemony* as the "point of confluence between objectivity and power," Mouffe understands "power" "not as an *external* relation taking place between two preconstituted identities but rather as constituting the identities themselves."[4] This conception of power is instructive for the hermeneutics of citizenship. It could enable processes that are simultaneously contestatory and (re)imaginative. By deploying postcolonial deconstructive tools of critique, these processes might denaturalize allegedly axiomatic narratives and conceptions of identity (a prepolitical "we") and facilitate alternative interpretations of identities that may be less exclusionary and chauvinistic and thus more consistent with demands of justice. My discussion of the cases of the Palestinian citizens of Israel and the Mizrahim in chapters 6 and 7 undertakes this task of denaturalizing the axiomatic presuppositions concerning the identity of Israel as exclusively Jewish (and Western), an identity that both secular and religious Zionist groups presume (as I demonstrate in chapters 1, 4, and 5).

Broadening the conversation in such a way embeds the analysis of justice in a thick hermeneutical questioning of subjective perceptions of belonging and identity—a questioning that may result in redrawing the thresholds of inclusion and exclusion. Denaturalizing the underlying connection between religion and nationalism inherent in nationalist narratives may in turn expand the (re)interpretive possibilities available for religious peacebuilding. The task of peacebuilding is not only to identify and bring to bear resources from within religious traditions that appear peaceful and justice-seeking but also to expose how religion fits into the invisible lines of discursive formations and how it may figure in redrawing and reframing the bounds of identity and power configurations. Reframing ontological identity claims, therefore, requires a multiperspectival lens that, while reclaiming and identifying pluralities within seemingly homogenous national historiographies, would also recognize how an exclusive reliance on one's own cultural, religious, and historical resources for peacebuilding might reinstitute and normalize meta-injustices.[5]

II. Political Theology

As I argued in the previous chapter, the liberalism of the Israeli peace camp reveals central flaws in the model of liberal nationalism. Of particular interest is the reliance on the interpretation of religion as "faith" and of religiosity as a distinct and separable component of social life (even if it assumes an occasionally obvious public relevance and presence). Such conception enables secular Israelis like Yossi Beilin to differentiate between Judaism qua national identity and Judaism qua belief, a dichotomy that obscures the need to contest the political theology of secular Zionism in order to illuminate and transform structural and cultural modalities of violence (see chapter 1).

Still, the view of nationalism as a theory of political legitimacy and as constituting a "belief" in "common descent," "providential mission," and "normative superiority" offers an important corrective to the models of liberal nationalism, as well as to the polycentric theories of multiculturalism. The latter overlook the relevance of religion to reimagining the "who" or the symbolic boundaries of the group. But even this corrected form of liberal nationalism—which remains the desired goal in the process of healing unhealthy, exclusionary, and illiberal forms of nationalism—does not provide sufficient resources for (1) identifying the blinders that enable the language of liberalism to gloss over meta-injustices and to misframe the justice discourse, and (2) reimagining the "nation" as something other than a thinly connected polity that carries certain presuppositions concerning religion's best practices in the public sphere.

While highly valuable, this liberal approach bypasses scrutiny of the dynamics of power to see how transforming them might (re)constitute social and cultural identities and practices. Even if relations of power are ineradicable (as agonistic theorists of democracy contend), it is important to recognize the need to transform them. Conversely, holding onto a liberal presupposition of and appeal to "a universal rational consensus" may mask the underlying patterns of exclusion under "pretenses of 'neutrality.'"[6] The case of the Israeli peace camp—in both its secular and its religious varieties—illustrates how the liberal framework could function myopically to conceal the underlying sources of conflict and consequently limit the horizons of possibilities.

The hermeneutics of citizenship, therefore, amounts to an introspective interrogation of the political theology underlying the definition of the modern "nation" and its institutions. The label "political theology" seems fitting for my analysis, though my use of this concept is different from its articulation by thinkers like Carl Schmitt and Leo Strauss.[7] Instead, my view of the modern nation as a form of political theology draws on the work of theorist of nationalism Anthony Smith's ethnosymbolist analysis of modern nationalisms.[8] Smith offers a critique of the modernist analyses of nationalism. He argues that—reflective of post-Enlightenment notions of human auto-emancipation—modernist approaches to the study of nationalism erroneously position the nation as an entirely secular category. He further adds that such modernist theories of nationalism—consistent with the classical secularism paradigm—view religion as a force of diminishing significance, as inconsistent with liberal values,[9] and as constituting the distant background[10] from which the modern nation emerged but eventually distinguished itself.[11] Other modernist theorists view the nation as an engineered invention to functionally respond to the need to control the masses in the post-Reformation and postindustrialization landscape.[12] Still other modernist theoretical frameworks argue that nationalism has nothing to do with religion and is exclusively the provenance of politics.[13]

In an effort to develop an alternative theoretical grid for the analysis of nationalism, Smith cites Elie Kedourie's reformed modernism as an insightful springboard for the study of the interrelation between religion and nation. Kedourie analyzes how the transplantation of the Western ideal and institution of the nation-state to African and Asian contexts involved a top-down manipulation of the "atavistic emotions" of the masses, generating the "pathetic fallacy" that he understands as "the belief that the interests, needs and preoccupations of the elites are the same as those of the masses."[14] Kedourie offers a second challenge to an unqualified modernist framework when he analyzes the modern phenomenon of nationalism as a secular version of millennial political religion. He views nationalism as "heterodox religion." On this account, while antireligion (that is, anticlericalism) has often been integral to the construction of national identity, the process of imagining a nation has appropriated "symbols, liturgies, rituals, and messianic fervor—which now come to possess new and subversive political and national meanings."[15]

Analyzing the nation as a "heterodox religion" accentuates the seeming contrast between the secular content and the religious forms assumed by various nationalisms. It also accounts for what may be viewed as cooptation or manipulation of religion in the service of secular political ends.[16] While other theorists identify the "cooptation" and "manipulation" of religion as a relevant variable for the analysis of the dynamics (not necessarily the causality) of conflict, the ethnosymbolist approach assists in clarifying the limits of such instrumentalist (and modernist) approaches to religion.[17] It also exposes what Benedict Anderson refers to as one of the "paradoxes" of modern nationalisms: their political power versus their philosophical weakness.[18] The ethnosymbolist approach underscores that unlike medieval millennialism, "nationalism is a distinctly this-worldly movement and culture." Nationalism, Smith explains, does not aspire "to flee a corrupt world" but rather "seeks to reform the world in its own image, a world of unique and authentic nations."[19]

While a central feature of millennialism is the expectation of total destruction of the existing order by way of an imminent, supernatural intervention, nationalists amplify the human act of auto-emancipation as a necessary step in fulfilling the destiny of a nation. Hence, Smith concludes that even though nationalisms appropriate religious motifs and symbols in the process of articulating themselves, they should not be viewed as a simple continuation of traditional religion. Nor should they be analyzed as "secularized versions" of religion. One needs to be more precise in the analysis of the relation between religion and nationalism because modern nationalisms are selective in how they relate to traditional religions. They tend to eschew notions of cosmic and otherworldly salvation.[20] Yet despite modern nationalisms' rejection of traditional religions and their constitutive this-worldliness, they do appropriate many religious motifs and popular forms. This insight leads Smith to suggest the need to uncover the underlying religious sources of the nation.[21]

Exposing the sacred sources of the nation becomes especially important when perceptions of nationhood seem to be directly relevant to questions of conflict and peace, as in the Palestinian-Israeli case. My analysis of the "nation" as a manifestation of political theology therefore echoes Smith's conclusion that the modern nation "is best seen as a form of culture and a type of belief system whose object is the nation conceived as a sacred communion."[22] But moving beyond ethnosymbolism, I stress the importance of deciphering the power dynamics undergirding national historiographies as they draw selectively upon antecedent traditions, legends, prejudices, and cultural praxes. This view, which also challenges the ethnosymbolist reliance on a modernist rendering of religion despite its critique of the modernist paradigm, is central to developing the hermeneutics of citizenship as an approach for scrutinizing the appropriation of traditional resources and symbols in the continuous process of imagining and reimagining the national group and its conceptions of origin, destiny, and self-fulfillment.

Examining the political-theological dimensions of nationalism requires interrogating various theological or religious motifs and traditions for their political agenda (either conscious or sublimated). The ethnosymbolist approach to the study of nationalism is therefore effective in highlighting the persistent religious motifs inherent in modern nationalism. It is also insightful in underscoring the this-worldliness of nationalisms, their emphasis on human self-emancipation, and their thoroughly "secular" character. These characteristics distinguish them from the religious foundations that they selectively appropriate. Instructively, a paradigmatic case for Smith is political Zionism, which rejects traditional Jewish notions of messianic redemption and insists instead upon the material, human-initiated redemption that is the return to the land.

There are two distinct yet interrelated advantages to the analysis of Zionism—even in its secular variety—as a *political theology*. First, it allows us to expose Zionism's conceptual blinders and underlying illiberality. Accordingly, we can illustrate how and why the Zionist ethnonational commitment limits the extent of Israeli liberalism as well as its modes of envisioning a justpeace for the Palestinian-Israeli conflict. Second, interpreting Zionism as a political theology enables a hermeneutics of citizenship, in which the religious and cultural symbolisms defining perceptions of nationhood are unmasked, interrogated, and contested.

A public process of reinterpretation—a process that would necessitate intragroup conversation—assumes a plurality of views, as well as a requirement to explore the legitimacy of political claims through intergroup exchange. In other words, analyzing the nation as a political theology or a heterodox religion challenges the inclination of nationalists to conflate "nation" with "religion" or "ethnicity" (when the latter constitute the primary principle of belonging). It also confronts the proclivity to essentialize such identities.

On my reading, the classification of the "nation" as a manifestation of political theology also points to what social theorist Max Weber identified as the "elective affinity" among indices of identity such as ethnicity, religion, and nationalism as well as to the possibility of reimagining how they may relate to one another.[23] Recognizing this complexity may be where the most innovative aspects of religious peacebuilding reside. Certainly, however, framing nationalism as a form of political theology and a "belief" does not amount to replicating the cognitive bias that has constrained the discussion of religion to the domain of "faith". Instead, because nationalism nests a set of embodied and embedded practices, change cannot be analyzed and acted upon merely through subjectivist and cognitive lenses.

III. Religious Peacebuilding

The field of religious peacebuilding emerged as a corollary to scholarly engagements with the question of religion and violence,[24] and thus it reflects similar assumptions.[25] The growing scholarship and field of practice that identify religion as a valuable dimension of peacebuilding and conflict transformation[26] have generally also subscribed to an unrevised modernist understanding of the "religious" and the "secular" as occupying distinct realms. This dichotomization constrained the industry of religious peacebuilding to focus on religion as falling within the realm merely of "soft power."[27] While underscoring the instrumentality and value of religious diplomacy, this trend only reaffirms the presuppositions undergirding Track I diplomacy, which frames diplomacy as a practice involving rational and mostly official actors who focus primarily on the geopolitical and thus "secular" implications of conflict resolution. In other words, the scholarship on religion and peace does not, for the most part, consider how recent debates on secularism may bear on understanding the role of religion in peacebuilding. Nor has it incorporated the insistence of postcolonial theory on reassessing the core beliefs of the "nation" from the point of view of its subalterns. Religious peacebuilding has thus been relegated to the sphere of "soft power" or Track II diplomacy as an auxiliary (albeit a necessary one) to the secular framework of official negotiations.[28]

Ethnoreligious national conflicts involve particular and contested interpretations of religious and cultural resources. Therefore, the involvement of religion in conflict transformation must entail more than mere Track II inspiration and activity.[29] It must also include a substantive engagement and sustained grappling with definitional questions pertaining to the formulation of national identities.[30] If this scrutiny is glossed over, religious peacebuilding (as I show in my account of the work of Rabbis for Human Rights in chapter 5) could, however inadvertently, become as complicit as secular peace activism in reaffirming the myopic and silencing function of national mythologies and political theologies.[31]

For the purposes of conflict transformation, it is necessary to expand upon the conventional approach to religion and peacebuilding. Indeed, the emphasis of the religion and peace genre on the requirement to recognize and acknowledge the creative potentialities of religious traditions and cultural/historical memories constitutes a central aspect of the task of religious peacebuilding. At the same time, especially in contexts where ethnoreligious claims form the primary vocabulary and modes of legitimization invoked by nationalist actors, religious peacebuilding also necessitates a thorough engagement with violent interpretations of religion. It calls for a contextualized and historically sensitive evaluation of how religion relates to nationalist agendas and to the construction and cultivation of systems of domination. This investigation goes beyond the confrontation of direct violence by exploring the ways that certain interpretations of religion, ethnicity, and culture contribute to systemic and symbolic forms of violence and, in particular, those forms born out of a commitment to the normative boundaries of the community. The hermeneutics of citizenship captures what I mean by this process of redescription and reimagining how religion relates to political identities.

I do not wish to privilege religion as a resource for reimagining the boundaries of identity but instead wish to point to the unavoidable task of both identifying and transforming the ways in which religion, in the case of Israel and other ethnoreligious nationalisms, relates to social and political boundaries. This is an unavoidable step in the analysis of conflict because exclusivist interpretations of membership constitute a form of cultural violence, which, in turn, undergirds institutional and direct violence. Yet the search for more inclusivist and palatable resources within religious traditions (as has been the focus of religious peacebuilding heretofore) does not sufficiently take account of the potential role of religious peacebuiliding in debunking symbolic boundaries and how that debunking might facilitate reframing social and political practices. The case of Israel exposes why this hermeneutical engagement needs to be expanded to include confrontation of the at times sublimated, particularistic religious and ethnic conceptions of identity that underlie national identity.[32]

This scrutiny is deeply contextualized and sensitive to power dynamics. The hermeneutical turn therefore needs to be supplemented with a context-specific, embedded exploration of individuals and groups on the margins and illuminate how their very experiences and hybrid locations (as Palestinian Israelis or Arab Jews, in the case of Israel) may not only challenge but also provide resources for rethinking received national historiographies.

This interpretive dimension of peacebuilding expands the scope of the field of religious peacebuilding by moving beyond the confinement of the "religious" to "background culture" and "Track II diplomacy." This effort involves drawing on the theoretical tools and conversations in religious studies and cultural theory. In particular, I engage theoretical approaches that highlight power as pivotal to any attempt to analyze and study religion. Such deconstructive modes of analysis offer effective tools for exposing structures of injustice. And yet ultimately these tools prove to be insufficient for constructively rethinking and reinterpreting identities, at least in a way that may be conducive to building peace. Hence, I put this critical and historicist scholarly approach to the study of religion and culture in conversation with constructive approaches to religion and peacebuilding that focus on resources within a tradition that may counter exclusivist conceptions of identity.

A multiperspectival focus on internal and external subalterns introduces the condition of relationality to religious peacebuilding, which otherwise consists comfortably with a modernist and phenomenological interpretation of religion as located outside discursivity, even if historically unfolding. While often offering constructive interventions in conflict zones, the conventional paradigms of religious peacebuilding, therefore, can become complicit with meta-injustices, if they focus monoperspectivally only on distilling peaceful motifs and practices. An exclusive reliance on this otherwise necessary introspection can replicate and gloss over the kind of chauvinism informing the very forms of direct and indirect violence that peacebuilding seeks to transform.[33]

IV. Constructive but Self-Critical

Pondering the task of historicizing and redescribing "religion," scholar of religion Russell McCutcheon has argued that religious studies scholarship has defaulted on its critical task and rendered itself publicly irrelevant because of a deep-seated metaphysical reductionism—"the longstanding but misguided assumption that studying religion provides deep, essential, absolute, or otherworldly insights into the very nature of things."[34] Presupposing "their datum and their work to have self-evident authority, relevance, and value" has led many scholars to become uncritical caretakers of traditions ("translators" or "color commentators").[35] Specifically, McCutcheon offers a critique of the longstanding and definitional phenomenological tradition of scholarship on religion, traceable to Friedrich Schleiermacher and the interpretation of religion as sui generis in the works of Rudolf Otto, Mircea Eliade, and Paul Tillich, to name a few notable examples. The thrust of this cultural reductionist and historicist critique of the phenomenological approach, therefore, is that it implicates the scholar of religion in the very dynamics of power driving insiders' conceptions of religion, culture, and identity. Instead of analyzing why certain interpretations of culture emerge, scholars of religion qua translators have "opted for the highly conservative practice of entrenching ideologies and rhetorics."[36] For scholarship in religious studies to have any kind of public relevance, McCutcheon argues, it needs to focus on "critiquing the strategies by which communities decontextualize and marginalize, mythify and deify one side in what is more than likely a complex situation."[37] Thus, the religion scholar as "critical rhetor" (to use McCutcheon's terminology) should be invested not in the art of translating but rather in exposing dominant normative discourses. Hence, the intellectual task is to recognize the constructed nature of society, text, nation, ethnicity, tradition, intuition, gender, myth, or even religion as well as the history of power and domination behind such constructs.[38]

One problem with this deconstructive approach is that it precludes thinking constructively about alternative modes of socializing that both redress past injustices and ask how religion may help refashion the thresholds of belongings or the criteria for determining full and meaningful citizenship in the polity. The task of moving beyond mere critique of the complicity of religion with dominating and unjust structures and sociopolitical boundaries must engage religion nonreductively. The hermeneutics of citizenship, therefore, deconstructs or denaturalizes the seemingly axiomatic claims of national mythologies but also, by focusing on processes of peacebuilding and conflict transformation, recognizes the less than universal hold of rhetorical formations.

The hermeneutics of citizenship and its preoccupation with deconstructing, in order to open up a multiperspectival avenue for reimagining, the subjective boundaries of otherwise axiomatic perceptions of identity answer the aforementioned culture reductionism and its binaries of critic versus caretaker. First, exploring the religious dimensions of self-identified secular nationalisms, as I do in the case of the Israeli secular peace camp, suggests the need to move away from an uncritical reliance on the religious-secular binary that informs modernist conceptions of political engagement. As I showed in the previous chapter, such reliance privileges certain paradigms of secularism, which typically reinforce orientalist views of the role of religion in international relations. The secularist construal of Judaism as a "faith," differentiated from Judaism as a "culture" or an "ethnicity," imposes a conceptual blinder that needs to be challenged as a part of thinking about justpeace in this context.

Comparative analysts like David Little have long focused on the human rights framework as pivotal in both the analysis of unjust political and social contexts and the redressing of such predicaments. This orientation underlies Little's comparative work with R. Scott Appleby on religious peacebuilding.[39] Appleby and Little advance what I call a "constructive" approach to the role of religion in peacebuilding. They underscore the irreducibility of religion to nation, despite frequent rhetorical arguments of nationalists to the contrary.[40] This irreducibility is in turn instrumental to constructive and peace-promoting engagement with nonviolent and justice-oriented resources of tradition, including religious leaders and institutions.

The significant point of departure of the constructive orientation is a recognition of the internal plurality of religions and the relevance of intragroup as well as extragroup contestations of questions of conflict and peacebuilding. In response to the deconstructive lens, then, the constructive approach could suggest (though this is not a preoccupation of this subgenre) that historicizing and contextualizing the "religious" does not preclude the relevance of phenomenological and hermeneutical scholarship.[41]

This is especially acute in ethnoreligious national contexts. In such instances, the mere recognition or recovery of "multiple interpretations of a given religious tradition" is not sufficient because the politics of secularism could impose conceptual blinders on underlying religious motifs and claims to entitlement. The case of Israel intensifies this point: the mainstream secular Zionist camp perceives itself as liberal and secular yet insists on the Jewish character of the Israeli state, an insistence that carries profound implications for questions of justice vis-à-vis the Palestinians. Significantly, the constructivist approach stresses the importance of engaging in a process of structural reform in order to redress the institutional causes of conflict. This process may include an interrogation of how religion and religious institutions relate to political, economic, and civic dimensions of the conflict under consideration. This focus on restructuring the underlying patterns of injustice already exemplifies that a religious studies contribution to this field will necessitate both a careful exploration and knowledge of the relevant religious traditions and a contextual, historical, and embedded confrontation of how religion relates to structural and cultural violence and to the systemic causes of conflict and how it and they may relate to strategic peacebuilding.

Hence, the constructive angle, as I reread it, retrieves phenomenological and hermeneutical methodologies in an effort to develop a thickly historical and analytical framework: one that not only recognizes how and why "religion" came to be interpreted in a particular way in a particular location in a particular time but also deploys broad historical and theological knowledge of alternative interpretations that may be available.[42] Subsequently, when deployed constructively and with a clear, normative human rights orientation to engage the dynamics of specific, historical circumstances, the phenomenological approach overcomes the cultural reductionist charge concerning the complicity of the "scholar as caretaker" in the underlying discourses of power. As I mentioned in chapter 2, the human rights approach is useful to the extent that it empowers and vindicates claims of repressed and wronged groups and individuals as well as enables the adjudication between competing narratives of victimhood and injustice. Still, the transformation of relational patterns and the underlying structures of injustice depend on *interpretive* rethinking of the boundaries of identities. The constructive approach begins to offer such a focus on the reinterpretation of the relations among religion, nation, culture, and ethnicity as key for imagining the transformation of ethnoreligious national conflicts.[43]

Therefore, the constructive approach represents a significant departure from mere color coding that explains *why* religious people and doctrines "erupted" to the fore or *how* religious politics challenges modernist and secularist presuppositions. It necessitates an exploration of religions and ethical traditions beyond their most immediate historical locations and dominant interpretations. Religion then is more than the sum of contemporary social institutions. To reiterate, this perspective does not entail a fossilized and ahistoric interpretation of religion. In fact, the very opposite is the case because the constructive approach does not only worry about explaining or redescribing how religion relates to dominating and unjust practices. Rather, it also attends to how religion could be related to restructuring and dismantling dominant discourses in light of the principles set forth in the

UDHR and subsequent human rights conventions—namely, through an embedded exploration of internal and external resources that could either provide alternatives or reform illiberal or exceedingly exclusivist national historiographies.

V. Contesting the Discourses of Secularism

But even if the constructive approach to religion and peacebuilding demonstrates the limits of a binary construal of critic versus caretaker, it still privileges the discourses of secularism. While the constructive approach to religion and peacebuilding dismantles the critique of the phenomenological approach—especially its inability to analyze the relation between religion and power and to have any public relevance—Appleby's reliance on Otto's conception of the sacred means that his approach still privileges a liberal conception of religion as a private, autonomous, and interiorized mode of being, related to the ultimate or the sacred—with the political corollary of having a "thin" view of nationalism. This orientation also permeates the field of practical religious peacebuilding, which Appleby and Little define as "the range of activities performed by religious actors and institutions for the purpose of resolving and transforming deadly conflict."[44] Thus, isolating the "religious" aspect of conflict transformation and peacebuilding bypasses the hermeneutical act of denaturalizing and rethinking collective identities that I argue is key for conflict transformation.

Indeed, the focus on how religion relates to the construction of group boundaries and to imagining and narrating a group's history suggests itself as an entry point to thinking about the role of religion in conflict transformation. This process involves denaturalizing dominant interpretations of identity and reimagining the interrelation between different facets of one's identity in a way that would exemplify greater consistency with human rights conventions. In zones of ethnoreligious national conflicts, this entails an emphasis on creating a more elastic and self-critical definition of citizenship and belonging that challenges a monocultural conception of the "nation." As in the constructive approach, this process also facilitates innovation within religion, recognized as thoroughly plural, multidimensional, and indeed historical. The degree to which religion is involved in authorizing unjust practices directly correlates with the degree to which the reimagining of religion vis-à-vis the "nation" would need to be integrated into programs for conflict transformation.

But this task cannot diminish, neutralize, or interiorize religion because such an approach would merely reinforce a lack of self-reflexivity.

Consequently, deploying a human rights orientation is crucial for the diagnosis; the mere recovery and appropriation of resources from within the dominant tradition/culture that show consistency with a "rights" orientation is not a sufficient framework for conflict transformation. Instead, as I also highlighted in the previous chapter, such a framework needs to integrate the analytic uncertainties that come with such notions as "multiple modernities" and "multiple secularisms" and explore what they might mean in every case.[45] Hence, while the human rights approach may introduce indispensible parameters for thinking about peace and justice as they translate into a "thin" interpretation of the role of government vis-à-vis cultures, religions, and ethnicities, it needs to be accompanied by a transformative, embedded, and therapeutic confrontation of the underlying causes of conflict. And this type of contextual engagement does not mean simply replicating liberal normative understandings about the supposedly correct place of religion in public life.[46] Neither does it mean dismantling and transcending normative commitments to individual freedoms and to deeply democratic and pluralistic political arrangements.

The scholarly trend of comparative secularisms or the prism of multiple modernities illustrates the contextual and embodied modes of negotiating or refashioning the interrelations between the "religious" and the "secular," situating such explorations within broader discussions of orientalism and empire.[47] This analytic angle, inspired by the deconstructive critiques of the phenomenological study of religion, opens the way for tracing and explicating the local and global power dynamics that produced certain interpretations of religion in every context and authorized certain political practices. This genre, however, provides an inverse of the phenomenology of religion, presupposing certain essential attributes of the secular condition, despite its manifold and contested forms.

Hence, despite an almost definitional allergy to normative presuppositions, the field of comparative secularisms, by virtue of its attempts to identify a diversity of secularisms in diverse cultural locations and of its concomitant preoccupation with rescuing the discussion from Christocentrism and the legacies of colonialism, does not relinquish the "secular." Neither does the method of the hermeneutics of citizenship envision change in terms of exposing the "secular" as an irrelevant category. Rather, the challenge in transforming exclusivist interpretations of identity in Israel is to expose the religious dimensions of a prevalent secularist self-representation while rendering it not merely a defective and blinded liberalism; instead, the goal is to illuminate how nationalism always constitutes a form of political theology and to show that what is at stake is hermeneutically interrogating, imagining, and transforming secular Israeliness. Without a theory of justice, situated with reference to a broad human rights orientation, the urgency of a hermeneutics of citizenship is not self-evident.

Hence, while grounded in a human rights perspective, the study of religion in conflict transformation is inherently contextual and multiperspectival (without being relativist). It takes into account a multiplicity of views in analyzing why certain interpretations of religion vis-à-vis political and social identification have gained prominence and whether such interpretations violate the dignity and life of other groups (including the "outsiders within" who elude normative conceptions of belonging). This approach is not relativist because it presupposes that certain actions, such as the imposition of collective punishment on the residents of the Gaza Strip, are unjust regardless of Israeli rationales and fears. There is therefore an important multidirectionality in the interrelation between religion and political frameworks that is not captured in an approach that tries to posit religion as an ahistorical reservoir of resources.[48]

I show above that the constructive focus overcomes a unidirectional understanding of the role of religion as a fixed category in conflict transformation. Historical circumstances may offer opportunities for reform that are deeply contextual. But the potential for change is not only located in how religious resources can be deployed to transform state or political praxis or to cultivate, through religiously informed activism, what Lederach calls a "peace constituency" along various axes of society (from grassroots organizing to policymaking).[49] Rather, the possibility of reform is also a function of how political and historical realities can dynamically transform the tradition. In fact, conflict that involves religion as it relates to national, ethnic, cultural, and/or geopolitical agendas offers a fertile ground for actively theorizing about religion and change. In conflict zones defined by ethnoreligious claims, whether the conflicts are intragroup contestations of identity or intergroup disputes, each group's perceptions of injustice and historiography need to be studied in light of the experiences of other groups that are also entangled in the conflict. Hence, the cultural reductionism that animates the brittle binary construal of critic versus caretaker, already shaken in the constructivist approach, is further *aufgehoben* in my focus below on the hybrid construct of a "critical caretaker," emerging through a multiperspectival prism that illuminates hybrid and counterhegemonic challenges to ontological identity claims and national historiographies. Critical caretaking is integral to the hermeneutics of citizenship.[50]

VI. Critical Caretakers

The multidirectional view recognizes religious peacebuilding as a constructive engagement with resources of religion that could challenge and transform structures of injustice. It also shows why a multiperspectival approach to justice that is thoroughly historical can dynamically reframe and innovate with elements of religious worldviews. This multidirectionality renders deconstructive approaches insufficient in themselves for thinking about transforming conflicts and underlying structures of injustice. It identifies pathologies but does very little to help rethink narratives and relational patterns.

Conversely, the potential multidirectionality of religious peacebuilding informs the hermeneutics of citizenship and its move beyond critique to a constructive scrutiny of how religion may relate to other dimensions of one's identity. It provides both a critique of the dominant discourses of religion and nation and a constructive engagement with the histories and counterhistories, memories, symbols, traditions, theologies, and embodied experiences of people, and suggests how they may relate to the alleviation of suffering and the reframing of unjust structures of control. In other words, the hermeneutics of citizenship deploys not only methodological reductionism in trying to explain, expose, and redescribe why and how certain interpretations of community or membership came into being and gained dominance, but also what alternative interpretations may emerge out of specific contexts and subaltern traditions and histories. It is precisely this task of thinking constructively about dominant structures and narratives that makes the religion scholar and activist potentially both a critic and a caretaker.

The scholar of religion is a caretaker insofar as she historicizes and contextualizes how religion relates to sociopolitical and cultural practices and identifies subaltern historiographies or narratives of the "outsider within" or the "domestic other." These are the sites that enable the process of exposing the pretensions of rhetorical claims about "who we are" as well as reimagining "who we could become." Notably, the process of exposing and contesting reigning discourses is not directed only toward ethnocentric conceptions of citizenship that are obviously "violent" and "exclusionary." The scholar as critical caretaker also aims to deconstruct how liberal and secularist interpretations of the nation and religion may have glossed over underlying and less obvious ethno- or religiocentric sets of entitlements. At the very least, the critical caretaker explores how these liberal-secularist underpinnings—despite their conventional construal as "peaceful" and indeed "civic"—may have contributed to conflict through the domestication of dissent and through the secularizing and compartmentalizing of identity indices such as ethnicity, nationality, and religion.

To be a constructive critic, the religious studies scholar as well as the religious peacebuilder needs to recognize the thoroughly historical and social characteristics of religion while also recognizing that it cannot be reduced to this context and history. This balancing act does not assume that religion is a sui generis and ahistorical first-order category. Rather, it acknowledges the multiplicity of histories, interpretations, and contexts located in different epochs (some may be inaudible and even nonexistent, indicating the potential for innovation). The aim is not only "to lay bare . . . mechanisms of power and control"[51] but also to imagine modes of redressing abuses, misinterpretations, manipulations, and unjust interpretations of religion vis-à-vis political, cultural, and economic organizations of social life. This exercise takes into account the centrality of the analyses of power and dominant discourses and also illuminates the irreducibility of religion to the structures of power and control and the possibility of agency and change. Indeed, the deconstructive approach exposes the mechanisms of power, but it forgets to ask how the subaltern counternarratives may offer what cultural critic Homi Bhabha refers to as "third spaces" or hybrid locations that challenge received narratives and provide alternative formulations of identity.[52]

Therefore, the constructive approach that invites the cultivation of knowledge about "religion"—one that transcends the most immediate "political" ramifications and historical constraints—can and should be supplemented with a deconstructive turn. This turn amounts to a careful exploration of subaltern counternarratives, which, when made audible, may contribute to the *process* of reframing ethno- and religiocentric conceptions of identity. This would involve amplifying a critique of the interrelation between power and religion already implied in the constructive approach. But it brings to full light the question of *why* recognition of the internal plurality of traditions and the irreducibility of religion to nation would need also to include the possibility of innovation and reimagining that may be located in hybrid identities. Such identities challenge, in their very experiences and historicities, purist and chauvinistic conceptions of membership and historiography.

Serbo-Croat identities, Arab Jews (Mizrahim), and Palestinian Israelis are only a few examples that can offer embodied alternatives to their respective dominant frames. These alternatives do not neutralize religion but rather reimagine its relationship to the conception of the nation in a manner that may enable the emergence of more just political practices. Hence, scrutinizing the internal plurality of the tradition is only one part of imagining the role of religion in conflict transformation. Another pivotal component involves an analysis of meta-injustices, resulting from underlying misframing of questions of justice.

Conclusion: The Hermeneutics of Citizenship as a Peacebuilding Process

The insights of the ethnosymbolist approach, pivotal for the hermeneutics of citizenship, are therefore qualified by the deconstructive insights of critical and postcolonial theory. The deconstructive lens interrogates the role of power dynamics in naturalizing the symbolic boundaries of identities, thereby vindicating sets of political, social, and cultural mechanisms that ensure the conservation and reproduction of those (inter)subjective boundaries. Though it does recognize the nation as a heterodox religion, ethnosymbolism does not address *why* certain interpretations of religious, cultural, and historical resources have gained dominance over others in the process of imagining a nation or *what* processes would bring about a reinterpretation of the relation between religion and nation. Such processes might necessitate a conscious effort to denaturalize the underlying assumptions about the defining characteristics and boundaries of a group. Nor does the ethnosymbolist approach enable an analysis of how and why the framework of the nation-state could introduce changes and reforms in how religious identities are or could be (re)imagined in light of a multiperspectival (contextual) approach to justice.

What I mean by the *hermeneutics of citizenship* is the reimagining of the interconnections among subjective notions of identity. I argue that for such reimagining to be meaningful as a peace- and justice-building tool, it needs, on the level of theory, to integrate some of the deconstructive insights of postcolonialism. On the level of practice, this approach needs to translate into the articulation of subaltern perceptions, counternarratives, and grievances. This articulation provides a space both for critiquing naturalized claims of identity and national historiography and for rethinking the parameters of belonging and justice. Indeed, the hermeneutics of citizenship with its focus on counterhegemonic experiences and narratives constitutes a long-term undertaking that needs to unfold on a variety of levels, from education reforms to literature to pop culture to social attitudes. Critical scrutiny therefore needs to be supplemented by a thorough exploration (and at times excavation and appropriation) of counterhegemonic narratives, subaltern experiences, and minority opinions. In other words, the hermeneutics of citizenship offers not only a second-order redescription of religion as a social construct but also a problem-oriented constructive engagement with histories, memories, and theologies. These two modes of analysis need to take place in tandem to avoid charges of ahistoricity, on the one hand, and overhistoricity, on the other.

This method of deconstructing and reimagining identities may be viewed as a strategic conceptualization of the possibilities for justpeace beyond what was imagined within the constraining frameworks of ethnoreligious national claims. As far as the Israeli case is concerned, the argument goes as follows: in order to engage in the hermeneutics of citizenship, it is crucial to come to terms with the view of secular Zionism as representing a political theology and as deploying the resources of tradition selectively. Such a realization opens a wide path for reinterpretations of its core motifs. This process would entail a context-sensitive reinterpretation from within the sources of Judaisms, Jewish histories, and Jewish people, one that is positioned with reference to human rights discourse as well as to subaltern embodied experiences.

While it may appear as theoretical belaboring, the purpose of the present and previous chapters has been to situate my project at the confluence of several bodies of literature: peace studies, religious studies, normative political theory, cultural theory, and nationalism studies. This theoretical exposition and bridging of often differentiated disciplinary silos is, in fact, a necessary precursor to the complex combination of theoretical moves I will make in the series of case studies that unfold across the remaining chapters of the book.

FOUR

Returning to Sinai: The Religious Zionist Peace Movement

For authentic memories, it is far less important that the investigator report on them than that he mark, quite precisely, the site where he gained possession of them. Epic and rhapsodic in the strictest sense, genuine memory must therefore yield an image of the person who remembers, in the same way a good archeological report not only informs us about the strata from which its findings originate, but also gives an account of the strata which first had to be broken into.

—Walter Benjamin

Introduction

The evaluation of the secular Zionist peace camp in chapter 1 demonstrated that this movement has not engaged in what I have called the hermeneutics of citizenship, an interpretive process that could not only expose operative myopic categories such as the Green Line but also enable the critical reimagining of an Israeli Jewish political theology. Rather, the movement holds to an ambiguous allegiance to the idea of a Jewish democratic state without substantially probing into the inconsistencies such a construct suggests.

To analyze the root causes and dynamics of conflict, one needs to produce what Walter Benjamin, in the epigraph of this chapter, portrays as "a good archeological report." Such a report "not only informs us about the strata from which its findings originate, but also gives an account of the strata which first had to be broken into." A thick analysis needs to approach the question of conflict like a good form of archeology in the Benjaminian sense.

The hermeneutics of citizenship calls for such "good archeology" because it necessitates a systematic diagnosis and careful scrutiny of the root causes of conflict. This scrutiny entails a reevaluation of the underpinning structures of control as well as the legitimizing national ethos. As indicated in chapter 3, this reevaluation entails retrieving and appropriating the creative potentialities located in counterhegemonic narratives. Those narratives are like the metaphorical strata in Benjamin's depiction of a good archeological report: on the one hand, they seem to raise an insignificant cloud of dust, but, on the other, they expose the violence and injustice inherent in unidirectional and exclusive cultural narratives. Because in Israel, as in other ethnoreligious national contexts, religion is so closely identified with the "nation," such counterpositions or interpretations may be located not only in the memories and realities of misrecognized and marginalized populations but also in those resources of religion or tradition eclipsed by an official or dominant interpretation of religion's interface with the nation.

In the case of Israel, using a hermeneutics of citizenship would amount to interrogating the Zionist interpretations of the Jewish nation-state. What do they mean? How does the right of Jewish return relate to the conflict with the Palestinians? How do definitions of *who we are* affect our interpretations of "justice"? How are the principles of inclusion in the Israeli nation-state determined? And how does the Zionist narration of Jewish history affect the understanding of the dynamics of diasporas versus homeland? These questions concerning Israel's theory of citizenship relate directly to the modes in which conceptions of peace and justice are formed and articulated. The interrogation of these questions by the critical caretaker scholar or activist necessitates critiquing and deconstructing the Zionist narration of Jewish history. This critique, which includes explications of the Eurocentric and orientalist attitudes as well as secularist presuppositions, constitutes a precondition for constructively reimagining Judaism(s) vis-à-vis Israel and for subsequently reimagining the horizons of justice discourse through a multiperspectival prism.

With a point of departure that posits Zionism as a form of political theology and nationalism, more broadly, as constituting a "belief system," it might be insightful to look at other attempts to radically (rather than merely cosmetically) reimagine a tradition. Feminist theory offers such creative tools for envisioning a reframing of religious traditions. In her now classic work *Standing Again at Sinai*, feminist scholar Judith Plaskow argues that in order to imagine Judaism according to feminist sensibilities, one needs to critically engage the tradition, especially the spaces of silences generated by male normativity. She writes: "The covenant community is the community of the circumcised (Gen. 17:10), the community defined as male heads of household. Women are named through a filter of male experience: that is the essence of their silence. But women's experiences are not recorded or taken seriously because women are not perceived as normative Jews. They are part of but do not define the community of Israel."[1] Plaskow argues that we cannot reconstruct and reimagine Judaism along feminist lines without challenging and critiquing the underlying male normativity of the tradition, a process that involves rescuing the silences—the sites of women's life excluded from the Jewish narration of history and law.

This feminist focus on silences provides a framework for thinking about systemic rather than merely cosmetic change, and it resonates with the hermeneutics of citizenship as a process designed to denaturalize identities and normative (though supposedly descriptive) claims about "who we are" by searching for those spaces of silences that fall outside the normative parameters of belonging. In the case of Israel, those spaces are primarily occupied by the explicitly religious communities, the Mizrahim, and the Palestinian citizens of Israel. Those groups challenge in their embodied experiences the secularist, Eurocentric, Ashkenazi, and ethnocentric self-perceptions of Israel. But the retrieval and appropriation of silences expand beyond the locality and the geography of Israel to the Jewish diasporas that occupy significant spaces in the symbolic boundaries of Zionism.

The point of this prism is not merely to offer a critique but also to imagine constructive change. Another crucial insight in Plaskow's work is her notion of return to the defining covenantal moment at Sinai, which entails a return through the lenses of critique that identifies and remembers the silences but also engages constructively in rethinking the parameters of Jewish life. Because of the recognition of the silences and the mechanisms of silencing (patriarchy, for example), what is meant by return to the definitional moment of the covenant is not restoration but rather transformation of the very meaning and perception of Judaism, a tradition that, after a deconstructive critique, needs to constructively rethink the normative boundaries of its community and gendered units.

The title of the present chapter, "Returning to Sinai," resonates with Plaskow's insights. In what follows, I discuss several Jewish thinkers associated with the religious Zionist peace camp who identify the return to Zion as a moment of great potentiality for internal Jewish reform and innovation after millennia of apolitical existence. The metaphor of the "return to Sinai" highlights the need to rethink Jewish identity in the contemporary world, underscoring the transformative dimensions of return.

Indeed, the idea that the modern Israeli political experiment might be pregnant with the possibility for theological innovations did not escape

Jewish religious thinkers. Because their primary interlocutors are militant religious ultra-Zionists, the religious peace camp emphasized that the covenantal moment occurred outside of the land of Canaan and viewed it as a key to both critiquing the idolatry of the land and articulating the Jewish meanings of contemporary Israel. This project included substantive conversations concerning the reconcilability of Judaism with the reality of the occupation of Palestinian territories, treatment of foreign labor, and discrimination against Jews affiliated with Reform Judaism.

Yet despite the emphasis on the covenantal moment, this chapter also highlights the reluctance of the religious Zionist peace camp to deconstruct the axiomatic parameters of Zionist identity. This reluctance has constrained its ability to imagine substantial alternatives to the Zionist paradigm. While critiquing specific repressive practices of the Israeli state by drawing on an extensive tradition of Jewish humanism, the religious peace camp does not contest the underlying discourses of injustices inherent in the Euro-Zionist historiography. This chapter illustrates that even while often significantly challenging the monopoly of Judaism by Zionism, religious Zionist peace organizations sidestep the possibility of retrieving, regenerating, or reimagining alternative Jewish modes of thinking about Jewish political existence in Israel/Palestine.

I. Judaism, Zionism, and Peace

The Status Quo

Religious Zionists have endeavored to increase the degree of consistency between Israel or Zionism and its particular interpretations of the sources of Judaism. The religious Zionist peace organizations indeed articulate their marginalized voices when they frame their critique of the occupation and oppressive Israeli behavior as a transgression of Jewish praxis as well as international conventions. Unlike secular groups, religious peacemakers convey their resistance by unapologetically and unequivocally alluding to religious vocabularies. To this extent, they challenge the historical, anti-religious militancy of the secular Zionist camp, its discrediting of the exilic condition as inauthentic, and its attempt to monopolize Judaism through sanctioning an official rabbinate.

The establishment of an official rabbinate, like the theme of the "negation of exile," points to the complex modes through which secular Zionists have interacted with explicitly religious themes and actors. Chapter 1 outlined the theological underpinnings of the motif of the "negation of exile," which is so central to Zionist mythologizing. This myth is grounded in a particular teleological conception of the Jewish messianic narrative. Yet Zionist historiography interprets this narrative of the return and ingathering of the Jewish diaspora as a historical, this-worldly event, generated and executed by human rather than divine agency.[2] The same way that secular Zionism appropriated the paradigmatic Jewish motifs of return and ingathering of the exiles, the leadership of the movement—in the defining moments prior to the declaration of the establishment of the modern Israeli state—labored to garner the support of religious parties, which had audibly expressed non- or anti-Zionist positions, prior to World War II.

What came to be known as the "Status Quo Agreement" came out of these efforts. The Status Quo Agreement is a shorthand description for the framework of interaction between the state and Judaism in Israel. The first prime minister of Israel, David Ben-Gurion, acting at the time as the chairman of the Jewish Agency Executive, outlined the agreement in a letter dated June 19, 1947, addressed to the ultra-Orthodox Agudat Israel organization. The letter reflects Ben-Gurion's attempt to garner a Jewish consensus to present to the newly formed United Nations Special Committee on Palestine (UNSCOP). The Status Quo, revised in some parts, remains a defining document.[3] While highlighting Ben-Gurion's commitment to ensuring a Jewish consensus for the Zionist imperative, the Status Quo Agreement also illuminates the influences of Jean-Jacques Rousseau's conception of the general will and Baruch Spinoza's fear of religious coercion guiding Ben-Gurion's own political theory, called "Mamlakhtiyut" or "statism."

In practice, the Status Quo amounted to the establishment of an official rabbinate that attained a monopoly over Jewish affairs. The official rabbinate gained control over the personal life cycle of individual Israeli citizens, regardless of their degree of adherence to traditional rituals of burial, marriage, and so on. The agreement also translated into the establishment of a ministry of religion, parallel educational systems for the religious and secular sectors, the institution of Shabbat as the national day of rest, the imposition of the laws of kashrut in official governmental offices, exemption of yeshiva students from military service, and other "symbolic" concessions. Those concessions to the non-Zionist and anti-Zionist religious countercultures were viewed as merely "symbolic" because, from the point of view of Ben-Gurion, they provided a necessary base for building a broad Jewish consensus while subordinating religion to the infrastructure of the secular nation-state. Although the initial intention was to subordinate the apparatuses of religion to the infrastructure of the state while granting religious authorities a few symbolic concessions, this institutional entanglement was, in fact, amplified by the character of Israeli parliamentary politics.[4]

As one who grew up in the secular sector of Israeli society, I resented the Status Quo and the seeming inconsistency between the presumption of a secular identity and a reliance on a rabbinate for the regulation of everything related to one's life—from birth to death. My friends and I experienced this framework as coercive, to say the least. Why did we need to go through the rabbinate for our marriage and burial? we asked.[5] There was also the added frustration that Haredi (conventionally translated as "ultra-Orthodox" but literally meaning "God fearing") Jews received tax exemption and could easily secure an exemption from military service while all of us in the tax-paying secular sector are mandatorily conscripted. Meanwhile, religious parties gained increasing leverage in the parliamentary politics of the Israeli Knesset and often voted in favor of military policies that endangered those of us who did serve in the military. What I did not realize until later—when I began to think more seriously about the Jewish meanings of Israel—was the complex symbiosis between religious and nonreligious Israeli Jews. Secular Israeliness was not devoid of and, in fact, depended on theological motifs and religious imaginations. Increasingly, political campaigns of even "shrimp eater" secular politicians, like Ariel Sharon and Benjamin Netanyahu, had to make obligatory stops in the residences and yeshivot of religious leaders.

By 2011, the secularist statist attitude that led to the Status Quo and to decades of accommodation and supposed utilitarian cooptation of Haredi political parties began to clash with mainstream Israeli society, possibly signaling a shift from a relationship of symbiosis to open confrontation. Country-wide campaigns against women spread beyond urban Haredi enclaves, partly owing to demographic realities and systemic Haredi "taking over" of Israeli cities, caused by high fertility and residential patterns.[6] Certain bus routes began to demand that women move to the back of the bus, advertisements featuring women were conspicuously removed from areas highly populated by Haredim (such as Jerusalem), signs indicated that women should walk only on designated sidewalks, and numerous other efforts imposed more "moderate dress" for women and segregated them in public spaces and the military.

In late December 2011, violent clashes erupted between a group of extremist ultra-Orthodox men and the police who attempted to remove street signs calling for sex segregation in the town of Bet Shemesh near Jerusalem. Previously, these signs had been tolerated by the authorities (not asymptomatic of the Status Quo). A national outcry finally unfolded as the upshot of a television interview with Naama Margolis, an eight-year-old girl from Bet Shemesh who recounted how daily walks to school involved being spat upon and cursed by extremist Haredim who condemned the dress code of the girl (who is from a religious family). After the airing of the story (that also involved a physical attack by Haredi activists on the journalists filming the story), thousands of Israelis rallied against ultra-Orthodox extremism in Bet Shemesh, getting the backing of Prime Minister Netanyahu, who reaffirmed a strong commitment to end gender segregation. Mainline secular Israelis were further shocked when a group of about three hundred Haredi protesters dressed up like victims of the Nazis, to equate the supposed infringement by the government on their freedom to the crimes of Nazism. This generated a broad Jewish uproar, even resulting in attempts to pass a bill outlawing "Nazi comparisons."[7]

On a different front, Benny Kazovar, one of the leaders of the settlement movement, spoke against the secular mainstream, claiming that the clashes can really be understood as a function of a broader leftist incitement against the so-called Hills' Youth (radical young settlement activists) and the Jewish injunction for moderate dress. He subsequently asserted that the days of Israeli democracy should come to an end, calling for the subordination of the state to Judaism.[8]

A few matters need to be fleshed out here. First, the theological shift of some elements within the settlement movement away from consecrating the state of Israel and its institutions, regardless of their secularity, suggests an ideological reorientation of the settlement movement. The ultranationalist veneration of Israel emerged from the theological underpinnings of this movement and specifically from the teachings of Rabbi Abraham Isaac Kook, whose dialectic framework enabled the acceptance of secular Israel as a necessary step in fulfilling the messianic drama of redemption.[9] Kazovar now suggests that Israeli democracy is no longer required. It has already fulfilled the role it was designed to perform in the dialectic unfolding of history. This statement echoes a wider discontent with Israel in the aftermath of the evacuation of the settlements in the Gaza Strip in 2005.

Second, the stressing of the two supposedly most critical principles of Judaism, namely, settlement of the land and modesty of dress (for women), suggests a curious potential alliance between Haredim and settlers. This alliance is curious because Haredim are mostly non- or anti-Zionist (see below). Further, the settlement movement (as is the case with frontier situations) challenged, in effect, assigned gender roles. Third, the calls to "subordinate" the state to Judaism and the increased confrontational attitudes of Haredim expose that the symbiosis with religious voices envisioned by Ben-Gurion in signing the Status Quo may have backfired. The so-called religious-secular cleavage within Israel, therefore, increasingly becomes a site for renegotiating the Jewish meanings of the nation-state. The trend seems to be toward the exclusivist pole (that is, toward illiberal forms of nationalism), partly owing to the secularists' myopic engagement with religious coercion as merely involving issues of rights and liberties. Likewise, the religious Zionist peace camp, despite its grounding in Jewish reasoning, reinforces this myopia.

Torah versus Territory

Unlike secular Zionist groups, such as PN and GS, Rabbis for Human Rights (RHR), which is the focus of the next chapter, did initiate an alternative (even if still constrained by the paradigmatic Zionist logic) Jewish Zionist conversation concerning the religious significance of membership in Israel, the independent relevance and raison d'être of Jewish sources, and the Jewish communities outside of Israel's political narrative. Its unique contribution rests on the relentless commitment of the rabbis and other affiliates to the demands and language of universal human rights. This commitment manifests itself in acts of solidarity with the Palestinians and through interrelated efforts to work toward social justice issues in Israel proper.[10]

It is important to situate RHR's position along a spectrum of responses to the theological dilemma posed by the Zionist movement and the establishment of Israel. The traditional Jewish opposition to Zionism, as represented in Neturei Karta[11] and the Satmar Hasidic group,[12] sees no theological ambiguities whatsoever in the Zionist ideology. These groups view Zionism and subsequently the modern state of Israel as blasphemous and illegitimate realities that have betrayed the principles of Jewish existence and redemption. Neturei Karta argues that "the Torah forbids us to end the exile and establish a state and army until the Holy One, blessed be He, in His Glory and Essence will redeem us. This is forbidden even if the state is conducted according to the law of the Torah because arising from the exile itself is forbidden, and we are required to remain under the rule of the nations of the world . . . If we transgress this injunction, He will bring upon us . . . terrible punishment."[13] While positioned on the other end of the spectrum, the religious ultra-Zionism that incubated in Kook's yeshiva and its offshoots similarly views Zionism and its place in the messianic drama in absolute, inevitable, and unequivocal terms.

Kook (1865–1935) was appointed the first Ashkenazi chief rabbi of the British Mandate for Palestine. Because of his attempt (highly influenced by his reading of G. W. F. Hegel's view of history) to synthesize the Zionist political and physical impulse with a particular interpretation of the kabbalistic traditions, he is often exalted as the father of religious Zionism. Under the leadership of his son, Kook's disciples perceive Zionism as the embodiment and inauguration of the messianic moment. They thus sanctify the institutions of the Israeli state as necessary instruments in the unfolding of a messianic drama and elevate the commandment to settle the land above all others. The "Kookists," as they came to be called, amplify the theological dimensions inherent in political Zionism,[14] and their approach undergirds the settlement movement in the territories occupied in 1967. The settlement movement reinfuses the concept of return to the land with explicitly religious content; accordingly, the return signals a messianic or metahistorical rather than a historical moment. But, as Kazovar declared in the winter of 2011, the dialectic interpretation of history guiding the settlement movement could also facilitate eventually discarding the instrumentality of the secular Israeli state in the redemptive process.[15]

As argued by the Israeli scholar of Jewish studies Aviezer Ravitzsky, the messianic ideology of the settlers, on the one hand, and the anti-Zionist critique of Neturei Karta and similar groups, on the other, represent two approaches to the theological problem posed by modern Zionism and the existence of a Jewish sovereign state located in the biblical territory of Israel. Both approaches, according to Ravitzsky, are deterministic, absolutist, and ahistorical. In between those extremes, the religiously motivated Zionist peace camp advances and cultivates alternative religious interpretations of the contemporary Israeli predicament. Unlike anti-Zionist orthodox Jewish groups like Neturei Karta and Satmar, religious Zionist peace groups direct their attention not to the blasphemous theological underpinnings of the modern state of Israel but to its practices as an expansionist violator of human rights and to disputing the (antipeace and bellicose) "land theology" preached by ultranationalist religious Zionists. In effect, the primary interlocutors of Oz veShalom (Strength and Peace) and Netivot Shalom (Paths of Peace)—two peace-seeking religious organizations that merged in 1985—are militant messianic settlers who, in their view, perverted the halakhah (the Jewish interpretive legal tradition) and the principles of Judaism. Accordingly, cultivating desire for and awareness of the messianic era cannot override the imperative to keep the halakhic way of life. The halakhah, such critics exclaim, ought to be guarded from being distorted by messianic tendencies. In other words, the territorial Sinai cannot eclipse Sinai as the symbol of the Torah.[16]

This tension between Torah and territory—between halakhic injunctions and intoxicated messianism—points to the effort on the part of the religious Zionist camp to argue against the militant and ethnocentric religious Zionism of the Kookist variety. One prominent religious critic of messianic Kookism was the Israeli public intellectual Yeshayahu Leibowitz, who voiced a critique of the Israeli state. Leibowitz drew on Maimonides's philosophy to discuss the possibility of cultivating a nonmessianic Jewish polity, on the one hand, and a Hobbesian instrumentalism, on the other.[17] Accordingly, like past Jewish kingdoms (the Hasmonean state, for instance), like all other political institutions, modern Israel carries no intrinsic religious value. Only matters oriented toward the Torah are religious for Leibowitz. He thus claimed: "Since the establishment of the State of Israel was not inspired by the Torah nor undertaken for the sake of the Torah, religiously speaking, its existence is a matter of indifference."[18] Further, in his unyielding critique of what he viewed as the underlying false and even dangerous alliance between Zionist atheists and the clerics (embodied in the Status Quo), Leibowitz argued for a strict separation between religion and state:

> We have no right to link the emergence of the state of Israel to the religious concept of messianic redemption, with its idea of religion regeneration of the world or at least of the Jewish people. There is no justification for enveloping this political-historical event in an aura of holiness. Certainly, there is little ground for regarding the mere existence of this state as a religiously significant phenomenon.[19]

While initially he had recognized Israel as a potential framework for substantial negotiation of the meanings of modern Jewish life (including the possibility of halakhic reform),[20] recurrent disappointments with Israeli politics and its cynical use and abuse of religion led Leibowitz to advocate a total separation between religion and state. The goal of such a separation was to save religion from its degradation and manipulation by, and subjugation to, the institutions of the Israeli secular state and the ultranationalist settlers. This kind of proposal, however, presupposes the possibility of state neutrality vis-à-vis culture, ethnicity, and religion. Leibowitz transposed religion per se into a private, autonomous, and nonpublic realm, thereby critically distinguishing between Judaism and the Jewish people. "The essential problem of the Jewish people," Leibowitz explains, "is that of Judaism, while Zionism is not a solution of the Jewish problem but rather . . . the means for the restoration of the Jewish people's national sovereignty."[21]

Notwithstanding Leibowitz's nonmessianic and secularist interpretation of Israel, he does acknowledge the legitimacy of Israel as a solution to the question of a nation's survival.[22] This point, which he chose not to "delve too deeply into,"[23] highlights Leibowitz's conceptual reliance on classical liberalism. This reliance is indeed consistent with his strict distinction between *she-lo li-shema* (not for its own sake), a religious practice motivated by extraneous reasons, and *li-shema* (for its own sake). This position, however, is as ambiguous as secular Zionism's inclination to interpret redemption solely in material and political terms. Its secularity illuminates Leibowitz's own historical location as the heir of a modernist construal of Judaism as a religion (viewed in a Protestant fashion as interior and even individuated "faith"), a thoroughly European development in profound tension with the noncompartmentalized conception and lived experiences of Jewishness in premodern and medieval Europe, and even more in dissonance with the lived religiosity of Arab-Jews.[24] To vindicate the establishment of Israel only in terms of the survival of Jews, and to frame it as having everything to do with "ethnicity" and nothing to do with "religion," as Leibowitz does, overlook the aforementioned intricate points of interface between religion, ethnicity, and nationality. Likewise, Leibowitz's critique of the aggressive policies of the Israeli occupation presupposes the legitimate existence of such a nonmessianic but Jewish state, supposedly devoid of any religious significance otherwise.

On the one hand, Leibowitz's outlook embodies a liberal-secularist interpretation of the place of religion in the political structure. On the other hand, his acknowledgment of the need for a demographic "solution" for Jews around the world is inconsistent with the ideal type of liberal nationalism. Rather than portraying Leibowitz's framework as a defective liberalism, his model highlights the limits of liberalism, which lends itself to compartmentalizing "nationality," "religion," and "ethnicity." To reiterate, this is not to argue that the values associated with liberalism need to be discarded, but instead to suggest the limitations of liberalism as a framework for conflict transformation in which the root of conflict lies in an ethnorepublican political project.

While voicing a strong challenge to the reigning Zionist interpretation of the link between Judaism and Israeliness, Leibowitz's secularism tightly distinguishes between categories such as the "political" and the "religious," and between the "Jewish people" (the "nation") and "Judaism" (the "religion").

Subsequently, his approach provides no resources for reimagining Israeli nationalism as an integral dimension of peacebuilding. In fact, vindicating the establishment of Israel in the manner that he did (as a necessary development for the survival of the Jewish people) reinforces the presumed "naturalness" of the borders of 1948 and the mythology that enabled the "return" of the Jews to the specific land of Palestine. Hence, despite his moral and religious critique of the settlement movement, Leibowitz was no different from the mainline peace movement. He operated within the same misframing that placed the moral burden on the occupation of the territories conquered in 1967.

Because Leibowitz held onto a secularist interpretation of religion as a private affair, his approach does not enable an engagement with the political theology underlying Zionism. To him, the manipulation of religion by secular and religious Zionists was cynical and idolatrous, respectively. Moreover, secularism—understood as the neutralization of the relevance of religious resources to political concepts of identity—seems especially misleading in the Jewish case, where the categories of religion, ethnicity, and nationality do not lend themselves to easy analytic differentiation.

A student of Leibowitz and a philosopher of contemporary Judaism, David Hartman, recognizes this limitation in Leibowitz's teachings. Hartman's emphasis on the covenantal model as a source for reevaluating the religious significance of Israel and his insistence, contra Leibowitz, on the inextricability of "peoplehood" and Judaism[25] expose the central problems inherent in Leibowitz's secularist approach. Affirming the covenantal interpretation of the relationship between God and Israel, Hartman underscores the need to "appreciate the role of memory, community, or historical consciousness in the life of faith."[26] Instead of emphasizing the Exodus story, Hartman highlights the role of the state of Israel in enabling the possibility of a normative return to the covenantal moment of Sinai in order to (re)assess its Jewish significance outside the narrative of messianic redemption.

This imperative to *return* to the Sinai moment is central to the conceptual framework of the Zionist religious peace camp. Yet the question remains whether the symbolic return to the covenantal moment at Sinai would also signal (as Plaskow's feminist critique urges) a renegotiation or reimagining of the normative or/and axiomatic boundaries of intra-Jewish conversations. This reimagining needs to deploy a multiperspectival approach to justice. The same way that an awareness of the spaces of silence occupied by Jewish women necessitates changing the normative meanings of Jewish life, could revisiting the covenantal moment in Hartman's evaluation of Jewish nationalism overlook the silences occupied by Palestinians and marginal groups within Israel? If those silences are taken into account, how would this transform the modes by which the Jewish national project is imagined and operationalized? How would applying a multiperspectival looking glass redraw the contours of peace platforms?

Like Hartman, Ravitzsky emphasizes the need to cultivate nonabsolutist and historical Jewish models that would advance alternatives for thinking religiously about the significance of the modern state of Israel. He underscores a nondeterministic and dynamic interpretation of the covenantal quality of Judaism. It is one based on a relationship of reciprocity and the importance of evaluating historical events not only from the messianic perspective of the end time but from partial and preredemptive historical predicaments. The contemporary concept of Jewish return, he argues, should be modeled not on the messianic "ingathering of the exiles" but on the eras of the Judges, the Kingdom of Judah, the Kingdom of Israel, the Second Temple period, or the Hasmonean Kingdom. Unlike the messianic era, these instructive moments are open to critique and fraught with lessons about human fallibility. This appreciation of the historical, the human, and the fragmented constitutes, according to Ravitzsky, the defining attributes of Jewish life and survival throughout millennia.[27]

Ravitzsky sets this alternative voice of religious Zionism, retrieved from within the sources of Judaism, against the settlers' ultranationalist arguments: "Are our entire lives and existence henceforth to be based on one principle alone—that of *shelemut ha'aretz*, the completeness of the land—which will override any and all other principles? Is this how the paths of Torah are portrayed in our classical sources? Is this to be the exclusive focus of the battle of Torah?" he asks rhetorically. "They tell us," he continues, "there is a scale of values for the exile, and a scale of values for the redemption, for the return to Zion. There is a Torah of the diaspora, and a Torah of the land of Israel. These two scales, these two Torot, are not the same, but differ from each other; and today all must be set aside in favor of the reckoning of the redemption of the land." To such a theological and ideological maneuvering, he contrasts fallibilistic approaches to Jewish political sovereignty:

> Did not prophets, sages, and kings rise up and lead the people of Israel while still in its own land? And both prophet and sage knew how to stand up to king and society and fight the battle of Torah. What was the scale of values *they* set forth; what was *their* Torah of the land of Israel? . . . Didn't they also live during a period of Jewish sovereignty . . . what were the issues with which they were concerned as they confronted the Israelite community?

How concerned were they over the question of the borders of the land, and to what extent did they call for *hesed*, loving kindness, *mishpat*, justice, and *tzedakah*, righteousness, for "restraining your feet for the sake of the Sabbath" (Isaiah 58:13) in the land? . . . How concerned were they with the ever fluctuating boundaries of the land, and how concerned were they with Torat Hayyim, with the Torah of life, with shaping the *people* in its land?[28]

Ravitzsky, in this fashion, seeks to deconstruct and historicize the theological claims central to the settlement movement, while nonetheless capturing the complex and divergent positions of Jewish Orthodoxy and traditions on messianism's relation to history. He views the elevation of the commandment to settle the land above all of the other values and mitzvot as a perversion of Judaism and Jewish history. Yet focusing primarily on diverse religious responses to Zionism and Israeli statism, he retains an axiomatic attitude toward the Jewish significance of the Zionist idea, thereby suggesting that the problem is located solely or primarily in the perverse Kookist notion of settling already-populated regions of the land.[29]

Therefore, this critique of the messianic settlement is disconnected from a wider consideration of the legitimacy of pre-1967 Zionist settlement or colonization of Palestine and how this historical turn of events bears on the conflict with the Palestinians. In other words, it reinforces the decontextualized and ahistoric bias characteristic of the secular Zionist peace camp. This bias is born out of imbuing Zionism with secularized and ambiguous interpretations of messianic themes, such as the "ingathering of the exiles," "return," and "redemption." Hence, it makes sense to interpret Zionism as a political theology, a political ideology with equivocal theological claims.

I have also noted that the decontextualization of the conflict with the Palestinians was achieved through the appropriation of the Holocaust as a vindication of the Zionist agenda as well as through the assimilation of classical Jewish diasporic narratives of victimization into this pivotal Israeli ethos. Such narratives as a "people that dwells apart," "from destruction to redemption," and "the few versus the many" were compounded by the perception of Israel as sharing the values and culture of the West and thus serving as the West's agent in the struggle against the "East."[30] All of these decontextualized narratives, which represented the Palestinian in the image of the classical (Amalek) or modern (Hitler, the "Arabs") enemies of the Jewish people, as well as the ahistoric notions of return and redemption, needed to be sustained in order to legitimize the Zionist establishment of the Jewish nation-state, an undertaking that implied systematic displacement, military subjugation, and discrimination.[31]

A thick analysis of the mechanisms undergirding the sustenance of a state of emergency and the subjugation/occupation of another group exposes the conceptual limitations of dichotomized secular and religious interpretations of nationalism.[32] Ravitzsky and other religious Zionist advocates of peace, however, overlook the critical relevance of addressing the ahistoric bias informing Zionism as a political theology for the peacebuilding effort.

Indeed, the Israeli context of the debate enables such authorities on religious sources to engage and expose the fallacies of the theological arguments of the Kookists in an open and democratic forum. Notwithstanding the importance of such debates, these critics leave the theologically laden yet secularized Zionist interpretation of the "nation" intact. As stated in chapter 2, the revised liberal presupposition of the "nation" as legitimate and unproblematic is a luxury that perhaps can be afforded only in North American and European contexts, not in Israel. Thinkers like Hartman and Ravitzsky, who recognize the covenantal tradition as a source of potential reframing of the Jewish significance of Israel, nonetheless uphold an ahistoric understanding of the Zionist concept of "return" to the "land of Israel." The unproblematic treatment of the notion of return and the sense of historical or biblical ownership of the land eclipse the history of the colonization and displacement of the Palestinians. Any conversations about the religious meaning of Israel, however, cannot be divorced from this legacy. Further, a creative return to the covenantal moment will also need to include a careful consideration of how the narratives of Mizrahi Jews may challenge Zionist truisms and historiography.

A former executive director of Oz veShalom, Yehezkel Landau, realizes the importance of recognizing the connection between the need to determine the Jewish identity of Israel and the possibility of reconciliation with the Palestinians. Accordingly, he explains that the objective of Oz veShalom "was to be a bridge between all Jews—observant and nonobservant, Israelis and those in the Diaspora—who each had their own views of what might constitute an authentic Jewish state."[33] While negotiating the question of Israel's Jewish identity is consistent with my method of the hermeneutics of citizenship, Landau's framework is still confined by the force of the paradigmatic demographic and homogenizing argument of secular political Zionism. He remarks: "For us [Oz veShalom–Netivot Shalom], human life, justice and peace were holier than territory. It was a Jewish imperative to sacrifice territory in Judea, Samaria, and Gaza . . . for a Palestinian state so that Israel would remain Jewish, ethnically and religiously."[34] Landau's statement indicates that while Oz veShalom–Netivot Shalom has challenged the monopoly of Gush Emunim over the religious interpretation of Zionism as well as the monopoly of secular groups like PN and GS over the interpretation of peace, it has nonetheless operated within the Zionist boundary of acceptable debate, with its fundamental and undergirding metahistorical bias.

In other words, its interpretation of events took the existence of a legitimate Israeli Jewish hegemony in the pre-1967 territories as an axiomatic point of departure. It was only the occupation of the West Bank and the Gaza Strip that was subsequently rendered illegitimate and immoral from a Jewish point of view. The negotiation of a common Jewish moral and political agenda is, Landau emphasizes, a precondition for genuine reconciliation with the Palestinians. Nevertheless, this desired common framework of understanding does not include the possibility of a nonhegemonic Jewish existence in Israel. This is because it attributes an essential redemptive quality to the Zionist notion of return and the conservation of a Jewish majority. The cultivation of an ethnically and religiously Jewish state implies nondemocratic practices, even if this state is extricated from the territories occupied in 1967. To this extent, Landau's religious Zionism is aligned with the secular variety, even though his theology is intentional and explicit rather than sublimated and implicit.

To conclude this section: the exposition of the views articulated by thinkers and activists such as Leibowitz, Hartman, and Landau highlights the strength as well as the limitation of the religious Zionist camp. Its strength lies in its general ability to challenge the theological claims of ultranationalist religious Zionists by deploying counterinterpretations of the sources of Judaism. Its limitation, however, is linked to its acceptance of a hegemonic Zionist discourse. Because they grounded their arguments exclusively within Jewish traditions, they offer but a monoperspectival, and therefore limited, argument about justice. The primary challenge posed by religious voices of peace, then, is directed primarily at the invocation of religious warrants for the continuation of the post-1967 occupation. Thereby they contribute to the normalization of the pre-1967 occupation and the reinforcement of the political theology inherent in secular Zionism.

Another related challenge would entail drawing connections between the domestic discussion concerning the so-called religious-secular cleavage and the conflict with the Palestinians. The inclination has been to frame the discussion by using the language of multiculturalism or rights to segregate the so-called religious/secular cleavage from the "international" or external question of the occupation of Palestinian territories. In contrast, the hermeneutics of citizenship exposes the self-deception underlying the conceptual differentiation between the various internal social cleavages in

Israel (secular versus religious, Ashkenazi versus Mizrahi, Jewish Israeli versus Palestinian Israeli, and so forth) and external concerns regarding justice for the Palestinians.

II. Negotiating the Boundaries:
The Question of Judaism (Synagogue) and State

The hermeneutics of citizenship involves the exploration and negotiation of the mythologies, philosophies, and ambiguities inherent in the normative definition of the state of Israel in relation to Palestinian and other subaltern alternative perceptions. This process requires redefining and challenging the mainstream Israeli self-perception as secular and Jewish, a self-perception that is reinforced by the modernist liberal compartmentalization of these indices of identity. In recent years there have been constructive efforts to negotiate the normative boundaries of Israeli identity on a variety of interrelated fronts. One front frames the debate as raging along the "religious-secular cleavage" in Israeli society. The second frames the debate more broadly along various social fissures, including the religious-secular divide, and focuses primarily on questions of social justice. For the purposes of the present chapter, I intend to address the conversation that has concentrated mainly on the religious-secular divide. Isolating the religious-secular cleavage as a distinct issue enables the framing of "religious extremism," when coopted by ethnocentric and militaristic agendas, as the primary impediment to peace.[35] This construal of a supposedly dichotomous relation between "secular" and "religious" Israelis overlooks important continuities between the political theology underlying secular Zionism and the settlement movement.[36] Exposing those politicotheological continuities provides an explanation as to why the secular (and religious) peace camp, despite its good intentions, ends up reaffirming a misframed discourse of justice. One prominent example of this set of conversations, intent on negotiating the symbolic and normative boundaries, is the drafting of "A Comprehensive Proposal for Dealing with Issues of Religion and State in Israel" or, in a literal translation of its original Hebrew title, "A Foundation for a New Social Covenant between the 'Free' [hofshiyiim] and Observant [shomrei mitzvoth] Citizens of Israel" (2003). The term "free" connotes the persistence in the self-perception of secular Israelis of the Enlightenment mythology of triumphalist secularism, entailing a process of liberation from the shackles of tradition and religion. As mentioned in the introduction, the New Covenant was drafted by Israeli professor of law Ruth Gavison and Rabbi Yaakov Medan, who became closely associated with the influential religious

Zionist Yeshivat Har Etzion that facilitates military service combined with religious learning.

The drafting of the Gavison-Medan Covenant attests to attempts by prominent public intellectuals and religious leaders to scrutinize the defining parameters laid down in the Status Quo Agreement. Distinguishing the Gavison-Medan Covenant from other proposals or charters is its time frame. The authors engaged the central questions and issues for over three years before producing this document. Further, the end product includes lengthy explanations of their positions.[37]

The Covenant articulates the following principles. First, it expands the principle of return to "every 'member of the Jewish people.'" In a significant departure from the Status Quo, the "Jewish people" would include "the child of a Jewish father and a person who has converted through a recognized procedure. Even someone who converted in a manner that diverges from the tradition of the 'Shulhan Arukh.'"[38] This expansive interpretation of the principle of return to Zion indicates the negotiation of the boundaries of Judaism and the willingness to accommodate a plurality of Jewish choices from Reconstructionist to Orthodox to secular atheism. This indeed signifies a deviation from the trajectory set out by Ben-Gurion and his interlocutors in Agudat Yisrael, as one of the outcomes of the Status Quo was the establishment of one religious authority in the form of an official rabbinate, thereby instituting a "church" where it had never previously existed.[39] The Covenant rejects the monopoly of the rabbinate and halakhic interpretations of the parameters of the Jewish people.

The second principle is consistent with the reasoning of the first and is aimed at challenging the monopoly of the rabbinate on the question of "personal status." The Covenant states: "The law of the state will permit weddings conducted according to any ceremony the couple chooses, and the marriage will be recorded in the population registry."[40] Here again a conscious effort is made to expand the definition of Jewishness and thus the boundaries of the community.

Third, Gavison and Medan also challenge the previously strict interpretation of the Sabbath. They define the Sabbath as "the official day of rest in Israel," but they state that "cultural events, entertainment and a reduced schedule of public transportation will be permitted to meet demand."[41] The Sabbath has been a site of great contestation among secular and religious sectors in Israel, and the total imposition of rest has often been interpreted by secular Israelis as a form of religious coercion. By allowing some leniency during the Sabbath, the Covenant attempts to resolve this contestation.

The fourth principle—the "principle of noncoercion"—underlies the previous three. This principle would entail "the elimination of any monopoly exercised by a particular group on overall arrangements; at the same time, the right of every group to preserve its own lifestyle according to its own conception and interpretation will be respected. The same will hold true in matters of burial, dietary laws, the Sabbath, religious services and prayer arrangements at the Western Wall."[42] This principle of noncoercion addresses an important issue of contention along the secular-religious divide in Israel. It pertains especially to the Status Quo, whereby the marking of events central to personal status and life cycle (weddings, burials, and so forth) is monopolized by the rabbinate. Indeed, the Gavison-Medan Covenant demonstrates a difficult process of renegotiating the boundaries of the Jewish community (by expanding the threshold of the right of Jewish return) and of recognizing the validity of many modes of being Jewish (by challenging the monopoly of the rabbinate).

Yet this rethinking of the question of Jewish pluralism proceeds in a decontextualized manner that overlooks the importance of deconstructing the monopoly of Zionism over the interpretation of Jewish history. Both authors subscribe to a teleological, universalizing, and unidirectional Zionist historiography. Neither author questions the right to "return" itself, nor do they reflect on the implications of the act of "return" for the Palestinians. Limiting the conversation to the topic of intra-Jewish plurality is both parochial and ahistorical. Most critically, it enables separating the "conflict" from substantive reflections on issues of social "domestic" justice.[43]

To understand why the Covenant reaffirms the underlying misframing of the justice discourse, it is instructive to explore the motivating rationales of Gavison and Medan in renegotiating religion-state relations. Gavison applies the framework of political liberalism as the most appropriate model for defending liberal and secular "free-thinkers," as well as enabling the respect and flourishing of other Jewish sectors. Medan approaches the Covenant by situating himself in the tradition of Kook's religious Zionism, especially the demand to preserve social unity despite internal fragmentation and the recognition (along kabbalistic lines) of the worth and holiness imbued in secularist activities and actors even if they are unaware of this holiness. Zionism and Zionist historiography delimits the parameters of the conversation of these two public figures.

For example, Medan's main impetus in drafting the Covenant with the secularist, liberal jurist Gavison was a recognition of the need to preserve the Jewish community as "a single historical unit."[44] Medan provides the metaphor of "a single ship" to denote this sense of mutuality: "The meaning of the mutual responsibility that connects all Jews . . . refers not only to a shared struggle for existence and mutual aid, but also to the collective fulfillment of the commandments required to uphold the Sinai covenant. This mutual responsibility affords the nation its identity. The individual has no escape from this framework, much as a person who sails on a ship cannot abandon the ship of his commitment to its safety in mid-ocean."[45] Locating himself conceptually in the tradition of religious Zionism, Medan says that the modern Israeli state "included an important foundation that was for the sake of Heaven, even if not all its components were 'kosher.'"[46] This perception, Medan continues, entails "a perpetual struggle over the character of the country's laws, in order to mold them as far as possible in the image of the Torah, or at least an imperative to do the utmost to preserve the *status quo* and prevent deterioration."[47]

Following the teachings of Kook, Medan differentiates "between a belief and the deed that follows it."[48] He explains that while the first generation of secular Zionists were not observant of the Torah and commandments, they did accept three fundamental principles found in the Book of Genesis[49]: "the children of the three patriarchs are a single people with a single fate and a single destiny," "longing for the Land of Israel," and "practicing righteousness and justice" ("in contrast with the ways of the Canaanite peoples of Sodom and Gomorrah"). Here Medan's analysis of secular Zionism highlights the underlying political theology of this movement. He agrees with Kook's recognition that even unself-conscious holiness can be found in the secular project of Zionists who may be inadvertently leading the Jewish camp in the direction of redemption.[50] It is, however, the responsibility of the explicitly religious sectors to reveal the true values inherent in the Zionist political project.[51]

Medan's approach, like Kook's, resonates with the teleology of Zionism and the presupposition of the unitary and unidirectional character of Jewish history and destiny (an orientation, as I demonstrate in chapter 7, that has come under scrutiny by Mizrahi thinkers). For Medan, then, the most important goal is to maintain a level of consensus or social cohesion, despite differences (which, in the final analysis—following the synthetic approach of Kook—he does not portray as profound or unbridgeable). Medan defines the imperative to maintain cohesion in terms of a "responsibility for the wholeness of the Jewish people and its continued existence."[52] Further, he argues from within the sources of Judaism against religious coercion.[53] Thus, he recognizes the necessity of a "joint resolution" with nonobservant sectors of the population because, he concludes, *a failure to decide between the two possibilities is tantamount to an explicit choice to sever Israeliness from Judaism with all that this entails.*[54]

In contrast to Medan's insistence on the "one ship" metaphor, Gavison describes her rationale to engage in such a conversation with these words: "From my standpoint, the purpose of my personal prologue is to explain how a liberal Zionist secular Israeli Jew, committed to democracy and human rights, believes that the covenant initiative is not merely consistent with these commitments, but is actually dictated by them." Reminiscent of other liberal theorists, Gavison underscores the consistency of Judaism with the principles undergirding human rights conventions and liberal values. For her, it is a matter of exemplifying those consistencies and engaging in a constructive intra-Jewish conversation that will enable the protection of a variety of lifestyles within Israel. "In my opinion, the covenant fulfills two key functions," she writes. "First, it promotes the secular lifestyle and creates conditions which will allow it to flourish. Second, it promotes the state, which enables both the fulfillment of the first function (conditions that allow the secular lifestyle to flourish) and the flowering of other forms of life. The covenant helps make it possible to maintain a shared political framework among people with conflicting world views."[55] Gavison's conceptual apparatus, therefore, echoes the discourse of liberal multiculturalism; accordingly, her political framework mediates among different and at times competing worldviews. The institution of the state is designed to safeguard nonreligious orientations while nonetheless recognizing the right of religious sectors to flourish as long as they do not abrogate the principles, boundaries, and sensibilities of liberal secularism.

In explicating her position, Gavison unsurprisingly cites John Rawls's notion of political liberalism as a key for thinking through the complexities of life in Israel. Rawls advances a political consensual framework in which social unity is grounded in the acceptance of the political conception of "justice as fairness," through the formulation of an "overlapping consensus" between otherwise irreconcilable "comprehensive worldviews." The underlying motivation of Rawls's version of social-contract theory is to attain a stable and "well-ordered" society that translates politically into a form of constitutional democracy, reflective of cooperative virtues and attentive to the idea of the individual as a free and equal citizen, regardless of attributes such as religion and class. Thus, in the contractual moment or the "original position," the contracting parties should proceed in devising a set of fixed, regulative "constitutional essentials," as if they were positioned behind a "veil of ignorance" as to their real-world social locations.[56]

In appropriating Rawls's conceptual orientation to the Israeli case, Gavison writes explicitly: "I . . . agree with the philosophical school headed by Rawls who argues that only political liberalism (as opposed to liberalism as an ethical teaching) is a necessary implication of humanism. Political liberalism recognizes as a fundamental fact that in social and political life there are a multiplicity of groups and interests and that this is an unavoidable and even desirable state of affairs. It follows from this that there is a need for a joint political framework that allows these assorted groups, each of which has its own unique characteristics, to live and thrive side by side."[57]

In Rawls's theoretical framework, conflict is prevented or mediated because of the supposed neutrality or impartiality of the government with respect to comprehensive schemes. Notably, the conflicting views Gavison discusses are those of the various Jewish currents and denominations within the Israeli state rather than a broader interreligious relationship. Equating the boundaries of pluralism with ethno-religious national boundaries, in the way Gavison does, accentuates what critics have portrayed as the "conceptual problems" of liberalism more broadly.

Theorists such as Alasdair MacIntyre, Michael Sandel, Charles Taylor, and Michael Walzer,[58] among many others, have objected to Rawls's proclivity to devalue the community and the relevance of tradition and social context to the formation of political reasoning and identities. Instead, they view the political community as articulating specific values and cultural bonds. Thus they consider the classical liberal requirement to abstract the individual from what Rawls calls "the background culture" to be an analytic fiction.[59] According to the critics of classical liberal political theory, societal bonds ought to be more particularistically robust and embedded than the Rawlsian framework of "constitutional essentials," and his view of individuals as unencumbered selves, allows for. For Gavison, however, the Rawlsian framework of political liberalism not only enables methodological nationalism but is also consistent with a particularistic commitment to the Jewish national project. Severing the particular from the universal conception of citizenship simply does not provide a constructive or transformative framework for reimagining the "political." It is methodical nationalism that needs to be tackled because, as the case of Gavison suggests, it hampers a multiperspectival approach to justice.

Likewise, a postnationalist stance as articulated in Jürgen Habermas's notion of "constitutional nationalism" is vacuous and, in effect, synonymous with liberalism, and thus it too inadequately responds to the problems that may arise from *jus soli* definitions of citizenship.[60] Indeed, in charged zones of ethnoreligious national disputes, a Habermasian proposal fails to address the root causes of conflict because these causes—as is the case in the Sudan, Sri Lanka, and Israel/Palestine, to list only a few such instances—revolve precisely around the degree to which particularistic conceptions of collective identity relate to the question of membership in the polity. Gavison's liberalism does not even pretend to transform Israel into a state for all its citizens. Her liberalism unapologetically affirms Jewish majoritarianism.

In line with communitarian liberals like Yael Tamir, Taylor, and Will Kymlicka,[61] Gavison highlights the universality of a people's right to national self-determination and collective recognition. She claims no contradiction between the particularistic needs of groups and the humanist and liberal values underlying her conceptual orientation. She says of critics who argue for inconsistency between her Zionist allegiances and her philosophical tone: "I . . . reject the claim that there is a built-in contradiction between the Jewish national movement of Zionism and human rights that differs in some essential way from the tension that always informs the relationship between universal values and a particular culture."[62]

Having established her point about the legitimacy of national projects of self-determination by locating this claim in a broader discourse of human rights and political liberalism, Gavison suggests pluralism as the most appropriate framework for Israeli society, one that will enable "bolstering and developing a secular Jewish identity."[63] However, Gavison's understanding of the "secular" in the compound identifier of "Jewish" and "secular" is located in an ambiguous juncture between the Enlightenment critique of religion and the particularistic, Jewish meaning of the Zionist national project. On the one hand, she stresses the importance of pluralism and of protecting her secular and liberated lifestyle from the shackles of tradition. On the other, she remains unapologetic concerning the undemocratic social, cultural, and political institutional frameworks implied by the Jewish character of Israel.

Indeed, Gavison reiterates her view of Jewish national self-determination as consistent with universal premises of collective rights. She underscores that this recognition is pivotal to her defense of the principle of Jewish return and "arrangements that stress the Jewish character of the state on the cultural and symbolic levels (such as the Hebrew language, the Sabbath, and Jewish holidays). It goes without saying that the history of the Jewish presence in Eretz Israel and the Jewish people's ties to this land are of cardinal importance as components of the universal claim."[64] Here is an example where relying on the human rights framework could vindicate particularistic conceptions of justice at the expense of others' rights, needs, and narratives of justice.

Gavison's discussion of democracy provides a further uncovering of the liberal myopia: "Israel must be (and can be) a democracy that upholds human rights, including freedom of religion and conscience and the right to equality, while fulfilling the Jewish people's right to self-determination (which is also derived from human rights).... [Democracy] generally enables a society to make decisions according to the preferences of the majority (so long as this does not violate the rights of those who do not support these decisions)."[65] This interpretation of democracy is unreflective of how the maintenance of a Jewish majority entails structural and cultural violence, manifested in bypass roads, checkpoints, segregation policies, and military occupations, to list a few examples.

Nor does Gavison ponder the political theology undergirding the right of Jewish return. Characteristic of other Israeli liberal thinkers, Gavison reinterprets Judaism as "culture," devoid of divine and/or theological content yet providing a source of inspiration and identity. She writes: "I am a secular Jew, who wants to feel fully at liberty to seek inspiration, solutions and elements of identity in every facet of human culture, while remaining aware that my unique culture is the Jewish Hebrew one, in all its shades and with all its components. A pluralist framework affords me and others like me the freedom to engage in the urgent and vital task of infusing such a Jewish identity with meaning."[66] In her call to pluralize the meanings of Jewish Israeli identity, she subsequently stresses the need to disestablish religion from the state—a celebrated principle of political liberalism:

> The state must choose between "surrendering" to one concept of Judaism or another or refraining in general from adopting any position on the matter, contenting itself with stipulating the conditions for *civil* religion of Jewish identity for its own purpose. Once it becomes clear that the state is not presuming to answer the religious question of "Who is a Jew," its determination does not detract from the religious freedom of any side. This is an *egalitarian* approach to the different streams of Judaism.[67]

The pluralism Gavison proposes seeks to safeguard against religious coercion in Israel without overwhelming the variety of modes of being Jewish by one secularist interpretation of Judaism: "The success of the covenant initiative will relieve us all from the struggle for liberty and against coercion, freeing us to develop features of the 'good life,' in accordance with our respective understanding of what that entails."[68] The outer limits of Gavison's vision of the pluralistic state are determined by the requirement to continue and cultivate Jewish majoritarianism in Israel. "Israeli society is characterized by a range of concepts of Jewish identity, and it is comprised of different cultures and different religious communities," she avers. But this disclaimer about the need to consider the well-being of minorities is selective because it is unreflective about the history, ideology, and policy that turned Palestinians into a minority group within Israel.

Certainly Gavison is unapologetic about the seeming inconsistency between liberalism and ethnocentrism. Her pluralistic model, therefore, exposes some of the conceptual problems of the liberal discourse more broadly. Will Kymlicka, as I showed previously, is most closely associated with the discourse of liberal multiculturalism. His model of group-differentiated citizenship is consistent with Rawls's contractual notion of an "overlapping consensus" and its relevance to a well-ordered and stable liberal democracy. Integral to this framework of liberal democracy is, according to Kymlicka, "the requirement of a shared civic identity that can sustain the level of mutual concern, accommodation, and sacrifice that democracies require."[69] Thus, Kymlicka's project, which underscores the need to defend minority rights in multinational contexts, is founded on individualistic rather than communitarian logic—on logic, that is, whereby cultural belonging or national identity is interpreted as vital to the well-being of the individual and as consistent with basic liberal principles of social justice and individual autonomy.[70]

In this respect, Kymlicka's notion of the "ties that bind" distinct ethnicities in one political framework may be subject to the same kind of critique leveled at Rawlsian notions of "overlapping consensus" and "constitutional essentials." The presumption of the neutrality of an umbrella civic arrangement overlooks the legitimacy question: the infrastructure of power that is the "state" ought to always be legitimated by a particularistic conception of the "nation," even if such a conception may be interpreted in more or less liberal terms. Certainly, the closer a definition of the nation is to a "liberal" ideal type, the lesser the chance for the eruption of direct violence and exclusionary practices. However, the liberal framework, as my analysis of the Gavison model suggests, can reify and vindicate deeper modalities of structural and cultural violence.

Another challenge to Kymlicka's thesis is found in the work of Iris Marion Young. She agrees with Kymlicka about the demand of differentiated citizenship[71] because she portrays the universality of citizenship as fundamentally unjust.[72] Yet she criticizes Kymlicka's typology of differentiated rights as too rigid, presupposing the willingness and wish of new immigrants to be integrated into the larger society.[73] Other critics of Kymlicka's argument fear that the recognition and granting of differentiated collective rights may constitute a pretext to abrogate the basic rights of individual members of these communities.[74] The liberal multicultural framework also encourages the reification of differentiated cultures, legitimates unjust practices internal to the "culture,"[75] and may detract from the struggle for equality, redistribution of resources, and social justice.[76] Finally, liberal multiculturalism does not adequately address the power asymmetry between center and periphery because it encourages the continuous marginalization and ossification of minority groups.[77]

In sum, the program of differentiated citizenship still retains many problematic characteristics of the tradition of political liberalism. First, it overlooks the legitimacy question. Indeed, its legitimacy derives from general, abstracted principles. Yet, because of its continuous reliance on the principle of governmental neutrality and abstracted, constitutional essentials, the liberal approach to multiculturalism offers no explanation as to what specific cultural, religious, historical, and social factors would confer legitimacy upon the overarching civic arrangement linking diverse communities together. Second, as a theory of justice, the liberal framework of differentiated citizenship favors either questions of recognition over demands of redistribution or vice versa. Third, a prioritized focus on the principle of recognition essentializes the differentiated communities and consequently may contribute to the perpetuation of intragroup discriminatory practices and continuous inequality. Conversely, and fourth, a prioritized focus on the principle of redistribution neutralizes and brackets contextual factors such as history, tradition, and memory.

Whereas the later Kymlicka begins to think through the discourse of liberal multiculturalism as a model of conflict transformation outside the contexts of Western liberal democracies,[78] Gavison's deployment of the language of liberal pluralism replicates many of the critiques of the liberal discourse cited above and betrays strong underlying illiberalism or meta-injustices. Accordingly, Gavison encourages the recognition of plural voices only so long as the normative bounds of the society remain intact. Further, the underpinning dichotomy Gavison reiterates between the groups that uphold religious observance as a way of life and the "freethinking" secular Jews[79] suggests an unreconstructed, secularist, liberal interpretation of religion as "faith" or belief—a compartmentalized mode. Likewise, the perception of cultural neutrality on the level of political state mechanisms blinds the liberal discourse to the importance of engaging the undergirding doctrines of nationalism and especially evaluating how a particularistic interpretation of the interrelation between religious identities and national claims (as in the case of Gavison's view of the Jewish claim for national self-determination) relates to structural and direct forms of violence. Restricting the discussion of religion to questions of free exercise, as Gavison does, bypasses the critical imperative to scrutinize the question of religion vis-à-vis nationality.

Significantly, Gavison's reliance on a Rawlsian conception of political liberalism does not enable renegotiating the political theology underpinning Zionist mythologies and thus proves ineffective as a framework for conflict transformation. Certainly, the Covenant did not intend to redress past injustices and the broader Israeli-Palestinian conflict. But my scrutiny of the conceptual limitations of the document suggests how it reinforces, under the pretenses of liberalism and pluralism, structural modalities of violence that, as we saw in both the religious and the nonreligious currents of the Israeli peace camp, limit the possibility of moving toward justpeace. The Gavison-Medan Covenant engages in the discussion concerning the relative spaces to be occupied, across the Israeli social, political, and religious terrains, by different Jewish lifestyles. This conversation takes place in a historical vacuum, disconnected from the realities of injustice experienced by the Palestinians and others.

Thus, the liberal models of multiculturalism would all leave the underlying power structures and discourses intact. The next three chapters show that the polycentric approach to multiculturalism confronts (and deconstructs) some of these attributes. For now, it suffices to underscore that the use of political liberalism for a vision of intra-Jewish pluralism takes place in a context defined by detrimental exclusions. The polycentric outlook recognizes these exclusions. While exposing the liberal myopia, the polycentric model, as typified in Israeli sociologist Yehouda Shenhav's critique of Israeli liberalism and proposal for reframing the geopolitical space as a loosely connected confederation of cantons divided along religious and other communal lines,[80] still needs to address the question of how we might redraw the concomitant symbolic boundaries that would authorize this new political entity. The redrawing of symbolic boundaries would need to move beyond a deconstructive exposition of the fallacies undergirding dominant discourses.

More than the mere veneer of liberalism is needed to substantially contribute to processes of peacebuilding and conflict transformation—those that address the root causes of injustice and structural and cultural violence. This point also highlights why the human rights orientation to peacebuilding—one that champions the *goal* of instituting a "thin" conception of government vis-à-vis so-called comprehensive worldviews—needs to engage in a long *process* of exposing the undergirding myopia caused by ethnocentric conceptions of membership and by ahistorical and *volkist* biases concerning national entitlements. I argue that this process of self-scrutiny, which also includes reimagining the boundary of the "we" in an agonistic and transformative manner, is deeply hermeneutical and deeply contextual.

Conclusion

The foregoing exposition of the Gavison-Medan Covenant highlights the ethnonational limitations of the conversation about pluralism in the Israeli state. Similar to the contradictions of the secular Israeli peace camp discussed in chapter 1, Gavison's reliance on Rawlsian liberalism and an unreconstructed liberal definition of religion as a private affair stands in tension with her approach to the identity of Israel as Jewish and her interpretation of a secular Jewish identity as "cultural," "national," and "historical."

Medan, for his part, reasons that the concessions he is willing to make to non-Haredi currents of Judaism as well as secular Israelis are key for maintaining social cohesion and enhancing the ethnonational and cultural boundaries of the Israeli nation-state. Hence, rather than engaging the discourse of multiculturalism in order to reimagine the subjective boundaries of the nation through an investigation of the monopoly of Zionist interpretations of Jewish histories, the Covenant reinforces the underlying Zionist discourse and axiomatic national claims like the "right to Jewish return." As noted above, because of these discursive blinders, the discussion of intra-Jewish plurality in Israel becomes ahistorical and decontextualized like a Rawlsian thought experiment. Those blinders, in turn, constrain questions of peace and justice in regard to the Palestinians.

Conceivably, in a different historical constellation and location, the Gavison-Medan Covenant could have been written as an exercise in mediating various currents of Judaism in a Jewish democratic state. Yet overlooking the important Benjaminian insight that good archeology accounts for the "strata which first had to be broken into," and overlooking internal Jewish critiques of the occupation of Palestinian lands and the idolatry of nationalism, as in Leibowitz's work, diminish the creative possibilities implied by a covenantal effort to redefine social boundaries, such as the one presented in the case of Gavison and Medan. This critique now enables the introduction of the innovation offered by Rabbis for Human Rights, which attempts to connect various sites of conversations: intra-Jewish plurality, domestic social justice in Israel, and the question of the occupation of the Palestinian territories and people.

FIVE

Rabbis for Human Rights
and Reclaiming Alterity

Introduction

While the Gavison-Medan Covenant represents one front where the boundaries of Israeli identity stand to be negotiated along the religious-secular cleavage, the work of Rabbis for Human Rights (RHR) is consistent with the second, interrelated front of multiculturalism and social justice activism. This line of critique attempts to connect various spheres of contention and social gaps in a mode that highlights the plights of the marginal and the subaltern. One prominent "secular" example is represented in the work of the group Shatil ("Seeding" in Hebrew). Shatil's vision is the promotion of "a society based on social, economic and environmental justice, human and civil rights, and cultural and religious pluralism."[1] Shatil's projects of religious pluralism include, among others, a principled struggle to decentralize the Haredi monopoly over matters of marriage, burial, and rabbinical courts; helping liberal Orthodox organizations develop and cultivate fertile conversations regarding the equal status of women in religious communities; and the promotion of alternative rabbinical courts.[2]

Unlike the Gavison-Medan framework, Shatil's approach challenges traditional practices and endeavors to cultivate organic transformation within the various religious communities, especially on women's rights. This scrutiny and transformation cannot be supported by the liberal pluralistic model undergirding the Gavison-Medan Covenant. The Covenant is not only restricted to intra-Jewish pluralism but also enables the reification and ghettoization of various strands and practices of Judaism (including the secularist one).

But beyond this focus on internal religious pluralism and encouragement of intra-Jewish reform, Shatil, as indicated, integrates its project of religious pluralism into a broader vision of social justice in Israel. For example, the organization promotes governmental accountability for the welfare of the community. It also encourages participatory models of democracy and the advancement of alternative forms of sustainable economic development. The focus of this activism is marginalized sectors such as Bedouin women in the Negev and Mizrahi women and immigrant women from Ethiopia.[3]

Shatil also designs programs for moving beyond the paradigm of "mutual tolerance" between Palestinian and Jewish citizens of Israel. It has therefore established a variety of contexts for building the leadership capacity of Arab-Jewish alliances and has developed models of joint living based on a careful examination of the city of Haifa and the central Galilee region with their high concentrations of Palestinian Israelis.[4] Through local empowerment and policy activism, the organization also promotes the equal allocation of resources and services as well as the reunification of families separated after 1967 as the result of changing geopolitical realities.

Like Shatil, RHR also focuses on broad questions of social justice and structural violence. An explicitly religious organization, however, RHR grounds its vision and practice in a particular understanding of Jewish humanism. The rabbis of RHR are keenly attuned to structural violence, and they hold the Jewish state accountable for meeting certain human rights norms. Nonetheless, the organization does not question the basic premises of Jewish nationalism or the centrality of the Zionist experiment vis-à-vis Judaism.

The limitations of RHR and similar organizations are located in their inability to disassociate their activism from the basic underlying and dominating ethos of Zionism. In the absence of such distancing, any conversation that focuses merely on internal pluralism—whether in the unrevised liberal sense of the Gavison-Medan Covenant, which affords a system of intra-Jewish mutual tolerance, or in the thicker, more comprehensive social-justice orientation of organizations such as Shatil and RHR—will fall short of addressing the undergirding narrative of injustice, and thus permit only a limited vision of a justpeace vis-à-vis the Palestinians. Moreover, my analysis of RHR will also focus on the limitations of this form of religious peacebuilding. RHR's role as a "critical caretaker" is restricted by its reliance on a particular nationalist framework (even if humanistic and pluralistic). A hermeneutics of citizenship is in order.

I. Rabbis for Human Rights

Background

I first encountered RHR on a shuttle ride from Ben-Gurion Airport to Jerusalem in the days following the eruption of the Second Intifada in the year
2000. I shared the ride with one of the rabbis leading the organization. I
had never before met a jeans-wearing, "hip" rabbi and was slightly taken
aback by the sight. This American-born rabbi, who raised his family in Jerusalem, told me sadly that he felt the experiment that is Israel had failed.
By the time of the Second Intifada, the euphoria that had brought him to
Jerusalem in the aftermath of 1967 had completely dissipated. But, he said,
his disappointment was also a source of motivation to continue to negotiate
the Jewish meanings of Israel on a deep level.

Founded in 1988 in response to the abuses of human rights by the Israeli military, RHR defines itself as "the only organization in Israel today
concerned specifically with giving voice to the Jewish tradition of human
rights" and as "the rabbinic voice of conscience in Israel."[5] David Forman,
the founder of RHR, further underscores the prophetic role of the organization: "It was founded to give a voice to a Jewish tradition, which speaks of
a prophetic vision of social justice, equality and humanity. As such, RHR
offsets a portrayal of Judaism in Israel that is often characterized by a chauvinistic theology, in which a national ego is projected onto God, and any act
is justified as a Divine right."[6] RHR is the only pluralistic rabbinic organization, comprising Reform, Orthodox, Conservative, and Reconstructionist
rabbis and affiliated students. The organization was established in light of
the failure of other religious organizations and individuals to react to the
suffering of innocent people as a result of the First Intifada. This was the
background for the emergence of RHR and its advocacy of what it portrays
as the "other face of Judaism": "the age-old Jewish tradition of humaneness
and moral responsibility or the Biblical concern for 'The stranger in your
midst'—even in the face of the danger to public order and safety which the
uprising represented."[7]

The rabbis and other activists involved in RHR record and publicize human rights violations, concurrently exerting pressure on the relevant channels of political influence in order to redress the injustices. The objectives of
the organization expand beyond the territories occupied in 1967 to include
ecumenical and educational engagements and specific involvement with
social and ethical issues, such as the status of foreign workers, the trafficking

of women, the Israeli health care system, and the campaign for an Israeli bill of rights.

Because of the organization's commitment to social justice and its solidarity with Palestinian victims of Israeli policies, it was the recipient of the Niwano Peace Prize, awarded to individuals who engage in interreligious cooperation to promote peace. At the ceremony, Rabbi Ma'ayan Turner, the RHR chairperson, received the award on behalf of the organization and explained its comprehensive vision of peace and the interrelation between questions of social justice and broader issues of peace and security:

> Every member of Rabbis for Human Rights acts out of a boundless love for Israel—the people, the land, and the State. We pray and we act in order to make the people of Israel a light unto the nations, the Land of Israel a house of prayer for all people and the State of Israel a model of social justice that does not oppress the orphan, the widow and the stranger, a responsible democracy, striving toward the prophetic vision: nation shall not lift up sword against nation. Some accuse us of being unrealistic idealists. To them we reply in the words of Theodore Herzl, the father of modern Zionism: "if you will it, it is no dream." And others accuse us of undermining the State when we criticize its actions and policies. To them we reply in the words of rabbi Abraham Joshua Heschel: "In a democratic society some are guilty, but all are responsible." If we do not decry the abuses of power and the injustices of our country, then they will remain with us, destroying our society from within much more effectively than any enemy without. And we do have enemies. The State of Israel and the Jewish people are still objects of hate for some individuals and nations. Terrorism poses a very real threat to Jews, to Israelis, and it is the responsibility of the State to do all that it can to protect its people. Yet our tradition teaches that justice must be reached by just means. The careful balance between security for Israelis and fairness toward Palestinians and the right of both to self-determination and most importantly to life, cannot be treated lightly.[8]

Turner's statement outlines the vision of justice of RHR. Propelled by its prophetic calling, RHR aspires to cultivate a just society that cares for the poor, the weak, and the stranger. This striving toward moral and social perfection also, however, highlights RHR's conceptual dependency on the axiomatic perception of Israel as democratic and Jewish.

Many assumptions go into the seemingly benevolent framing of Palestinians as "strangers," not the least of which is the Green Line paradigm that unproblematically glosses over and authorizes the histories of Palestinian displacement and the mechanism of Israeli control that enable the cultivation of a "Jewish-democracy" within the borders of 1948. The protest of RHR is directed not against the central tenets of Zionism or devoted to questioning its underlying legitimacy but rather against the failure of the Israeli state to live according to its potential and initial aspiration as stated in its Declaration of Independence. The obligation of the rabbis of RHR, whose Hebrew name means "guardians of justice" (Shomrei Mishpat), is to hold Israel up to what they view as the ethical requirements of Judaism. Turner underscores the special obligation of Israel to be "a light unto the nations" and thus to provide an exceptionalist "model of social justice" and "a responsible democracy." Not unlike socialist Zionism in the founding decades of the Israeli state, RHR envisions the independent state of Israel not only as a place of refuge from pogroms and extermination attempts but also as a framework for exemplary social redemption as well.

It is important to underscore that RHR's vision of justice is embedded in a markedly American notion of religious prophetic activism and conception of the liberal state. The invocation of Heschel in Turner's speech is not accidental; hence the necessity of examining the biographical, philosophical, and religious roots of the predominantly American-born rabbis of RHR.

American Jewish thinkers like Joseph Dov Soloveitchik, Heschel, and Mordechai Kaplan sought to establish a modern interpretation of Judaism that would apply to both Israel and the United States in a consistent and compatible manner, without undermining the independent significance of Jewish life outside the state of Israel.[9]

Israeli scholar of Jewish studies Yoel Finkelman explains that Soloveitchik, for instance, saw potential for a dialectical relation between secular and religious currents of Zionism, which would lead eventually to a broadly embraced, uncoerced, and genuine religious existence. In this respect, Soloveitchik's approach is not inconsistent with the Gavison-Medan framework.

Heschel's existentialist approach to religion sees individual religious experience as central to public morality. In his view, religion's vocation in public life is to be restricted to its moral dimensions as set forth by extraordinary prophetic voices. As a result, Heschel overlooked the need to theorize the relevance of religious institutions, symbols, rituals, and dogmas to the public arena and to the framing of social and national boundaries, arguing for the primacy of the prophetic function of religion vis-à-vis public institutions and practices.

In his discussion of Israel, however, Heschel did recognize the possibility of living a thoroughly public Jewish life. But unlike the ingrained Zionist ethos that sees the return to Israel as the *negation of exile*, he advanced a romanticized vision of the Eastern European shtetl as a model for authentic Jewish life in the Israeli state. Like Soloveitchik and cultural Zionists such as Ahad Ha'am and Martin Buber, he rejected secular Zionism's primary focus on physical normalization and imitation of secular Western cultures. He argued that Israel's focus on the negation of exile had resulted in the negation of spirituality and thought—an outcome of its rejection of the diasporic existence in the shtetl.[10]

While Heschel based his views on an existentialist notion of religion, Kaplan held a Durkheimian social understanding of religion. Consequently, he defined Judaism in civilizational terms, encompassing aspects of social and cultural life, without necessarily depending on belief. He thought of the Zionist experiment as an opportunity for the Jews of Israel to fully ground their lives in Judaism. He realized that this desired model could not be replicated in the diasporas because only being in Zion can provide the opportunity to fulfill the land-centric commandments. Thus, American Judaism (which constituted his primary concern) should operate according to the principles and values of American civilization.[11] This implied a profound respect for and active support of American democracy and an advocacy for cultural pluralism. Pluralism, in Kaplan's view, would provide a mechanism to constrain fascistic and totalitarian potentialities. Along the same lines, he was not a supporter of Jewish political hegemony in Israel. Instead, he preferred a multinational political framework, which would prevent the same type of fascism he feared might materialize in a nonpluralistic United States.[12]

The teachings of these American religious thinkers provide both a background for interpreting RHR's vision and activities in Israel and a point of entry for deconstructing the Gavison-Medan Covenant by revealing its axiomatic and unapologetic vindication of Jewish majoritarian hegemony. The philosophical frameworks advanced by thinkers like Heschel and Kaplan challenge secular Zionism's unidirectional and dominating interpretation of the Jewish diaspora and the concomitant reduction of Judaism to political notions of identity. While studying the Jewish significance of Israel, they primarily focused on the dynamics and realities of American Judaism. Because of their existentialist notion of religion and their conceptual reliance on the principles of American liberalism, as they interpreted them, both Soloveitchik and Heschel exhibited a level of discomfort with the Jewish experiment in Palestine.[13] Yet they celebrated the possibility of a Jewish spiritual revival and a fully integrated Jewish public life. While a degree of uneasiness with the reduction of Judaism to an ethnonational project may have situated such voices outside of acceptable Zionist debates, a deep engagement with the writings of these thinkers on the part of the prototypical peace groups in the prestate period rescues their approaches from easy dismissal by Zionist frames.

Of the three thinkers alluded to above, Kaplan is perhaps the most relevant to Jewish activism in Israel, and indeed his pluralistic stance suggests resources for rethinking the boundaries of Jewish political life in Israel. In fact, influenced by Kaplan's notion of Judaism as a civilization and his position on Zionism, the Reconstructionist movement published a report of its Israeli Policies Task Force (2004), in which it highlights why elucidating the place of Israel in Reconstructionist Judaism constitutes a critical step in formulating a specific and coherent approach to Israel's political predicament.[14] In other words, the task force recognizes the link between hermeneutically debating Judaism qua nationality and geopolitical concerns with peace and justice.

The task force affirms Kaplan's view of Reconstructionism and Zionism as organically interrelated: "For both, Jewish peoplehood . . . is central. For both . . . democracy is a religious value." "Following Kaplan's teaching," the task force report continues, "democracy in our communities and in the Jewish state is essential to achievement of salvation of the Jewish soul and spirit. Under these conditions, Kaplan always hoped that Jewish civilization in Israel would lead the way in revitalizing Jewish religious practice, radiating to the Diaspora."[15]

However, Kaplan, like Heschel and Soloveitchik, accepted the existence of the "Jewish state" as a given and did not question the "right of return" or Israel's "right to exist." Like them, he questioned only "how it existed." Hence, it is no wonder that Zion's dependency on the structures and discourses of colonialism and the Eurocentric and historical biases of the Zionist movement are absent from his treatment of Israel. Furthermore, a sense of Jewish exceptionalism embodied in the optimal configuration of the Israeli state likewise reverberates in Kaplan's view of the Zionist project and his understanding of how the excellence of the Jewish state would be transmitted to, and come to permeate, Jewish life in the diasporas, thereby substantiating the teleological mode central to the Zionist/Israeli ethos. This ethos presumes Israel to be the fulfillment of Jewish destiny, thereby devaluing the "diaspora" as a site of a lesser authenticity (despite the Reconstructionist effort to rescue Jewish diasporas from this overwhelming logic). At the same time, Israel has assumed a position of centrality vis-à-vis the diasporas (peripheries), functioning as their mouthpiece, as if Jews have one history, one voice, and one destiny.

The Reconstructionist task force illustrates why, despite its intention to innovate, this Jewish denomination still operates within the conventional Zionist paradigm of Jewish history. By this account, Jewish history unfolds as the story of one historical unit—"the Jewish people." The diasporic communities are akin to tentacles of one body that ultimately reconnect in the land of Zion after millennia of disembodied existence. As I discuss in chapter 7, assimilating non-European Jews into a particular historical paradigm consisting of dispersion, repeated pogroms, and eventual return universalizes the experience of European Jews. Any substantive discussion of justice will have to challenge this normative interpretation of Jewish history and its subjects.

The innovative component of the task force, to which I allude above, is that it recognizes the need to think of Zionism as *"a way to reconstitute the Jewish people"* beyond *"an ideology of refuge."*[16] The report of the task force therefore clarifies that Jewish attachment to Israel cannot be based merely on its status as the birthplace "of our foundational myths and focus of future hope" or as a land of refuge from a constant threat of annihilation and anti-Semitism.[17] The report further underscores that profound cultural differences exist between various Jewish centers around the globe, with the Orthodox hegemony in Israel constituting a significant obstacle to plurality in unity. The report recommends continuing incipient efforts to cultivate partnership among various Jewish organizations (including secular Jewish Israeli ones) with the objective of broadening the connectivity among the "centers of the Jewish people"[18] and, indeed, *reconstituting* Jewish identity on more than the mere imperative of physical survival. What is at stake, in this discussion, is the Jewish meaning of Israel.

While the task of emboldening the interconnectivity among Jews challenges the simplicity of a one-note historical narrative of return and refuge (or redemption), the Reconstructionist line, as stated, does not sway significantly from this paradigm (a characterization I unpack in detail below). Nonetheless, observing the insufficient hold, in practice, of the rhetoric of "survival" as a common thread among Jewish centers and the sense of mutual estrangement experienced by Israeli and non-Israeli Jews brings to the fore the possibility that the hermeneutics of citizenship may entail localizing Jewish Israeliness as a distinct national framework in the same way that Catholicism in Spain, for instance, is distinct than Catholicism in Mexico. Recognizing the distinction does not entail abrogating their common Catholicism but rather underscores their distinct embodiment in historical and social contexts. Israelis in the diaspora, referred to by the pejorative term "yordim" (literally "those who descended," an antonym of the Hebrew word "olim," which means "those who ascended" to the land or immigrated), usually associate with other expatriates (or Israeli citizens, temporarily away from home) and feel estranged from the local Jewish scenes. They long to speak Hebrew and eat Israeli-made cheese rather than attend the local Jewish temple.

In 2011, an ad campaign targeting (presumably secular) Israelis in the United States (the estimate is that there are about 600,000 as of 2011), instigated by the Israeli Ministry of Immigrant Absorption in order to entice former Israelis to return home, focused on the threat of losing one's Israeli identity. The campaign was abruptly discontinued as the result of an outcry from the American Jewish community (a significant source of financial and political support for the Israeli state), outraged by the commercials' suggestive and caricaturing tone that portrayed marrying American Jews as a recipe for losing one's secular Israeli identity. One such commercial featured a woman lighting candles for Yom HaZikaron (Israel's official Memorial Day) and her partner mistakenly interpreting this ritualistic act as a romantic overture. The voiceover reminded the viewer that the American Jewish man can never truly comprehend what those candles signify to an Israeli.

The source behind the Jewish American reaction is the perception that this campaign contradicts the conventional Zionist framing of Israeli and non-Israeli Jews as one community. Israeli death in the battlefield is a Jewish loss, not just an Israeli loss.[19] And yet distinctions between Israeli and non-Israeli Jews are significant, suggesting possibilities for reimagining Judaism qua Israeliness without diminishing or eradicating Jewish Israeliness. Later in the chapter, I show that younger generations of American Jews and Jews in other diasporas increasingly feel no special attachment to Israel. This development further indicates the growing possibility for engaging in a hermeneutics of citizenship that reimagines the Jewish meanings of Israel. The Reconstructionist line, however, retains the basic Zionist commitment to "the unity of the Jewish people,"[20] even if this sense of unity cannot rely exclusively on the ideology of refuge but needs, rather, to reflect more deeply on Jewish rejuvenation.

The task force report attempts to undertake this task. This document outlines an understanding of a New Zionism that would translate into "a state of Israel that represents the Biblical promise of redemption and liberation to a Jewish people that has suffered historic persecution and is, as such, viewed by Jews, as a national homeland with sacred spiritual and religious significance."[21] This statement affirms the metahistorical bias that draws a direct and causal relation between the biblical promise and presence in the land and the legitimacy of a Jewish return. The statement also replicates the Zionist historiography of continuous Jewish sufferings and persecutions and similarly betrays an interpretation of the act of return as redemption from this diasporic fate.

The report, however, qualifies the latter proclamation with a strong emphasis on the principles of equality and democracy. It states that "as important as is the creation of a Jewish homeland and society which utilizes all of the symbols, language and culture of the Jewish tradition, the state of Israel must also be committed to uphold equal rights and opportunities for all of its citizens, regardless of race, religion, nationality, gender and sexual orientation."[22] Kaplan's approach, echoed in the report of the task force of the Reconstructionist movement, is consistent with the transformative interpretation of the act of "returning," which I highlighted in the previous chapter. Correspondingly, the return to the land of Zion is embraced only to the extent that it generates self-reflexive rethinking about the substantive meanings of Jewish life. The concept/process of return is a redemptive moment, conditioned upon just praxis and a deepening of the Zionist discourse beyond the mere paradigm of survival.

In sum, the report emphasizes the biblical promise of the land as well as the redemptive and teleological function of the modern state of Israel. It does not, however, problematize the concept of "redemption and return" beyond stressing the imperative to live up to the principles of Jewish humanism. Nor does it explore the profound repercussions of such a concept for its Jewish and non-Jewish victims alike. RHR's positions and philosophical underpinnings reflect similar oversights. As in the case of the secular peace camp as well as Oz veShalom–Netivot Shalom, RHR's approach to the conflict with the Palestinians is decontextualized and metahistorically biased. While World War II and the establishment of Israel anchored the discussion over the question of Judaism and modernity in the paradigm of Zionism, a fuller understanding of RHR necessitates situating it in a broader spectrum of Jewish responses to modernity.

Judaism and Modernity: Historical Paradigms

In many respects RHR follows in a more expansive and systematic manner what I have already identified as the principles underlying Oz veShalom–Netivot Shalom. Whereas the secular Zionism of the Israeli variety carries the Spinozan legacy of suspicion and reluctant recognition of the psychological and sociological truths of religion,[23] both peace-seeking organizations of religious Zionism may be situated in the theological "school" associated with Moses Mendelssohn and his emphasis on the consistent relationship and continuity between reason and revelation.

Mendelssohn was a key figure of the Jewish Haskalah (Enlightenment) and German Enlightenment. A close associate and interlocutor of Gotthold Ephraim Lessing, Mendelssohn sought to increase civic rights for Jews in Germany. He saw no contradiction between reason and revelation and articulated the possibility of harmonizing German public life with private Jewish religiosity. In his *Jerusalem, or On Religious Power and Judaism*, Mendelssohn underscored the principle of tolerance with respect to religion by arguing that neither the state nor the church can coerce one's conscience. He further suggested that this argument for freedom of conscience is consistent with the revealed truths of Judaism.

Israeli scholar of Jewish thought Eliezer Schweid correctly observes that while Spinoza viewed religion as irrational yet instrumentally necessary for the operation of the state and recognized only its anthropological and social truth and functionality, Mendelssohn attempted to present Judaism as rational and compatible with natural religion, thereby creating a synonymy between ethical-religious and political frameworks.[24] RHR similarly endeavors to employ the universal principles of human rights as a prism through which to reread biblical notions of justice.[25] Its mission is similarly guided by a "religious humanism" that advocates equal ethical obligations toward Jews and non-Jews alike.

Influenced by the Jewish American philosopher David Novak's discussion of religion and human rights, however, RHR interprets the life of Jews as representing a qualitatively different value from that of the life of non-Jews. Novak derives this outlook from a distinction between the Noahide laws, which are, in his view, consistent with universal human rights as they echo the divine covenant with humanity and, on the other, Jewish law, which constitutes the special covenant of God with the Jews.[26] Novak's attempt to locate compatibility between the universal and the particular represents a contemporary variation of Mendelssohn's conversations with his Christian interlocutors, in which he underscored the compatibility of Judaism with the notion of "natural religion" and explained away the particular duty of the Jews to obey the specific commandments of the Mosaic law as a private obligation. Similar to Mendelssohn's framework, RHR's notion of human rights elevates individual conscience and thus necessitates cultivating corresponding civil and political liberties and institutions. Accordingly, the role of RHR in this context is to serve as the prophetic voice that reminds the dominant power of the Israeli state of its equal ethical obligation to each and every human being.[27]

The Mendelssohnian prototype, as reframed by RHR, depends conceptually on the idea of the liberal state as classically construed. Hence, it becomes vulnerable to the same kind of critique leveled against Yeshayahu Leibowitz's secularism, in which a privatized interpretation of religion as exclusively involving relations between the individual and the Torah enables, in contexts defined by ethnic parameters of belonging, what becomes an untenable differentiation between civic and religious modes of identification. RHR's religious humanism compels the organization to perform admirable acts of solidarity with the Palestinians in the territories and with other groups and individuals whose rights have been violated by the Israeli state. Yet it does not consider how the framework of the Israeli state itself, including the unilateral right of Jewish return, has violated the rights of the Palestinians inside and outside Israel proper.

This oversight points to the conceptual blinders that enable RHR, like PN, to hold onto a belief in the possibility of fulfilling the ideal of Israel as a Jewish liberal nation-state. The case of Israel exposes not only the fallacies of Israeli liberalism but also the limitations of the liberal framework more broadly. Despite its undergirding principles of equal rights, liberalism lends itself to the same conceptual blinders and biases I identified in my analysis of the Israeli peace camp in chapter 1, and my exposition of Gavison's liberalism in chapter 4. Thus liberalism as a framework for conflict transformation is limited and even, on occasion, reinforces symbolic violence.

Indeed, theorist and historian of nationalism Anthony Marx identifies a form of "collective amnesia" regarding the "dirty, bloody secret" of the founding of the "nation" as a central motif in the process of *imagining* every Western European form of liberal nationalism.[28] Marx explains that state making and the consolidation of "nations" in Western Europe fed on and manipulated religious passions, fanaticism, and sectarianism. But eventually, once their distinct political identities were consolidated, they moved toward more secularized and civic definitions of national identities. This move enabled the forgetting of the illiberal building blocks of liberal societies—an amnesia central to classical and revised political liberalism.[29]

While France can afford to forget the Saint Bartholomew's Day Massacre and the United States can relegate the genocide of Native Americans to periodic commemoration, Israel's persistently ethnocentric definition of nationalism and its daily implications for the Palestinians cannot be masked by the cloak of human rights activism or the transplantation of Novak's liberal discourse of rights from the American to the Israeli landscape. France and the United States can afford doses of "collective amnesia" because those defining "bloody" chapters are, in many respects, settled and/or far from sight (e.g., on American Indian reservations). But even in those two contexts, the provinciality and ethnocentricity of their respective forms of liberalism were exposed with the eruption, in the first decade of the twenty-first century, of the rhetoric of Islamophobia. This rhetoric reproduces orientalist and Judeo-Christian symbolic boundaries, which in turn authorize exclusionary political and social structures as well as interventions in Middle Eastern affairs.[30] Indeed, built into the liberal national framework is a self-fixing mechanism that enables the broadening of the community, moving away from its definitional exclusivity and "bloody" moments of inception. It could also move in the other direction toward greater exclusivity or illiberality. The processes of defining and redefining national identity are neither predetermined nor unidirectional and depend on interfaces with religion, ethnicity, and culture.[31]

Israel cannot afford the kind of amnesia that the Israeli liberal discourse affirms with its naturalization of the 1949 armistice line and its intricate system of bypass roads to avoid the 1967 territories. It cannot afford it because such amnesia enables the silencing of the events of 1948 and the dispossession that preceded this watershed date. It cannot afford it because it normalizes an illiberal interpretation of Israeli citizenship and because this underlying illiberality constrains the possibility for redressing past injustices done to the victims of this national project. But such amnesia nonetheless permeates Israeli peace activism. As stated in earlier chapters, it is not only that Israeli liberalism is defective. An analysis of its flaws also exposes the limitations of the political philosophy of liberalism as a guiding framework for conflict transformation.

As I argued in the previous chapter's discussion of Gavison's position, the Israeli case accentuates what critics of political liberalism have already identified as the limitations of the liberal framework for questions of peace and justice. Novak's notion of human rights also presupposes a civic and liberal definition of nationalism. The root cause of human rights violations in Israel/Palestine lies in the very definition of the polity—its geopolitical boundaries as well as its subjective notions of community. Israel's insistence on the automatic right of Jewish return and its commitment to the continual cultivation of demographic advantage indicate that peace activists cannot afford liberal amnesia. Until they have addressed the Zionist legacy of ethnic cleansing, the plight of Palestinian refugees, the Jewish right of return, and the automatic naturalization of all Jews as Israeli citizens (if they choose to immigrate and thus ascend or "make aliyah"), the activists' visions of peace will fall short of a multiperspectival engagement with justice. The multiperspectival prism is the metric by which I evaluate peace agendas,[32] regardless of whether holding such a prism is a prerogative for the peace activists in question. A multiperspectival engagement demands that the plight of the Palestinians and of subaltern groups within Israel—their stories of displacement, humiliation, and marginalization—become central in the process of reframing the debate and rethinking the complex relations between Judaism, "Jewishness," and Israel. Indeed, even those most motivated by empathy for the victims may be shortsighted owing to an overwhelming discourse. The pivotal fallacy of RHR, then, is the transplantation of a liberal religious humanism into a context where the key issue is the definitional ethos and illiberality of the nation-state.

The Limitations of the Liberal Model

Certainly, illiberal exclusionary practices constitute definitional moments in the emergence of liberal nationalisms. Likewise, the liberal model is not yet capable of redressing foundational historical injustices (like the genocide of Native Americans) and dealing with the implications that redressing these histories may have for the definition of citizenship in the nation (here lie its limitations as a model of political [re]conciliation).[33] Yet, as noted, liberalizing the scope of membership in such contexts as the United States, England, France, and Spain is possible owing to their definitional amnesia about the founding moments of their national consciousnesses. In the case of the Israeli Jewish democracy, the "skeleton in the closet" is the ethnic cleansing that took place in 1948. In the end, a group's "ownership" of territory and geopolitical space is a function of robbery, one way or another. In the volatile landscape of Israel/Palestine, the victims, despite bypass roads and closures, will simply not go away, resurfacing periodically in the Israeli national consciousness for a "Thanksgiving dinner" (of falafel and humus). In fact, they increase daily. Therefore, liberal amnesia amounts, in some instances, to actual blindness and delusion concerning the moral standing of Israeli liberalism within Israel proper. This delusion leads, as I explain in the next chapter, to framing the question of Palestinian Israelis in terms of "minority relations" and dismissing them as a mere "addendum" to peace negotiations with the Palestinians beyond the Green Line.

It is against such amnesia that a small circle of primarily Israeli critics began to break down what they unmasked as the fallacies of political and spatial categories such as "Israel proper" vs. "the occupation," "right" vs.

"left," and "religious" vs. "secular" because these distinctions gloss over the centrality that 1948 needs to represent in any discussion of peace and justice.[34] That 1948 is singled out and not, for instance, 1917 (the Balfour Declaration) as the defining moment is not coincidental. It denotes, at least according to sociologist Yehouda Shenhav, that even while denaturalizing the category of "Israel proper" and exposing the ideological continuity of the political "right" and "left," Israel as a historical fact needs to be reconceived along post-Westphalian lines, not discarded.[35] Relinquishing the 1967 paradigm advanced by the Zionist peace camp would generate this rethinking and move beyond the illiberal constraints of the Israeli liberal discourse. But what is required is not only breaking down and correcting defective spatial and political categories but also recognizing that reframing those categories cannot return to 1948 as if six decades of history, including Jewish Israeli history with its distinct qualities and meanings, did not take place. Nonetheless, remembering 1948 and its implications provides a nonmyopic lens through which Jewish Israeliness can be hermeneutically and multiperspectivally reimagined. The point is not to dismiss Jewish Israeliness but rather to reconfigure it—a process that needs to involve non-Israeli Jews as well. As noted, this opens the road for localizing Jewish Israeli identity, stressing its distinctiveness in relation to other Jewish communities and thereby problematizing the homogenizing logic of Zionism.

Indeed, an analysis of the task force of the Reconstructionist Zionist movement and the orientation of RHR illuminates their conceptual consistency with the approach of an organization like Shatil. All of these organizations deeply negotiate the boundaries of belonging in Israel by underscoring concepts such as multiculturalism and by focusing on concerns about structural and cultural violence. For a secular organization like Shatil, the conceptual framework enabling a social critique and a vision of change is located in the discourses of multiculturalism and sociocultural and economic justice. In the cases of RHR and the task force, the language of multiculturalism and social justice is supplemented and colored by an explicit countering of a Zionist monopoly over the interpretation of the Jewish meanings of the Israeli state.

The analysis of the Israeli peace camp, including RHR, shows an enduring reliance on and acceptance of Zionist historiography, however. When I asked one of the authors of the Reconstructionist task force, an American-born activist rabbi in RHR, about her vision of peace and justice,[36] she first said that the "promise" of the land is contingent upon the ability of the Jews to live and cultivate a life guided by the principles of social and economic justice in a pluralistic and multicultural framework.[37] She also underscored that the current anthem and flag, as well as other state symbols such as the menorah, are the symbols of the Jewish people rather than of the Israeli state. She thus welcomed the challenge of envisioning a creative multicultural and pluralistic infrastructure and cultural symbol system.

Still identifying herself as a Zionist, the activist rabbi intimated her support of the "two-state solution." While she highlighted the importance of granting a *symbolic* right of Palestinian return as a precondition for commencing the healing process, she thought this right should be constrained by the familiar demographic argument that insists on the cultivation of a Jewish majority within the Green Line. It is not clear how this pluralistic vision and nonhegemonic position on the issue of the state's symbols is to be reconciled with a conception of justice that favors separation and adherence to the classical demographic logic of political Zionism (and the normative distinctions between the pre- and post-1967 territories it presupposes).

This inconsistency is symptomatic of RHR's conceptual apparatus. It also exposes the limitations of the liberal model of multiculturalism as a potential framework for conflict transformation in ethnoreligious national contexts. Granting certain concessions, including regional autonomies and just distribution of resources, introduces a degree of structural and social reframing, but it does not enable a substantive interrogation of the ethnoreligious national thresholds of the debate. Hence, the demands of the hermeneutics of citizenship as a method of peacebuilding are only partially satisfied. While confronting the theological chauvinism of ultranationalist Jewish settlers by invoking their alternative interpretations of Judaism and Jewish resources, RHR overlooks the need to similarly engage the more sublimated political theology underlying Israeli liberalism and the deployment of particular interpretations of Jewish concepts by mainstream definitions of the "nation." Instead, RHR accepts those definitions, thereby failing to address the root causes of the conflict.

RHR's mission and activism in Israel/Palestine therefore testify to the advantages, but also the limitations, of the liberal model of multiculturalism as a framework for conflict transformation. In his discussion of the possibility of a global diffusion of liberal multiculturalism, Kymlicka underscores the importance of "desecuritizing" the question of minority rights, thereby undermining possible renderings of minorities as a potential "fifth column" or "demographic threat." This, Kymlicka perceives, would be a welcome development conducive to conflict transformation, primarily by reducing xenophobic currents and chauvinistic impulses.

Despite recognizing a strong systemic connection between questions of social justice within the Green Line and the patterns of occupation within the territories of 1967, RHR differentiates the "occupied Palestinians" from the Palestinian citizens of Israel. As the next chapter highlights, the logic of "desecuritization" also informs the struggle of the Palestinian citizens of Israel for minority rights. The process of "desecuritizing" or domesticating minorities serves, in the case of Israeli liberalism, to (1) reinforce the metahistorical bias that normalizes the borders of 1948 and distinguishes between the problem of the "occupation" of 1967 and Israel proper, and (2) reframe the question of the Palestinian citizens of Israel as an instance of negotiating minority rights. This points to the limitations of the multicultural vision of RHR: it does not go far enough in illuminating that at the root of the conflict and the memories of injustice is the definitional moment of 1948, which turned those Palestinians who had remained within the Green Line into a "minority."

This oversight is not merely an indication of a flaw in the liberal lens for conflict transformation. It also reveals that the liberal framework is not equipped with the resources to address the definitional illiberality of the national project and thus deeper issues of justice. Liberal sensibilities may acknowledge those "dirty secrets" that are masked by the "collective amnesia," but the liberal model does not provide any resources for radically rethinking and restructuring the symbolic boundaries of the "nation" in a way that touches upon definitional meta-injustices. Rethinking symbolic boundaries can profoundly affect the restructuring of unjust social and political boundaries.

The theological assumptions championed by the rabbis involved in RHR are reflective of their American liberal sensibilities and philosophical influences, as found in the writings of Heschel, Novak, and Kaplan. In the Israeli context, however, the liberalization and humanization of state practices cannot be detached from critical discussions of the subjective boundaries of the "nation" as construed by the persistently dominant Zionist narrative. RHR does not engage in the latter set of conversations. The problem with RHR and other Israeli religious and secular peace groups is their inability to see beyond the conceptual blinders dictated by Zionism (its particular historiography and ethos) and consequently to recognize that these very blinders are, in effect, at the root of the conflict. Only by addressing these blind spots can peace activists rethink the parameters of conflict transformation and peacebuilding to redress justice concerns in a multiperspectival manner. I now turn to discuss why the hermeneutics of citizenship can enrich RHR's activism, liberalism, and modes of envisioning peace and justice.

II. Critical Caretakers?

RHR and Religious Peacebuilding

As explicated in chapter 3, the hermeneutics of citizenship entails becoming a "critical caretaker" of the tradition.[38] Accordingly, peacebuilding objectives are grounded in the denaturalization of ethnoreligious national claims; the widening of the debate concerning the interrelation between religion, culture, national identity, and ethnicity; and a centralization of marginal and counterhegemonic accounts as a way of assessing presuppositions concerning identity and history. This process involves three essential tasks: a critical deconstructive critique of reigning discourses; an imaginative and constructive engagement with hybrid spaces generated by conflict; and a similar engagement with traditional, historical, and religious resources that may also occupy marginalized positions in dominant ethnonational narratives.

In many respects RHR constitutes a perfect case study for the growing field analyzing religiously motivated efforts at conflict transformation and peacebuilding.[39] Undeniably, RHR draws on its particular interpretation of the Jewish prophetic tradition and engages in intense "consciousness-raising" activities and religiously inspired advocacy for strengthening civil society and redressing human rights abuses. The rabbis perform symbolic acts of solidarity and exhibit empathy for the victims of Israeli policies, thereby demonstrating how religious peacebuilding supplements interfaith dialogue (IFD) with symbolic acts, nonverbal modes of communication, and gestures of reconciliation and solidarity.[40] The rabbis of RHR also engage in educational activities, thereby establishing what John Paul Lederach refers to as the "infrastructure" and "constituency" of peace.[41]

While admirably dealing with practical subsystemic problems such as house demolitions, poverty, foreign labor rights, and uprooted olive groves, RHR has not been able to address the systemic problems that have grave repercussions for the conflict. The analysis above suggests that the organization (1) naturalizes the boundaries of 1948; (2) overlooks the colonialist and orientalist undertones of Israeli society to the conflict with the Palestinians; (3) transplants philosophical-religious frameworks more appropriate for the American discourse of religion and politics into Israel; and (4) accepts axiomatically the basic theopolitical presuppositions of mainstream secular Zionism.

The intention here is not to minimize or dismiss the relevance and crucial importance of RHR as an agent for peace and reconciliation. Indeed, this organization constitutes a courageous undertaking by rabbis and activists who have felt compelled to try to transform the Israeli-Palestinian conflict. RHR as well as other religiously motivated peace groups and peacemakers in Israel address some of the ambiguities and deficiencies inherent in secularist frameworks of peacemaking. In particular, RHR's conscious integration of social justice issues internal to Israel proper demonstrates the organization's effort to make the Israeli nation-state, its infrastructures, and its political practices consistent with its interpretation of Judaism, Zionism, and justice.[42] This effort entails confronting the "land theology" championed by the settlers and their ideological supporters and subsequently challenging their religious monopoly. RHR also addresses substantially the significance of cultivating Jewish political sovereignty—a question that is often overlooked by secular Zionist peace groups or reduced to demographic arguments, seasoned with ambiguous historical and biblical allusions and justifications. However, RHR does not challenge the political theology underlying political Zionism. In fact, it still operates within it.

Inherent in RHR's call to treat the "stranger in your midst" with respect and dignity is the unproblematized assumption of legitimate ownership. Scholar of development Bettina Prato asks rhetorically: "Are human rights a way to retroactively depoliticize certain historical processes and to normalize their crystallizations in the present by reducing everything to the issue of how to 'humanize' a polity that, more than any other, is often called to justify its origins?"[43] RHR has challenged the practices of the state of Israel but has nonetheless evaded scrutiny of the colonialist and Eurocentric underpinnings of the Zionist nation-state, as well as the possible strategic relevance of such a deconstructive stance to reconciliation and peacebuilding as a reimagining of Jewish Israeliness within its Middle Eastern context. Such an evasion indicates that RHR's vision of justice relies on a naturalized interpretation of Jewish-Zionist polity in Palestine/Israel. Its underlying intention, however, is to make this polity righteous and compatible with RHR's exceptionalist understanding of the Jewish tradition of human rights.

RHR: A Critical Caretaker?

Animating the hermeneutics of citizenship is the idea of the "critical caretaker." This hybrid construct signals a move beyond a dichotomous positioning of the caretakers or apologists of tradition, on the one hand, and the critics of structures of injustice, on the other. This dichotomy reflects a view of religion, and of a certain thread of scholarship about religion, as always complicit with the status quo within a religious community and in how it relates to sociopolitical structures. The analysis of RHR illuminates the simplicity of such a binary.

RHR offers a penetrating critique of the infrastructures and practices of the Israeli state. This critique is grounded in a particular interpretation of the meanings of Judaism and is propelled by an aspiration to reframe Israeli policies and institutions to conform to Jewish values. To this extent, when juxtaposed with the religiously inspired militancy of the religious settlers, RHR's peace-seeking and nonviolent militancy recalls R. Scott Appleby's thesis concerning the "ambivalence of the sacred." RHR also illuminates the relevance of religion both for examining the conflict and for imagining processes of peacebuilding. Unlike the Gavison-Medan Covenant, RHR's agenda is grounded in and reflective of the injustices perpetrated by the Jewish state. RHR's mission is precisely to argue from a distinct and unapologetic Jewish point of view against what universally may be deemed unjust practices. RHR does not reify various modes of being Jewish under an umbrella of multiculturalism. Rather, the organization identifies some structural and discursive connections between social injustices and discrimination in Israel proper and the occupation of the territories of 1967.

However, while interjecting Jewish values and countering the Zionist monopoly over the interrelation between religion and nationalism, and while enriching the debate over the internal plurality of Judaism, RHR's approach is still limited to basic axiomatic Zionist presuppositions. Nevertheless, the activism of RHR and similar organizations suggests the importance of confronting ethnoreligious national claims through an explicit hermeneutical engagement with the theological and historical resources of the tradition. Even while assuming the role of the "caregiver" of Judaism, this mode of religious peacebuilding does not overlook the centrality of an analysis of power and structural violence in the Israeli context. And yet this is only one aspect of the process of the hermeneutics of citizenship. To reimagine justice outside the bounds of acceptable debate, this process must break beyond an intra-Jewish contestation of the sociopolitical and cultural landscape and engage in a multiperspectival interrogation. Simply remaining focused on intratraditional critique and caretaking could, as indeed it does in the case of RHR, reinforce, however inadvertently, meta-injustices.

The critical caretaking mode that the hermeneutics of citizenship calls for would denaturalize axiomatic assumptions about Israeli and Jewish identity by focusing on the counternarratives of groups that do not fit into certain normative assumptions about belonging to the Israeli nation-state. The critical contextual probe into subaltern and other identities born out of the realities of conflict could constructively supplement the possibilities available for religious peacebuilding. Here religion is not reduced to political and/or national identities. But the hermeneutical possibilities are not merely self-contained within the pages of Jewish sacred sources or historical chapters; rather, they are fully embodied by the realities of others' suffering, displacement, and dispersion, and by the experiences of hybrid communities. In other words, religious peacebuilding would involve more than deploying explicitly religious sources to resist perceived perversions of religion (as in the case of religious critiques of the settlement movement) or enlisting the participation of religious leaders in the cultivation of a broad and multilayered "peace constituency." It would entail sustained critique and reimagining of underlying assumptions concerning identity. A move beyond a fossilized conception of religious peacebuilding as involving merely a process of retrieval facilitates access to the creative outlets of lived religions. In the case at hand, the emergence of a distinct Israeli Jewish secular identity, largely estranged from non-Israeli Jewish outlooks and worlds of associations, could provide a creative space for localizing Jewish Israeliness. On a different front, the theological devaluation of the Israeli state by certain segments within the settlement movement, as well as the Jewish diasporants' resistance to the homogenizing and universalizing logic of a Zionist interpretation of Jewish identity and destiny, further illustrates that the Jewish meanings of the Israeli nation-state are contestable from within.

Clearly, RHR is not the only Jewish voice that critiques the Israeli nation-state. In the previous chapter, I discussed (in addition to Jewish anti-Zionist voices) the prophetic voice of Leibowitz and other influential Jewish and Israeli thinkers who both reject the idolatry of nationhood and view the possibility for creative reform within Judaism as the result of the "return" to the land. But for this line of critique to transform the prospect of peace and justice, it needs to be expanded to include a sustained discussion of the root causes of the conflict or of the "meta-injustices" that refer to basic acts of "misframing" the "who" to whom justice applies.

Although Nancy Fraser's analysis effectively refocuses the discourse of justice on the "who" to whom justice may apply, thereby challenging the geopolitical and conceptual framework of the nation-states, in the case of Zionism's relation to Judaism it is precisely the boundaries of the "who" that need to undergo a transformation attuned to the demands of justpeace. The "who"—in this case the "Jewish people"—is not a unitary body, nor can it be reduced to political Zionism.[44]

A discussion of the root causes of the Israeli-Palestinian conflict thus would inevitably involve an intra-Jewish hermeneutical renegotiation of the boundaries of identity and the underlying Zionist ethos, through a multi-perspectival rather than merely intratraditional prism of self-scrutiny. To move beyond the current ethnoreligious national lines, it is necessary to confront the constituent features of what I have identified as their underpinning political theology. These include the enduring monopoly of Zionist historiography over contemporary interpretations of Jewish identity, the conflation of Judaism with Zionism, envisioning Israel as the official representative of a supposedly monolithic body called the "Jewish people."

As noted, both inclinations of rejecting the idolatry of nation-statehood and embracing the creative possibility of religious reform presented by the physical return to the land reflect a general acceptance of the Zionist ethos in which the establishment of the modern state of Israel and the trajectory of the return to Zion signal a process of redemption from the darkness, passivity, and ahistoricity of millennia of diasporic existence. This presupposition suggests a perception of Israel both as the telos of Jewish history and as the center of Jewish contemporary life. It translates into granting an automatic "right of return" to Jews around the world, a policy with profound ramifications for the conflict with the Palestinians. This gains dramatic expression with the "Birthright" pilgrimage to Israel, primarily by American youth, for whom this free visit potentially defines their Jewish identity in a more pronounced way than their bar or bat mitzvah ceremonies. This contemporary pilgrimage reinforces a dominant Zionist reading of Jewish history, which is, however, being increasingly contested by Jewish scholars and activists alike. I turn now to those who endeavor to move away from an ethnonationalist framework of identification by retrieving alternative meanings of exile.

Alterity and the Exilic Condition

Despite the hegemonic hold of the logic of political Zionism and Israel-centrism, there are noteworthy non-Israeli Jewish voices of critique. One prominent example is the American rabbi Michael Lerner. The editor of the *Tikkun* progressive and interfaith magazine, Lerner has rejected ethnocentric interpretations of the Torah. He has been outspoken against the Israeli occupation of the West Bank and has broadly supported the principles outlined in the Geneva Accords.[45] Likewise, he has rejected as counterproductive and inflammatory the inclination of strong lobbies like the American Israel Public Affairs Committee (AIPAC) and the Anti-Defamation League (ADL) to equate critiques of Israeli policies with anti-Semitism.[46]

Still, Lerner does not go beyond the level of critical caretaking of Judaism engaged by the rabbis of RHR. He expresses sadness concerning the perversion of "the loving message of Judaism into a message of hatred and domination" and outlines his vision of peace and justice as including the following initiatives on behalf of Israel: "a massive Marshall Plan in Gaza and in the West Bank to end poverty and unemployment, rebuild infrastructure and encourage investment; dismantle the settlements or make settlers become citizens of a Palestinian state; accept 30,000 Palestinian refugees annually back into Israel for the next 30 years, apologize for [Israel's] role in the 1948 expulsions and offer to coordinate a worldwide compensation effort for all that Palestinians lost during the Occupation; and recognize a Palestinian state within borders already defined by the Geneva Accord of 2003."[47]

Lerner's proposal may provide important orientating goals, but it and similar agendas cannot simply be imposed. Instead, if it were to be translated strategically into transformative processes of peacebuilding, it would necessitate more than denouncing the simple conflation of Judaism and Zionism and more than articulating objectives. Lerner's proposal would necessitate a hermeneutics of citizenship that might even challenge the principles of the Geneva accord. This accord still relies on the two-state principle and thus on certain presuppositions concerning the thresholds of membership in Israel.

Likewise, the platform put forward by the U.S.-based Jewish Voice for Peace (JVP) targets the Israeli occupation of the West Bank, Gaza, and East Jerusalem in its critique. "Inspired by Jewish tradition," JVP's mission statement reads, the members of this organization are committed "to work together for peace, social justice, equality, human rights, respect for international law, and a U.S. foreign policy based on these ideals." The statement further supports the "aspirations of Israelis and Palestinians for security and self-determination." While JVP does not explore what "security" and "self" might entail, the organization, like Lerner, challenges the conflation of Judaism with Zionism and the positioning of Israel as the representative of all Jews. The mission statement reads emphatically: "We are among the many American Jews who say to the U.S. and Israeli governments: 'Not in our names!'"[48] Such voices are important because they are grounded in particular interpretations of Judaism that are self-consciously in conflict with Zionist presuppositions about the unity of Jewish identity and history, and with the practices such homogenizing presuppositions authorize. Yet for such critiques to translate into constructive frameworks of conflict transformation, a scrutiny of the substantive meanings of the principle of self-determination is pivotal. If JVP and American Jews more broadly do not wish Israel to act on their behalf, then a contestation of the Jewish identity of Israel becomes urgent. And this contestation moves beyond questioning the legitimacy of certain Israeli policies from a Jewish point of view to a substantial engagement with the Jewish meanings of Israel as well as with the meanings of Jewish life outside of Israel.

The Indispensability of Nonbelonging

> We are outside ourselves before ourselves and only in such a mode is there a chance of being for another.
>
> —Judith Butler

The words of the subhead of this section encapsulate the American Jewish philosopher Judith Butler's reflection on the interrelation between Zionism, Israel, and Judaism. She is especially troubled by the general inclination to brand any kind of critique of Israeli state policies as anti-Semitic. She underscores that while some critique of Israel indeed amounts to anti-Semitism, the automatic equation is particularly bothersome because of the rich tradition of Jewish social criticism.[49] After all, the public criticism of state violence is, Butler exclaims, "a Jewish thing to do."[50] Recognizing how the dominant Jewish discourse heralds Israel as the representative of the "Jewish people," Butler aspires to rescue and reinvigorate what she deems an "anti-identitarian" Jewish tradition. Because Israeli state violence is done in the name of Jews everywhere, it is an intra-Jewish ethical obligation to retrieve nonnationalist Jewish ethical traditions in an attempt to critically examine and reimagine the Israeli political project and its reliance on Jewish resources.

Butler does so primarily by highlighting the thought of two Jewish German thinkers: Hannah Arendt and Walter Benjamin. The ethical tradition represented by these two thinkers may gesture toward alternative antiteleological and antihomogenizing modes for conceptualizing modern Jewish history in a way that may generate greater empathy for the interrelated plights of Palestinian displacement and repression as well as frameworks for innovative postnationalist modes of cohabitation in the land. By an "anti-identitarian" Jewish orientation, Butler alludes to an ethical tradition that views the patterns of relations to non-Jews or "co-habitation" as the underlying "norms for sociality."[51] The reimagining of "religion in public life," she writes, "is . . . a question of understanding the very relation to the non-Jews."[52]

As noted, for Butler, reimagining the justice discourse, however, cannot exclusively emerge out of the various resources of Judaisms and Jewish histories but ought to be grounded in the kind of ethical relationality that links the Palestinian predicament of subjugation and exile with Jewish diasporic ethical traditions of unchosen cohabitation in radically diverse contexts. In articulating her critique of Zionism, Butler retrieves Jewish plurality to combat the hegemony of Zionist historiography. But in her imagining a political ethics of cohabitation, she moves beyond an intra-Jewish frame by engaging the kind of multiperspectivity offered by the ways in which Palestinian scholar Edward Said and Palestinian poet Mahmoud Darwish articulate their conceptions of justice and injustice. Ethical reframing cannot happen without integrating such a consideration of why the question is not about "cleaning up the act of present-day Israel or implementing reforms, but of overcoming a fundamental and ongoing structure of colonial subjugation that is essential to [Israel's] existence."[53] This is where I see Butler's form of critical caretaking radically departing from RHR's effort to humanize Israel without addressing a definitional reliance "on dispossession and expulsion."[54] As already anticipated in the introduction to this book, the hermeneutics of citizenship diverges from Butler's preconditioning of ethical reframing and cohabitation on dismantling, through a definitional embrace of alterity, the force of collective passions (political Zionism) as they relate to political projects of self-determination.[55] I return to this point below.

Through a retrieval of diasporic polyvalence, the focus on ethical cohabitation subsequently signals a contestation of Zionist monopoly as the representative of "Judaism" and the "Jewish people."[56] Butler's reference to critiques of political Zionism articulated by earlier thinkers like Arendt and Franz Rosenzweig denaturalizes and reorients the presuppositions undergirding the discussion of the interrelation between Judaism, the "Jewish people," and Zionism. For Rosenzweig, the substance of Judaism was located in "waiting and wondering" rather than in "inhabiting."[57] This reading of Rosenzweig recovers a conversation that focuses on the question and ethical demands of cohabitation.[58]

Likewise, Butler reads Arendt's reflections on Zionism and Jewish identity as highlighting "alterity" or strangeness as constitutive of *who* one is. This insight resonates with Said's reflections in his *Freud and the Non-Europeans*, in which recognition of overlapping stories of Palestinian and Jewish displacement and subsequent heterogeneous cohabitation may suggest that the diaspora and the condition of alterity can be historical resources and guiding principles for thinking about justice in the Palestinian-Israeli conflict.[59] To denaturalize a sense of ownership through a reclamation of alterity would attune the discussion of justice to the sufferings glossed over by a commitment to Jewish hegemony. Justice as a form of cohabitation rejects the presumption that one can choose with whom one co-inhabits the earth or a given territory. Such a presumption could lead to genocidal practices (as it did in the case of Nazism).[60] Justice as cohabitation, however, embraces heterogeneity that is not only the condition of alterity but also inherently diasporic.

This concept of alterity and diaspora or "nonbelonging," Butler comments, resonates with the kabbalistic tradition of scattered lights (*sefirot*) and gestures toward Arendt's reading of Benjamin's countermessianic view. By the designation "countermessianic," or rather a counterteleological reading of Jewish history, Butler along with other thinkers such as the Israeli scholars Gabriel Piterberg and Amnon Raz-Krakotzkin demonstrate the divergences between a Benjaminian approach and indebtedness to the kabbalistic tradition, and a reading of Jewish history by the influential scholar of Jewish mysticism Gershom Scholem. The latter imbued the establishment of the Israeli state with redemptive and messianic significance. Echoing the Zionist ethos of the "negation of exile," Scholem thought that the establishment of the state signaled a return to "history" from a diasporic void of nonexistence.

As philosopher Richard Bernstein observes in his analysis of Arendt's relation to the "Jewish question," both Arendt and Benjamin want to move away from the modern inclination to interpret history "as the progressive development of 'victorious' causes." Instead, they wish to focus on "those defeated causes—those causes which were forgotten, marginalized, and obliterated from most historical accounts and memory."[61] This critical lens is evident in Arendt's critique of the modern nation-state and its presumption of cultural homogeneity, in *The Origins of Totalitarianism*.[62] This presumption necessitates, by default, a condition of statelessness or a massive "refugee problem." This historical insight refuses to treat the establishment of the Israeli state on the basis of Jewish sovereignty as a "unique" exceptional case. As a result, Arendt gravitates toward political frameworks that encourage heterogeneity such as "postnational and postsovereign federalism."[63] These frameworks are supported by an embrace of the principle of plurality as a "regulative ideal."[64]

According to Arendt's regulative ideal, plurality is not merely about internal differentiation. The latter interpretation, as we saw in the analysis of the Gavison-Medan Covenant, is unreflective about its boundaries, and in particular, the commitment to an ethnocracy. Instead, pluralization must be reconceived as a process that is also marked by dynamic relationships with the "outside" and that subsequently could transgress its presumed boundaries in ways that cannot be preconceived.[65] Therefore, within Arendt's ethical frame, the amnesia of 1948 is clearly at the heart of the Israeli-Palestinian conflict. Confronting this amnesia would also constitute the point of departure for an ethical reimagining of the basis of sovereignty and justice through reinterpreting the meanings of citizenship. On this point, Arendt significantly diverges from Martin Buber and other proponents of binationalism in the earlier, prestate period who, while stressing the need to curtail the Zionist expansionist agenda, still operated within the impulse for homogeneity.[66] This is the reason that Buber's cohort's visions of binationalism are erroneously retrieved as an "alternative" to the Israeli political project.

Benjamin, like Arendt, challenges a victorious Zionist narrative of historical redemption by exposing the ethical ramifications of such triumphalism. He advances an alternative to the teleological and anthropocentric interpretations of the messianic moment.[67] For Benjamin—as Arendt comments in her influential introduction to his *Illuminations*[68]—the messianic moment amounts to a fleeting memory of suffering from another time. This memory functions to disrupt and reorient the events of the present. This memory takes momentary shape as a form of light (alluding to the *sefirot*) and shakes beneath the ordinary surface of national amnesia.[69] "Redemption" subsequently amounts to rethinking the story of one's own exile in light of others' accounts of dispossession and dispersion. This mobilization of memory or "remembrance"[70] and the revalorization of exile, Butler concludes, would enable the rewriting of a more comprehensive history of oppression.[71] Such rewriting would be integral for what I have termed a "multiperspectival" approach to justice. Benjamin's thesis of history thus constitutes "an ethical impulse to redeem the oppressed," and, as such, Butler classifies it as an "anti-messianic messianism" that bears some complex relation to the kabbalistic tradition.

Arendt also rejected Scholem's messianic interpretation of Jewish history. In reaction to Arendt's famous argument concerning the banality of evil in her analysis of the Eichmann trial in Jerusalem, Scholem accused her (in a correspondence of 1963) of lacking "love of the Jewish people" (*ahavat yisrael*). In response to this accusation, Arendt wrote to Scholem: "You are quite right—I am not moved by any 'love' of this sort . . . I have never in my life 'loved' any people or collective . . . I indeed love 'only' my friends and the only kind of love I know of and believe in is the love of persons . . . I do not 'love' the Jews nor do I 'believe' in them; I merely belong to them as a matter of course, beyond dispute or argument."[72] Arendt's response clearly indicates that she resisted the homogenizing project of political Zionism. Her lack of "love" for the Jews as a people branded her as a persona non grata in Israel and as a "self-hating" Jew, a label often deployed against Jews who diverge from a prevailing script concerning Jewish history and destiny.

Like Benjamin, Arendt worried about the implications of a narrative of Jewish return and domination for the Palestinians.[73] Centralizing the notion of alterity and the principle of "nonbelonging," the exilic moment becomes definitional for Arendt. Likewise, in Butler's reading of Arendt, the very possibility of ethical relations depends upon a certain dispossession from a national framework of belonging.[74] Hence, justice can be imagined only through a process of denaturalizing "my self-referential notion of belonging."[75] Therefore, Butler concludes that "we are outside ourselves before ourselves and only in such a mode is there a chance of being for another."[76]

Reinforcing the insights already found in the work of Israeli critics such as Raz-Krakotzkin,[77] Butler's denationalist approach and subsequent emphasis on the exilic not only as a definitional dimension of the Jewish condition but also as a marginalized Jewish ethical tradition provide a creative mode for reimagining the scope of Jewish identity beyond the confines of Zionist historiography.[78] She conjectures that "to practice remembrance in the Benjaminian sense," exposing amnesia as trauma of dispossession, "might lead to a new concept of citizenship, a new constitutional basis for that region, a rethinking of binationalism in light of the racial and religious complexity of both Jewish and Palestinian populations, a radical reorganization of land partitions and illegal property allocations, and even, minimally, a concept of cultural heterogeneity that extends to the entire population, which is protected rather than denied by rights of citizenship."[79] Dispelling amnesia through remembrance, therefore, introduces one ethical basis for reframing the ideological landscape so that it will no longer enable both structural and cultural forms of violence. It opens the possibility to reframe the interface between Judaism, Jews, and Zionism. The denationalist lens stresses a multiperspectival approach to suffering as central to reforming the ethical relations in Israel-Palestine. Indeed, this hermeneutical angle draws on a Jewish ethical tradition that focuses on the *silences* of history as well as on the intersubjective dynamics of belonging and alterity.[80] Subsequently, it clarifies why the emphasis of the hermeneutics of citizenship on hybrid and marginalized identities can be mobilized for thinking imaginatively and from within the sources of Judaism and Jewish intellectual history about conflict transformation and strategic peacebuilding.

And yet, focusing on alterity and nonbelonging, and reclaiming the diasporic as constitutive of Jewish identity, are by themselves insufficient as a framework for peacebuilding. This is because the argument about the exilic as constitutive of Jewish identity is still a decontextualized and ahistoric argument about Judaism that offers few concrete insights into the process of reframing the boundaries of Israeli citizenship or into the embodied experiences and attitudes of Israeli and non-Israeli Jews. This denationalizing approach and especially the rereading of Jewish history through the lenses of Benjamin and Arendt position Butler as an example of what I have called a "critical caretaker" of Judaism, at least to the extent that she draws on Jewish resources in order to offer both a discursive critique and a constructive reframing of the terms of the debate, and with unrelenting awareness of the sufferings of the Palestinians. This critique and reimagining are not merely an intellectual exercise but an expression of moral outrage concerning violence perpetrated and sustained in the "name of the Jews."

Through "dispossessing" herself from "belonging" to a homogenizing interpretation of Jewish identity, and through articulating her moral outrage about the practices and ideologies of the Israeli nation-state, Butler becomes a critic of Zionism's manipulation of Judaism. But it is through a lucid reclaiming of a counterhegemonic and thus antinationalist Jewish intellectual tradition that Butler becomes a "critical caretaker." Nonetheless, such an approach needs to engage specifically with how subaltern or marginalized Jewish and non-Jewish experiences of (and in) Israel could constructively shape the reimagining of "belonging" as a mode of peacebuilding.

Here Butler's reliance on Arendt's work is limiting. On the one hand, Arendt's lack of *ahavat yisrael* enables the critical internal differentiation Butler stresses in her effort to break away from the homogenizing hold of Zionism. Paradoxically, on the other hand, Arendt's claim that she belongs to the Jewish people simply "as a matter of course, beyond dispute or argument" leaves intact certain "fixed" boundaries of the Jewish community. This presumed fixity precludes the possibility of reconceiving those boundaries despite the ethical urgency to dispossess ourselves of self-referential clarity concerning "who we are." Butler translates Arendt's point about cohabitation into a redrawing of the geopolitical space that still does not respond to the earlier critiques of the multicultural framework: what, beyond a commitment to a set of abstracted political principles (i.e., equality and participatory decision-making) might be the collective ties that would bind a polity together, despite its recognized deep plurality? Arguably, this deficiency is grounded in Arendt's relegation of passions to the private realm, which reflects her articulation of the basis of citizenship as "respect," understood as a kind of political "friendship" ("without intimacy and without closeness").[81] This analytic move tends toward a reimagination of Jewish Israeliness as most basically individuated, and perhaps ultimately private. By evacuating these elements from political space, Arendt offers limited resources for hermeneutically rethinking citizenship by contesting the political theology of Zionism. The approach prescribed by the hermeneutics of citizenship, as I have developed it, stresses the necessity of recognizing and reconfiguring public passions, illuminating and contesting thick interrelationalities among identities that are often irreducibly hybrid and interlaced. Appealing to abstract principles without reimagining public passions (e.g., the *ahavat yisrael* that Arendt eschewed in particular) jeopardizes the legitimacy of the kind of geopolitical restructuring desired by Butler and other post-Zionists.

Subsequently, while Butler's critique of Zionist ideology complements RHR's approach, the analysis above suggests that it is still insufficient in itself. The hermeneutics of citizenship complements both the denationalist outlook of Butler and the humanizing approach of RHR because it strives for both a discursive critique and a constructive, contextual reimagining of the thresholds of belonging. This process may also encompass the possibility of reframing normative interpretations of the Jewish traditions.

Unlike the denationalist orientation, which embraces the principle of nonbelonging, the hermeneutics of citizenship illuminates alterity as encapsulating embodied possibilities for the reframing of belonging. In other words, it engages nonbelonging only insofar as such resources are indispensible for reimagining the boundaries of belonging. Unlike RHR, the hermeneutics of citizenship denaturalizes axiomatic and definitional interpretations of Israeli historiography through dispelling myopias. The hermeneutics of citizenship aims to access silences as a mode of challenging ideational certainties and of reimagining the boundaries of identity in light of the sufferings and experiences of others whose histories intersect with one's own. Instead of individuating Jewish Israeliness as a way to reframe the question of citizenship, the hermeneutics of citizenship explores lived and localized interpretations of collective identity that resist homogenizing paradigms. It finds the debris of state- and nation-making not only through a retrieval of Palestinian experiences of dispossession but also through an exploration of the silences within.

III. Silences

It is necessary now to expand the conversation to the diasporas in order to further rethink and decenter the relations of homeland-diaspora in this particular context. Multifaceted sites of silences are located in the various diasporas. In their study of these landscapes, Caryn Aviv and David Shneer develop a decentered model.[82] They ask: "Why is Zion still so central to the construction of Jewish identity in a global world? How did Jews' ideas of home change once the mythic had become the real, once the ghost of Jewish sovereignty had come 'back to life,' once Jewish nationalists had established political hegemony over the place that had been a place of memory?"[83] Aviv and Shneer challenge the centrality of Israel to Jewish life, stressing that Jews have always had multiple homes. The Zionist diaspora discourse, and what the authors term the "diaspora business" (the financial philanthropic support of Israel by non-Israeli Jews), began to erode after Israel's invasion of Lebanon in 1982. In 1994 the British chief rabbi Jonathan Sacks commented that the outpouring of Jewish money to Israel indicates that British Jews have internalized that they are somehow on the margins of the Jewish world. Sacks as well as other Jewish communal leaders questioned this logic.[84] Likewise, scholars of Jewish diasporas Danny Ben-Moshe and Zohar Segev explain that while Israel functioned as a form of "civil religion of Diaspora Jews," the younger Jews are and the more removed from the formative events of the Holocaust and the creation of Israel, the less likely they are to identity with Israel.[85] This in turn suggests the weakness (already pointed out above in my discussion of the Reconstructionists) of grounding Jewish nationalism solely in an ideology of refuge.[86]

Renowned Israeli scholar of diaspora studies Gabriel Sheffer observes similar patterns in the Israel-diaspora relations and sense of unity (of being "one people"): "Israel is regarded by many Diaspora Jews as a mediocre state. Some of its scientists may get the Nobel Prize, but on the whole neither its cultural nor scientific achievements are very impressive. Consequently, few Diaspora Jews view Israel as a source of inspiration or target of full identification."[87] Whether this statement provides an accurate description of the sentiments on the proverbial "Jewish street," that a scholar who specializes in Jewish diasporas would say such a thing signals a change. Early reverence of Israel as the culmination of Jewish creativity was embodied in miraculous images of Israeli heroism and innovative spirit that, as Israeli and Jewish folklores recall, "made the desert bloom"—images that circulated widely and permeated the popular imagination, especially in North America.[88] Another diaspora scholar, Ofira Seliktar, identifies the First Lebanon War of 1982—widely viewed as an offensive war of choice—as the moment that "turned Israel from a focus of shared identity into an agent of polarization."[89] No longer was Israel a mythical entity; it was now a regular powerful state.

Hence, as a result of the changing tide and the distancing from the direct experience of the Holocaust and its aftermath, "many Diaspora Jews," Sheffer continues, "have realized that the revival and continuity of Jewish culture in the Diaspora does not depend on the knowledge of Hebrew, or on Israeli cultural achievements."[90] Notably, yet another diaspora scholar, Chaim Waxman, points to internal variations in the degree of attachment to and identification with Israel based on denominational affiliation. Accordingly, Orthodox Jews experience more attachment than Conservatives, who feel a greater sense of attachment than Reform and Reconstructionist Jews.[91]

These findings bring to the fore a question concerning whether Israel still should occupy a space of centrality in Jewish life. Jewish American essayist and scholar Steven Bayme affirms that the degree of religiosity informs the degree of attachment to Israel, subsequently alluding to the relative weakness of mere nationalism in instilling a sense of peoplehood. Bayme contends:

> Distancing from Israel cannot be understood apart from Jewish matters generally. Herein lies the strong connection between the agenda of Israel-Diaspora relations and that of Jewish continuity. Those most committed to Judaism are most likely to be committed to Israel. Secular Jewish identity, so prevalent in Israel, evokes few echoes among American Jews. Rather, those who are not identifying with religious frameworks are least likely to be attached to Israel. Religion for many . . . may be the way of practicing one's ethnicity in America today . . . As assimilation proceeds unimpeded, one of its most critical expressions is indifference to Israel as a Jewish state.[92]

The complex interconnections between the American landscape of multicultural politics and Jewish attachments to Israel also signal a departure from a view of Zionism as representing the modern secular Jewish identity, one that is "national," "ethnic," or merely "cultural," with only residual "religiosity." Seliktar refers to this earlier mode of identification as "Judaism as Israelism," "Israel worship," and "Israelotry."[93] But the intensification of ethnocentric tendencies in Israel and its aggressive policies "did not sit well with the progressive sensibilities of secularized American Jewry,"[94] signaling an acute polarization within diaspora communities concerning the support of Israel.[95] Hence the estrangement from American Jews expressed by (usually secular) American Israelis (as I cite above) is mutual, denoting the possibility of reimagining the Jewish meanings of Israel—the symbolic boundaries of the "nation"—and, subsequently, what might be the implications for peacebuilding.

The decentered analytic prism for the study of Jewish diasporas highlights that since the 1980s and 1990s, there have been attempts to rethink Jewish secular identity outside the Zionist paradigm that reduced Judaism to Zionism and to the mandatory bar mitzvah (and Birthright) trips to Israel. One outlet was found in retrieving, reviving, and remembering the Yiddish culture of Eastern Europe. Aviv and Shneer explain that "many of the people who began this search—often progressive, feminist and queer Jews, but also the Haredim (ultra-Orthodox) who nostalgically remember pre-Holocaust Eastern European Orthodox culture as the apex of religious Jewish life—felt marginalized by the dominance of Zionism and Israel in American Jewish culture."[96]

The return to Yiddish and to the nostalgia for Eastern Europe amounts to an embrace of the antithesis of the self-remade Israeli. The celebration of Yiddish culture as the zenith of Jewish religious life interferes with Zionist historiography and the interpretation of the diasporic as empty ahistorical time, a huge abyss that connects the two critical points in Jewish history—expulsion and return. The proliferation of Yiddish offerings on university campuses, *klezmer* concerts (a musical tradition of Ashkenazi Jews of Eastern Europe), and Yiddish theater, among other cultural productions, signifies a conscious effort to challenge Zionist and Hebraic hegemony and to reinvent the meaning of contemporary Jewish life in the diasporas in a way that would not reduce it to Zionism and Israel.[97] Yiddish studies began to gain currency in Israel as well, with centers opening in secular universities and other private institutions of learning, denoting an interest in reclaiming dimensions of Jewish heritage repressed by an ethos of "negation of exile."

The decentered outlook also focuses on why the retrieval of Mizrahi and Sephardi cultures and histories provides another space for broadening the discussion over Jewish contemporary life. As in the case of the "dead" Yiddish culture, Mizrahi cultures and histories have been overshadowed by and assimilated into the Zionist teleology. In chapter 7, I discuss how Mizrahi and Sephardi players enter the Zionist drama as it unfolds in the chronicles of Zionism only at the moment when the global return of Jews to the land of Palestine commenced. Centuries of cultural productions and flourishing Jewish communities in the Middle East and North Africa are rendered irrelevant. The silencing of Mizrahi cultures, like the silencing of Yiddish cultures, indicates the hegemonic status of the Zionist paradigm. But the silencing of the Sephardi experiences also points to the thoroughly Ashkenazi and Eurocentric underpinnings of political Zionism as well as the dominant ethos of the Israeli state.

In the United States the process of retrieving Sephardi Judaism manifested itself in "the incorporation of the American Sephardi Federation into New York's Center for Jewish History, the production of Ladino plays and educational projects designed to challenge Ashkenazi hegemony."[99] In Israel, the retrieval of Sephardi cultures had significant sociopolitical ramifications with the emergence of the Shas movement. Shas—a Haredi Mizrahi political party—offers an alternative framework for the question of Judaism and the Zionist state, which brings into sharp contrast the conceptual Eurocentrism of the Zionist religious peacemakers I have reviewed thus far.

Shas (Shomrei Torah Sephardim or Sephardic Torah Guardians) is classified as an anti-Zionist or, more frequently, a non-Zionist political party. Initially, under the patronage of the Ashkenazi rabbi Eliezer Shach, Shas assumed the traditional anti-Zionist Jewish stance. However, since the emergence of Rav Ovadia Yosef (a former chief rabbi of the Zionist Israeli state) as the sole spiritual leader of the movement, the strict anti-Zionist position has subsided, and Yosef's critique of Zionism has assumed different shapes. His ultimate position, nonetheless, rejected the view of Israel as an expression or actualization of Jewish redemption.[100] An Israeli scholar studying the Shas party and ideology, Tzvi Zohar, explains that Yosef agreed with the Ashkenazi elite of the early decades on several counts. He too accepted the negation of diasporic customs and saw no need to import the Judaism that had incubated outside the geographical parameters of the land of Israel and its native religious scholarship. Like Ashkenazi Zionists, he subsequently underscored the requirement to uphold the *authentic* as opposed to the *diasporic* model of Judaism. But while the Ashkenazi elite imagined a new notion of the Jew as antithetical to the diasporic Jew of the European shtetl, Yosef argued that the authentic image of the Palestinian Jew had already been articulated by the fifteenth-century rabbi Yosef Karo in his magnum opus *Shulchan Arukh*, a comprehensive and authoritative work on halakhah.[101] Yosef desired halakhic unification for all of Israel's Jews, regardless of their ethnic and geographical variation. By maintaining that *minhag hamakom,* or "local customs," take precedence over transplanted ones, Yosef resisted what he perceived as Ashkenazi religious colonialism.[102]

Other leaders of Shas underscore their critique of the secular and Ashkenazi version of and monopoly over the idea of Zionism and suggest that they are, in effect, the real Zionists. When asked whether they are Zionists, they say they wish to reclaim the definition of the concept. Zionism, Yair Peretz claims, can never amount to "compromising the Halakha—not even for the land or the state of Israel." Likewise, Shlomo Benziri asks: "What is Zionism? If it means the settlement of the land of Israel, then I am a Zionist . . . If Zionism means the building of a Halakhic state . . . then I am a super-Zionist. But if Zionism is the opposite of this demand—I am not ashamed to say that I am not a Zionist . . . you cannot disconnect the settlement of the land from the Torah."[103] Shas and its leadership accept the Israeli state as the arena for renegotiating the meaning of Zionism, revitalizing and recovering the glory of Sephardi and Mizrahi traditions and cultural, religious, and social lives, and subverting the Ashkenazi-secular hegemony. Hence it is incorrect to classify this movement as anti-Zionist or even non-Zionist.

The Ashkenazi hegemonic hold also extends to conversations concerning the role of religion in public life. The Zionist state's ideological emphasis on the negation of exile, the ingathering and amalgamation of the diasporas, and the socialization of a new Jew derived, as we saw, precisely from modernist and secularist sets of conceptual dichotomies. Conversely, as a scholar studying Shas and the Mizrahim in Israel, Roni Baum-Banai, explains: because the ideas of the Haskalah and Zionism had filtered into Islamic contexts only in the late nineteenth century, Mizrahi Jewry's exposure to secularization and modernization was more gradual or relaxed and less traumatic or abrupt than Ashkenazi Jewry's.

Mizrahi Jews had not been forced into a choice between "religion" and "progress." However, upon their mass migration to Israel in the 1950s, they were suddenly confronted by the paternalistic and dismissive attitude of Ashkenazi Zionism and its republican, homogenizing melting-pot policy. Most of the Mizrahim chose to leave their religiosity and cultures partially behind in order to integrate into Israeli society. This group is often characterized as "traditional." Notably, the Ashkenazi Haredi segments within Israel sought to gain control over the education of the Mizrahi youth, which led to hybrid identity and enculturation. The leadership of Shas eventually emerged in 1984 out of this context: a sense of profound rejection from both the mainstream secular and the Haredi-Ashkenazi communities.[104] Shas articulated an alternative Sephardi-Haredi identity and, since its dramatic entry into the Israeli political landscape, has negotiated and debated the values underlying the Israeli state and Israeli Judaism.[105] Shas represents a unique Israeli hybrid of Haredi religiosity, on the one hand, and acceptance (whether instrumental or eventually ideological) of the Zionist framework, on the other. This signals a departure from conventional

Haredi opposition to the secular Jewish project. Because Shas's leadership and constituencies have a profound experience of victimhood vis-à-vis the Zionist Ashkenazi hegemonic state and Ashkenazi Haredi monopoly of religion, they are uniquely positioned in a "third space"—a liminal "place in between" homogenizing categories of identity.[106] By virtue of this location, Mizrahiyut (or Mizrahiness) in Israel contains resources to challenge the totalizing boundaries of official narratives by regenerating alternative decentered, marginalized, and local histories. Conversely, RHR is demographically as well as ideologically identified with the normative history as written by a privileged Ashkenazi orientation and subsumed within Eurocentric conceptual frameworks.

While Shas is not a peace movement, its alternative interpretation of Zionism explains why its leadership, on various occasions, has exhibited ostensibly dovish positions on the question of territorial compromises. Prominent analysts of this movement suggest that Shas's dovish image is, however, misleading. The party's primary concern is questions of social justice and reactionary reclamations of the lost glory of the Sephardi tradition. Many of its heterogeneous constituencies associate the peace processes with the same Ashkenazi hegemony that has continuously victimized Mizrahim.[107] Nonetheless, the inclination to classify Shas as dovish is based primarily on Yosef's famous invocation of the halakhic injunction *pikuah nefesh*—the principle that the commandment to save life overrides all of the other commandments—to sanction the evacuation of Sinai. Shas's participation in the Labor-led coalitions of Yitzhak Rabin and Ehud Barak in the 1990s has further reinforced this image. But a careful scrutiny of Yosef's views demonstrates that his justification for territorial compromises is based not on a recognition of Palestinian rights for self-determination or of the immorality inherent in the occupation of another people (as in RHR's platforms or Butler's "remembrance"), but rather on traditional halakhic quietism. Yosef's call for quietism also encompasses a deep mistrust of and even fearful revulsion against the "Arab world."[108]

Nevertheless, while Shas's occasional inclinations toward peace concessions do not withstand scrutiny, if one analyzes its platforms from a justpeace orientation, the movement's position of marginality and social critique as well as its alternative readings of the Jewish character of life in Israel may enable the positioning of Shas as a potential partner in a coalition of marginalized voices. Such a coalition would function both to illuminate the interrelatedness between social injustice within Israel and the Israeli-Palestinian conflict and to offer resources for reimagining the meanings of Israeli citizenship—an endeavor that would bear important implications for the transformation of the Israeli-Palestinian conflict. But, in order to substantially, and not merely pragmatically, assume a peace-oriented stance, Shas—on the level of both its leadership and its wide base—would need to deconstruct the kind of perception that posits the "Oriental Jew" and the "Arab" as mutually exclusive identities, demarcated by geopolitical and sociocultural boundaries. Such a curious estrangement from a Mizrahi's Arab identity reflects the enduring internalization of the Eurocentric biases inherent in the dominant Zionist frame.

The strong articulation of the Arab as the "other" substantiates Shenhav's account of how Mizrahi Jews were socialized and incorporated into the dominant Zionist narrative and Israeli polity in the early decades of the state. Shenhav explains that the Zionization of the Arab Jews entailed concurrent processes of de-Arabization and Judaization. Judaism, subsequently, became the primary entry channel into Zionist and Israeli frameworks—an ironic twist given the antireligious militancy of secular Ashkenazi Zionists.[109] Chapter 7 explores these dynamics, and how the de-Arabization of the Arab Jews affected and defined the history of the conflict with the Palestinians. For my purposes here, it suffices to illuminate Shas's hermeneutical engagement with what it has perceived as Ashkenazi religious colonialism. Shas provides yet another example, along with diasporants, non-Orthodox Jews, and even secular Jewish Israelis, of the many interstices and crevices throughout an otherwise homogenizing and universalizing interpretation of Jewish history and identity. All of those fault lines provide resources for reimagining Israel's Jewish meanings without necessarily individuating and privatizing them, which appears to be a recurrent limitation and impulse of postnationalist proposals for reconfiguring the geopolitical spaces of Israel/Palestine.

The systemic experiences of discrimination, marginalization, displacement, and effacement by the hegemonic Ashkenazi structures have enabled the Shas movement and its leadership to challenge and offer alternatives to the normative mainstream definitions of Zionism or Israeliness. They wish to reinterpret the question "Who are we?" in a fundamental way. Yet their conceptual compass is Judeocentric and lacks empathy for and awareness of the relevance and centrality of the "other"—the Palestinian in Israel proper and in the territories. It lacks the ethical insights of Buber, Benjamin, Arendt, and Butler. Nevertheless, unlike RHR and other religious peace organizations, the case of Shas, even if the group is uninterested in universal human rights conventions and largely unreflective of its Arabness (due to an internalization of the Ashkenazi Zionist discourse), highlights the significance of exposing and historicizing the colonialist and orientalist legacies interlaced with Zionist history. This scrutiny, undertaken from within the Jewish Israeli context, is integral to the hermeneutics of citizenship. This process involves a resuscitation of Sephardi and Mizrahi religiosity and cultural productions.

Lost Jewish cultures are retrieved in other contested sites as well. The revival of Yiddish cultures, especially in the United States and Europe, and the reclaiming of Sephardi cultures and Mizrahi histories and religiosity, especially in Israel, signal conscious attempts to challenge Zionist hegemony and to reimagine Jewishness in the contemporary world. These attempts necessitate recovering and appropriating the silences created by the dominance of Zionist historiography. Likewise, the nonnationalistic thread of modern Jewish thinkers represents another location of silence. In this context, the diasporas represent "diversity" rather than "rootlessness." The decentered approach and its confrontation of Zionist teleology contribute to the valorization of the diaspora and to overcoming the impulse for violence on the basis of hegemonic political aspirations.[110]

Of course, neither the valorization of the diaspora nor the celebration of Yiddish, Ladino, or alternative and plural narrations of Jewish history and life on its own can expand the horizons of peacebuilding and conflict transformation in Israel/Palestine. But conversations that explicitly engage Jewish resources, memories, and repressed traditions nonetheless enable the deconstruction of the dominant ethos and illuminate the possibility of reframing the interrelation between Jewishness and Israeliness. Reimagining the teleological relation between homeland and diaspora, recognizing Ashkenazi cultural, political, and religious dominance, and focusing on alterity as authentically Jewish as well as on the kind of "remembrance" that dispels amnesia—all of these counterhegemonic threads could be translated into a substantive reimagining of the thresholds and meanings of Jewish membership in the Israeli state.

To conclude, RHR as well as other religious Zionist peacemakers fall short of the demand for the hermeneutics of citizenship, partly as a result of their conceptual reliance on the theory of religious humanism and partly owing to their immersion in North American and European notions of liberal citizenship and unrevised interpretations of the interrelation between religion, nationalism, and the infrastructures of the state. Hence, in order to move beyond the Zionist paradigm in approaching the question of peace and justice, RHR would need to reassess and reform its political theory. This turn could facilitate a hermeneutical engagement with the underpinning theology of secular Zionism in addition to a confrontation with the messianic-Kookist variation.

Because the hermeneutics of citizenship necessitates a negotiation and a reimagining of the Jewish significance of Israel, and in particular a re-thinking of the homogenizing teleology of Zionism, this conversation, by definition, would need to capture the plurality of Jewish voices, both inside and outside Israel. This would involve engaging Jewish diasporas and the meanings of Jewish identity in the contemporary world as well as reclaiming non-Ashkenazi or Mizrahi interpretations of Judaism. Beyond retrieval and appropriation, however, reimagining can also emerge out of the lived interpretations of Jewish Israelis of their culture and identity as distinct from those of non-Israeli Jews, paving the way for reconceiving a Jewish Israeli identity along local lines. Such reassessment would also entail exploring the structures of power that facilitated the production and endurance of a particular discourse of political Zionism.

SIX

Subaltern Visions of Peace I: The Case of the Arab Palestinian Citizens of Israel

Introduction

As of 2012, the Palestinian Israeli sector constitutes 20 percent of the Israeli population. Growing up in the privileged and mostly Ashkenazi secular sector, however, I seldom encountered a Palestinian Israeli who was not a laborer or a service provider. I never perceived this as problematic. While my grandfather's generation celebrated Hebrew labor, my generation grew up thinking it was normal for an "Arab," from either the territories or the Green Line, to be employed in manual labor. I was fortunate enough to receive self-critical insight on this state of affairs at home, as my parents were active in challenging those realities and in resisting the systematic discrimination against Palestinian Israelis and Palestinians in the territories occupied in 1967.

My parents stood in front of the demolition bulldozers that intended to raze the homes of Palestinians, and my father published observational accounts of these events and critical essays in his weekly newspaper columns in *Ha'Olam Ha'ze* and elsewhere. When I was eight years old, we moved to a "mixed" neighborhood in Jerusalem. There I had the opportunity to play on the streets with my friends from the Arab Palestinian part of the neighborhood. These idyllic moments ended with the eruption of the First Intifada and an attempt to blow up the gas containers outside my family's apartment building. I wish my childhood memories of playing with my Palestinian neighbors could have been shared by subsequent generations of Israelis. I wish I had spoken Arabic as well as all my Palestinian friends spoke Hebrew. As I recognized only in hindsight, that Hebrew was the lingua franca of our neighborly playtime illuminates that my serene cohabitation with Palestinian kids took place, in effect, under conditions of occupation in which I was the occupier. Why didn't I speak their language? Arabic was and still is not a required language in Israeli schools. It is an optional second language after English, and primarily taught for the purpose of cultivating future IDF intelligence officers (this is despite occasional attempts to make the teaching of Arabic required for certain grades).[1]

Such efforts to introduce Arabic studies into the curriculum are countered by exclusivist currents that aspire to assert the Jewish character of the Israeli state. This is acutely evident in efforts to legislate a "loyalty oath" (October 2010), which would require Palestinian and non-Jewish citizens to state their allegiance to a "Jewish and democratic" Israel. In a last-moment attempt to save the public-relations disaster that such an oath generated both in and outside Israel by extending it to Jewish citizens as well, the Israeli cabinet glossed over the undergirding systemic problem that such a proposal brings to light. Neither the introduction of Arabic studies into the schools nor the requirement of all new citizens to swear an oath of commitment to a certain national identity tackles the root cause of the conflict. Instead, the focus on Arabic studies domesticates Arabic and turns it into a cultural artifact in a Jewish nation-state. The oath—even when extended to Jews—affirms the exclusionary character of the Israeli political project.[2]

Even though my parents forced me to think self-critically about systemic injustice of which I was a part, I began to explore the Arabic language only as a first-year college student at the University of California, Santa Barbara. This is indeed an ironic twist. I had to journey all the way to Santa Barbara to realize that coexistence might mean more than just playing soccer with my Arab Palestinian neighbors and using Hebrew as our means of communication. That Hebrew governed our play indicated the structures of power endured by my Palestinian friends—structures that as a child I was not able to understand.

Palestinian Israelis are citizens. And yet, as Scandar Copti, the director of the Oscar-nominated Palestinian Israeli film *Ajami* (2009), announced: even though the film was nominated as an Israeli film, he does not represent Israel, because Israel does not represent him.[3] This controversial comment illuminates the complex relations between Palestinian Israelis and the Israeli state and society. The focus of this chapter, therefore, is precisely the complexity of the Palestinian Israeli sector. Specifically, I explore how their experiences and unique hybrid locations provide resources for rethinking the meaning of membership in the Israeli state. Paradoxically, we will see, embracing their hybridity reinforces the underlying misframing of the justice discourse with respect to the broader Israeli-Palestinian conflict.

I. The Vision

The defining moment for Palestinian Israelis is the Naqba, which denotes the events from 1947 to 1949: the rejection of the UN partition plan, the war against the Jews in Palestine, the subsequent expulsion of about 750,000 Palestinians from their homes, and the demolition of hundreds of Arab villages (to be replaced by new Jewish settlements). The journey of the Palestinians in Israel also included a systematic policy of land confiscation, disenfranchisement, and socioeconomic neglect and discrimination. The Palestinian citizens of Israel likewise commemorate a few other critical interactions with the authorities as central in the consolidation of their political and social outlook. First, the protest against the state policy of land confiscation in the Land Day of 1976 resulted in six killed demonstrators and many other casualties. Second, the October events of 2000 saw the Israeli police act brutally against Palestinian citizens who protested against Israeli policies concerning the Palestinians in the territories occupied in 1967, following Ariel Sharon's provocative visit to the Haram al-Sharif.

The tragic demonstrations of 1976 and 2000, as well as other similar events, lurk in the background of attempts later in the first decade of the twenty-first century to clarify the status of the Palestinian Israelis through an embrace of their Palestinian narrative of displacement and discrimination, on the one hand, and of their Israeli civic identity, on the other. Precise reflection upon these later attempts requires examining "The Future Vision of the Palestinian Arabs in Israel," a document published in 2006 by the National Committee for the Heads of the Arab Local Authorities in Israel, a wide consensus of Palestinian Israelis. The Vision and related documents (for example, the "Democratic Constitution" issued by Adalah and the "Haifa Declaration" issued by Mada al-Carmel, both in 2007) call for recognition of the minority and indigenous status of the Palestinian citizens of the state of Israel, and they underscore the legal consequences to be drawn from such recognition. The Vision, therefore, may be viewed as one document among a series of similar proposals that stress an alternative vision of the status of the Palestinian citizens of Israel, specifically, and of Israel, more broadly. Privileging restorative and distributive conceptions of justice, these "Vision documents" demonstrate the need to confront the underlying meta-injustices born out of a commitment to an ethnorepublican conception of membership in Israel.[4]

The Vision advocates granting collective rights, including a dual-language system, which would enable the effective representation of the Palestinians within official institutions; a veto right to be exercised in relation to issues particularly relevant to Palestinian Israelis; self-rule in the fields of education, religion, culture, and media; equal distribution of resources; the right of Palestinian Israelis to cultivate their own connections with the rest of the Palestinian people and other Arab nations; the confrontation of controversial questions such as the right of return, the Islamic *waqf* (a religious endowment that entails the right to manage sacred spaces), unrecognized Arab villages, and land confiscation; and, finally, an official acknowledgment of the historic injustices perpetrated against the Palestinians in general and Palestinian Israelis in particular, accompanied by corrective measures.

The "Democratic Constitution" addresses these issues in a juridical fashion, grounded in human rights conventions, international law, UN resolutions, and examples from other contexts like postapartheid South Africa.[5] The "Haifa Declaration" complements the "Democratic Constitution" because it involves an exposition of internal systemic problems, such as discrimination and violence against women within Palestinian society (including the practice of "honor killing"). Moreover, it sets these problems within the Israeli framework and the broader Palestinian story of displacement and occupation. Drafted by prominent Palestinian Israeli intellectuals, the document focuses on internal social issues, the relationship between the Palestinian citizens of Israel and the Israeli state, the relationship of Palestinian Israelis with the Palestinian people, and the meaning of a Palestinian Israeli national identity. The "Haifa Declaration" therefore involves telling the story of Zionist settlement in Palestine and subsequent events from the point of view of the Palestinian inhabitants of the land. It reads as follows:

> Our citizenship and our relationship to the State of Israel are defined, to a great extent, by a formative event, the *Nakba*, which befell the Arab Palestinian people in 1948 as a result of the creation of the State of Israel. This was the event through which we—who remained from among the original inhabitants of our homeland—were made citizens without the genuine constituents of citizenship, especially equality. As we are a homeland minority whose people was driven out of their homeland, and who has suffered historical injustice, the principle of equality—the bedrock of democratic citizenship—must be based on justice and the righting of wrongs, and on the recognition of our narrative and our history in this homeland. This democratic citizenship that we seek is the only arrangement that guarantees individual and collective equality for the Palestinians in Israel.[6]

The argument of the drafters of the "Haifa Declaration" is that recognition of this history of injustice as experienced by Palestinians must be at the heart of any attempt to reframe the institutions of the Israeli state and its ideological infrastructure. This recognition is also pivotal to any attempt to remedy past injustices (thus the Haifa document broadens and complements the legalistic formulations in the "Democratic Constitution" of Adalah).[7] The prospect of reconciliation, therefore, entails a systemic and subsystemic transformation. The "Haifa Declaration" underscores this point:

> We look towards a future in which we can reach historic reconciliation between the Jewish Israeli people and the Arab Palestinian people. This reconciliation requires the State of Israel to recognize the historical injustice that it committed against the Palestinian people through its establishment, to accept responsibility for the *Nakba*, which befell all parts of the Palestinian people, and also for the war crimes and crimes of occupation that it has committed in the Occupied Territories. Reconciliation also requires recognizing the Right of Return and acting to implement it in accordance with United Nations Resolution 194, ending the Occupation and removing the settlements from all Arab territory occupied since 1967, recognizing the right of the Palestinian people to self-determination and to an independent and sovereign state, and recognizing the rights of Palestinian citizens in Israel, which derive from being a homeland minority. Furthermore, such an historical reconciliation between the two peoples must be part of a comprehensive change in Israeli policy, whereby Israel abandons its destructive role towards the peoples of the region, especially in the context of a hegemonic U.S. policy which supports certain Arab regimes in oppressing their citizens, stripping them of their resources, obstructing their development, and impeding the democratic process in the Arab world.[8]

Acknowledging the right of Jews to live peacefully and securely in the region is also essential to any process of reconciliation worth the name. It will require empathetic understanding of the enduring psychological and spiritual impact of the catastrophe that befell European Jewry during World War II. Still, according to the drafters of the "Haifa Declaration," the manipulation of this tragedy to vindicate the dispossession of Palestinians diminishes the moral lessons of the Holocaust. They write:

> This historic reconciliation also requires us, Palestinians and Arabs, to recognize the right of the Israeli Jewish people to self-determination and to life

in peace, dignity, and security with the Palestinian and the other peoples of the region. We are aware of the tragic history of the Jews in Europe, which reached its peak in one of the most horrific human crimes in the Holocaust perpetrated by the Nazis against the Jews, and we are fully cognizant of the tragedies that the survivors have lived through. We sympathize with the victims of the Holocaust, those who perished and those who survived. We believe that exploiting this tragedy and its consequences in order to legitimize the right of the Jews to establish a state at the expense of the Palestinian people serves to belittle universal, human, and moral lessons to be learned from this catastrophic event, which concerns the whole of humanity.[9]

This way of narrating the history of Palestinian-Israeli relations, with its emphasis on reconciliation, echoes the proposals outlined in the Vision and the "Democratic Constitution." Accordingly, the "Haifa Declaration" demands a transformation of the definition of membership in the Israeli state—one that abandons systemic privileging on the basis of race, religion, ethnicity, nationality, and gender.

The Vision (which broadly encompasses the "Haifa Declaration" and the "Democratic Constitution") is a focal point for my discussion because its conception of justice is articulated from the perspective of Israel's non-Jewish citizens. In this respect, it marks a departure from the interpretations of PN, Gush Shalom, and RHR. Indeed, it represents a counterhegemonic interpretation of membership in the Israeli state. While groups such as PN and RHR have operated within the Zionist status quo, the arguments and grievances articulated by the Palestinian citizens of Israel challenge the Zionist paradigm and contest the legitimacy of Zionism as a state ideology. Their particular location in the stratified Israeli society enables the Palestinian citizens of Israel to identify and denounce the biases and blind spots inherent in Zionist peace platforms.[10] The Zionist logic underpinning the two-state solution is thereby confronted in its myopia. Inadequate as ideology no less than as history, it has attempted to rationalize the myths of return and redemption in a Jewish nation-state while overlooking the legitimacy of Palestinian historical presence in the land.

The various Vision documents, therefore, are entirely consistent with Judith Butler's call for intra-Jewish, yet relational, reimagining of the ethics of cohabitation, upon the remembrance of 1948. The Vision exposes the myopia of the Zionist Israeli peace camp by stressing the Naqba as a defining tragedy. Any discussion of justice will have to challenge the presumption of normalcy within the Green Line. And yet, while confronting homogenizing conceptualizations of Jewish Israeliness by stressing the principle of self-estrangement or "nonbelonging," the cohabitation model paradoxically relegates religion to private and individuated spaces. This is limiting because it rejects the imperative to reconfigure political and collective passions.

The reimagining of religion qua nationality is pivotal for authorizing the kind of radical institutional restructuring entailed by the model of cohabitation. Likewise, the Vision relies on multicultural proposals that frame the struggle of Palestinian Israelis in terms of individual and collective rights, subsequently overlooking why decentering Judaism within the Israeli landscape needs to be supplemented with a reimagining of Israel's political theology. Clearly, it is not the responsibility of Palestinian Israelis to reframe the Jewish narrative that they view as a root cause of injustice. But the models of multiculturalism that they aspire to cannot acquire legitimacy without the kind of reimagining called for by the hermeneutics of citizenship. Because of their presuppositions about the fixity of identity markers and their presumption that a polity can cohere on the basis of abstract principles or a thin overlapping consensus, such frameworks can offer necessary but not sufficient insights into conflict transformation in zones drawn by ethnoreligious national claims. The task of the remainder of this chapter is to unpack this argument.

A historical analysis of the various political currents shaping the Palestinian-Israeli conflict shows a growing recognition by Palestinian Israelis of the link between the struggle for equality within Israel proper and the question of peace with the Palestinians in the territories occupied in 1967. Noteworthy in this analysis are the gradual politicization of the Palestinian street, the emergence of a nuanced Palestinian Israeli identity that recognizes its own hybridity, and the growing confidence of activists who seek to restructure the system from within and challenge Israel to act in accordance with its proclaimed commitment to democracy. Following this presentation, the chapter explores the Vision, including the drafters' appeal to international law and human rights conventions in order to substantiate their grievances and demands for full equality. It then focuses on a conceptual critique of the Vision with implications for peacebuilding processes.

II. The Palestinian Citizens of Israel

In order to understand the Vision of the Palestinian citizens of Israel, one needs to explore the Palestinian political sector in Israel by considering how the struggle for equality within Israel has been linked to the broader

Palestinian conflict, and how Palestinian Israelis have interpreted the relation between the Palestinian and the Israeli dimensions of their identities. Do they view these dimensions as contradictory or compatible? The drafters of the Vision endeavor to strike a balance between their demands for civic equality as Israeli citizens and for recognition of their Palestinian national identity and culture. The processes of political formation leading to the Vision are testimony to a deepening Palestinian Israeli consensus.

While major distinctions do exist among the different Palestinian political currents in Israel, one may identify a gradual consolidation of a position that centrally links (even if at times only implicitly or reluctantly) the principle of equality in Israel proper to the question of peace. Regardless of their particular orientations, the different Palestinian Israeli political movements prioritize either the struggle for equality or the national agenda (and in the case of the Islamist movement, the Islamicization of Palestinian society). Historical developments such as the PLO's recognition of Israel and the internal processes of political maturation and confidence building have contributed to the emergence of a widening consensus that sees no contradiction between the demand for full and meaningful equality for the Palestinian citizens of Israel and their complex relations to the broader Palestinian community. This consensus embodied in the Vision and similar proclamations may have profound implications for peace and justice in the Palestinian-Israeli conflict. The Vision's call for reimagining the meaning of membership in Israel constitutes a space from which the terms of peace may be reconceived.

Palestinian Israeli scholar As'ad Ghanem provides intriguing insights into the political formation of Palestinians in Israel. Ghanem's account of the Palestinian Arab minority in Israel since 1948 stands in tension with previous studies, which tend to classify the various political currents of the Palestinian citizens of Israel by analyzing their degree of acceptance or rejection of the Jewish Israeli infrastructure.[11] Instead, Ghanem offers a multidimensional approach, classifying the different political streams among the Palestinian citizens of Israel by exploring their broader ideological orientation, organizational basis, degree of radicalism, rhetorical style, and key motifs as well as internal ideological coherence.[12] On the basis of these criteria, he identifies four primary political and ideological currents relevant to the experience of the Palestinian citizens of Israel: the Israeli Arabs, the communists, the nationalists, and the Islamists.[13] It is important to understand the history and political fluctuations of the different Palestinian political currents in Israel in order to analyze and appreciate the significance of the Vision and its potential implications.

The Israeli Arab Stream

The Israeli Arab stream (presupposing, by this designation, the impossibility of an Arab Jewish Israeliness as embodied in the Mizrahim—as if only Palestinian Israelis are also "Arabs") is characterized by its commitment to operate legally and nonviolently within the Zionist establishment. It is also characterized by its prioritization of civic equality over other topics that may be critical for the Palestinian population, its pragmatic agenda, and its conciliatory tone.[14] Up until the 1970s, the leadership of this stream articulated its identity in terms of a fundamental bifurcation between its Israeli and Arab dimensions, thereby internalizing the Jewish-Zionist definition of this group as an Arab minority to be distinguished from the Arab world and the Palestinian people. Instead of the notion of a basic conflict between the Arab Palestinian and Israeli components of this group's identity, the 1980s witnessed the emergence of more synthetic notions of identity.

The onset of the First Intifada in 1988 marked a critical shift in the history of the Israeli Arab stream. Abdulwahab Darawshe had resigned from his position as a Labor member of the Knesset (MK) in protest of the Israeli government's response to the uprising in the West Bank and the Gaza Strip. Darawshe's resignation precipitated the founding of his new Democratic Arab Party (DAP or ADP). The DAP promptly gathered wide support within the Palestinian Israeli landscape, from local council heads to academics to religious leaders. The platform of the DAP for the 1988 elections emphasized the need to implement the principle of equality for all Israeli citizens, regardless of race or religion, as well as the need to establish a viable Palestinian state alongside Israel with the intention to solve the broader conflict. The DAP platform, therefore, overtly denied any contradiction between the loyalty of the Arab citizens of Israel to their Israeli civic identity and their strong affinity with the Palestinian people. "This view of the identity as complex rather than bisected," Ghanem stresses, "stemmed from a growing awareness of their simultaneous affinity with two spheres, the state of Israel and the Palestinian people, and the desire to preserve both of them."[15]

Yet the DAP consistently underplayed its Palestinian identity and thus was perceived as unthreatening to the Zionist establishment. Consequently, Palestinian scholar Nadim N. Rouhana defines it as a "non-ideological political party."[16] Rouhana's understanding of the DAP suggests persistent and close proximity of the political party to the positions held by Palestinian Israelis who remained under the auspices of the Zionist political parties. Like them, the DAP sought to integrate into the Israeli political landscape without shaking its ideological foundations. Rouhana concludes, however, that despite this ideological ambivalence and integrationist objective, the party failed to become a coalition partner of any substance, a problem inherent precisely in the ideological superstructure to which it submitted.[17] Rouhana's critical dismissal notwithstanding, Ghanem argues that the establishment of the DAP indicates the changing attitudes of the Israeli Arab stream, especially with regard to matters of equality, institutional discrimination, and integration.[18]

Hence, over the decades since the Naqba, one may observe dynamic transformations in the modes by which Palestinian citizens of Israel have participated in the Israeli Zionist political landscape, as well as how they understand themselves in relation to Israel, Arabness, and their Palestinian identity. They began to perceive a closer link between the conflict and their prospects for full and meaningful integration. This perception of the connection between the principles of equality and peace is consistent with their gradually more nuanced (re)interpretation of their complex identity as Palestinians in Israel.

Furthermore, the Israeli Arab stream has increasingly gained the confidence to broaden its platforms from a narrow preoccupation with municipal and civic goals to broader political topics such as land expropriation, the Palestinian-Israeli conflict, and the Palestinian problem in general. This broadening grew out of a process of politicization. The changes are also indicative of the aspiration to integrate into the Israeli state—a struggle for equality that is distinct from the struggle of the Palestinian people for self-determination.[19]

While secondary to the question of equality in the Israeli system, over the years the relevance of the conflict to the predicament of the Palestinian citizens of Israel has become more and more clear in this stream's platforms and attitudes. Consequently, it moved from support for, or formal indifference to, Israel's policies to a public articulation of the demand for an independent Palestinian state, as well as to an official recognition of the PLO as the sole legitimate representative of the Palestinians.[20] After the Yom Kippur or October War (1973), and as a result of growing international awareness of the Palestinian predicament, this political stream reoriented its approach to the conflict, thereby coming closer to the position advanced by the Israeli communist political current since 1967. Accordingly, Israeli Arabs did not shy away from expressing their positions concerning the conflict. Instead, they publicly advanced the return of territories and compliance with Security Council Resolutions 242 and 338. The conflict came to be interpreted as an impediment to coexistence and full integration in Israel.[21] Reversing the logic informing this outlook, some analysts of Palestinian Israeli affairs began to recognize that without reconfiguring internal concerns with equality and cultural and collective rights, the so-called peace process with the Palestinians in the occupied territories would remain derailed.[22] This point is consistent with my argument that questions of peace and justice are thoroughly contingent upon rethinking the basic norms of national identity and political practices.

The Communists

The communists, unlike the Israeli Arab stream, organize on a Jewish Arab, non-Zionist basis. The communist stream has centralized its dual commitment to equality and peace, seeing them as interlinked objectives. Further, it has advocated radical change by explicitly calling for the eradication of Zionism as the overarching state ideology. The Israeli Communist Party (ICP) unequivocally identifies Zionism as the primary impediment to equality for the Palestinian citizens of Israel. Discrimination against the Palestinian citizens of Israel, it insists, cannot be dismissed as mere bureaucratic malfunction but rather indicates the operation of an extensive ideological framework.

Consequently, their tone is more acerbic than the one characteristic of the Israeli Arab stream with its attentiveness to Jewish Zionist sensitivities. Nonetheless, the communist stream has developed a commitment to coexistence, articulated both on its organizational level in its ideological formulations. Hence, rather than calling for the eradication of Israel, the communists are committed to a reframed conception of Israeliness.

Accordingly, the ICP has chosen to focus on the struggle against Israeli land expropriation and the Judaization of the Galilee, and the battle for the recognition of the Palestinians in Israel as a national minority. It has also perceived the conflict with the Palestinians as another critical barrier for advancing equality. After the October War, the communist stream began to refer explicitly to the need to establish an independent Palestinian state alongside Israel, thus endorsing the two-state solution. Further, unlike the Israeli Arab stream, the communists have believed from the start that there is no irreconcilable conflict between their national Palestinian identity and their Israeli civic one.[23]

The ICP (or "Maki," as it is known in Hebrew) was formed in 1948.[24] Initially, the political party consisted predominantly of Jewish activists, but by the mid-1950s, as a result of increased Soviet hostility toward Israel, the party had become gradually Arabized. The ICP split in the mid-1960s. One group, under the leadership of Shmuel Mikounis, retained the name Maki and remained mostly Jewish in membership. The other faction, under the leadership of Meir Wilner and Tawfiq Toubi, was named the New Communist List, or Rakah, and attracted primarily Arab Palestinian activists. In 1969, Maki failed to pass the parliamentary threshold, thereby clearing the way for Rakah as the sole representative of the Communist Party in the Knesset.[25]

From its inception the Communist Party not only defended the rights of the Arabs in Israel but also mounted opposition to domestic and foreign Israeli policies. It called for the return of the Palestinian refugees, the termination of the policy of land expropriation, and the establishment of an independent Palestinian state alongside the Israeli state in accordance with the UN partition resolution of 1947. Jewish Israeli analyst of the politics of the Palestinian Communist Party Ilana Kaufman adds that it was only in 1965 that the ICP finally articulated its vision of a just peace as based on a mutual recognition of the right for self-determination of the two peoples.[26] The statute of the ICP, she notes, envisioned the resolution of the class conflict as a catalyst and condition for the resolution of the national conflict. However, subsequent variations of the party's platform suggest a reversal of this progression, whereby the establishment of a just and lasting peace would stimulate an effort to resolve the capitalist-socialist tension. It would also facilitate the struggle for equality of the Palestinian minority in Israel.[27]

From the early 1970s until the mid-1980s, the communists were able to garner significant support on the Palestinian streets (in the elections of 1973, 1977, and 1981 it won the plurality of the Arab vote, and in 1977 it won the absolute majority). These years may be characterized as the "golden age" of the Communist Party.[28] Rouhana insists that the wide support for the Communist Party indicated a protest against the impotence of the Israeli Arab stream rather than an endorsement of communist ideology. The Arab Palestinian public supported the party's commitment to fighting discrimination, land expropriation, and similar official practices.[29]

But as in other countries in the Middle East, the Israeli Communist Party has suffered decline since the mid-1980s. This decline may be attributed to its failure to revise its platform and the absence of a positive definition of the notion of equality. In other words, the party failed to articulate its vision of the Israeli state. In addition to this internal crisis, Rakah was also faced with external factors that contributed to its decline: the emergence and increasing strength of new political organizations (such as the Progressive List for Peace [PLP], the Islamic movement, and the DAP) and the dissolution of the Soviet Union.[30] The DAP, as mentioned, also linked the question of equality to the broader Palestinian conflict and thus presented an alternative to the ICP's framework. Similarly, Kaufman explains that the emergence of the PLP in 1984 on the national scene (after local success in Nazareth in 1983) marked the end of the ICP's monopoly over the intelligentsia and presented an alternative to the ICP's position on the Palestinian issue. The success of the PLP also suggested the emergence of a strong nationalist rather than class-based Palestinian Israeli orientation (see below).[31] The nationalist stream criticizes the ICP for focusing on the category of class as a primary lens through which to analyze the broader concerns of the Palestinians.

Finally, the emergence of the Islamic movement further challenged the communists' secular style and their claim to be the sole representation of the Palestinian position.[32] Nevertheless, while it failed to update its platform, the communist camp has expanded its interpretation of Jewish-Arab equality over the years and has intensified its calls for recognizing the Palestinians in Israel as constituting a national minority. It has also reinforced its view that no contradiction is posed by the seeming tension between, on the one hand, the Palestinian national facets and, on the other, the civic Israeli facets inherent in the identity of the Palestinian citizens of the state of Israel.[33]

Rakah's most successful initiative has been the Democratic Front for Peace and Equality (DFPE) or Hadash. It was established to broaden the influence of Rakah by downplaying the communist ideological framework. Hence, its platform called for "achieving a comprehensive and stable Israeli-Palestinian and Israeli-Arab peace, defending workers' rights, achieving equality for Arabs in Israel, advancing the status of women, abolishing communal discrimination, and protecting the interests of the poor neighborhoods and development towns."[34] Notably, the ICP has critically linked the question of equality to the broader issues of conflict resolution and peace with the Palestinians outside the 1948 borders. It has underscored the two objectives of equality and peace as primary and coextensive and has encouraged cooperation with Jews who concur with its reading of the Palestinian predicament.[35] In its platform, for instance, Hadash describes its daily efforts for advancing peace, equality, labor rights, and the rights of minorities and women as a struggle based on mutual trust and respect.[36]

Hadash has continuously defined itself as a Jewish Arab (Palestinian) movement. It has been consistently involved in struggles for social equality in Israel and in efforts to advance its vision for a just Israeli-Palestinian peace settlement. In its platform for the 2006 Knesset elections,[37] the party articulated the principles of a just peace: evacuation of all settlements and other forms of Israeli presence from the territories occupied in 1967,

including the West Bank and East Jerusalem; establishment of an independent sovereign Palestinian state alongside the Israeli state in the West Bank,
Gaza, and East Jerusalem; the declaration of West Jerusalem as the capital of
the Israeli state and East Jerusalem as the capital of independent Palestine
(the settlements would guarantee cooperation and free movement between
East and West and free access to sacred spaces); a just resolution of the refugee problem, in accordance with UN resolutions; peace agreements with
Lebanon and Syria; and the return of the Golan Heights to Syria. Hadash
sees this struggle for peace as intricately linked to its social agenda. It views
the Israeli political right as an agent both in deepening the occupation and
in implementing neoliberal policies that precipitated the total collapse of
the social state, unemployment, poverty, and broadening gaps between rich
and poor.[38]

Hadash, in other words, explicated the interconnections between supposedly internal issues of social justice and the broader external Israeli-
Palestinian conflict. It linked peace to the imperative to redefine Israeli
nation-statehood, illuminating the problems posed by both its ethnoreligious commitments and its increased embrace of neoliberal outlooks.
This linking was further elucidated in the 2000s with the coalescence of
the Vision documents, growing dissatisfaction of Palestinian Israelis with
the Jewish majority and the history of systemic and cultural violence, the
abovementioned series of chauvinistic legislation in the Knesset[39], and the
development of a distinct Palestinian Israeli struggle for collective rights
within Israel.

Hadash's insights provide an earlier challenge to the conventional rendering of Palestinian Israelis as a "problem," distinct from the predicament
of the Palestinians in the occupied territories and the diasporas. This convention, informing decades of negotiations between Israel and the representatives of the Palestinians, began to crumble toward the end of the first decade
of the twenty-first century, with the already-alluded-to analysts' increased
acknowledgment that domestic "minority rights" are deeply connected to
the broader conflict, and that a "solution" will necessitate redefining Israeli
nation-statehood. Since 2005, this point became all too clear, with the in-
cessant demand of successive Israeli governments that the Palestinian Authority (PA) officially recognize Israel as a "Jewish state." This issue became
a precondition for peace negotiations.[40]

Certainly, Hadash articulated the interrelations between internal questions of identity and social justice and the Israeli-Palestinian conflict much
earlier than the 2000s. But it was criticized by nationalists who not only
called for a radical change in the status quo but also advocated the establish-

ment of a unitary secular and democratic state on the entirety of the land of mandatory Palestine (referring to the geopolitical space that fell under the British Mandate, preceding the establishment of modern-day Israel).

The Nationalists

The initial platform of the nationalist stream was anti-Israeli, and it organized on an Arab national basis, in contrast to both the ICP's insistence on organizational coexistence and cooperation and the Israeli Arab stream's use of Zionist political infrastructures. Because it derived its ideological orientation from Palestinian nationalism, the nationalist stream also amplified the consistency and contiguity between Palestinians in and out of Israel. Yet as in the previous two cases, this stream also has adapted over the years. It has begun to recognize (even if reluctantly) the Israeli dimensions in the identity of the Palestinian citizens of Israel. It has also granted limited support for joint campaigns with Jewish activists as well as for limited cooperation with Zionists when deemed strategically beneficial.[41]

The nationalist stream was slow to materialize as a significant player in the Palestinian political landscape in Israel.[42] The 1967 war and the subsequent renewed contact with Palestinians of the West Bank and the Gaza Strip precipitated a Palestinian national renaissance, despite the conditions and the shock generated by the military defeat. Out of this context, the Ibanna al-Balad (Sons of the Village) emerged in 1972, under the leadership of Muhammad Kewan. The Sons of the Village had initially called for the establishment of a democratic secular Palestinian state on the entire territory of historic Palestine.[43] But afterward, starting in the late 1980s, activists affiliated with this movement expressed recognition and acceptance of UN Resolution 242 and a willingness to consider the establishment of an independent Palestinian state in the West Bank and Gaza, which amounted to a de facto acceptance of Israel as a geopolitical fact.

This modification was catalyzed by the Intifada and the PLO's recognition of Israel—events that necessitated recognizing the distinct identity of the Palestinian citizens of Israel. Previously, one of the fundamentals of the nationalist stream had been a refusal to acknowledge that the Palestinians in Israel were any different from their brothers and sisters outside of the artificial boundaries of the state.[44] This modification in the general attitude of the nationalist stream is epitomized in the PLP, founded in 1984. The Progressives' platform, which underscored the need for mutual recognition of the two peoples and mutual recognition of the two states, was based on an alliance with the Jewish Alternative group of Uri Avnery and Matti Peled.

The establishment of the National Democratic Alliance (NDA or BALAD) also represents the consolidation of a nuanced nationalist agenda that distinguishes between the predicament of Palestinians in Israel and the broader conflict. Founded in 1996, the NDA is composed of a variety of small, left-wing political groups. The party describes its orientation as "based on the idea of Israel as the state of all its citizens, Jews and Arabs." Its objective, therefore, is to "fight for equal rights for the Arab citizens while preserving their Palestinian heritage and links."[45] Therefore, the platform of the NDA signals a general shift toward positions akin to the communist stream's. Accordingly, the party has strongly supported the creation of a Palestinian state, with East Jerusalem as its capital. The party has also called for the dismantling of all settlements in the 1967 territories and the reframing of Israel as a "state of all its citizens," a demand that implied granting the Arab minority a degree of cultural autonomy. However, the NDA continuously derives its ideological orientation from Palestinian and Arab nationalism.[46] While the communists regarded progress on the peace front as critical for their struggle for equality within Israel, the nationalist stream has increasingly underscored the struggle for equality as a strategic maneuver in the general struggle for national liberation. For this reason, it has been designated by Jewish Israel and other analysts working within the Zionist discourse as a radical political stream.

Azmi Bishara, the leader and founder of the NDA,[47] belongs to a new Palestinian-Israeli generation that, in the words of Israeli author and co-founder of the Alternative Information Center (AIC) Michael Warschawski, "demands its civil rights and refuses to beg for these rights; a generation which takes the Israeli self-definition of being a democratic state very seriously."[48] Indeed, Bishara, unlike individuals associated with the Israeli Arab stream, is not content with a mere cosmetic semblance of equality in the sphere of individual liberties. Instead, he emphasizes the systemic dimensions of discrimination. For him, the only acceptable resolution entails Israel's transformation into a state for all of its citizens. Bishara writes:

Today we make up 20 percent of Israel's population. We do not drink at separate water fountains or sit at the back of the bus. We vote and can serve in the parliament. But we face legal, institutional and informal discrimination in all spheres of life . . . Israel acknowledges itself to be a state of one particular religious group. Anyone committed to democracy will readily admit that equal citizenship cannot exist under such conditions . . . The Israeli authorities are trying to intimidate not just me but all Palestinian citizens of Israel. But we will not be intimidated. We will not bow to permanent servitude in the land of our ancestors or to being severed from our natural connections to the Arab world . . . If we turn back from our path to freedom now, we will consign future generations to the discrimination we have faced for six decades.[49]

Bishara and other leaders and activists in the NDA identify Zionism and the ethnocentric definition of Israeli nationalism as the primary obstacle for fulfilling their democratic aspirations. Their position echoes Edward Said's understanding of secular equality as a necessary foundation of just peace. Said stresses the need for "common secular citizenship, not of ethnic or religious exclusivity, with its culmination first in two equal states, then in a unitary state."[50] He views the secularization of identity as a liberating vehicle and as a key for instituting a long-term, just political framework. "Citizenship," Said contends, "should be based on the just solidarities of coexistence and the gradual dissolving of ethnic lines."[51] He subsequently interprets "secularization" as a process of "demystification," which demands "an irrevocably critical attitude towards self, society, and others, at the same time, keeping in mind the imperatives and principles of justice and peace."[52] The NDA Party expresses similar criteria in evaluating, challenging, and articulating its demands from the Israeli infrastructure.

What this demystifying angle conceals is that a reconfiguration of the category of membership in Israel/Palestine would necessitate a hermeneutics of citizenship, or contestations from within Jewish (and Muslim and Christian) sources of the boundaries of belonging. Similarly to the "remembrance" of 1948 as an occasion to reconceive ethical relations of cohabitation as I discussed in the previous chapter, the move away from exclusionary practice and symbolic violence cannot take place merely by "evolving" out of religious and ethnic trappings. Instead, attempting to approximate inclusivity and dehegemonized national boundaries would entail a process of reframing that takes seriously the meanings people attach to their political and social identity markers. The nationalist stream appears almost universally threatening to the Jewish Israeli and non-Israeli communities because it translates into erasing one's core conception of selfhood. The hermeneutics of citizenship illuminates, however, that a transformation of symbolic boundaries can occur without diminishing the authenticity of one's identity and sense of self. But it also suggests the possibility that what is "authentic" is contestable and elastic and thus open to (re)interpretation. In fact, as I illustrated in chapter 5, there are numerous sites where such reinterpretations already take place. In the present instance, the onus for the hermeneutics of citizenship rests upon Israeli and non-Israeli Jews. Still, this discussion exposes the blind spots inherent in a secularist program like the one advanced by the Palestinian Israeli nationalist stream. The Islamist movement with its explicit focus on the Muslim meanings of a Palestinian society likewise gestures toward the need to engage in an intra-Palestinian substantive hermeneutics.

The Islamists

The Islamic stream emerged only in the mid-1980s.[53] As a political alternative to the other streams, it was articulated initially by Sheikh Abdallah Nimr Darwish of Kafr Qasim. The Islamic stream is primarily represented by the Islamic movement that entered the Knesset in 1996 as part of an alliance with the Democratic Arab Party. The Islamic movement, however, has operated primarily on the local level through mosques and local councils. The movement (influenced by the model of the Muslim Brotherhood in Egypt) has focused on education, welfare, and the Islamicization of Palestinian society. Like the Israeli Arab stream, Israeli Islamists base their struggle for equality on an official acceptance of their minority status in a Jewish majority state. This acceptance does not involve questioning the Zionist logic as acutely as in the case of the NDA (although anti-Israel sentiments are routinely expressed in different publications of the movement).

The entrance of the moderate wing of the Islamic movement (initially headed by Darwish) into national politics in effect signified a pragmatic move toward accepting the state and its sovereignty. It also marked recognition of the need to integrate into the Israeli state while still maintaining the Muslim identity of Palestinian citizens.[54] Hence, unlike the nationalist stream, the Islamists underscore the religious dimensions of a Palestinian identity, though without falling into reductionism. They do, consequently, demand control over the sacred sites of Islam by invoking the Islamic principle of *waqf*.[55] Owing to its acceptance of its minority status, the pragmatic wing of the Islamic movement in Israel does not follow similar movements' cries for instituting an Islamic state. Yet the movement does reject the democratic-civic vision of society, thereby advancing principles for establishing a religious social order.[56] Nonetheless, the Islamist's concerns are incorporated into the Vision, demonstrating the document's effort to represent a wide consensus of the Palestinian sector.

The preceding overview of the different political attitudes of the Palestinian citizens of Israel demonstrates dynamic changes. The Israeli Arab stream has gradually intensified its demand for equality and integration, has recognized the complex layers of the identity of Palestinians in Israel, and has endorsed the two-state solution as an inevitable formula for the resolution of the Palestinian problem as well as a critical step toward implementing the domestic platform of coexistence and integration. Despite its consistent demand for equality, this stream has accepted the Jewish character of the Israeli state and has operated within the Zionist establishment. Conversely, the communist stream has advanced a non-Zionist agenda that has called for uprooting Zionism as state ideology. Notably, the communists have not demanded the eradication of Israel but rather promoted its reimagining alongside an independent Palestinian state.

Whereas the Israeli Arab stream began to link the broader Palestinian problem to the question of civic equality for the Palestinian citizens of Israel only at a later stage in its development, the communist stream has always considered the objectives of equality and peace as intricately interlinked. The Israeli Arab and communist streams are significantly different from the nationalist stream because neither calls for the eradication of Israel. But, as indicated above, even in the case of the nationalist stream, there has been a movement toward a de facto recognition of Israel as a geopolitical entity and thus a consideration of the so-called two-state solution as an interim option, anticipating the eventual institution of a secular democratic state on the entire land of mandatory Palestine. The nationalist stream has also approached the general outline of the communist position by gradually (following the watershed moments of the First Intifada and the Oslo Accords) paying attention to questions of civil rights in Israel, and by drawing distinctions between the experience and identity of Palestinians inside and outside the Green Line. The Islamic stream similarly recognizes the complex but not necessarily irreconcilable dimensions of the identity of Palestinians in Israel.

Regardless of their political affiliation, the Palestinian citizens of Israel have clearly undergone profound processes of formation in order to determine their position vis-à-vis the state of Israel, on the one hand, and to reimagine their connection with the Palestinian people, on the other. The Palestinians who remained within the 1948 borders of Israel found it necessary to articulate their relationship to the Zionist state, the territories occupied in 1967, and the Palestinian diasporas. With the exception of radical elements within the nationalist and Islamist streams, a gradual coalescence of the different streams has put Palestinian Israelis in a position that fundamentally links questions of civic equality in Israel to the resolution of the conflict with the Palestinians, without diminishing the uniquely Israeli aspects of their identity.[57]

Of particular interest, however, are the Israeli Arab and communist streams (as well as some currents within the nationalist stream), owing to their preference for the transformation rather than the eradication of the Israeli state and their commitment to operating within the state's legal confines. The Vision represents a clear demand for full integration and equality within a substantially reformed Israeli state. The authors of the document acknowledge as much: "The project aims at answering the question, 'who are we and what do we want for our society?'"[58] And they continue: "we are moving towards a new era of self-recognition, where it is necessary to create our future path, crystallize our collective identity and draw up our social and political agenda."[59] Indeed, the document states their grievances, explicates the root causes of their experiences of injustice, and charts a way toward redressing past injustices.

The Vision, therefore, represents a merging and aligning of the different political orientations of the Palestinian citizens of Israel in a position reminiscent of the communist stream. It highlights the importance of granting the Palestinian citizens of Israel collective as well as individual rights. It consequently brings to the foreground the complex location of Palestinians in Israel as an indigenous group now in the minority. In line with the Islamic stream, the Vision also stresses the issue of *waqf* because it falls under the rubric of the demand for recognition and collective rights. The document thus articulates a commitment to an Israeli identity as well as a strong and continuous link to Palestinian history and culture. In articulating its link to a Palestinian identity, the Vision centralizes the return of the Palestinian refugees, the demand for an official apology and compensation for the events of 1948, and the need for mechanisms of corrective justice.

The Vision, consequently, challenges official Israeli tendencies to classify the Palestinian citizens of Israel as a domestic "security threat" or as a "demographic problem" and to occasionally draft proposals for territorial swaps and population transfers. It also challenges in a fundamental way Israel's failure to consider the status of Palestinian Israelis in deliberations concerning the so-called final settlements with the Palestinian Authority. In other words, while Palestinian Israelis have begun to reimagine their identity and their connection to the Palestinian experience and to Israel (without negating either), their Jewish Zionist counterparts have not. Thus, the Vision and similar attempts to propose a redefinition of Israeliness are generally interpreted as calls for the eradication of Israel or as anti-Semitic.

Critics of the Vision

A few thinkers situated in the Jewish sector welcomed the Vision and similar formulations as an opportunity for reevaluating the fundamental and definitional problems of Israeli ethnocracy. Renowned historian Meron Benvenisti, for example, stresses the importance of the Vision for renegotiating the underpinning logic of Jewish hegemony over all of Israel/Palestine. "From the moment the demon is allowed out of the bottle," Benvenisti writes, "there's no returning it, and the emergence of consociational democracy that creates a new balance of collective rights is only a matter of time."[60] Likewise, political geographer Oren Yiftachel welcomes the Vision as a significant challenge to the ethnocratic infrastructure of the Israeli state:

> The document articulates . . . the demands of the Arab-Palestinian community in Israel in a manner that challenges most of the foundational premises of the Jewish state. It does not accept the historical Zionist narrative or the magical formula of a "Jewish democratic state." It presents the destructive results of the Jewish settlement of the country for the Palestinian nation in general, and specifically for the Palestinian minority in Israel, and painfully describes in detail the results of long-standing discrimination, including a self critique of the weakness of the Arab-Palestinian society in Israel. Most important—the Vision presents a program for a democratic struggle and peaceful co-existence, despite the arduous, persistent yoke of the occupation of the territories.[61]

Both Benvenisti and Yiftachel understand the Vision as signaling a critical opportunity for reimagining Israel outside the axiomatic taboos of Zionist conversations. Yiftachel, in particular, focuses on the Vision's articulation of the impact of ethnocratic practices on the Palestinian citizens of the country. Such an articulation from the perspective of the subaltern functions as a critical check on the legitimacy of such practices.

In contrast to the favorable reception of the Vision by these two Jewish Israeli scholars, however, Jewish Israelis have generally greeted the Vision and similar efforts negatively and with suspicion. The most common response interprets the proposals as one-sided formulations, implying the eradication of Israel and the demise of the two-state solution. For instance, Yossef (Tommy) Lapid, a journalist turned politician running on a radical secularist (antireligious) agenda as the leader of the Shinui Party, writes that "the Arab public representatives' demand to change the character of Israel from a 'Jewish State' to a 'state of all its citizens' is a transparent attempt to drain all content from Zionism . . . This will not work, because if we relinquish the nature of Israel as a Jewish state, then there is nothing left for us here."[62] Jewish Israeli historian Alexander Jacobson echoes Lapid's line in explaining the Vision's threat to the integrity of the Zionist principle of Jewish self-determination: "It is obvious that this idea represents explicit abandonment of the principle of 'two states for two peoples'—a principle whose application requires two separate nation-states, one Jewish Israeli and the other Palestinian Arab."[63] Scholar of Palestinian Israeli politics Elie Rekhess confirms that the primary problem with the Vision is that it "is based on a zero-sum game in which civic equality cannot be realized as long as the Jewish nature of the state is not abolished."[64]

Other critics of the Vision read the document as a domestic manifestation of a broader Arab and Islamic rejection and delegitimization of a Jewish state. For example, analyst of Palestinian-Israeli strategic relations Yossi Alper writes:

> That Israel's Arabs demand equal land and education rights is of course fully justified. But this document goes much further. Most disturbing of all—and here the years of neglect cannot be blamed—the document can be understood to bring its authors into line with those in the Arab and Islamic world who refuse to accept the existence of a Jewish people at all, much less one with legitimate roots in the Middle East. The future vision document rejects the principle of a democratic Jewish state that lies at the heart of the Oslo solution of two states for two peoples. It positions the Israeli Arab community as very much a part of the broader Palestinian problem.[65]

Alper's approach typifies Israeli liberalism. He underscores his general support for civil liberties to be granted to the Palestinians of Israel. Yet this struggle for equality cannot jeopardize the Jewish definition of the Israeli state. Alper in effect rejects the logic underlying the demand for collective rights.

Likewise, in an open letter to the drafters of the Vision, Shimon Shamir, a former member of the Or Commission,[66] expresses explicit concern about the detrimental implications of the Palestinian Israeli proposal for the Jews of Israel. He argues that the Vision presents a one-sided formulation that delegitimizes the Jewish Israeli identity, attributes the establishment of Israel solely to colonialism, and rejects the Jewish right for self-determination as a nation-state. "It is difficult to shake off the feeling that the purpose of your one-sided definition is to strip away the identity of the Jews of this land," he accuses the drafters of the Vision. Because of this one-sidedness that delegitimizes the national claims and aspirations of the Jews and reduces their identity to a mere "religious or ethnic group," all paths for productive dialogue are blocked, Shamir announces. Reducing the analysis of the state of Israel to a simple argument about colonialism also insinuates, he continues, "that the apologetic process of de-colonialism in the world will come and put an end to it."[67]

Shamir urges the drafters of the Vision to recognize that the changes they seek can be attained only by means of a dialogue with the Jewish citizens of Israel, not by searching for external frameworks such as human rights conventions and trends of decolonization. Hence, reducing the Zionist project in the land to a colonial enterprise and seemingly rejecting the identity of the Jews in Israel will only generate fear and mistrust. "The only way to achieve your rights passes through the Jewish society. Salvation will not come from outside," he writes. "You will make progress in achieving the equality that is your due, only to the extent that the Jewish citizens and their institutions recognize that equality is not merely just but also essential. Unfortunately, the document you composed does not promote this process but reverses it."[68]

The critiques introduced by Alper and Shamir exemplify the response of the Israeli liberal camp to any proposal to fundamentally negotiate membership in Israel. Analyst of Israeli peace activism Reuven Kaminer sharply identifies the illiberal dimensions of Israeli liberalism as they surface in reaction to the Vision:

> The "Future Vision of the Palestinian Arabs in Israel" "succeeded" in evoking a storm of liberal disapproval. The (very illiberal) liberal message was quite clear, to the point of being menacing: I, as a liberal Jewish Israeli, am willing to support you, in principle, in your battle for full individual rights. But the demand for collective rights arouses suspicion as to your real intentions. It is therefore catastrophic. If you were to abandon this fiction about collective rights, which would damage the nature of Israel as a Jewish state, we could make some serious advances on the path of equality.[69]

This irony-filled account of Israeli liberals and their almost universal suspicion of the Vision substantiates the argument that while the marginality of Palestinian Israelis poses an uncontested and necessary critique of Zionist hegemony, a constructive reimagining of membership in Israel will have to invite a hermeneutical intra-Jewish reframing of Jewish nationalism. Without this, the Vision with its reliance on so-called external frames like human rights and international law is viewed as an existential threat to Jewish Israeli identity and ontological certainty. This reinforces the suggestion made in chapter 3 that for the act of critique to offer constructive insights for conflict transformation, it needs to be supplemented with critical caretaking.

Kaminer, however, is also critical of the Vision's evasion of the relevance of the broader occupation to the plight of the Palestinians in Israel. He finds it "disturbing" that "the impact of the occupation and its relation to the development of the Palestinian Arabs in Israel" is minimized in the document. "Of course, the Arabs in Israel have every reason and justification to look inwards in search for ways to influence their future," he admits, "but any analysis that fails to deal with the impact of the overall struggle of the entire Palestinian people at this stage would be painfully incomplete."[70]

Member of Knesset Jamal Zahalka (at the time, NDA chairman) is similarly critical of the document's failure to incorporate the broader Palestinian conflict into its formulations. "What is infuriating about the document is its disregard of the Palestinian issue . . . No [mention of] occupation, '67 borders, Jerusalem, Right of Return, Golan, Fence, settlements, or international resolutions." He fumes: "What's going on here? Did the occupation end and the refugees returned without anyone informing us about it?"[71]

By demonstrating their commitment to coexistence and full equality in Israel, the drafters of the Vision have undoubtedly responded to the accusations raised by Jewish Israeli critics such as Lapid who view the document as representing a zero-sum game that signals the demise of Jewish Israel. Palestinian Israeli commentator Amal Helow powerfully articulates such a response:

> Israeli Jews need to recognize that only when our narrative is taught to Jewish children just as the Jewish narrative is taught in Arab schools, will Israel be on its way to becoming a true democracy. Displaying Palestinian symbols does not negate Jewish symbols; quite the opposite: it sends a strong and true message of mutual respect . . . When a state affords democratic rights to only some of its citizens it is not democratic.[72]

Helow underscores the Vision's explicit intention to expand and reimagine the definition of Israel without diminishing the contextual particularities of its citizens as well as to hold it accountable to its commitment to democracy.[73] The drafters' exclusive emphasis on the question of the Palestinian citizens of Israel, however, complicates their potential response to accusations such as those raised by Kaminer and Zahalka that they fail to link the struggle for equality in Israel proper to the broader conflict and condition of occupation.

Indeed, the Vision documents clearly outline the normative framework necessary for instituting measures for the protection and respect of collective rights in Israel. The focus of those documents is on establishing the minority and indigenous status of Palestinians in Israel according to human rights conventions and international norms. Hence, references to the relevance of their formulations to the broader conflict with the Palestinians are vague and implicit at best. Certainly, the documents emphasize the Naqba as a defining moment and demand acknowledgment of the far-reaching repercussions of this historic event, an apology, and mechanisms for redressing the refugee problem and the long-term experience of discrimination. Further, in establishing the demand for collective rights, the documents labor to explain the deep connection between Palestinian Israelis and the broader Palestinian community, a connection that bears no contradiction with their desire to integrate as full equals into the Israeli landscape.

Yet they are careful to maintain their focus on the topic of the Palestinian citizens of Israel and their aspirations for full and meaningful citizenship. The omission of an explicit consideration of the broader conflict may be attributed to the effort to establish the entitlements of Palestinians in Israel through the invocation of human rights conventions. The link to the Palestinian community and history outside the 1948 borders is articulated only insofar as it establishes the claim for collective rights. Hence, it seems as if the Vision subscribes to the spatial and historical biases inherent in the logic of the two-state solution as articulated in the platforms of PN and other Zionist movements. Accordingly, the problems of the occupation of the territories of 1967 and the discrimination against the Palestinian minority in Israel are viewed as distinct from one another. This distinction points to how completely the powerful party determines the terms of the conversation across the spectrum.[74]

Notably, the Vision subscribes only partially to this spatial and conceptual bifurcation. Indeed, it stresses the democratic self-perception of Israel proper (as distinct from the military occupation) as a resource for advancing the narrower and differentiated claim for equality of the Palestinian citizens, thereby acknowledging a spatial and political separation from the Palestinian conflict. On the other hand, however, the Vision does identify the ethnocratic logic of the Israeli state as the source of Palestinians' condition of discrimination as well as the root cause of the protracted conflict with the broader Palestinian community.

For this reason, despite what may seem like a conspicuous exclusion of broader Palestinian issues, my earlier analysis of the different political currents of Palestinians in Israel showed the growing mainstreaming of the interlinking between the struggle for independence and self-determination in a Palestinian state, on the one hand, and for equality in Israel, on the other. Even though the Vision documents avoid a direct discussion of the broader Palestinian-Israeli conflict, their proposals carry profound implications for its resolution, management, and transformation. Their drafting captures a moment in the history of the Palestinians in Israel when Israel's ethnocratic character was scrutinized by a wide consensus of activists, leaders, and academics.

Israel has systematically buttressed its Jewish character symbolically and concretely by creating "facts on the ground" (through settlements, population transfers, immigration policies, land expropriation, policies concerning capital flow, military occupation, and a corresponding array of legal stipulations). This Judaization has resulted in a rigid system of institutional segregation and stratification, not only between Jews and Palestinians, but also among Jewish ethnoclasses.[75] In the same manner that the Judaizing project in the land (viewed as one contiguous unit of analysis) brought about the erosion of civic definitions of Israeliness and concomitant "de-Arabization," the rethinking of Israeliness in the Vision aspires to reverse the ethnocratic logic of settlement, control, and stratification of citizenship. The paradox of this reversal, however, is that it subscribes to the spatial differentiation that enables the differential treatment of social-justice issues in Israel proper and the territories occupied in 1967. Even if Israel's treatment of its minorities were to directly bear on Israel's position with respect to the broader peace process, the hermeneutics of citizenship suggests that substantive challenges to Jewish hegemony will have to move beyond reframing religion or cultural identity as a "right" for individual practice and collective representation. A reliance on abstract ideas of equality and sociocultural justice as articulated within both the liberal and the polycentric frameworks is necessary but not sufficient. In what follows, I explore the intricacies of this paradox in more detail.

III. The Vision of Palestinian Israeli Citizens: A Conceptual Critique

Highlighting Ethnocracy as a Fundamental Challenge for Equality and Justice

The Vision underscores that the very definition of Israel as a Jewish state is at the root of the problem and thus is consistent with the position held by the communist and nationalist Palestinian Israeli streams. Both political currents insisted that Zionism as a state ideology is detrimental to the principle of equality. Unlike the Israeli Arab stream, they consequently insist on changing the Zionist character of the state. The Vision echoes this understanding of the ethnocratic definition of the state of Israel itself as the most basic obstacle to equality:

Defining the Israeli State as a Jewish State and exploiting democracy in the service of its Jewishness excludes us, and creates tension between us and the nature and essence of the State. Therefore, we call for a Consensual Democratic system that enables us to be fully active in the decision-making process and guarantee our individual and collective civil, historic, and national rights.[76]

The statement recognizes and bemoans the implications of the Zionist imperative for maintaining and cultivating a Jewish and democratic state for the Palestinian citizens of Israel. What is articulated by Zionists as a just and justifiable undertaking—Jewish political self-determination after millennia of persecution—amounts to a profound experience of injustice from the point of view of the subaltern who is excluded from the definitional parameters of the nation yet included within the boundaries of the state as a "domestic other." While critical of the ethnocentric character of the nation-state, the authors underscore their aspiration to attain a full and meaningful membership and citizenship.[77] Accordingly, this aspiration can be approximated only through reimagining the meaning of Israeliness and reforming the state infrastructures. Hence, they advocate a consensual democracy[78] that would resist the domination of an exclusionary ethnocentric agenda.[79] This democratic framework (akin to the Belgium model for Flemish and French speakers) would involve proportional representation and power sharing in a central government and autonomy for the Palestinian community in educational, cultural, and religious matters.[80]

Promoters of consensual democracy often recognize the need to institute a constitutional framework. In June 2005, the Mossawa Center, an advocacy center for Arab citizens in Israel, organized a roundtable discussion on the issue of collective rights for the Palestinian citizens of Israel. The discussion drew on a diversity of viewpoints: the head of the High Follow-Up Committee for Arab Citizens in Israel (Shawki Khateen), Palestinian scholars, lawyers, NGOs, and MKs. The roundtable discussion and relevant sessions of the Knesset's Constitution, Law and Justice Committee eventually resulted in a position paper composed by Palestinian legal scholar and civil rights activist Yousef Jabareen.[81] Titled "An Equal Constitution for All? On a Constitution and Collective Rights for Arab Citizens in Israel," the paper reaffirms the demands for equality and recognition outlined in the Vision. In the words of Jafar Farah, the director of the Mossawa Center, the document "provides rationale for the inclusion of the Palestinian Arabs' constitutional protections and collective rights as a national minority into any discussion or proposal for an Israeli constitution."[82]

The underlying "ontological questions" of a constitution, Jabareen writes, amount to whether "the purpose of the anticipated constitution [will be] to substantially equalize the status of Arab citizens with that of Jewish citizens, or will the constitution settle only for improving the position of Arab citizens? Will it be a constitution of full equality, or only of 'improvement'?"[83] This view leads Jabareen to stress the importance of neutralizing the power differentials between the parties involved in the drafting of the prospective constitution. "There should be no distinction between the process of establishing the constitution and its content," he exclaims.[84]

Notably, the debate over whether to draft a constitution has been fought along a Jewish secular-religious divide, conspicuously excluding a consideration of the relevance of the Palestinian citizens of Israel to these sets of conversations.[85] Jabareen complains that while the High Follow-Up Committee for Arab Citizens in Israel represents the aggregate interests of local authorities, Knesset members, and extraparliamentary movements, this body has never been engaged in a substantive dialogue over constitutional questions concerning the state of Israel.[86] Jabareen insists that such a meaningful dialogue can take place only if every constitutional principle and every societal taboo can come under scrutiny. No single group can monopolize the conversation: "Social consensus requires that all aspects of the constitution, all its headings and principles, shall be open to debate . . . Such an open discussion precludes issues considered 'taboo' or based on axioms. No single group or individual can have a monopoly on truth or justice or on the social good which we, as citizens of the State, aspire to formulate in the constitution."[87] Jabareen's paper, therefore, echoes and reaffirms the Vision's claim that all forms of discrimination endured by the Palestinians emanate precisely from the essential definition of the Israeli nation-state as Jewish.[88] Israeli law relates to Palestinian Israeli citizens with remarkable normative duality: unequal laws, distinguishing between Jews and Palestinians in favor of the former, alongside laws forbidding discrimination between Jews and Arabs. Yet the dominance of the unequal laws in Israeli public life raises the inevitable question: is it really possible to establish true equality for Palestinian citizens in areas where the antidiscrimination laws apply, such as in employment or provision of public services?[89] Jabareen further explains that the Palestinians in Israel are subject to two intertwined levels of discrimination: formal-symbolic and socioeconomic. The formal discrimination manifests itself in the normative arena of state symbols because the latter exclusively highlight the Jewish dimensions of Israeli identity.[90] The socioeconomic level of discrimination corresponds to the formal discrimination against the Palestinians and their inferior status in Israeli society.[91] Jabareen consequently argues that full equality can be attained only through rectifying the discrimination or exclusion of Palestinians from the formal definition of the Israeli state.[92] This insight exemplifies the connection between symbolic violence and sociopolitical mechanisms. As French theorist Pierre Bourdieu recognized, symbolic violence enables the misrecognition of power relations. A substantive rather than a cosmetic transformation will necessitate reframing symbolic boundaries. I deploy the concept of *reframing* as opposed to *eradicating* with the awareness that social and political interrelations are always constituted by power.

Jabareen's focus on the definitional question indicates a critical dissatisfaction with the fallacies of Israeli liberalism and with the kind of benevolent symbolic violence it reproduces. Accordingly, liberal reforms and cosmetic improvements in the condition of Palestinian Israelis can no longer gloss over a failure to recognize the connection between the definition of Israel as a Jewish democracy and the fact of social, political, economic, and moral discrimination against the Palestinian citizens of Israel.[93] Jabareen proceeds to outline specifically how the systemic discrimination against Palestinian Israelis is rooted in the ethnocratic definition of the Israeli state. He raises the issue of the right of Jewish return or immigration as a central indicator for the link between ideology and discriminatory policies.[94]

He likewise catalogs a list of additional legal stipulations that have operated to secure the ethnocratic logic. Section 7A of the Basic Law: The Knesset; section 5 of the Political Parties Law, 1992; the opening sections of the Basic Law: Human Dignity and Liberty; the Basic Law: Freedom of Occupation; and section 2(2) of the State Education Law 1953—all of these legal provisions function to specify the character of Israel as "Jewish and democratic" or as the "State of the Jewish People."[95]

These legal stipulations also suggest a "conceptual duality" in the attitude of Israeli law to Jews and non-Jews: a collective approach with regard to the Jewish majority and an individual approach with regard to non-Jewish citizens.[96] Added in 1985, section 7A of the Basic Law: The Knesset, for instance, blocks the participation of political parties or individuals in the Knesset's elections if they hold positions that may be interpreted as threatening to the idea of Israel as a "Jewish and democratic state."[97] Clearly, section 7A functions to prevent the participation of political parties that wish to challenge the ethnocentric definition of Israel, such as by advocating proposals for full civic equality or binationalism articulated primarily by the Palestinian sectors of the population.[98] The so-called Loyalty Law alluded to at the outset of this chapter provides a later, intensified exclusivist and ethnocentric interpretation of Israeli citizenship. Unlike the conventional

212 / Chapter Six

reasoning of the Israeli peace camp, the exclusivist tone is not distorting but rather highly consistent with the political theology of Zionism.

In its attempt to identify and articulate the root causes of the Palestinian Israeli experience of injustice, the Vision also highlights the profound reliance of the Zionist undertaking in Palestine on the structures and logic of colonialism. This entails emphasizing the elitist and European background from which modern Zionism emerged and attributing the implementation of the Zionist agenda to colonial powers that generally facilitated the settlement project in Palestine. Indeed, the settlement of Palestine was not in any way inconsistent with colonial practices in other colonial domains.[99] The document identifies the elitist, European, and colonialist undertones in the Israeli state's policies of discrimination and internal colonialism as well as its orientalist self-perception as Western, European, and enlightened.[100] The document further alludes to the centrality of the Holocaust and World War II for the fundamental international decision to sanction the establishment of the Jewish state in 1948. The recognition of this background, in which the sufferings of the Jews overlap and interrelate with the sufferings of the Palestinians, anchors the Vision's analysis of the contemporary state of affairs as well as its recommendations as to how to move from exposing symbolic and sociopolitical violence to transforming those systemic obstacles. The programmatic component of the document tackles those connections between symbolic violence and sociopolitical injustice.

The Programmatic Dimensions

In addition to outlining the root causes of their experience of injustice and articulating their vision for the future implementation of a consensual democracy, the drafters of the document also stress the importance of acknowledging past injustices, symbolically as well as in deeds. In particular, they call for the recognition of the War of 1948 as experienced from the point of view of the Palestinians, both those who remained in their homes and those who became and remain refugees. The Vision also suggests the possibility of financially redressing this defining experience of injustice.[101] This is where "remembrance" of 1948 needs to result in a reframing of the question of justice as articulated in the model of ethical cohabitation. The Vision not only identifies the Naqba as a traumatic event for Palestinians in and outside of Israel but also interprets it as the defining event for Palestinian citizens of Israel, an event that separated them from the larger Palestinian experience and led to their status as a national indigenous minority, entitled to full citizenship rights, including the right to voice an opposition to the policies of the nation-state.[102] The Vision also calls on Israel to correct the injustices inflicted by its ethnocratic logic by implementing policies of affirmative action.[103] The Vision underscores the need to institute a careful system of accountability, transparency, and oversight, which would be consistent with international conventions of human rights:

> The legal system should adopt the anti-discrimination laws in all aspects of life individually and collectively. This legal system should also include the creation of an independent commission (or commissions) for equality and human rights. Such a commission should focus on guaranteeing the implementation and surveillance of anti-discrimination laws. It should also adopt the international conventions pertaining to the protection of human rights and be obliged to them . . . so that the terms of these conventions would become an indivisible part of the internal law enforced in the country.[104]

As this excerpt demonstrates, the Vision represents a meticulously developed Palestinian Israeli position. The fact that it was drafted by a wide consensus of activists, intellectuals, and leaders of the Palestinian community in Israel[105] signals a critical shift from the earlier acceptance, on the part of the Israeli Arab stream, of the Zionist frame of reference. Gradually, the cautious and even apologetic mentality rooted in the earlier instinct for survival—a sort of "don't rock the boat!" attitude—began to change. Helow writes that over the last twenty years, "Palestinians have begun taking their rightful place within Israeli society: in universities, as professors or students; in political parties; in the media; in the cultural arena." By interacting with Palestinians in the territories and valorizing their struggle for freedom from Israeli occupation, Helow explains, "we also became reacquainted with ourselves. This in turn helped give us the confidence to assert our national identity."[106]

Certainly, the document demonstrates a substantive engagement with questions of Palestinian identity and membership in the Israeli state. It also mounts a significant challenge to the status quo. It nonetheless aspires toward reform rather than obliteration of Israel, thereby reaffirming a commitment to redressing grievances of Palestinian Israeli citizens and cultivating their status as full citizens within the Israeli state and through its legislative instruments. Among the factors that have contributed to this position is the exclusion of the question of the status of the Palestinian citizens of Israel from the Oslo Accords and subsequent negotiations. In addition, there is an increased acknowledgment of the complexity rather than the contradiction inherent in the identity of Palestinian Israelis. The language of the Vision also demonstrates the empowering relevance of the framework of international human rights conventions to the predicament of the Palestinians in Israel. This framework, which draws on concepts such as collective rights, is especially helpful in situating the Palestinian citizens of Israel as an indigenous minority population.

The Appeal to International Legal and Moral Frameworks of Analysis

The Vision's call for a consensual democracy intimates the yearning of the Palestinian citizens of Israel to attain and deepen the collective, historical, and national dimensions of their identity as well as their civic rights. This point is noteworthy because the Israeli Arab stream has generally been reluctant to apply and expand its struggle for civic equality to collective and national rights. Conversely, the communist stream insisted that there was no contradiction between the Israeli civic facets of their identity and the Palestinian national, cultural, and social ones. The Vision echoes this sentiment:

> There are two facts that must be taken into consideration in crystallizing the legal status of the Palestinian Arabs in Israel. 1. The Palestinian Arabs in Israel are the indigenous people of the country and their historic and [what must be taken into consideration is their] material relations with their homeland emotionally, nationally, religiously and culturally. 2. They are an integral vital and inseparable part of the Palestinian People.[107]

While the struggle for recognition of collective rights is thus more consistent with the communist stream and its unswerving insistence on recognizing Palestinians in Israel as a national minority, the Vision indicates a growing awareness of comparable conversations concerning the rights of minorities in other contexts, such as Turkey, Sri Lanka, Latvia, Lithuania, Estonia, and Canada.[108]

Highlighting the comparative aspects among those cases plays a role (at least rhetorically) in further legitimating the particular grievances of the Palestinian population in Israel. The authors of the document argue that the case of the Palestinian citizens of Israel may be analyzed by deploying some of the same conceptual frameworks that render such practices against minorities unjust elsewhere.

The authors similarly draw on the language of human rights in articulating and reinforcing their position and rights as a national minority. Consequently, the document clearly states that "Israel should acknowledge the right of minorities in line with international conventions." This would translate into a recognition of Palestinian Israelis as an indigenous cultural and national group, entitled to "international protection, care and support according to international conventions and treaties."[109]

Certainly, explicit references to the international framework and terminology of human rights are intended to underline the minority and indigenous status of Palestinian Israelis and thus to substantiate their claim for equality and to call for transforming Israel into a consensual democracy. "The State has to acknowledge that Israel is the homeland for both Palestinians and Jews," the document reads. This means that "the two groups should have mutual relations based on the consensual democratic system (an extended coalition between the elites of the two groups, equal proportional representation, mutual right to veto and self-administration of executive issues)."[110]

Similar to the Vision, Jabareen's formulation extensively draws on the vocabulary of international legal norms in order to demonstrate the minority and indigenous status of Palestinians in Israel. He argues that the fact that "the indigeneity of the Arab minority is hardly given expression in the Jewish-public discourse on a formal constitution in Israel" amounts to a total contradiction of international norms, "whereby the original-indigenous character of a minority group (in contrast to an immigrant minority group) should make the collective rights of the group doubly valid and should justify them both legally and morally."[111]

In order to understand their own status and experience of injustice, the Palestinians in Israel do not need to be fluent in the conventions of human rights. The invocation of the international framework and comparative cases is nonetheless empowering. In reference to an envisioned constitution, Jabareen's allusions to international conventions accentuate their capacity not only to legitimate claims of injustice but also to provide legal and conceptual resources for imagining change. While, Jabareen contends, "it cannot be expected that the legal norms in themselves will succeed in totally neutralizing the socio-political dominance of the majority group," they do provide an imperative "to cleanse the law of all bias that favors the majority."[112]

The question that arises, however, is whether international conventions of human rights provide a sufficient framework for reimagining membership in Israel. Moreover, to revisit the theoretical discussion in chapter 2, is such a human rights approach adequate as a theory of justice and peacebuilding in zones of ethnoreligious national conflicts? The aspiration and struggle of Palestinian Israelis to attain collective rights within a consensual framework may provide an opportunity to evaluate the efficacy of group rights theories developed by Will Kymlicka, Charles Taylor, and others for conflict transformation and peacebuilding.

As I have argued, that the liberal thread of multicultural theory may provide certain corrective measures and ensure a more equitable and just relationship among different groups in a pluralistic society is clear. Nonetheless, the liberal model does not put forward the tools for reimagining of the justice discourse in order to redress the root causes of conflict. Indeed, it may itself be implicated in symbolic and cultural forms of violence. For this reason, to move from the merely cosmetic to the substantive, the application of human rights and international norms as well as the rethinking of citizenship along multicultural lines need to be supplemented by the hermeneutics of citizenship.

The Vision and the Limits of Liberal Multiculturalism

In his discussion of the congruence between his theories of group-differentiated citizenship and the basic principles of a liberal democracy, Kymlicka identifies three types of minority rights: "special group representation," "self-government," and "polyethnic."[113] "Special group representation rights" ensure the inclusion of national or ethnic minorities in decision making. "Self-government rights" entail a decentralized system in which decisions about education, language, and other areas of importance for minority groups are vested in the care of subnational bodies. Similarly, "polyethnic rights" are instituted in order to protect particular religious and cultural practices. Further, in responding to claims that his theory of differentiated citizenship may jeopardize individual liberties, Kymlicka highlights the importance of distinguishing between two types of demands that may be advanced by a national or ethnic group: "the claim of a group against its own members" and "the claim of a group against the larger society." For these two types of claims, there are two sets of restrictions designed to protect minorities from various kinds of destabilizing forces like internal dissent and broad political decisions.[114] "External protections" focus on intergroup relations, while "internal restrictions" apply to intragroup concerns. Kymlicka explains that granting external protections to groups is not necessarily inconsistent with individual freedoms, as his critics would argue. Kymlicka advances external protections as a means to facilitate justice among groups and to ensure the survival and flourishing of substate national minority groups and the well-being of their individual members. He nonetheless rejects the imposition of internal restrictions that may prohibit the individual group member from questioning, reforming, or exiting intra-group modes of interactions. This position relies on a particular individual-istic philosophy of the human person and of religion as a matter of choice and right. This individualistic and cognitive conception of the human per-son limits the capacity of the liberal framework to reimagine religion qua nationality as key for threading together disparate and internally pluralizing communities under a broader political framework.

While the Vision echoes the kind of radical restructuring found in poly-centric multiculturalism, its interpretation of the consensual model draws on each of the three types of differentiated citizenship outlined within Kym-licka's liberal framework. The document consequently reflects a preoccupa-tion with the external protections of the collective and thus is vulnerable to the usual critique of consensual democracy as a group-centric model, privileging the protection of groups over individual liberties and elites over grassroots strata.

Brian M. Barry, a critic of Kymlicka's liberal theory of multicultural dif-ferentiated citizenship, is quick to highlight the fact that "voluntary associa-tions do not have to have internal rules satisfying the demands that liberal principles make on political bodies."[115] Furthermore, Barry is critical of the liberal model of multiculturalism and the politicization of culture in gen-eral on the grounds that "a politics of multiculturalism undermines a poli-tics of redistribution" and thus constitutes an incoherent theory of justice.[116] Undoubtedly, because the Vision conforms to the liberal thread of multi-culturalism, it too is subject to the same kind of egalitarian critique as well as a postcolonial critical appraisal of political liberalism.[117] Indeed, the Vi-sion as an application of a liberal theory of multiculturalism does not offer resources for a constructive reevaluation of the "nation" because it affirms the minority status of the Palestinians in Israel. This affirmation vindicates the majority status of Israeli Jews and thus justifies a de facto commitment to maintaining this status quo.

Defining the case of the Palestinian citizens of Israel in this way brackets the occupation of the 1967 territories and the so-called Israeli-Palestinian conflict as a related yet distinct area of concern. As in the case of the Gavison-Medan Covenant with its reliance on the framework of political liberalism and as in the case of RHR's naturalization of the 1948 borders of the Jewish nation-state, the Vision's framing of the question of the status of Palestin-ian Israelis as primarily one of minority rights glosses over connections to the broader Palestinian-Israeli conflict. As such, even while rejecting Jewish ethnocracy, it offers only a cosmetic correction to the Zionist peace camp's normalization and vindication of Israel proper as a Jewish nation-state.

The Vision constitutes a mere surface correction because, even when stressing the need for a deeply pluralistic process for drafting a constitution, it presumes that Israeli democratic values and infrastructure contain self-correcting mechanisms that will enable eventual fulfillment of the proclaimed commitment to democratic practices and values. Therefore, the Vision documents presume that by heralding constitutional principles and human rights conventions, they will cause the inconsistencies between Israeli commitments to democracy and Jewish hegemony to dissipate. Once again, this assumption that loyalties can be reconfigured merely on the basis of allegiance to abstract principles allows only one option for reimagining religion qua nationality, that is, privatization (whether on the level of individual conscience or the collective version of religious and/or cultural, autonomous enclaves).

Therefore, to recall the polycentric critique of liberal multiculturalism from chapter 2, the liberal model—even when articulated from the marginalized location of Palestinian Israelis—advances only a limited framework for conflict transformation. The polycentric approach to citizenship sees the liberal view of differentiated citizenship as involving the mere cooptation of minority groups without rearranging the structures of power. Indeed, as outlined above, critical Palestinian assessments of the Vision have underscored the inadequacy of the document on the question of the occupation. Accepting the Green Line as a demarcation, distinguishing Palestinian Israelis from Palestinians in the territories occupied in 1967, limits and bifurcates the scope of the justice discourse in a way akin to the critique of Jewish Israeli liberalism.

This critique notwithstanding, the Vision does propose a radical reconfiguration of membership in the Israeli nation-state. It seeks institutional reframing by decentralizing national symbols and ethos. This strong commitment to reforming the Israeli framework is also reflected in recent efforts to develop a constitution, which Israel has lacked. These proposals are aligned with the objectives and conclusions of the Vision and reflect the general desire to rethink the parameters of citizenship in Israel. The challenge from the hermeneutics of citizenship is that institutional restructuring cannot be accomplished without rethinking the subjective boundaries of Jewish national identity. This rethinking cannot be attained solely by hoping that Israeli and non-Israeli Jews will come to realize that justice resides in a thin interpretation of the political. Unsurprisingly, the Vision evoked a strong negative reaction from the rank and file of Israeli liberalism, who were suddenly confronted by their underlying illiberality.

Probing into the conceptual underpinnings of the Vision and other related proclamations illustrates that, as a platform for justice and conflict transformation, the Vision exhibits both advantages and limitations. Deploying the diagnostic tools of a human rights approach, the Vision certainly challenges the ethnocentric ethos and institutions of the Israeli nation-state. It calls for a radical restructuring of the geopolitical space as well as for a reconfiguring of formal and symbolic practices. Consequently, consistent with the liberal thread of multicultural theory, the Vision's consensual platform offers an alternative interpretation of the parameters of meaningful citizenship by envisioning a more just intergroup balance within Israel.

However, while the deep pluralizing of Israeli citizenship and the commitment to liberal and noncoercive state institutions may be a desired end point (one that will most certainly transform positions on the broader Israeli-Palestinian conflict), the primary limitations of the Vision and, by extension, of the liberal model of multiculturalism include its tendency to naturalize the categorization of the Palestinian sector in Israel as a minority group. (Their indigenous status is invoked in reference to their claim for cultural autonomy and only vaguely as a way to link the question of their Israeli citizenship to the occupation of 1967 and the broader Palestinian-Israeli conflict.) Treating the case of the Palestinian Israelis solely as a matter of "minority rights" exposes the potential complicity of a human rights discourse with historical injustices. After all, how did Palestinians become a minority group? How might this process relate to the broader ethos that enables the conventional peace camp to categorically differentiate Israel proper from what happens beyond the Green Line? This domesticating of the Palestinian Israelis exposes how the human rights approach integral to the Vision could inadvertently normalize undergirding meta-injustices. The interrelated discourses of liberal multiculturalism and minority rights (often with a focus on religious freedom and liberty), in presupposing the majority-minority relation as a given, deflects contesting meta-injustice and misframing of the justice discourse.[118]

As I argued in chapter 2, the typology that links inclusivist interpretations of religion and nationalism is grounded in the human rights framework that guides the adjudication of ethnocultural and intranational questions of justice. This orientation, however, despite its emphasis on equality and minimal views of government, is insufficient as a framework for conflict transformation. This is especially true for instances, such as the

Gavison-Medan Covenant (see chapter 4), in which the language of religious freedom and minority rights cloaks meta-injustices.

In the case of the Vision, the limitations manifest themselves not in its commitment to a semblance of a multicultural and multinational polity, but rather in its reliance on secularist views of religion. This reliance bypasses the imperative not only to deconstruct the political theology informing Israeli nationalism but also to reframe the meanings of membership in the Israeli nation-state through substantive intra-Jewish and intra-Israeli conversations. The Jewish meanings of Israel cannot be decentering or dehegemonized merely by subscribing to secularist political frameworks that prescribe a noncoercive role for religion and culture or proclaim, as "post-Zionists" often do, that Israel is a "state of all its citizens." This language, under the façade of equality and justice, decontextualizes and ahistoricizes the predicament of the Palestinian Israelis.

To reiterate, the problem is not only that Israeli liberalism is flawed, that it focuses on intra-Jewish plurality within the boundaries of an ethnocracy. As a framework of conflict transformation, the liberal discourse has conceptual limitations. However, this critique does not amount to a rejection of liberal institutions and values or of their relevance to questions of individual freedoms from moral and religious coercion. To be sure, a counterhegemonic, polycentric project need not entail letting go of a basic adherence to universal human rights. Instead, it requires distinguishing between the principles and values undergirding liberal democracies and the systems of domination that rearticulate and limit their implementation (see chapter 2). Nor does the critique of Israeli liberalism amount to a rejection of the basic premises of the typology that correlates liberal religion with inclusivist nationalism. Instead, it points to the inability of this framework to identify meta-injustices born out of the misframing of the justice discourse. Arguably, framing the issue of Palestinian Israelis as a matter of "minority rights" represents such a misframing. The misframing is grounded in the domestication of the question of Palestinian Israeli citizens that affirms the myopic normalization of 1948. This indicates the paradoxical character of this discussion. On the one hand, Palestinian Israelis embody the misframing by virtue of their transformation into strangers in their own homeland, who, despite their status as citizens, can never embrace the amnesia that defined their dislocation. On the other, their lived realities as Israelis differentiate them from Palestinians in the territories of 1967. The Green Line that encapsulates their trauma also defines their distinctive identity.

This paradox is not addressed in the model of cohabitation, because despite its focus on historicizing a political Jewish identity, its recommendations (see chapter 5) gloss over the hybrid identities that ethnocracies tend to produce by virtue of the symbolic boundaries they impose. Hence, this process that involves the remembrance of 1948 cannot erase the hybridities and solidarities that emerged out of the ensuing geopolitical constellations. The hybridity that Palestinian Israelis occupy does make their case distinct from the broader Palestinian predicament and thus replete with creative possibilities for a meaningful conversation concerning the redrawing of the symbolic boundaries of Israel. Certainly, the primary burden in reframing ethnocentric definitions of identity resides with Israeli and non-Israeli Jews and their engagement in the hermeneutics of citizenship.

Yet the Vision's framing of "religion" as a "right," subsumed within the autonomous conscience of the individual (even if this does not preclude the public relevance of religion), suggests the limits of this proposal as a platform for transforming Israeli identity. These limits echo the already-articulated conceptual flaws of liberal multiculturalism, namely its (1) inability to account for what substantially will connect the distinct and multifaceted subgroups within a polity (beyond a set of civic or constitutional commitments) and (2) potential complicity with meta-injustices.

Conclusion: Reimagining Peace from the Point of View of the Subaltern

Unlike the conception of alterity and nonbelonging discussed in the previous chapter, the Vision's proposal of cohabitation is born out of authentic lived experiences within the particular constraints of the Israeli nation-state. The hybrid location of the Palestinian Israelis (and the Mizrahim, as I show in the next chapter) affords the possibility of challenging the parameters of identity, primarily by critiquing its axiomatic presuppositions and the practices these presuppositions authorize. The exposition of the Vision shows the link between reimagining the parameters of identity (probing the definitional question of *who we are*) and peacebuilding. It also demonstrates that such reimagining may emerge out of the third spaces where received axioms and taboos are challenged by the embodied experiences of subaltern voices.[119]

The identities of Palestinian Israelis are constituted by and through their localized experiences within the framework of the Israeli nation-state. While Palestinian Israeli identity is undoubtedly grounded in Palestinian history and reality, the framework afforded by Israeli citizenship also functions as a critical resource in its formation and reformation.[120] Their location between the forces of Jewish and Palestinian nationalisms and their acceptance of their Israeli civic frame of reference undergird the emergence of a distinct form of ethnoregionalism among Palestinian Israelis—a process that has entailed a collective reimagining of their distinct and hybrid location vis-à-vis Palestine and Israel.[121]

The analysis of the Vision exemplifies how alterity or nonbelonging both challenges the ethical underpinnings of the political system and offers creative alternatives. This is reminiscent of Walter Benjamin's insight about history as a momentary eruption of the memory of oppression into homogenous empty time and into the characteristic and definitional amnesia of national contexts. But as Judith Plaskow's concerns with the transformative implications of the "return to Sinai" suggest, Judaism after a feminist critique ought to change significantly and perhaps even definitionally. Judaism's principal actors cannot be exclusively men (see chapter 4). Likewise, the audibility of a critique from a place of alterity and the empathic remembering of silenced Palestinian sufferings would necessitate a reimagining of Israeliness and its parameters of belonging that no longer affirms the spatial and metahistorical biases that created the hybrid category of Palestinian Israelis in the first place. This is the paradox of the Vision as a definitional critique that nonetheless reaffirms a broader misframing of questions of peace and justice with respect to the Israeli-Palestinian conflict.

The analysis of the Palestinian Israeli sectors and their substantive demands (including the decentering of Jewish cultural hegemony) points, on the one hand, to why the concept of agency cannot be understood merely as the outcome of a binary tension between external social impositions and internal dynamics. The Palestinian Israeli platforms explicate reform on formal-symbolic as well as sociopolitical and institutional levels. From the point of view of the hermeneutics of citizenship, the secularist decentering of Israel's Jewish identity (as is the case with the proposal for cohabitation elaborated in the previous chapter) provides insufficient resources for imagining the "political" beyond principled abstractions connoted by the labels of "multiculturalism" or "consociationalism." On the other hand, the Vision's acceptance of the Palestinian Israeli "problem" as a matter of "minority rights" amounts to a concomitant subjectivization that reaffirms (albeit while critiquing) the dominant discourse that presupposes justice as a function of resolving minority-majority relations within Israel.

I deploy "subjectivization" here to allude to Michel Foucault's view of what becoming a "subject" of a discourse entails. It means occupying a position that enables the greatest consistency with the dominant frame. Hence, in some respects, everything is determined by discourse. In her effort to pluralize interpretations of what constitutes agency beyond the dichotomy of acceptance and outer resistance or overthrow of the reigning structures, anthropologist Saba Mahmood illustrates that the process of subjectivization can provide the grammar and context for the emergence of self-conscious agency. This is most certainly the case for the Egyptian pious women Mahmood studies. In fact, agency in this case amounts to inhabiting what the Egyptian women understand to be the norms of feminine Muslim piety, including humility, modesty, and subversiveness. Still, by inhabiting Muslim norms of piety, these women have contributed to significant shifts in Egyptian society and especially to a poignant and transformative critique of Egyptian secularism. As Mahmood conceives it, the inhabitation of these norms, however, does not afford interrogating whether these norms are just or whether they gloss over unjust definitional structures such as patriarchy.[122]

While different, the case of Palestinian Israelis and their process of "subjectivization" cannot be analyzed outside the Israeli context or in the mere dualistic sense of oppressor-victim; rather, it must be analyzed in a deeper and more constitutive sense. To say that their moral claims rest solely upon the language and logic of "minority rights," however, reaffirms the misframing of the discourse of justice. This was recognized by the aforementioned Palestinian critics of the Vision's acceptance of the spatial and ideological differentiation between Israel proper and the occupied territories. They reject this differentiation because it operates within the Zionist discourse of justice, perhaps despite itself.

To move beyond the overwhelming paradoxical presence of the Zionist discourse—to move beyond the paradox of a critique that reaffirms the norm while exposing its flaws—the counterhegemonic reimagining of the structures of power needs to be supplemented by a comparable reimagining of the "nation." Such reimagining may be equally counterhegemonic; in any case, it would require taking ethnonational and religious claims seriously and would thus prompt a reevaluation of the interrelation between religion, nationalism, and ethnicity. The hermeneutics of citizenship subsequently intends to defamiliarize one's identity. In turn, this de-essentializing process may offer transformative ways for rethinking the terms of the conflict and its negotiable and nonnegotiable aspects. It is only in the context of the hermeneutics of citizenship that a substantive rather than a cosmetic reimagining of the discourse of justice can take place.

In other words, the comprehensive human rights framework for thinking about a justpeace for the Palestinian-Israeli conflict cannot be dissociated from the demands and grievances articulated by the Palestinian citizens of the state of Israel. Nor can it be dissociated from a hermeneutical reframing of the intersubjective boundaries of Israeli nationalism, a process that calls for a probe into the Jewish meanings of Israel and Israeli citizenship. One limitation in rendering the polycentric account a useful tool for the study and transformation of ethnonational religious conflicts is therefore exposed in the analysis of the Vision. The Vision is consistent with the polycentric emphasis on counterhegemonic restructuring of power configurations. But like the polycentric model, the Vision glosses over the need to interrogate how religion relates selectively to the symbolic boundaries that constitute social and political commitments.

The Vision's consistency with the polycentric frame is not surprising. While religion is indeed relevant to the identity of the Palestinians in Israel and while the Vision does stress the importance of the *waqf*, religion is not synonymous or conflated with Palestinian Israeli identity as it is with Jewish Israeli ethnonational identity. The defining narrative of the Palestinian Israelis is the occupation of 1948, their subsequent journey as citizens of the Jewish nation-state, and their ambiguous and complex relation to the broader Palestinian community and to the so-called Arab/Islamic problem. Accordingly, their conception of justice includes acknowledging their history and correcting their position as a minority that suffers discrimination, both individually and collectively. In contrast, the Zionist interpretation of the relationship between Israel, Judaism, and the Jewish people is not only a defining cornerstone of Jewish Israeli self-perception. The drafters of the Vision portray it as *the* root cause of their experience of injustice in Israel.

Precisely in this context where the definitional question ought to be raised, religion becomes a critical resource for conflict transformation and peacebuilding. R. Scott Appleby's notion of the "ambivalence of the sacred" is relevant here.[123] Despite what rhetorical formulations of nationalist demagogues might indicate, this "ambivalence" makes the relation between religion and nation one of irreducibility. Accordingly, the body of tradition may present a living reservoir for the excavation of alternatives to ethnocentric and chauvinistic conceptions of the nation. Yet the hermeneutical process in Israel cannot amount to simply overthrowing the structures and narratives of Zionism. Such a dualistic lens cannot lend itself to the complex and changing landscapes of identities. Reimagining the boundaries of membership in Israel, therefore, cannot remain a one-sided effort subsumed under a secularist agenda that compartmentalizes the discussion of religion under "rights." Nor can it merely retrieve the motif of alterity as the only modality for reconfiguring the ethical relations of cohabitation. The primary concern is not about "nonbelonging" (although denaturalizing what appears axiomatic is key), but rather about *reimagining* belonging, without dismissing and decontextualizing collective passions of solidarity. This process needs to involve the Jewish sectors in a meaningful definitional conversation,[124] which I have been highlighting here as a hermeneutical process invested in reimagining the symbolic boundaries of Israeli nationalism.

SEVEN

Subaltern Visions of Peace II:
The Case of the Mizrahim

Introduction

The predominantly Ashkenazi constituencies of the Israeli peace camp, as I have demonstrated, have internalized the dominant, Eurocentric, Zionist narrative, which construes the Israeli as a Western, cultured, and enlightened inhabitant of the land. The residency of this supposedly prototypical Israeli in the Middle East is almost incidental, despite the biblical, cultural, and historical roots that connect her to this foreign, oriental neighborhood. For me, home was my grandfather's apartment, with the royal stamp on the china collection from Poland, the silver from France, and the constant sounds of Bach, Beethoven, and Chopin. I have countless memories of four o'clock teas at my grandparents' house, where they would entertain other older European and mostly German Jewish Jerusalemites. Non-European Israeli Jews brought to the Israeli experience other smells, languages, sounds, and memories. This chapter tells the story of the marginalization they endured and demonstrates how it embodies an important critique of the dominant narrative of Jewish Israeli identity.

The previous chapter demonstrated how the hybrid and subaltern position of the Palestinian citizens of Israel has enabled them to mount a critique of the ethnorepublican character of the Israeli state and to demand its radical restructuring.[1] Now, the discussion turns internally to the predicament of the Mizrahim in Israel and how it may relate to broader concerns about peace and justice.

The term "ethnorepublicanism" underscores two critical and interconnected attributes of the Israeli nation-state: (1) a commitment to an ethnic project vis-à-vis non-Jewish (and especially Palestinian) inhabitants of the land and (2) a commitment to a particular republican definition of membership in Israel that reinforces the self-perception of the Israeli as Western,

228 / Chapter Seven

secular, liberal, and Ashkenazi. Hence, the application of the term "ethno-republicanism" implies external and internal boundaries, concurrently excluding and marginalizing non-Jews as well as non-Ashkenazi Jews. Recognizing the connection between these two basic commitments indicates that the proposal for radical restructuring advanced in the Vision would need to be supplemented by an intra-Jewish and intra-Israeli scrutiny of the meaning of membership in Israel. Such introspection would amount to the hermeneutics of citizenship—a reevaluation of the nexus of religion, nationalism, and ethnicity as it relates to the definition of Israeli citizenship. A focus on Israeli ethnorepublicanism also points toward Euro-Zionism as a common root cause of Palestinian and Mizrahi grievances and histories of discrimination, marginalization, and oppression. Cultural theorist Ella Shohat eloquently expresses this argument:

> The same historical process that dispossessed Palestinians of their property, lands, and national-political rights was intimately linked to the process that dispossessed Arab Jews of their property, lands, and rootedness in Arab countries while uprooting them from that history and culture within Israel itself. But while Palestinians have fostered the collective militancy of nostalgia in exile, Arab Jews, trapped in a no-exit situation, have been forbidden to nourish memories of having belonged to the peoples across the River Jordan, across the mountains of Lebanon, and across the Sinai desert and Suez Canal.[2]

This chapter argues that the new radical Mizrahi discourse in Israel offers alternative, localized resources for reimagining Jewish Israeli identity and experience. Ultimately, however, because this discourse does not go beyond polycentric secularism, it impedes the move from a deconstructive critique to a constructive reframing of symbolic boundaries and the sociopolitical mechanisms they authorize.

As I concluded in my discussion of the Vision in chapter 6, without a substantive engagement with Jewish ethical traditions, vocabularies, symbols, and historical memories, mere critiques and sociopolitical formulas are insufficient for conflict transformation and reframing the national discourse. Despite the radical restructuring afforded by the polycentric model of multiculturalism, it nonetheless relies on a secularist presumption about the fixity and distinctness of identity markers such as "religion," "nationality," and "ethnicity." The "who" who is the subject of justice in the polycentric framework is, in other words, only geographically contested (it need not necessarily be subsumed within the geopolitical boundaries of the nation-state), not hermeneutically.[3]

Certainly, the new radical Mizrahi discourse hermeneutically challenges the Eurocentrism and orientalism of the Zionist discourse, but it does not challenge its secularity. The impulse to privatize religion echoes the limitations of the cohabitation model (see chapter 5). This model also hermeneutically contests, from a space of nonbelonging, normative and seemingly axiomatic national claims, in order to ethically and multiperspectivally reframe the terms of cohabitation. Unlike the Mizrahi discourse, however, the ethical reframing advanced by this model can imagine only a deeply individuated Jewish Israeliness rather than a reframing of symbolic boundaries, collective passions, and loyalties. The limit of Mizrahi polycentrism, however, is that its reimagining of collective passions precludes engagement with Jewish sources that transcend the historicity and locality of the marginalized groups this model seeks to valorize. Without such a hermeneutics of citizenship, the kind of radical restructuring aspired to by Palestinian Israelis and Mizrahim cannot unfold.

The "new radical Mizrahi discourse" is articulated by what Israeli scholar and activist Sami Shalom Chetrit refers to as the "new Mizrahim." Chetrit subsumes under this heading individuals whose ancestral origins may or may not be traced to Islamic and Arab geographies and those who may or may not be Jewish or Israeli. Instead, the "new Mizrahim" refers to those who have participated over the last two decades in a discourse that encompasses community organizers, educators, academics, students, artists, journalists, and poets in an effort to form a radical critique of and an alternative frame of reference to the hegemonic Ashkenazi ethos.[4]

The hegemony of the Ashkenazi ethos runs deep despite social practices that may point to a different conclusion. For example, the fact that intermarriages between Mizrahi and Ashkenazi Israeli Jews are not strictly taboo (as is the case with intermarriages between Palestinians and Jews) and, in effect, constitute a relatively common practice does not change the basic line of critique offered by the new Mizrahim. The mere act of intermarriage and the mere reality of embodying "mixed" identities provide few resources to alter the dominant narrative and normative conceptions of "Israeliness."[5] The effort to renarrate seeks to complicate the basic dichotomies inherent in Zionism, understood as a Eurocentric, orientalist, and Ashkenazi hegemony, and its perceptions and treatment of non-European Jews in Israel. The new Mizrahim subsequently challenge the basic assumptions inherent in Zionism. As Chetrit writes: "The New Mizrahim reject the process of Zionization that they and their parents underwent . . . By the same token, the New Mizrahim want none of the Ashkenazi Zionist collective memory and seek to form a Mizrahi collective memory from which a Mizrahi consciousness and alternative vision for the State of Israel will emerge."[6] In order for such alternative subaltern voices to reconceptualize membership in Israel, there is a need not only to deconstruct the national ethos by exposing its ethnorepublican logic but also to hermeneutically reevaluate the link between religion and nation. Deploying postcolonial insights, the Mizrahi discourse calls attention to its subordinate position within Israeli society and hence focuses its efforts on deconstructing and reforming systemic manifestations of injustice. Its activities and platforms, however, evade an equally creative engagement with the sources of Judaism. Such an engagement could overcome the conceptual problems with Israeli secularism as defined and reproduced by the dominant Zionist discourse. Such scrutiny, that is, could not only challenge Israeli secularism but also offer a substantive alternative to Shas's interpretation of the relation between religion, nation, and citizenship in Israel.

The statistical fact that many Mizrahim have demonstrated support of the right-wing Likud Party and have rallied behind Shas, the Haredi political party with an ethnocentric focus, does not, according to Shohat, indicate some essential attribute of the Mizrahim but rather a misplaced protest against Ashkenazi oppression. This point is critical because, in the parlors of Israeli Ashkenazi liberal activism, the Mizrahim are often demonized. They are portrayed as exhibiting a strong inclination toward populist demagoguery, rightist militancy, and uncritical acceptance of authority—characteristics that are also attributed to non-Jewish Arabs. These "fanatical" tendencies are then contrasted with the "beautiful Israeli" represented by the liberal PN and its constituencies. The Mizrahi population in its support of an ethnonational citizenship discourse is represented as an obstacle to peace, akin to how the religious sector is portrayed by Israeli secularists.[7]

The dichotomization of the "beautiful and enlightened Israeli" versus the "fanatical and boorish" one is consistent with the orientalist and Eurocentric underpinnings of Ashkenazi Zionist hegemony and is no different from the earlier renderings of the Mizrahim as underdeveloped during the first decades of their "absorption" into Israeli society (see below). With this in mind, Shohat contends that "Arab-hatred when it occurs among Oriental Jews is almost always a disguised form of self-hatred."[8]

This "self-hatred" can be related to American civil rights activist and author W. E. B. Du Bois's notion of "double consciousness" with reference to the self-perception of African Americans. According to Du Bois, "double consciousness" denotes the African American internalization of white stereotypes about black people and culture as well as an internal conflict between one's American and African identities.[9] The self-hatred that Shohat discusses is also a result of socializing the Mizrahim to understand themselves and the Arabs as Other. Shas's anti-Arab rhetoric exemplifies this insight.[10] The movement's narrow focus on sectarian issues is also indicative of its internalization of the strict Zionist separation between the two sites of the conflict: the internal "ethnic" conflict and the external "national" problem posed by the military occupation. Indeed, as demonstrated in this work, this conceptual compartmentalization is also characteristic of the secular and religious liberal Israeli peace camps. Paradoxically, a conceptual differentiation between the occupied territories and Israel proper as two distinct sites of justice also limits the effectiveness of the Vision of Palestinian Israelis.

Shohat underscores this point concerning the conceptual distinction between, on the one hand, the "ethnic" and the "domestic" and, on the other hand, the "political" and the "external" problems of the Israeli state: "Even the progressive forces in the Peace Camp that support a Palestinian state alongside Israel seldom abandon the idea of a Jewish Western state whose subtext inevitably is the ethnic and class oppression of Sepharadim. Within such a context, it is hardly surprising that the membership of Peace Now is almost exclusively Ashkenazi, with almost no Sepharadi, or for that matter, Palestinian, participation."[11] Similarly, Israeli sociologist Yehouda Shenhav explains that any attempt to link the Palestinian and Mizrahi questions is profoundly threatening to the Zionist framework. Zionism relies on a strict conceptual separation between the two.[12] Hence, "ethnic discourse is permitted as long as it is defined as intra-Jewish discourse and perceived as an ephemeral phenomenon that poses no threat to national solidarity."[13]

Such separation is also evident in academia, where no overlaps may be detected between the research of historians studying the Palestinian-Israeli conflict and sociologists focusing on the "ethnic rift" and the so-called Mizrahi problem. For instance, the historian Benny Morris's prominent work on the birth of the Palestinian refugee problem[14] does not concern itself with the relevance of the Mizrahi refugees for understanding this historical moment.[15] Shenhav argues that this academic division of labor "depoliticizes the 'ethnic' issue and nullifies the possibility of addressing Mizrahi history and Palestinian history with similar tools, even though both those groups were forced to cope culturally with European Zionism."[16] Shenhav, therefore, proposes to highlight the interconnections and common critiques and causes threading disparate sites of injustice by deconstructing the fallacies of the 1967 paradigm informing the so-called Israeli left and broadening the discussion beyond the artificiality of geopolitical lines.[17]

The present chapter, likewise, stresses the link between Mizrahi and Palestinian histories and the important connection between "domestic" struggles for social justice and broader concerns with the Israeli-Palestinian conflict. My first contention here is that this theoretical insight (even if not yet translated into actual alliances on the ground) challenges what I have identified as the spatial and metahistorical biases inherent in how the Zionist peace camp (in its religious and secular varieties) imagines peace and justice.[18] A second and interrelated contention is that despite its penetrating deconstruction of the Zionist ethos, the new radical Mizrahi discourse overlooks the importance of reimagining the connection between religion and nation for reconstructing an alternative notion of membership in Israel. In other words, a focus on the radical restructuring of the systems of control by accessing subaltern histories of repression and subordination is not yet matched by an effort to radically reconfigure the relation between Judaism, Jews, and Israel. Nevertheless, the chapter concludes that Mizrahi experiences and histories potentially provide resources for a localized renegotiating and reimagining of Jewish Israeli identity.

The chapter is broken up into three main parts. The first explores the background and history of the Mizrahi experience in Israel. It discusses the mass Mizrahi immigration to Israel, the treatment of the Mizrahim by Zionist authorities, and the patterns of early Mizrahi protests. The second part explores the types of protest activities in which the radical Mizrahi discourse is involved and its attempts to advance alternative readings of Israeli history and to expose the underpinning premises of the Euro-Zionist hegemony. The third part analyzes the radical Mizrahi discourse and its relevance for justpeace. This section also studies the polycentric approach to multiculturalism as articulated by two theorists involved with the radical Mizrahi discourse and its potential contributions as well as its limitations for reimagining membership in Israel.

I. Background

The Mizrahi Immigration

As in the previous chapters, I anchor this chapter's discussion in the conceptual framework of one movement in order to access a broader field of inquiry, loosely defined as the "new radical Mizrahi discourse." Accordingly, in chapter 1, I focused the discussion on Peace Now in order to shed light on the premises undergirding the secular Zionist peace camp. In chapter 5, I studied Rabbis for Human Rights in order to identify the conceptual inconsistencies of the religious Zionist peace camp and its understanding of the relationship between Israeli nationalism, Judaism, and the Jewish people. Chapter 6 similarly scrutinized the "Future Vision of the Palestinian Arabs in Israel" in order to explore the challenges that the Palestinian citizens of Israel mount to the Jewish hegemony and the ethnorepublican logic of citizenship. Finally, the present chapter analyzes the conceptual field of the Mizrahi Democratic Rainbow—New Discourse or HaKeshet Hademokratit Hamizrahit—Siah Hadash (simply "Keshet" henceforth) in order to delve into the sorts of challenges to Ashkenazi Israeli hegemony that the Mizrahi citizens of Israel articulate and embody.

Before proceeding with my discussion of the Mizrahi challenge as represented in the Keshet, it is important to further clarify what I mean by the designation "Mizrahi." Like Chetrit, Shohat explains that since the 1990s the term "Mizrahim" (literally "Easterners" in Hebrew) has come to denote not only one's geographic origin but also the collective experience of non-Ashkenazi Jews in Israel. As such, the emergence of this umbrella identity signifies an unintended consequence of the systemic delegitimization of any manifestation of Eastern characteristics and cultural affiliation in Israel. The use of the term "Mizrahim" is intended to counteract the common application of the designation *bnei edot hamizrah* (descendants of oriental ethnicities). The latter, as well as the designation "Sephardim," was posited as the "other" in relation to the normative conception of the Israeli as Western and Ashkenazi.[19] The designation "Mizrahim," Shohat concludes, "condenses a number of connotations: it celebrates the Jewish past in the Eastern world; it affirms the pan-Oriental communities developed in Israel itself; and it invokes a future of revived cohabitation with the Arab Muslim East. All these emergent collective definitions arose . . . in dialectical contrast with a newly encountered hegemonic group, in this case, the Ashkenazim of Israel."[20] Like that of the Palestinian Israelis, Mizrahi identity can neither be reduced to nor explicated outside of the particular dynamics of Israel.

The Mizrahi immigration to Palestine began with the arrival of approximately ten thousand Yemeni Jews prior to the outbreak of World War I. This immigration was depicted in the parlors of Zionism in markedly racial and colonialist terms.[21] The Yemenites, and later a few thousand Kurdish and Persian workers, seemed to serve the Zionist principle and goal of Hebrew labor by substituting it for cheap Palestinian labor.[22] However, leaders across the Zionist spectrum strongly expressed their fear of the Levantinization of Zionism.[23] Reeling from World War II and the near extermination of European Jewry, Zionist leaders, worried about the demographic prospects for *Eretz Yisrael*, refocused their interest on the recruitment of the "Arab

234 / Chapter Seven

Jews" for the Zionist project. This recruitment process eventually resulted in the often-reluctant mass arrival of Mizrahim in the years following the establishment of Israel.[24]

Chetrit outlines the characteristics of this "oriental" immigration.[25] First, the impetus for this immigration was located in the ideological drive of Zionist institutions rather than in the aspirations of the immigrants. Second, the eruption of the War of 1948 signaled the automatic classification of the Jews of the "Orient" as Zionists based solely on their religion, thereby eliminating the common Arab cultural basis of Jews, Muslims, and Christians in the region. This conflation of Judaism and Zionism may be attributed to the recruitment efforts of Zionist emissaries as well as to the rhetorical maneuvers of Arab nationalists. Third, the absorption of Arab Jews into Zionism entailed the loss of the social and economic infrastructure of their communities and their subordination to, and dependency on, the Israeli Euro-Zionist hegemony.

For Arab Jews, Shenhav notes, religion has been the primary conduit into the Zionist undertaking, since they were recruited by mostly secularist and Ashkenazi atheist Zionist emissaries who had been dispatched to their countries of origin.[26] In analyzing the logic of Zionist efforts to recruit in the "Orient," Shenhav identifies a paradoxical component of secular modern nationalism like the one articulated by European Jews: "modern nationalism turns to religion in order to manufacture itself, and . . . it denies its religious underpinning and imagines itself as secular and modern."[27] (I shall return to this point in part 3 of this chapter.) In other words, the immigration of Arab Jews to pre- and poststate Israel, and their incorporation into the Zionist ethnorepublican undertaking, entailed a strict differentiation between their Arab ethnicity and their Jewish religion, which was equated with their nationality as Israelis. This basic differentiation between religion and ethnicity, and the concurrent systemic effort to depoliticize and suppress the Arabness of the Mizrahim, are consistent with the insistence of the Israeli liberal peace camp on regarding "ethnic" and "national" problems as two distinct sites of conversation and conflict.

Despite the Zionist mythologization of the rescue of the Jews from their captivity in Islamic and Arab lands, this turn of events necessitated the practice on the part of the Zionist leadership of so-called cruel Zionism, generating panic within the Jewish communities by planting bombs in synagogues and other places of Jewish gatherings and, in the case of Iraq, collaborating with local authorities. The efforts to provoke the emigration of the Mizrahim in the post–World War II era notwithstanding, the Ashkenazi leadership and elite continued to paint the Arab Jews in racist terms, as they had in the prewar days. This attitude resulted in far-reaching and systemic discriminatory practices that have since defined the Mizrahi experience in Israel.

One of the most scandalous episodes of this period was the kidnapping of hundreds of Yemenite babies and their adoption by Ashkenazi families. Many other indignities are associated with what was referred to as the "absorption," or *klita*, of the Arab Jews. Upon arrival, they were "disinfected" with DDT and transported to crowded *ma'abarot* (transit camps) and later to remote Ayarot Pituah (development towns), border moshavim,[28] or newly evacuated Palestinian neighborhoods in urban centers, thereby creating a geography of ethnic segregation.

In her groundbreaking essay "Zionism from the Perspective of Its Jewish Victims," Shohat explains that the economic development of Israel was made possible through the transformation of Mizrahim in poor, segregated regions into a cheap, unskilled "industrial proletariat," a condition that led to ever-increasing socioeconomic gaps. Despite a façade of equality (central to the ethos of the early decades of Israel), the division of labor was also reproduced by means of a segregated and unequal educational system, inequitable immigration policies, and skewed government subsidies.[29] As a participant in the new Mizrahi discourse, Shohat analyzes this systemic discrimination against the Mizrahim as a function of the orientalist, colonialist, and Eurocentric premises inherent in the Zionist movement. The maltreatment of the Mizrahim derived from the basic binary relation between the self-perception of the Ashkenazim as modern, European, Western, and enlightened and their categorization of the Mizrahim as premodern, oriental, and backward. This binarism has been infused with normative connotations positioning Ashkenazi Israelis in a place of superiority. This sense of superiority authorized practices designed to "modernize," "de-Arabize," "resocialize," and "reeducate" Mizrahi Jews and transform them into "Israelis" (i.e., Ashkenazi Jews).[30] As indicated above, this reliance on the premises of colonialism and orientalism also enabled the Zionist colonization of Palestine in the prestate era and the later repressive and discriminatory treatment of Palestinians under the regime of the Israeli state.[31]

Focusing primarily on the case of Iraqi Jews, Shenhav unravels the links that connect the Palestinian expulsion in 1948 and the mass immigration of the Mizrahim to Israel. The connection between the two is encapsulated in the so-called population exchange theory. Accordingly, the expulsion of the Palestinians during the War of 1948 is supposedly balanced by the expulsions of the Arab Jews from their countries of origin. Developed already in the 1950s by the highest echelons of the Israeli administration, this theory used the property that the Arab Jews left behind in their countries of origin as a bargaining chip to counterbalance Palestinian claims for compensation, reparation, or return. This population exchange theory reflects how the Israeli government in effect neutralized the claims of Palestinians who became refugees in 1948 to their property that had been impounded by Israel's Custodian General of Absentee Property and the claims of Iraqi Jews for compensation for their property that had been frozen or confiscated by the Iraqi government in 1951. The underlying logic that enabled the Israeli government to equate the two sets of claims relied on basic Zionist presuppositions whereby the Jews of the "Orient," by virtue of being part of the Jewish people, were de facto naturalized as Israeli citizens and their property nationalized, preventing any possibility for individual compensation. This conflation of Jewish and Israeli identity was mirrored by the neutralization of the Palestinian national identity, subsuming it under the generic "Arab nation."[32]

The equation between the Arab refugees of 1948 and the Arab Jewish immigrants was thus grounded on a basic denial of a distinct Palestinian identity.[33] Iraqi-born Israeli diplomat and politician Shlomo Hillel astutely observed the implication of the "accounting" logic central to the population exchange theory. He argued that it is inconceivable that Palestinian nationals would accept that their claims for return and monetary compensation from Israel had already been settled with Iraq.[34] Nonetheless, the theory about a de facto population exchange has remained a bargaining chip in attempts to negotiate the right of the Palestinians to return to Palestine and their claims for material compensation for confiscated property. This argument was factored into former prime minister Menachem Begin's negotiation of the peace agreement with Egypt and into former U.S. president Bill Clinton's announcement in 2000 that Arab Jews should be considered "refugees."

Probing into the population and property exchange theses thus exposes the intricate links between the ethnic and domestic Mizrahi issue and the external Palestinian question, which have traditionally been kept distinct. Shenhav's study of the World Organization of Jews from Arab Countries (WOJAC) further exposes this problematic distinction. In 1974 the Israeli government outsourced the task of assimilating the Arab Jews into a unified Israeli national memory to the newly established WOJAC advocacy group. This group comprised many prominent Mizrahim with strong ties to the establishment. Shenhav's reading of WOJAC's archival trail, however, shows that in its attempt to substantiate the Zionist framework, WOJAC inadvertently challenged some of the central building blocks of Zionist memory, especially its separation between nationality and ethnicity and the teleological logic of Zionist historiography. Indeed, as an instrument of the government, WOJAC supported the population and property exchange theories. It also, however, emphasized the deep-rooted historical presence of Jews in the Middle East. These three basic arguments were designed to underscore the rights of the Jews to the land and to delegitimize the rights of Palestinians to repatriation and compensation. Yet these three political assertions in effect deconstructed some of the basic assumptions inherent in the Zionist ethos.[35]

First, the primordiality thesis that claims a continuous and flourishing Jewish presence in the Middle East thwarts the Zionists' rendering of the exilic period as a cultural void and an era of territorial and temporal discontinuity with the land. The primordial claim also offers an alternative to the dichotomization of Europe versus Zion and homeland versus diaspora. It thus challenges the central Zionist themes of both "negation of exile" and Jewish "return to history." It also posits an alternative historical interpretation that rejects the Zionist dichotomization of Jewishness versus Arabness. Second, the conversations that took place among the members of WOJAC concerning the theses of population and property exchange afforded an opportunity for some of the participants (especially non-Israeli Arab Jews) to voice their rejection of the nationalization of their interests and properties by the Israeli state and their demand to distinguish between Jewish and Israeli affairs. Such challenges also threatened the Zionist emphasis on the delicate differentiation between ethnic and national discourses. The claims of Israeli officials that the state's investment in the absorption of immigrants from Arab and Islamic countries entitled its nationalization of, and bargaining with, Jewish Arab property was criticized by some of the individuals who attended WOJAC gatherings as cynical and offensive, considering the historical discrimination against those same immigrants.

Shenhav finally argues that while officially attempting to maintain the basic Zionist compartmentalization of the national and ethnic discourses, WOJAC had difficulty preventing intra-Jewish "ethnic" aspects from surfacing in its discussions of "national" matters. The primordiality thesis, for example, suggested a Mizrahi claim to the land and thus implied the "strangeness" or "otherness" of the European presence therein. This potentially constitutes a reversal of their representation as the "near other" of the Euro-Zionist prototype (the "far other" being the non-Jewish Arab). Further, the symmetry that was created between the Palestinian and the Mizrahi refugee conditions introduces into the argument the history of the absorption of Mizrahim in Israel (e.g., their initial dwelling in refugee or transit camps). This parallelism once again exposes (even if inadvertently in the case of

WOJAC) the coherence between the ethnic and the national discussions and between the Palestinian and the Mizrahi narratives. Even though the Mizrahim who spearheaded WOJAC's activity aspired to be integrated into the hegemonic Zionist discourse, their internal discussions and divergence of opinions indicate an inability to articulate a coherent national identity without addressing the ethnic one.

In sum, WOJAC exemplifies the radical Mizrahi discourse's preoccupation with the paradoxes, inconsistencies, and power dynamics inherent in the Zionist construction of Mizrahi identity in Israel. Accordingly, the "Oriental Jew's" ethnicity is denied by classifying her primarily as a "Jew"—a classification that Shenhav calls "unification" and that has come to be synonymous with "nationality" (further reducing religion to a particular interpretation of the "nation").

The assimilation of the Mizrahi into the Euro-Zionist teleology and orientalist construal of the Israeli Jew as modern, European, and enlightened also posited her in a dichotomous relation with the Arab Palestinian, who is portrayed as a backward savage. This dichotomization, which construed "Arab" and "Jew" as antonyms, is likewise central to the conventional distinction between the "national" conflict with the Palestinians and the "ethnic" internal gap between Ashkenazim and Mizrahim. Interestingly, this practice of "unification" of Ashkenazim and Mizrahim is, Shenhav points out, countered by a conflicting practice of "othering." As a result, on one level, the unification depoliticizes and domesticates the "ethnicity" of the Mizrahim, thereby rendering it a "culture" and denying its potential political links to the broader Middle East, especially to Palestinians in and outside of Israel. Conversely, as can be inferred clearly from their absorption into the Israeli state and their continuous marginalization, the "othering" of the Mizrahim renders them inferior to the Euro-Zionists. Through the application of the same orientalist language used to delegitimize the Palestinians, the Arab identity of the Mizrahi has positioned her in an inferior societal location, as the "domestic other" of the Ashkenazi Israeli Jew. The radical Mizrahi discourse challenges the cultural dynamics and power relations that have enabled the marginalization of the Mizrahim in Israel. As shown below, this discussion entails reclaiming the Mizrahi past from the universalizing logic of Zionist teleology and exposing the systemic structures of discrimination and exploitation.

Like the Palestinian Israeli identity, the Mizrahi one emerged out of the Israeli nation-state and its logic of stratified citizenship. Indeed, not unlike the drafters of the Vision, the Mizrahim involved with the Keshet have come to recognize their complex linguistic, cultural, and historical connections to the broader Arab world as well as their defining experiences within the Israeli nation-state. Nonetheless, neither Palestinian Israeli nor Mizrahi identities can be reduced to the conditions from which they emerged. In other words, while their particular experiences of discrimination and oppression in Israel/Palestine have generated distinct and localized collective memories and narratives, the cultural, historical, religious, and linguistic memories of these groups transcend those experiences. These memories can function as an empowering resource for renegotiating the meaning of membership in Israel.

While Judith Butler and other non-Zionist Jewish critics locate the source of creative rethinking in the exilic and definitional condition of the Jew as a pariah (the principle of "nonbelonging"), Mizrahi rootedness in the Middle East could advance alternative modes of reframing the boundaries of the debate and the question of cohabitation in Israel/Palestine. Scholar of literature Ammiel Alcalay stresses the need for "mapping out a space in which the Jew *was* native, not a stranger but an absolute inhabitant of time and place."[36] Alcalay underscores the exclusion of Arab Jewish scholarly works and thought from the canons of world history produced in the "West" and the suppression of Mizrahi culture as a result of the dominance of Euro-Zionism. Alcalay discusses the theme of "reclaiming nativity" through an analysis of contemporary Jewish and non-Jewish Israeli poets. He gives the example of poet Tikva Levi, who writes: "every melody is colonized / by the West / Homeni alone / holds the breach / but at the same time / arms deals / with Israel and the US / flourish / as long as Iraqis die / there is joy and jubilation in the Land." Alcalay notes that "references to this war are startling for a contemporary Israeli work, in which the tendency is simply to ignore the surrounding world unless it is an immediate concern, as in the case of Lebanon. Levi places herself at a crucial junction: she is at once a neighbor, a person who clearly identifies herself as an Iraqi, and an involved political observer."[37] Another poet, Ronny Someck, writes "Jasmine. Poem on Sandpaper":

> Fairuz raises her lips
> to heaven
> to let jasmine rain down
> on those who once met
> without knowing they were in love.
> I'm listening to her in Muhammad's
> Fiat at noon on Ibn Gabirol St.
> A Lebanese singer playing in an Italian car

That belongs to an Arab poet
from Baqa' al-Gharbiyye on a street named
after a Hebrew poet who lived in Spain.
And the jasmine?
If it falls from the sky at the end of days
it'll stay green for
just a second at
the next light

Alcalay illuminates the seeming cacophony captured in the poem: "Here, earth and heaven intersect in the quotidian possibilities that have not yet been formalized but certainly exist: as Fairuz invokes heaven, Hebrew and Arab poets, riding an Italian car on a Mediterranean street named after an Arab-Jew, look to an earthly light, if it not only turns but stays green, would signal the coming of the Messiah and a time of peace on earth."[38]

Alcalay and the poets above attempt, therefore, to reclaim nativity, not through the invocation of biblical narratives, but rather through the celebration of the sounds, cultures, and histories of cohabitation and the cacophonies of colliding universes of symbols. They envision cohabitation on the basis of belonging to the Middle East. This belonging is local and historical (rather than mythical and metahistorical), born out of centuries of coexistence with non-Jewish Arabs. Reclaiming this nativity deconstructs the dominant Euro-Zionist presumption of Israel as a stranger in a hostile neighborhood. In the same way that the model of cohabitation advanced by Butler is born out of the principle of nonbelonging, drawing on Edward Said's call to connect Palestinians and Israelis on the level of the historical experiences of alterity and dispersal (see especially chapter 5), this model of cohabitation revolves around reclaiming nativity, a process that demands deconstructing the orientalist undertones of the Zionist discourse. In both instances, however, what is at stake is the denaturalizing of Zionist historiography and homogenizing narrative. This focus on denaturalizing the logic of Euro-Zionism is also at the heart of Mizrahi activism in Israel.

The activism of Mizrahim in Israel aims to reclaim Mizrahi culture and history. It could potentially enable a reimagining of Israeli identity as Levantine rather than European. The process of retrieving rootedness in the region can facilitate new creative possibilities. Notably, this approach is different than the Canaanite doctrine, which highlights native rootedness over European and diasporic strangeness. Certainly, the primordial thesis also constitutes a critical aspect of the ideology of the Canaanite movement. This movement is an early example of an attempt not only to disentangle Judaism as a source of legitimacy from the state in Palestine, but also to generate an alternative symbolic formation of the meaning of citizenship.

Comprising intellectuals and artists, "Canaanism" emerged in the late 1940s and early 1950s under the leadership of the poet Yonatan Ratosh (1909–81). The Canaanite movement advanced a non-Zionist Hebraic conception of the nation. It advocated severing all ties with Judaism and the Jewish diasporas in favor of constructing a native Palestinian Hebraic identity. Indeed, the model advanced by the Canaanites reimagined the nation's legitimacy along local territorial parameters, but it nonetheless sought to establish a regional Hebraic supremacy—an obviously problematic vision. The point of contention between this movement and political Zionism was that the latter's initial intent to free itself from the Jewish diasporas was never realized. Thus, Ratosh and the Canaanites rearticulated Zionism's new Hebrew as a native Palestinian who bears no connection to Judaism and Jewish memory. The Hebrews of the Canaanites constituted a nation through their local ties to territory and language.[39]

On many levels, the Canaanites took Zionism's ethos of the "negation of exile" to its logical conclusions, conceptually solving some of the underlying inconsistencies between the notion of return as a liberation from the distortion of Hebraism in diasporic Jewish religiosity and the increased reliance on Judaism and Jewish imaginings for the consolidation of national consciousness and legitimacy. The Mizrahi reclaiming of Arabness and native connections to the Middle East does not entail a rejection of Judaism. In fact, Judaism, as Shas leaders point out, is as much Middle Eastern as it is Ashkenazi and diasporic.

The History of Mizrahi Protest in Israel

Mass Mizrahi protest first reached the Israeli mainstream in the "Upset of 1977," which marked the victory of the Likud Party over the Labor Party.[40] This electoral upset was made possible by the overwhelming support of the Mizrahim. A general dismantling of central Euro-Zionist myths contributed to the Mizrahim's ability to resist the overpowering hold of MAPAI. First, the Yom Kippur War, which was widely perceived by Israelis as a complete political and military fiasco, punctured the prevalent dichotomization drawn between the "few smart European Jews" and the "millions of backward Arabs." Second, a series of exposés of political corruption in the upper echelons shattered the myth of "solidarity and socialism" central to the Labor Party. Third, the protest of the Black Panthers (discussed below) revealed, and articulated in the form of mass protest, the hypocrisy of the

myths of the "ingathering of the exiles" and "melting pot," which had operated under the pretense of attaining integration and social equality.

By flocking to Likud, however, the Mizrahim aligned themselves with an
ethnonational agenda that contributed to their classification as "Arab hat-
ers," a classification indicative of a "self-hatred" that had developed during
the decades of Ashkenazi hegemony[41] as an upshot of the conflicting practices of unification and othering discussed above. Nevertheless, the expecta-
tions that Likud would effect a radical shift away from discriminating Labor
practices proved delusional. Despite its populist appeal, Likud retained the
basic structures of Ashkenazi hegemony, and by the late 1990s both parties
had become aligned with neoliberal ideologies. Despite coming to power
with the promise to significantly alleviate and reform the socioeconomic
conditions of the Mizrahim, Likud made a series of economic decisions that
ultimately facilitated the total erosion of the social state in the 1990s and
the perpetuation of the marginality of Mizrahi sectors.[42]

Established in 1981 by Aharon Abuhatzeira, the short-lived TAMI (the
Hebrew acronym for the "Movement for Jewish Tradition") attracted a wide
cross-section of Mizrahi society but fell short of advancing an alternative to
the Ashkenazi hegemony that it had rejected.[43] As the first independent Mizrahi party, TAMI represented a radical step. But, as some commentators suggest, TAMI's ideological ambivalence, fluctuating between an outcry against
socioeconomic inequality and a reluctance to embrace Mizrahi identity,
may have caused its rapid disappearance by 1984 in a time of increased
Mizrahi electoral protest.[44]

Out of this context, the Shas Party emerged in 1983 as an explicit response and challenge to the secular Ashkenazi Zionist hegemony. Especially after ridding itself of the tutelage of the Lithuanian chief rabbi Eliezer
Shach in 1988 and instituting Rabbi Ovadia Yosef as the undisputed spiritual leader of the movement, Shas increasingly grounded its political protest in the call to redress the social and economic inequality experienced by
the Mizrahim. Unlike TAMI, Shas advanced an unequivocal position and
thus has been perceived as the first Mizrahi independent political alternative. Its leadership has insisted that regardless of political orientations such
as "right" or "left," the secular Ashkenazi political infrastructure is to be
blamed for the inferior socioeconomic status of Mizrahim in Israel. In a
similar vein, Shas has attributed the abandonment of tradition and religion
to the same hegemonic scheme. Therefore, under the banner *Lehahazir Atara
LeYoshna* (literally: "To Return Glory to Its Rightful Place"), Shas has worked
toward reclaiming the glory and dominance of the Sephardic mode of interpreting Jewish texts and practices.[45]

Despite the wide influence of Shas's social and political activities, Chetrit explains, it has remained predominately a religious movement. Regardless of its highly developed awareness of Mizrahi concerns and its appeal to an alternative religious framework of interpretation, Shas has not provided an alternative social ideology that would accommodate the non-Haredi Mizrahim who are attracted to its form of social protest.[46] For the Shas Party to represent a genuine alternative to the dominant system, it would need to broaden its scope and democratize its practices. Chetrit concludes:

> How many steps beyond the synagogue will Shas be willing to take? Can it separate its political branch offices from the synagogue? Conversely, how many steps will Shas's secular voters be prepared to take in the direction of the synagogue and even into it? What is the ideal midpoint, and is it feasible in Israeli political reality? If such questions are not satisfactorily resolved, a new Mizrahi movement, social in its goals and democratic in structure, could well arise . . . precisely at that midpoint.[47]

In addition to locating a novel balance between religious, social, and political objectives, it would also be necessary to challenge Shas's ethnocentric focus, which is self-limiting. Transcending ethnocentrism would enable it (or any other political force) to link Mizrahi grievances against the Ashkenazim to those of the Palestinians (although the Palestinian condition is much more dire).

The radical Mizrahi discourse recognizes and explores this connection. However, to anticipate my conclusions in part 3, while this discourse has challenged the Eurocentric and orientalist dimensions of Zionist claims, it has retained a rather uncritical approach to the strict separation of religion and state called for by Israeli secularity. This modernist approach, I have argued, overlooks the importance of articulating the complex relation between religion and nation. Instead, even the radical Mizrahi discourse presumes that the "state" functions optimally as a neutral institution with respect to religion and culture. This presumption neglects asking what conceptions of the "nation" legitimate the "state." What is the place of Judaism in the envisioned definition of Israeliness? To this extent, the Mizrahi discourse falls into the same conceptual traps that prevent the Vision from moving beyond critique to reimagining the symbolic boundaries of Israeli national identity.

As highlighted by Shohat, the compartmentalization of the "ethnic" and "Palestinian" problems overlooks "the mutual implication of the two issues and their common relation to Ashkenazi domination."[48] Indeed, the new radical Mizrahi discourse as represented in the Keshet recognizes the relevance of the Ashkenazi hegemony and thus challenges the liberal compartmentalization of the two matters. While "new," this discourse should be understood as a chapter in the history of radical Mizrahi protest in Israel dating back to the formation of the Black Panthers (BP). Indeed, because the BP came into being through a conversation with the radical anti-Zionist groups of Matzpen and Siah, the connection between the struggles of the Palestinians and the Mizrahim had already been evident to its leaders in the early 1970s.[49] The Marxist Matzpen group, for example, explicitly stated in its fundamental principles the importance of integrating the struggle of the Mizrahim and the Palestinians as part of a broader internationalist revolutionary struggle for justice and equality.[50] Likewise, the BP embodied a radical social critique that, if taken to its logical conclusions, illuminated the interconnections between various sites of injustice.

The BP was born in the Jerusalem neighborhood of Musrara. Against the backdrop of repeatedly preferential treatment of European immigrants and the deplorable conditions of Mizrahi slums, the BP emerged, by the end of the 1960s, as a forceful protest movement.[51] Its first massive demonstration in March of 1971 mobilized in response to the government's decision to demolish and transform an old Palestinian neighborhood into a luxury district for new Ashkenazi immigrants. Drawing substantial popular support and spreading to other slums, demonstrations continued into the following year, with the demonstrators demanding fundamental socioeconomic reforms and the immediate redressing of Mizrahi conditions.[52]

The government, as in the case of its response to earlier mass outbursts, attempted to delegitimize the BP by offering individual solutions, stigmatizing its activists as criminals, and underscoring the movement's connection to the anti-Zionist left.[53] Nevertheless, certain attempts were made to inquire into the grievances raised by the BP. However, the diminishing ability to generate mass demonstrations, the failure of the newly established "Black Panthers–Israeli Democrats" to pass the electoral threshold following the 1973 war, and the subsequent internal splintering of the group all marginalized the Mizrahi struggle. A scholar of modern Arab politics, Joseph Massad, adds that the BP's inability to sustain the intensity of the protest may also be attributed to its lack of an economic base. Further, because they were anchored to the urban slums, the BP was far removed from the majority of Mizrahim, who resided in development towns and moshavim.[54]

The most critical obstacle, however, was the Ashkenazi hegemony that dominated all aspects of political, social, cultural, and economic life in Israel. In joining Maki (the Israeli Communist Party), Charlie Biton, one of the key figures of the BP, later demonstrated that the Arab Jewish Mizrahi identity could not be subsumed under the Euro-Zionist framework.[55] Regardless of its limited success and short-lived tenure as a mass protest movement, the BP has had a lasting influence. Its protests articulated for the first time the self-consciousness of a common Mizrahi experience and identity, an awareness that has paved the road for later political activism and demands for cultural rights by groups such as Ohalim (Tents) and HILA (The Israel Committee for Equality in Education).[56] The Keshet would continue pursuing the educational and cultural agenda of Kedma and HILA. "The importance of the movement," Chetrit concludes, "was that it broke the dam of silence, triggering an irreversible process of radicalizing Mizrahi political consciousness that would, by the early 1990s, mature into a movement of critique and proposed alternatives."[57]

It is thus important to situate the Keshet and the new Mizrahi discourse in this tradition of radical Mizrahi protest and to recognize the crucial place occupied by the BP in this trajectory. The name "Black Panthers" was chosen in order to underscore the links between the struggles of African Americans in the United States and Palestinians in Israel/Palestine.[58] It was the BP that was able, for the first time, to draw analogies to other revolutionary struggles around the world. Yet despite the radical nature of its protest, the BP engaged in what Chetrit calls "naïve protest." Its activists focused their attention on "material discrimination" and neglected developing an alternative *interpretation* of Israeli society. This naïve protest may also be attributed to the neutralization and cooptation of Mizrahi intellectuals (a familiar colonial practice) by the Zionist establishment, thereby inhibiting the possibility of imagining alternative outlooks. In fact, it seemed almost impossible to imagine alternatives "because on the surface there was no subjection or oppression, but rather the 'ingathering of exiles' of 'a single nation' with 'a single religion,' 'a single history,' and therefore a 'single fate.'"[59] In order to articulate a more "mature protest," one needed to challenge those axiomatic premises of the Zionist discourse. Once again, Shohat's statement in this regard is discerning because she underscores the need to articulate the connections between Palestinian and Mizrahi histories through exposition of how they are told and studied in reference to the Zionist narrative and practices of unification and othering. She writes:

> What is desperately needed for critical scholars is a de-Zionized decoding of the peculiar history of Mizrahim, one closely articulated with Palestinian history. Rather than segregate Palestinian and Mizrahi histories as two unrelated events, we must see their intricate links. This conceptualization does not see

the Mizrahi question as simply internal to the study of Israel (as though outside of the question of Arab nationalism) or without implication for the question of Palestine. Making such links serves to 're-orient' the debate, bringing
together two absolutely crucial currents of critique within a multiperspectival
analysis.[60]

The BP's recognition of the link between Palestinian and Mizrahi grievances reverberated in public manifestations of solidarity with the Palestinians in the 1980s. Mizrahim formed a large contingent of the Committee
for Israeli-Palestinian Dialogue (established in 1986). Despite the Counter-
Terrorism Act, issued to prevent Israeli contact with the PLO, the Dialogue
Committee conducted meetings with PLO officials in Romania and Buda-
pest in 1986 and 1987, respectively. These meetings initiated a Mizrahi-
Palestinian dialogue, which was marked by a meeting in Toledo, Spain,
in 1989. This meeting was attended by a considerable number of Mizrahi
intellectuals and key figures from the Palestinian side, including the future
Palestinian president Mahmoud Abbas and the Palestinian poet Mahmoud
Darwish.[61] These meetings already indicated the emergence of the new radical Mizrahi discourse, which had attempted to challenge the central taboos
undergirding Israeli society. The Palestinian-Mizrahi conferences signified
a conscious move away from the internalized self-hatred and official Zionist construal of the "Arab" and the "Jew" as antonyms. This march toward
self-assertion and reclamation of the Arab dimensions of Mizrahi identity
and history also entailed recognizing the links between the Mizrahi and
Palestinian predicaments. It has evolved into a stream of resistance known
as the Keshet.

II. The Keshet

The Keshet was established in 1996 by a group of second- and third-generation
Mizrahim. Its membership consists of a variety of professionals, including
academics, artists, educators, business people, and journalists who have
endeavored to articulate a new radical Mizrahi discourse and to generate
momentum for mass organizing. As explained by Moshe Krif (the first
spokesperson of the movement), despite their own individual success and
established status, those who became involved with the movement aspired
to transform the public discourse that has relegated the Mizrahim to a marginalized position in Israeli society and mounted structural and ideological
obstacles to any form of Mizrahi socioeconomic, political, and cultural mobility. They have thus called for nothing short of systemic change.[62] The or-

ganization consequently defines itself as "an apolitical, non-parliamentary social movement whose goal is to affect the current public agenda in the aim of bringing a change into Israeli society as a whole and to its institutions."[63] The Keshet underscores its identity as Mizrahi in its objectives and as universal in its underlying values. It is committed to advancing its principles and transformative goals through the necessary democratic channels. Those principles and goals include the advancement of social justice, the respect for human rights, and the cultivation of multicultural frameworks of engagement within Israel. Its activities concentrate mainly on the just distribution of land use, unemployment, education, and coalition building.

Consistent with the new radical Mizrahi discourse, the Keshet is engaged in a variety of cultural activities designed to raise consciousness in the broader Israeli society and empower the Mizrahim and other marginalized sectors to question the dominant discourses and to regain agency. One example was the Mizrahi Jewish and Arab Visual Art project (2004–5), which highlighted the common aspects of their cultures and backgrounds. This traveling exhibition of Arab and Mizrahi art also intended to raise awareness not only of the common cultural and regional background of Mizrahim and non-Jewish Arabs but also of their common experiences of discrimination. The Keshet also employs other forms of consciousness-raising, such as holding discussions, lectures, and conferences in order to study different aspects of Israeli society and questions of social justice.[64] The radical Mizrahi discourse as articulated by the Keshet challenges the Zionist paradigm by reclaiming Mizrahi history and the Arab dimensions of its identity.

Another important area of activity of the movement has revolved around land struggles, including public housing and the implementation of standards for equitable distribution of land. The privatization and liberalization trends of the 1990s were translated into the rezoning of agricultural lands affiliated with the kibbutzim and moshavim. The projected astronomical monetary profit yielded from this undertaking was designed to exclusively benefit the kibbutzim and moshavim in question. Here the Keshet demanded that past injustices committed against the Mizrahim be corrected and that the need to operate according to the principles of distributive justice be recognized. Its activists contended in no uncertain terms that the rezoning arrangement pushed by the strong agricultural lobby would perpetrate the socioeconomic inequality inherent in the Israeli system. It would benefit primarily the Ashkenazi middle class whose presence on the properties under consideration already reflects the history of preferential treatment by the Zionist establishment and absorption practices. Once again, an entire segment of the population, the Mizrahi blue-collar class in the urban slums and development towns, is unaware of the ongoing, officially sanctioned robbery of their real estate.[65] The Keshet thus linked its critique of the historical, inequitable distribution of land and the systemic maldistribution of resources to its concrete struggle for legislation in support of public housing rights.

Following in the footsteps of earlier initiatives and organizing (HILA and Kedma, specifically), the Keshet's struggle for social justice and equality also focuses on the Israeli educational system. In particular, the Keshet has attempted to expose the institutionalized "vocational track" as an instrument for perpetuating the poverty and marginality of the Mizrahi sector. The vocational track constitutes another structural obstruction blocking the possibility of social and economic mobility.[66] Among other areas of educational policy, the Keshet has also resisted cutbacks and privatization of the educational system, a trend symptomatic of the official embrace of the neoliberal framework, regardless of political affiliation. Furthermore, the Keshet has engaged in a variety of coalitions advancing such questions as inequalities in education and cultural representation.[67]

The Keshet has subsequently advanced the inclusion of Mizrahi issues in school curriculum. In 2003, it achieved minor success when the Knesset decided to officially incorporate two chapters on Jewish oriental history into the mandatory matriculation exam in the subject.[68] Yet this success is still very limited because, as noted by Shenhav, the representation of the history of the Jews from Arab and Islamic countries in textbooks is saturated with distortions and inaccuracies. In particular, the description of the sufferings and discrimination experienced by Jews in Islamic and Arab countries is misleading, ideological, and indicative of the problematic logic of Zionist teleology.

Indeed, these textbooks are designed to subsume the histories of the various Jewish diasporas in the chronology of the Zionist movement. In other words, the Jewish communities come to light in these history books only insofar and when their paths intersect with Zionism. Clearly, Mizrahi Jews cannot be featured in this storyline since Zionism originated as a European movement. Hence, Zionist historiography diminishes the history of the Arab Jews, especially since the latter have not experienced the same intensity of pogroms and sufferings as the European Jewish communities have. Likewise, the political history of the Mizrahim is absent from the curriculum. An exploration and a reclaiming of this history would expose the underlying premises and discriminatory practices of Zionism.[69]

Without a doubt, because it identifies Ashkenazi hegemonic claims as the source of the problem, the Keshet implies a radical form of protest that may result in an alternative understanding of membership in Israel and thus in a reassessment of questions of peace and justice relevant to the Israeli-Palestinian conflict. However, while echoing the work of earlier radical movements, most notably the BP, radical Mizrahi protest is still a marginalized phenomenon. The Forum for the Study of Society and Culture under the auspices of the Van Leer Jerusalem Institute in Jerusalem understands the Keshet as working to deconstruct the dominant perception along with the academic construal of the Mizrahim as primitive and underdeveloped or as an obstacle for peace. The former characterization is attributed chronologically to the first generation of the 1950s and the 1960s when the modernization and melting pot theories determined both the production of knowledge about the Mizrahim and the formulation of discriminating and humiliating political and social practices.[70]

The rendering of the Mizrahim as an impediment to peace derives from the emergence in the 1990s of the already-alluded-to liberal post-Zionist thread of analysis that views the Mizrahi as ethnocentric and militant. Just as in the earlier application of the modernization paradigm, the Mizrahi is interpreted in opposition to the developed, enlightened, secular, and peace-seeking liberal Ashkenazi. Drawing on the insights of postcolonial theories and conceptions of multiculturalism, theoretical works reflective of the "radical Mizrahi discourse," however, have been able to advance a critique of the dominant modes of interpretation and representation of the Mizrahim in Israeli society. Chetrit contends that only through a radical restructuring of the ideological and institutional apparatuses of the Ashkenazi establishment would it be possible for an authentic Mizrahi protest to materialize and gain momentum. He thus concludes:

> What is clear is that the Mizrahim will not aspire to become a political collective as long as they identify and cooperate within the paradigm of Ashkenazi Zionism. This paradigm is broad enough to create the illusion that it can encompass everything: Right/Left, peace camp/nationalist camp, religious/secular, Israeli-born/new immigrants, and a multiplicity of political views. The Mizrahim are invited to integrate themselves into this paradigm and "be like everyone else." But in fact, the basic social infrastructures of the economy and capital, of education and culture still serve mainly the Ashkenazi collective, with all of its divisions and political camps.[71]

In short, a defining aspect of the radical Mizrahi discourse entails a conscious confrontation of the homogenizing Euro-Zionist paradigm. In order to become political and to effect systemic change, Chetrit argues, the

Mizrahim need to challenge the Euro-Zionist dominance over the parameters of acceptable public conversation concerning the normative meaning of membership in Israel. Challenging the unifying and universalizing Zionist teleology in this way necessitates the reclaiming of one's agency and history.

In many respects, the Mizrahim are in a better location than Palestinian Israelis in that, beyond the critique they embody, their Jewish identity and thus normative positionality within the Israeli framework (despite their marginality) can offer constructive Jewish reinterpretations of Israeli citizenship. Those alternatives need not rely on a supposedly external mechanism that will nullify domineering impulses through secularist practices or theological tracts. Nor can the rethinking of a Jewish Israeli identity as the upshot of an intra-Jewish conversation be misunderstood as a zero-sum game as has been the usual reception of the Vision by Jewish Israelis. The Mizrahi critique and reclaiming cannot be domesticated and pacified through the language of minority rights. Such a critique, instead, calls for a fundamental reimagining of Jewish Israeli history. A hermeneutics that deconstructs the basic premises of who we are could, in turn, drastically affect the broader justice discourse as it pertains to the Palestinians in the occupied territories.

III. Analysis: The Keshet and the Prospect of Justpeace

Deploying a postcolonial deconstructive framework of analysis, the radical discourse of the Mizrahim as represented most recently by the Keshet contributes to dispelling the binary logic of Zionism that rendered Jewish Arabness oxymoronic through the practice of othering.[72] The representation of the Arab as the "enemy" by construing her as analogous to the Nazi,[73] as well as the self-perception of Israel as "Western," further delegitimated the Middle Eastern and Arab dimensions of Mizrahi identity. "Arab Jews were urged to see Judaism and Zionism as synonyms, and Jewishness and Arabness as antonyms."[74] Shenhav notes that by construing the Galut (i.e., the diaspora) as an undifferentiated metacategory, the Euro-Zionist master narrative collected the diverse sites of diasporic memories into one hegemonic and overarching teleological national memory.[75] Because the shaping of a collective national memory involved the creation of a territorial consciousness, the ancient presence and sovereignty of the Jewish people in the Land of Israel was celebrated, commemorated, and longed for as the objective of the Zionist movement. In contrast, the diasporic era was portrayed "as a lacuna, a dark interim space bereft of political sovereignty and therefore a time to be forgotten."[76]

This Zionist theme of the negation of exile[77] enabled the cultivation of the two motifs of the Jewish people as continuously existing in this diasporic void and as constituting "one people" who persistently yearned for the return to Zion. Hence, "the existence of the void," Shenhav continues, "enabled a single historiographic narrative line to be stretched from the ancient to the modern era. Upon its establishment, the state of Israel expropriated the multiple exilic memories of its citizens and recast them as the national memory."[78] That the *farhoud* (the anti-Jewish riot in Iraq that broke out in June 1941) was assimilated into the twin Zionist narratives of the negation of exile and the history of the Jews as a series of persecutions exemplified this point. Zionist historiography about the *farhoud* subsumed this one isolated event into the narrative of "Shoah and Awakening," thereby expunging and dismissing the long and rich history of Iraqi Jews in Iraq.[79]

Reimagining the national ethos therefore would involve retrieving the eclipsed histories, cultures, and languages of the diasporas and deciphering the links between Euro-Zionist cultural hegemony and its enduring discriminating practices. These connections are underscored in the above analysis of Mizrahi representation in Israeli textbooks. They are also reflected centrally in Yossi Yonah and Shenhav's articulation of multiculturalism as it may pertain to the case of Israel.[80] In their *What Is Multiculturalism? The Politics of Difference in Israel*, these two authors argue that it is impossible to understand the political and economic inequality among the different groups in a given society without scrutinizing the role of national ethos and culture in generating this inequality. Accordingly, a successful struggle for socioeconomic equality and distributive justice cannot be disconnected from a struggle for cultural recognition. In the case of Israel, such an effort would involve understanding an Israeli ethnorepublican type of nationalism. Subsequently, Yonah and Shenhav—both active in the Keshet—introduce Nancy Fraser's program of multiculturalism, which insists that the cultural identities of marginalized groups struggling for political, civic, and economic rights be respected.[81] Indeed, the Keshet's range of activities, including housing and land issues as well as education policies, is consistent with Fraser's elucidation of the connection between misrecognition and maldistribution.[82]

However, as I have argued repeatedly throughout this book, this insight that the multicultural struggle involves deconstructing the national ethos and reconfiguring the power structures needs to be supplemented with a reimagining of the intricate relation between "religion" and "nation" through the hermeneutics of citizenship. This is especially urgent in contexts defined by ethnoreligious and national collective entitlements. Therein, nationalism, understood as a theory of political legitimacy and as a political theology, draws selectively on religion to justify exclusive and/or repressive state policies.[83] In other words, the polycentric model of multiculturalism, anchored in the task of deconstructing the Zionist ethos, overlooks the significant role religion may play in reimagining the meaning of membership in Israel. In this particular application, but also more broadly, this model (which stresses the political and historical contingencies involved in the formation of collective identities) indeed de-essentializes and defamiliarizes reified representations of the "nation" and thus may offer tools for undertaking self-assessment. Rethinking what is essential to one's identity could result in reevaluating what might be negotiable in the broader conflict with the Palestinians.

Still, de-essentializing the Zionist master narrative through an articulation of the voices and histories of the Mizrahim is not sufficient. Deconstructing historiographies needs to be expanded to incorporate a constructive engagement with the relationship between Judaism and Israeli citizenship. Such an engagement would entail not only a challenge to the political practices of Euro-Zionism and to its monopoly over Jewish history but also an attempt to reimagine the nexus of religion, nationality, and ethnicity in Israel and throughout Jewish communities around the world. By underscoring the Mizrahi experience of marginality as well as Mizrahi approaches to the multiple traditions and histories of Judaism, such an exploration may offer an alternative to the ambiguous secularism and concomitant political theology informing the Israeli liberal left as represented by Meretz or PN.[84] It would also challenge the monopoly of Shas over the religious aspects of Mizrahi identity in Israel.

Therefore, the next section explores the advantages and limitations of the polycentric model of multiculturalism in its application to this context. I ask to what degree this model is consistent with the criteria set forth in this book for thinking about peace and justice in zones of ethnoreligious national conflicts and to what extent it complements the cohabitation model discussed in chapter 5.

The Polycentric Framework

Yonah and Shenhav advance a polycentric understanding of multiculturalism that emphasizes the deconstructive turn necessary to articulate a counterhegemonic protest and program of action. However, they stress that postcolonial and postmodern critical modes of analysis may also enable the formulation of reconstructive proposals, such as the establishment of a binational state or the granting of cultural and national collective rights to the Palestinian citizens of Israel.[85] Accordingly, in this Israeli version of polycentrism, multiculturalism is transformative because it negates an essentializing view of identities that may reinforce and reproduce rather than challenge and correct the basic structures of inequality. While agreeing with Fraser's position on multiculturalism, these authors insist that, owing to the essential illiberality of the nation-state, the demand for civic equality would necessitate a radical transformation of the common thread that would optimally link different groups together within the political framework. In Israel, such a process would focus on a scrutiny of Zionist hegemony and its policies toward the Palestinians and the Mizrahim. This hegemony may be challenged through reforms in education policy and in the principles guiding the redistribution of resources.

Hence, this polycentric multicultural position aspires to expose the cultural premises that inform and legitimate discriminatory and repressive political practices and invoke cultural difference as a tool for political empowerment. However, it also draws a distinction between sectoral and multicultural struggles. In sectoral struggle, groups such as Shas and Shinui fail to form broad coalitions with other groups within the society and thus operate only to advance their own particularistic interests. In multicultural struggle, a group like the Keshet acknowledges the universal values of distributive justice and seeks to build alliances with other groups subject to similar economic and cultural repression and discrimination.[86] Indeed, the positions and activities of the Keshet, as illustrated above, exemplify this insight and the aspiration not only to reform the principles of redistribution but also to radically transform the basic structures and premises that enable the reproduction of the structures of control and exploitation.

While underscoring the centrality of the principles of social justice and the overarching re-envisioning of the socioeconomic political order as integral to identity politics in Israel, Yonah and Shenhav criticize essentializing communitarian accounts that portray collective identities as fixed entities. Instead, the authors emphasize the fluid or arbitrary character of the emergence and reproduction of those identities. This historicized view of collective formulations of identity leads Yonah and Shenhav to qualify their support for the respective rights of self-determination of Jews and Palestinians. Echoing the model of cohabitation, historicizing through "remembrance" of the interrelated tragedies of the Palestinian Israelis and the Mizrahim problematizes the homogenizing and seemingly axiomatic

renderings of these identities as well as the perception of the two-state solution as the most just. Perceptions both of fixed uncontested identities and
of the justness of a separationist peace agenda are products of historical
and circumstantial dynamics. A shift away from the historical determinism
and primordialist claims prevalent in nationalist rhetoric and its representation of the "nation" as an ahistorical truth makes it possible to reimagine
and redefine these identities in a way that would overcome the separationist
impulse of the "two states for two nations" solution.

For this reason, even if such a reconceptualization seems farfetched at
the moment, the contextualization of collective notions of identity could
challenge and nuance essentialist claims and the historical determinism
that has marked nationalist discourse. In fact, Shenhav and Yonah support
a polycentric multicultural interpretation of the proposal for reinstituting
Israel as a liberal democracy and a state for all its citizens. Such a formulation means that while Israeli Jews retain their right of self-determination
and their understanding of Israel as their national home, this right cannot
be interpreted in exclusivist terms. Such an understanding, in short, does
not necessarily conflict with the possibility of transforming Israel into a
binational state with institutional recognition of cultural differences within
its own society.[87]

In his later work *The Time of the Green Line*, Shenhav, as I discussed in
previous chapters, illuminates the limitations of a one-state solution. Especially, he suggests that reframing the geopolitical space of Israel/Palestine as
"a state of all its citizens" could lock Jews and non-Jews in a demographic
race. Instead, he proposes an alternative consociational model of loosely
threaded independent cantons. In this work, Shenhav challenges the 1967
paradigm that defines most of the discussions of peace within the so-called
liberal Israeli left. He contends that the liberal longing to relinquish the
legacy of the occupation of 1967 is grounded not only in a fear of being
overwhelmed by non-Jews, corrupting the possibility of a Jewish democracy
but also in a fear that Israel will become a Mizrahi-majority and increasingly
religious society. It is a form of "nostalgia" for the "good old days" of Euro-
Zionism.[88] It reflects a clinging to a self-perception of Jewish Israelis as accidental guests in the heart of the Arab world. The ties that connect the "left" to
this Middle Eastern land are mythical (biblical), even if read as "historical"
(see chapter 1, especially). Israeli polycentrism challenges the Eurocentricity
of the liberal left but does not engage hermeneutically the political theology
enabling *being in* without *becoming of* the Middle East. I identified a similar
limitation in the model of cohabitation in which reframing ethical inter-

relations between Jews and non-Jews is not context dependent. While the push toward reframing requires a historicist maneuver (a "remembering" of the defining amnesias of a national project), the political constellation Butler imagines in Israel/Palestine is decontextualized. It could have described ethical relations of Jews and non-Jews in Warsaw as well as Jerusalem. Israeli polycentrism is highly contextualized, perhaps even to a fault. I explain this point further in the next section. At this juncture, however, it suffices to underscore that Mizrahi polycentrism complements the conceptual model of cohabitation in that it draws on the experience of nonbelonging in order to reimagine a national identity or solidarity rather than eliminate collective passions and loyalties. To combat the mythology of mainstream Zionism—the political theology that enables Euro-Zionists to be in the Middle East without belonging to it—the Mizrahi discourse focuses on reclaiming its integral belonging to the historical and cultural landscapes of the region. In the remainder of this section, I explicate where Mizrahi polycentrism works effectively in challenging and in reframing hegemonic interpretations of Jewish Israeli identity.

For Israeli polycentrists, any effort to reimagine national identity would involve the historically sensitive recognition of the power relations undergirding the formation and transformation of identities. The transformative framework of multiculturalism, in the Israeli context, would indeed enable the deconstruction of the relationship between the metanarrative of the dominant group and the systematic discrimination against groups that fall outside the normative scope of this narrative. Therefore, Mizrahi polycentrists conclude that identity politics may provide an effective tool of protest against discrimination and oppression when utilized by subjugated and marginalized groups.[89]

To a significant degree, this approach to identity politics has informed the positions and activities of the Keshet. It is deployed as an instrument for rediscovering one's roots and for uncovering the systems of injustice integral to the making and remaking of the dominant normative conception of the "nation." Indebted to the postmodern and postcolonial turn, in the case of Israel, these processes of rediscovery amount to the deconstruction of the basic binaries underlying the dominant structures of control. Here I refer to the dichotomies of Arab versus Jew, secular versus religious, Ashkenazi versus Mizrahi, and so forth. The effort of the radical Mizrahi discourse to provoke an alternative conversation involves an exercise in historical imagination in which counterfactuality is employed in order to resist the logic of historical determinism inherent in Zionist historiography (teleology) and its long-term systemic consequences.[90] Here, an agonistic resistance to the presupposition of a "natural" and "fixed" prepolitical "we" may become a constructive and perhaps even transformative orientation (see also chapter 2).

Indeed, the polycentric framework of multiculturalism reflected in the activities and platforms of the Keshet conceptually corresponds with Pierre Allan and Alexis Keller's notion of "thick recognition," which is a necessary step in outlining a framework for a just peace (see chapter 2). It involves a recognition of the other's humanity and particular identity as well as an introspective look at one's own identity. National identities are plastic and changeable, Allan and Keller argue. Accordingly, effective negotiations may result in "the discovery that accommodation of the other's identity need not destroy the core of the group's own identity."[91]

This position is consistent with the polycentric view of multiculturalism in Israel that introspects and deconstructs the definition of the "nation" as construed by the hegemonic Zionist patterns of unification and othering. The polycentric approach is in accordance with the demand for thick recognition in that it too insists on accepting and respecting the other's identity without relinquishing one's own; indeed, it highlights the contextuality of such formations.

Thick recognition and the polycentric approach to multiculturalism both rely on a conscious effort to de-essentialize the conceptions of the "self" as reified in nationalist rhetoric. To this extent, they are consistent with the call for reclaiming the alterity pivotal for the model of cohabitation. While Allan and Keller do not specify how to approach this demand for reimagining the national self, Mizrahi polycentrism utilizes the theoretical tools developed by postcolonial and postmodern critical thought in facilitating the de-essentialization of the national ethos. Their analysis substantiates my insistence on the critical role that subaltern groups or the "domestic others" (such as the Mizrahim or the Palestinian citizens of Israel) play in deconstructing the national ethos and the underlying discriminating and repressive state practices.[92] The application of postcolonial and postmodern interpretive frameworks thus shows the relevance of analyzing power structures to the process of thick recognition. The histories and experiences of the subaltern not only challenge the coherence of the dominant discourse but also may offer alternative modes for imagining the "nation." Subsequently, reimagined conceptions of the "nation" may facilitate reframing the broader Israeli-Palestinian conflict. Hence, as discussed above, the polycentric multicultural model could signal a departure from a two-state solution and an eventual embrace of a more integrative political arrangement and even a consociational democratic framework that moves beyond the axioms of Westphalian logic and beyond the fallacies of Israeli liberalism.[93]

The Missing Dimensions of the Polycentric Multicultural Model

Notwithstanding the transformative potential of the polycentric model of multiculturalism, two general aspects of this approach need to be further developed for evaluating visions of peace and justice. The first relates to the problem of building broad coalitions across national and spatial divides, despite theoretical recognition of the connection between "domestic" and "foreign" in instances of injustice. In addition to recognizing the power variable and the importance of reimagining the political order through the dynamics of identity politics, the polycentric approach also underscores the importance of linking the struggles of oppressed and marginalized groups, thereby avoiding sectoral political focus and highlighting the interconnections among different sites of discrimination (even if those extend beyond geopolitical boundaries). Oren Yiftachel's analysis of Israel/Palestine as a unitary space representing a system of creeping apartheid and Shenhav's work on the connections between Mizrahi and Palestinian predicaments pinpoint the ethnorepublican ethos of Israel as a root cause of both the unjust socioeconomic, political, and cultural configuration at home (i.e., Israel proper) and the continuous conflict with the Palestinians in the territories occupied in 1967. The interrelation between the sites of injustice is more complex than the mere demarcation entailed by the Green Line. This is because of the presence of a poor, disadvantaged population (mostly Mizrahi) in the settlements in the occupied territories of 1967. This sector, in many respects the victim of neoliberal policies within the Green Line, remains dependent on the generous statist welfare system that is the settlement project—the last bastion of an otherwise eroded welfare socialism that defined the early decades of the Israeli nation-state.[94] Demolishing and evacuating the settlements (a key ingredient of the two-state solution), Shenhav argues, would constitute an unjust act that is oblivious to the political and social realities of the settlers. Therefore, he proposes to move beyond the rigidity of Westphalian premises and to recognize the multifaceted and occasionally curious interrelations between those various sites of injustice. Viewing the settlers as victims as well as villains certainly complicates rendering them as the primary obstacle for peace. This observation refocuses the settlement infrastructure within a broader conversation concerning the presumed axioms of an Israeli identity. Located beyond the Green Line, the settlements, in other words, cannot be reduced to the religious messianic impulse to settle the Greater Eretz Yisrael but also involve the historical, economic, and social complexities of Israeli nation-statehood.

However, this crucial recognition of the link between the "domestic" struggles of the Mizrahim and Palestinian Israelis for social justice and the "external" struggle of the Palestinians for national self-determination has not yet been translated into the formation of broad and effective coalitions and collaborative acts of protest. Nonetheless, this understanding of the strong connection between questions of social justice and the so-called peace process deeply challenges the spatial biases of the loyal left or the peace camps. According to this view, a confrontation of the domestic "ethnic" problem would need to await a resolution of the conflict. In fact, the designation "left" is something of a misnomer because this camp predominantly holds (neo)liberal views on socioeconomic "domestic" issues. The radical Mizrahi discourse, in the tradition of the BP, astutely identifies this problem with the liberal "left" in Israel. While the Keshet's activities revolve primarily around "domestic" concerns with education and housing, the potential for broadening the struggle beyond national divides— as was already attempted in the 1980s in a series of Mizrahi-Palestinian dialogues—is indeed consistent with the basic theoretical insights of this discourse.

The second area where the polycentric multicultural framework needs to be further expanded is more substantive than the practical and strategic problem of building broad coalitions across geopolitical zones of conflict. The polycentric approach to multiculturalism overlooks the relevance of supplementing the deconstructive effort to de-essentialize conceptions of the "nation" by using a constructive hermeneutical engagement with the resources of religion. Certainly, it engages innovatively in a constructive reimagining of Jewish Israeliness, but this effort is thoroughly focused on retrieving and appropriating Mizrahi historical and cultural belonging to the topography of the Middle East and North Africa as a way to combat the orientalism of the Zionist establishment. This effort also entails, perhaps inadvertently, challenging the historical bias of political Zionism and how the secularization of the Tanakh enables the territorialization of Jews in Palestine. But beyond the reclamation of historical presence and the concomitant aspiration to localize and normalize Arab Jewish Israeliness, the polycentric model needs to scrutinize and hermeneutically engage a political theology that enables the endurance of the mythos of return and ingathering. It is only through such contestations that the geopolitical space could be radically restructured. For this to take place, however, two interrelated issues need to be addressed. First, in order to reach a modified understanding of the polycentric multicultural proposal, the theoretical presupposition concerning the dynamic fluidity and contingency of collective identities—central to this model—requires alteration. Second, in order for the polycentric configuration to facilitate meaningful debates concerning the Jewish character of the Israeli nation-state, it would need intentionally to overcome the monopoly of sectoral groups such as Meretz and Shas over the normative definitions of Israeli secularity and religiosity, respectively.

In other words, the "religion" variable enters the conversation not only in the form of a retrieval of resources from within Judaism and Jewish history that are consistent with the demands of human rights and justice (e.g., RHR and Butler). Nor does it enter merely as a factor in coalition building.[95] Religion also enters the conversation through a radical Mizrahi critique that interrogates axiomatic narratives designed to homogenize and universalize the Jewish experience. Therefore, this critique challenges and deconstructs the construal of Judaism qua Israeliness.

While Shas rescues Sephardi religiosity from the perceived monopoly of Ashkenazi interpretations of Judaism, this kind of retrieval is not sufficient as a form of critique and sociopolitical transformation. In fact, in order to move Shas away from the ethnocentric dimensions of Israeli identity, its efforts to reclaim the "glory" of oriental Judaism need to be supplemented by a Mizrahi critique of structural and cultural violence in Israel proper, a critique that logically extends beyond the Green Line. Its efforts also need to be joined with RHR's ethical and humanistic orientation and empathy for the victims of Israeli policies, illuminating the striking connections between the plights of the "domestic" and "external" others of Euro-Zionism.

Awareness of the contingency and, in fact, arbitrariness of collective identities enables the polycentric model of multiculturalism to deploy postcolonial and postmodern deconstructive tools. These tools would help to expose the ideology, power dynamics, structures of oppression, discourses (e.g., colonialism, orientalism), and historical circumstances that incubated this or that conception of identity. Indeed, as mentioned above, the interpretation of identity as a product of circumstances intends to contest and transform primordialist formulations and representations of national identity as unchanged, ahistorical, and inflexible. Scholar of nationalism Umut Özkirimli suggests that the primordialist approach represents nationalism as "a 'natural' part of human beings, as natural as speech, sight or smell . . . [that] have existed since time immemorial."[96] I showed above that in an effort to empower subaltern elements within the society and to denaturalize the representation of the "nation" and its history, Mizrahi polycentrism challenges this primordialist presupposition through the articulation of counternarratives of the nation as told from the margins of society, be it feminist, queer, Mizrahi, or Palestinian.

The polycentric approach likewise offers a conceptual and political challenge to the communitarian formula of a monocultural nation-state. In resisting liberal, individualist, legalistic, and alienating interpretations of public life, the communitarian argument underscores the importance of cultivating a unified sense of community based on a common ethos and shared values. Such a program lends itself to an assimilationist attitude vis-à-vis minorities and to a minimization of cultural differences and heterogeneity.[97] In contrast, by introducing postmodern and postcolonial insights (as well as feminist and queer theories), the polycentric model analyzes the role of power relations and the normative conception of the "nation" (or the dominant discourse) in the complex and hybrid formations of persons and groups, as is evident in the cases of Palestinian Israelis and Mizrahim in Israel. The complex conditions that led to the formation of such groups point to the ethical problems inherent in implementing a homogenizing and communitarian cultural agenda and in representing the nation as an ahistorical entity. Analyzing and understanding collective identities within and in light of their ambiguous contexts and historical circumstances rather than in a primordialist, ahistorical, and essentialist fashion is of critical importance.

Indeed, undergirding the polycentric vision is the assumption of the fluidity, arbitrariness, and contextuality of collective notions of identity.[98] While this assumption makes the multiculturalist model transformative and empowering, it also limits the resources from which alternative modes of the "nation" may be imagined. In the case of Israel, it deconstructs the Eurocentric and Ashkenazi ethos through the dynamics of identity politics and through reclaiming (historical rather than biblical) belonging to the Middle East. In other words, it risks an overly reductionist approach to conflict transformation. The radical Mizrahi discourse, as I mention above, is particularistic but not sectoral and thus attempts to redefine the underlying character of the broader society in accordance with universal principles of justice. Hence, the effort to debunk the binaries that have defined Israeli nationalism—Arab versus Jew, Mizrahi versus Ashkenazi, European versus Oriental, and secular versus religious—must be accompanied by an equal emphasis on reconstructing and rearticulating alternative interpretations of the "nation." The problem with de-essentializing and denaturalizing collective articulations of identity is that it risks reducing them to their contexts by overlooking the influence of cultural, historical, and religious resources that transcend these contexts (even when they are rhetorically conflated with them, as in the case of Israel).[99] The hermeneutics of citizenship comes into play precisely at this intersection.

To be sure, overly historicist theoretical approaches to religion fail to advance a multidimensional and nonreductive account of the role of religion and culture in the formation and reformation of the nation. Benedict Anderson's notion of "imagining"[100] lends itself to the hermeneutics of citizenship as a transformative engagement—one that is consistent with a comprehensive approach to peacebuilding that focuses not only on the reduction of direct violence but also on the transformation of underlying attitudes and relational patterns.

Indeed, as discussed in chapter 2, Anderson's representation of imagining as a creative act provides a point of departure for reimagining the nation along more equitable lines with a conscious redressing and remembering of its past injustices. In order to recognize the plight and worth of marginalized groups, this reimagining would build on the postmodern and postcolonial deconstructions of the hegemonic nation. But the act of reimagining would further call for an engagement with the cultural and religious resources available for a given community.

RHR's ethical impulse to stand in solidarity with the Palestinians—an impulse grounded in a humanistic interpretation of Judaism—exemplifies this point. The impetus for RHR's activism is a particular interpretation of Judaism that, as I showed in chapter 5, challenges Israeli policies of discrimination against the Palestinians and other groups. Rather than absolute, RHR views the "promise of the land" as conditional, depending upon just practices. RHR challenges Israel to live up to and fulfill its Jewish identity. This identity, the rabbis affiliated with this organization contend, cannot be expansionist, repressive, or exclusionary. Such practices contradict their view of Judaism as inherently attuned to social justice and human rights. (They cite the commitment to the Noahide laws and to the prophetic tradition as well as to modern Jewish humanist thought.) Israel, they exclaim, cannot celebrate its own victimhood while inflicting suffering on others. Likewise, explicitly Jewish peace activism critiques the secularist framing of Judaism as merely "ethnic" or "national" and pushes the national conversation to use the act of "return" as an opportunity for reassessment, innovation, and reform—for rethinking Judaism in light of the new predicament of political self-determination.[101] Critics like Ravitzsky and Leibowitz worry about the idolatry of nationhood exhibited by secular and religious Zionists alike, which they deem a profound contradiction to Judaism. They retrieve Maimonides's nonmessianic interpretation of "Jewish return." They do so by excavating the stories of the Hasmonean Kingdom rather than those depicting the messianic end-time (a narrative that political Zionism has secularized).

Unlike the aforementioned religious critics, the Mizrahi discourse, while also retrieving a nonmessianic interpretation of Jewish Israeliness, contests the presumption of "promise" not on its theological content but in reference to the kind of symbolic and structural violence it enabled. It does so by reclaiming the histories of Jewish physical presence in the region. Beyond the need to redress injustices and reconfigure the political system, there is nothing special about Jews in Israel/Palestine as opposed to Jews in Iraq or Iran. The normative resource for the ethical reframing advanced in Mizrahi polycentrism is the human rights discourse, which, as I argue, is insufficient as a framework for conflict transformation. Notably, this understanding challenges the reduction of the nation to the dynamics of politics[102] as well as the contention of Mizrahi polycentrism about the arbitrariness of national identities.

The reconceptualization of the nation—especially in zones where the conflation between religion and nation is perceived as a root cause of conflict—may thus entail a hermeneutical conversation concerning the relation between nation and religion. This argument is based on an understanding of nationalism essentially as a theory of political legitimacy and on a synthesis between Anthony Smith's nation-centric approach and Anthony Marx's state-centric analysis. The former, ethnosymbolist thinker underscores the enduring relevance of religion to the definition of the nation, while the latter's modernist analysis suggests the diminishing pertinence of religion owing to a general trajectory he identifies in the history of Western European nations from their founding moments of bloodshed, exclusivity, and discrimination against the "domestic other" to their ever-increasing liberality, tolerance of minorities, and inclusivity.[103]

A synthesis of these two approaches accords with Marx's point about the potential of the modern "state" to effect changes in the definition of the "nation." It likewise concurs with Smith's insistence on the continuous and lasting role of religion throughout this process. This synthetic interpretation is indebted to a clear recognition of the continuous relevance yet irreducibility of religion to the "nation." It also highlights the need to contextualize each instance of nationalism through a careful examination of how the dynamics and institutions of the state may have transformed the relevant religion or religions and vice versa, thereby introducing a historically sensitive approach to the study of religion as well as to the study of nationalism. What this approach implies for the contemporary case of Israel and Judaism is thus *a transformation of both the nation-state and also Judaism* via a dialectical encounter, via both counterhegemonic institutional reform (as advanced by postcolonial critics) and intra-Jewish contextualized engagement with the hermeneutics of citizenship (a process of reimagining).

Furthermore, this view of the relationship between religion and the modern institution of the nation-state points to the hermeneutics of citizenship as a method of peacebuilding and conflict transformation. The focal point of this argument is outlined in chapter 3. A hermeneutics of citizenship calls for a sustained critique of the hyperhistoricity of reductionist analyses of religion and culture as false consciousness, on the one hand, and of the ahistoricity of secularist approaches that posit religion as removed from political and ideological formations, on the other.

So far I have discussed the requirement to reevaluate the reductionist interpretation of the "nation" as contingent upon political structures and historical circumstances as well as the demand to partake in hermeneutical discussions about the interrelation between nation and religion in a manner that would not rely on unrevised secularist conceptions of citizenship. Additionally, the polycentric model, as envisioned by the theorists of the Keshet, would need to overcome the monopoly of sectoral groups, such as Meretz and Shas, over definitions of Israeli secularity and religiosity, respectively. The Keshet understands the radical Mizrahi discourse as extending beyond the confines of sectoral politics and agendas.

The articulation of its identity as Mizrahi yet universal also constitutes a central issue for the Keshet. The movement has intended to advance a broad social alternative to Israeli society, and thus it distinguishes itself from a political actor like Shas, which is focused on advancing particularistic and sectoral interests.[104] "Mizrahiness," Krif exclaims, "constitutes a political and moral position."[105] He contends that the choice of advancing the struggle for social justice and restructuring from the Mizrahi point of view indicates a realization that "the Jews who will choose to continue their residency here would need to (sooner or later) acknowledge their natural environment [in the Middle East] and thus it is not inconceivable to argue that under these conditions the state of Israel would become more Mizrahi and more Jewish."[106] In other words, dismantling the orientalist and Eurocentric Zionist discourse would entail coming to terms with the geographical location of Israel and reevaluating its self-perception as a Western outpost.

Krif also underscores the place of the Jewish tradition as an integral dimension of Mizrahi identity and experience; thus, Mizrahi secularity amounts, in his view, almost to an oxymoronic proposition. Indeed, he holds an unrevised (and thus inadequate) notion of secularism as the absence of religion. Similarly, despite his call to connect "Mizrahiness" and

Jewish conceptions of social justice, the founding committee of the Keshet was unable to reach an agreement about the issue of Judaism and the Israeli state.[107] It has continuously advanced its support of the separation of religion and state, despite recognition that the secular-religious polarity has constituted another manifestation of Ashkenazi hegemonic control and has reflected the Ashkenazi experience of enlightenment and suspicion of religion (foreign to the experience of Mizrahim in their countries of origin). For example, Mizrahi activist Simon Biton argues that "the movement supports the separation of religion and state. Yet it views the heated secular Ashkenazi contempt expressed against the folklorist traditionalism of the Mizrahim as another instrument for the humiliation and marginalization of the Mizrahim."[108]

In the final analysis, however, the movement has advanced a rather unrevised interpretation of the principle of separation between religion and state (not unlike Meretz) and has not focused its attention on accessing the sources of Mizrahi traditions to engage in a meaningful reimagining of the interrelation between religion and nationalism. It has subsequently enabled Shas to continue its monopoly over questions of Mizrahi religiosity. The articulation of a postsecular interpretation of Israeli secularity—one that would overcome the modernist binary of religion versus secular and the idea of the "state" as culturally and religiously neutral—would necessitate a critical evaluation of the relation between Judaism and Israeliness. Such a process would entail a recognition of the political theology underlying secular Zionism as well as a substantive and multifaceted engagement with the interrelations between Judaism, the Jewish people, and the state of Israel—a process that is thoroughly polycentric (currently unfolding, for example, in Jerusalem, New York, and Moscow).

How would the hermeneutics of citizenship translate into the process of reimagining Judaism-qua-nationality and ethnicity? Shas's celebration and retrieval of Arab Jewish cultural and religious resources could reinforce the radical Mizrahi critique of the entrenched, Eurocentric, teleological narrating of Jewish history. At the same time, the Mizrahi discourse curtails Shas's ethnocentric impulses. This echoes Alcalay's call for reimagining the Jew as a "native" rather than a "stranger" in the Middle East. This sense of rootedness is not to vindicate the occupation of the land but rather to reconceive the relation Jews may have to the space that is Palestine/Israel and more broadly to the Middle East. This relation is not necessarily theological and messianic, but it will have to overcome the orientalism that interlaces Euro-Zionism.

This rethinking also entails an interrogation on the level of the community on a case-by-case basis in the various Jewish centers around the world. This should not be an exclusively Israeli conversation because the dominant, universalizing, Jewish history told by the Zionist paradigm perpetuates the Israeli-Palestinian conflict and the ethnocentric logic of citizenship in Israel. Unlike the Canaanites who envisioned rootedness only as a function of stripping away the trappings of religion (a total "negation of exile"), this reimagining would amount to celebrating historical Jewish life in the Orient and its intimate relations to Arab cultures as well as authentic sentiments of Jewish Israelis who see their connection to Israel as grounded in their Jewish identity.

The ethical impulse of the humanist Judaism of RHR, Shas's attempt to decolonize the Ashkenazi hegemony over Judaism, and the radical Mizrahi critique of the Israeli ethos all open creative new pathways for synergistically reimagining the Jewish meanings of Israeli citizenship and nationhood. This introspection is clearly distinct from Butler's retrieval of a Jewish ethical tradition valorizing the "diasporic" and the "stranger" as constitutive of Jewish identity and as key for rethinking the relations between Israel, the diasporas, and the Jewish people. The impetus for both kinds of approaches, however, is an ethical impulse for cohabitation or coexistence in Palestine/Israel—an aspiration radically departing both from the ethnocentric national ideologies (deemed inherently unjust) and from the underlying rigidity of persistent modernist paradigms that conceive of the "nation" in monocultural terms.

Reimagining Israeli Judaism as distinctly Middle Eastern rather than projecting Hannah Arendt's sense of estrangement or alterity (a distinctly European experience) could contribute to reevaluating the relations of Israel to Jewish diasporas (and other Jewish centers) and the meanings of Jewish national self-determination. This process of reimagining would necessitate not only deploying the ethical principles of RHR, propelled by a commitment to the humanity of the occupied Palestinians and a compassion for the "stranger in our midst," but also rethinking those principles in light of my earlier critique of RHR's reliance on the axioms of the Zionist narrative, especially the themes of "return" and the "ingathering of the exiles."

Likewise, while the Mizrahi discourse exposes the fallacies and ramifications of an Ashkenazi-dominant narration of Jewish history, for Mizrahi protest in Israel to offer a framework of peacebuilding, one that fully interrogates cultural and symbolic forms of violence and offers an agonistic transformative prism, it would need to also interrogate the place of Judaism in the national ethos. This last area still requires engagement. In an effort to distinguish its type of protest from the one espoused by Shas, the radical Mizrahi discourse adopted a secularist approach to religion that, as my critique of liberal Zionism and post-Zionist orientations suggested, insufficiently addresses the root causes of internal and external injustices; thus I understand it as offering only a limited arena for peacebuilding.

The hermeneutics of citizenship focuses on the stories of marginalized groups in an effort to expose and challenge the basic premises of the ethno-republican Israeli state and to radically reconfigure its structures of control. However, it is also crucial that this process be accompanied by alternative interpretations of the interrelation between nation and religion from within the sources of Judaism and Jewish histories as well as the third spaces highlighted in the polycentrist model. The counterhegemonic struggle involves reasserting and reclaiming the histories and rights of the marginalized and displaced, recognizing and compensating for past injustices, and calling for radical and multiperspectival reconceptualization of the redistribution of resources. The restructuring of ethical and geopolitical relations, however, would also involve a similar struggle against Zionist interpretations of Judaism, Jewish history, and the relation between Israel and the diasporas. Thus, the task of reimagining the nation-state needs to include a contextualized deconstruction of the underlying ethos, an introspective study of subaltern perspectives, and a denaturalization of conceptions of the "self" as suggested by the cohabitation model as well as the polycentric framework of multiculturalism and as practiced to a certain degree by the Keshet. Likewise, it requires a constructive exploration of the resources of religion, including but not restricted to theological formulations and positions advanced by religious leaders and other authoritative interpreters of the tradition.

In my reading, the polycentric model does not preclude—indeed, it demands—bringing religious resources and living voices to bear on reimagining the nation and radically transforming its institutions. Notably, Shenhav's analysis of the nexus between ethnicity, religion, and nationalism could lend itself to an imaginative exploration of the interrelation between religion and nation as it has unfolded in the case of Israel.[109] Shenhav argues that religion, ethnicity, and nationalism have been critically intertwined in the construction and reproduction of Zionist identity: "Each of these categories is a necessary but insufficient condition for the whole, and each category requires the other two in order to produce the 'Zionist subject.' Only when these three categories co-appear do they succeed in manufacturing a coherent Zionist identity."[110]

Shenhav's thesis applies theorist Bruno Latour's analysis of modernity as consisting of the contradictory and concomitant dynamics of "hybridization" and "purification" to the case of Zionism. According to Latour, modernity signals the concurrent "hybridization" of distinct elements and their "purification" or construal as antonymous.[111] This theoretical insight enables Shenhav to reread the history of the Mizrahim, especially that of Iraqi Jews, in a way that identifies the reliance of Zionism on the structures of colonialism and the ideological frameworks of Eurocentrism, orientalism, and nationalism. Extending Latour's analysis of modernity to the scrutiny of Zionism also enables a recognition of the unique position of the Mizrahim in a third space, which significantly challenges the purification of the categories of ethnicity, religion, and nationalism. Indeed, by virtue of their experiences of discrimination and marginalization alone, the Mizrahim challenge the dynamics of "purification" and thus introduce the possibility of reimagining the interrelation among the categories of religion, ethnicity, and nationalism.[112]

This analysis of the symbiotic interrelations between religion, ethnicity, and nationalism, as well as the recognition of the need and possibility of renegotiating those links from within the third spaces, is instructive. Reading this analysis in conjunction with the insights of the polycentric model of multiculturalism substantiates the argument that polycentrism may expand not only to include the debunking of the symbiosis of religion, nationalism, and ethnicity and their simultaneous construal as ontologically distinct, but also to suggest a constructive rethinking of how religion, nationalism, and ethnicity may relate to one another in multicultural contexts. Furthermore, deploying the Latourian framework of hybridization and purification (construing the symbiotic yet differentiated categories of "ethnicity," "nationality," and "religion") also points to the importance of exposing the underlying political theology of Israeli secularism. This effort could encourage a meaningful conversation concerning the contours of Israeli secularism.[113] Such a conversation needs to go beyond the conceptual blinders of Israeli liberalism, which holds to an unrevised notion of secularity as the binary opposite of religiosity—a pretense that, as the discussions of PN and RHR highlight, does not survive scrutiny.

The limitation of Mizrahi polycentrism and, by extension, of a proposal for a loosely connected consociational democracy is that it neutralizes this need to hermeneutically engage the political theology enabling the reification of the Green Line. Mizrahim, to reiterate, reclaim their belonging to the Middle East through accessing the memories, histories, and languages they became estranged from owing to their Zionization. The Mizrahi discourse uses these sources to critique and reimagine Israeliness. To this extent it functions as a "critical caretaker." Critiquing the orientalist and Eurocentric motifs of Ashkenazi Zionism, the Mizrahim also reclaim memories of being an integral part of the Middle East and North Africa, not accidental residents. While the resources retrieved and appropriated are not theological but rather historical, social, economic, and cultural, the Mizrahi discourse offers constructive possibilities for localizing Jewish Israeliness. Yet, as I argued, a reconfiguration of the geopolitical space will have to confront the underlying political theology that enabled the reification of the Green Line in the first place. Thus, Mizrahi polycentrism, like the cohabitation model, offers a limited framework for change.

The hermeneutics of citizenship, therefore, amounts to a synthesis of the insights found in the models of polycentrism and cohabitation. It is a synthesis between ethically reframing the geopolitical space, initially through historicizing Jewish political hegemonic claims about Jewish identity, on the one hand, and remembering the plight of the Palestinians as an occasion for this ethical reframing, on the other. But this reframing wants to impose another form of amnesia, a resetting that pretends decades of Jewish-Israeliness never happened, with the kind of loyalties and cultural formations that it generated. It is essentially about reclaiming the diasporic condition as the most authentically Jewish one—a counterhistorical imagination as if Israel never happened. This is despite the emphasis of the cohabitation model on relationality and remembrance. In contrast, the polycentric model relies on estranged and marginalized identities born out of decades of Israeli statehood. For both models, the principle and the experience of nonbelonging become the primary resources not only for historicizing and remembering counterhegemonic histories but also for reconstructing the geopolitical space and its ethical relations. The polycentric model complements the cohabitation one by imagining the possibility of reconfiguring rather than dissolving solidarities—a process that does not erase Israel but profoundly reframes it from within, while still claiming alterity (ironically through reclaiming indigeneity). This valorization of the "stranger within" needs to be complemented by an intra-Jewish conversation that transcends the historicity of Israel/Palestine.

Certainly, the understanding of Zionism as a political theology or a heterodox religion enables engagement in the hermeneutics of citizenship as a means for conflict transformation. This method highlights those religious dimensions inherent in the conceptions of the secular nation. Second, from within the tradition, it suggests alternatives that would more consistently cohere with the universal norms and demands for equality and justice articulated by those who fall outside the normative and hegemonic definition of nationhood. It also, however, enables the contextualized transformation and reform of religion, thereby questioning essentialist and ahistorical interpretations and maintaining fluidity, flexibility, and adaptability to new historical circumstances. Hence, whereas the view of the nation as a "heterodox religion" or "religion surrogate" exposes the underlying religious motifs of secular nationalisms, such as the one articulated by Meretz and PN, it offers no conceptual tools for reimagining the relation between those motifs and a group's ethnonational claims. For this reimagining to occur, it is crucial to introduce into the discussion how institutional dynamics may influence and reshape conceptions of nationhood.

Conclusion

This chapter argues that like the Palestinian citizens of Israel, the Mizrahim occupy a space of social and political marginalization, but also a space where the logic of Israeli ethnorepublicanism may be challenged and renegotiated. The general argument that has emerged in these chapters is that the two subaltern groups of the Palestinian Israelis and the Mizrahim confront the structures and ethos of the Euro-Zionist hegemony in their experiences and platforms of social justice. They challenge the dominant institutions and ideology by exposing the systemic patterns of discrimination and injustice. Indeed, these two sectors call for a radical restructuring of the power dynamics and a radical reconceptualization of membership, thereby recognizing the link between national ideology and power arrangements and the need to reimagine this ideology in order to redress past injustices and to establish a more just arrangement for the future. While this process of reimagining involves a reevaluation of the nexus between religion and nation, both groups fall short of engaging hermeneutically with the sources of religion in their effort to offer an alternative narrative.

Unlike the Jewish but non-Israeli probe into nonnationalist traditions that valorize the diasporic rather than the rooted as the most authentic Jewish condition (per Butler), the Palestinian Israelis and the Mizrahim offer alternatives born out of their contextualized experiences as victims of Ashkenazi Zionism. Both identities emerged from this context and are defined by it, even if nonreductively. The previous chapter shows that Palestinian Israelis relied principally on the international norms of human rights in order to frame their critique of the institutions and underpinning ideology of the Israeli nation-state. But I also noted that this approach needs to be supplemented and reciprocated with an intra-Jewish and intra-Israeli reimagining of the relationship between Israel and Judaism. Without such an interrogation and rethinking, the struggle of Palestinian Israelis, despite its

profound critique of Zionist hegemony, remains subsumed by this dominant discourse that detaches it from the broader Israeli-Palestinian conflict.
This delinking reflects the historical and conceptual blinders informing the
conventional peace camp. Likewise, the Mizrahi discourse discussed in this
chapter pushes for the radical reconceptualization of the Israeli power infrastructure as well as the legitimizing narrative of the nation. Like the Future
Vision of the Palestinian Arabs in Israel, the Mizrahi argument attributes
the systemic inequalities characteristic of the Israeli "state" to its exclusivist,
ethnorepublican definition of the "nation." While the Palestinian Israeli
document invokes the legal framework of human rights, the Mizrahim primarily use postcolonial theoretical tools to articulate their grievances and
expose the colonial, Eurocentric, and orientalist dimensions of Zionism and
the Israeli state. Indeed, this process of deconstructing the Zionist ethos (by
its Jewish victims) signals the initiation of an intra-Jewish/Israeli conversation concerning the meaning of membership in the Israeli nation-state.
The Mizrahi discourse challenges the normative definition of the Israeli and
Israel as Western and European by exposing its underlying conceptual fallacies. This critique necessarily involves reimagining the nexus of religion,
nationalism, and ethnicity.

However, the radical Mizrahi discourse, possibly in an attempt to distinguish itself from Shas, overlooks a careful debate over the role of religion in
the construction and reconstruction of notions of citizenship and nationalism in Israel. What is necessary is a broadening of the intra-Jewish conversation beyond the focus on Mizrahi and other Jewish and non-Jewish Israeli
sites of alterity to include other marginalized spaces (theologies, memories,
nonnationalist ethical Jewish traditions, and so forth) not subsumed within
the geopolitical constellations of Israel/Palestine. A second overlooked
insight is the profound connection between the Palestinian and Mizrahi
predicaments. Mizrahi protest has tended to focus on "domestic" questions of inequality rather than on forming alliances with the Palestinians.
Hence, the link between the discrimination against the Mizrahim and the
Palestinian-Israeli conflict has not yet yielded a coherent, unified platform.
Nevertheless, as suggested by the early Mizrahi-Palestinian conferences
of the late 1980s, such an alliance may present a transformative challenge
to the modes in which peace and justice may be imagined.

The Hermeneutics of Citizenship:
The Missing Dimension of Peacebuilding

This study of the Israeli peace camp has shown that Zionist peace groups reinforce and reproduce Zionist historiography, orientalism, and Eurocentrism. Moreover, their political theology is taken directly from the worldview of secular Zionism. Despite their apparently increased commitment to liberalism (reflected most sharply in the neoliberal transformation of the Israeli economy and in the legislation supporting broader individual liberties in the 1990s), Meretz and PN nonetheless exhibit a secularism characterized by support of the ethnorepublican rationale that has defined the Israeli state since its inception.[1] This rationale reflects a commitment to the cultivation of conditions favorable to the persistence of Israel as a Jewish and democratic nation-state. According to this study, the view of the modern secular nation as a heterodox religion enables the scrutiny of Zionism as a political theology.

Regardless of the negation-of-exile motif and its other historically antinomian characteristics, Zionism requires a rather explicit retrieval of certain traditional, theological modes of justifying the "nation." Indeed, Zionism's charged and contested nature demands of its proponents a certain ironic, if subtle, acknowledgment of Israel's "sacred" origins and destiny. The Israeli liberal left, however, is uncertain as to how this legitimating political theology shapes (or should shape) its positions on the Israeli-Palestinian conflict. Clearly, the imperative to secure the survival of Israel as a Jewish democracy lies at the heart of the Zionist peace camp's support of the two-state solution. This solution neatly secures the "ethnic" project through a geopolitical separation between a future Palestinian state and Israel. Similarly, adhering to the two-state formula also leaves unchallenged the logic pivotal to the "republican" project, which defines Israel as Ashkenazi, secular, and enlightened through the suppression and marginalization of Israel's "others": Palestinian Israelis, non-Ashkenazi Israelis, religious Israeli Jews, and Jews in the diasporas. The ethnorepublican rationale constrains the ability of the "loyal" peace camp to envision any alternative modes of responding to the question of peace and justice vis-à-vis the Palestinians. It enables the Green Line to mark not only spatial but also normative differentiation that profoundly limits the vistas of the discussion.

In order to envision ethical alternatives, it is necessary to deploy a multiperspectival approach to justice by focusing on history as told from the point of view of Israel's Jewish and non-Jewish victims. That is the central thesis of this book. This task entails debunking the colonial and orientalist dimensions of Zionist teleology. Reimagining the "nation" likewise necessitates a critical reexamination of Zionism's foundational political theology through an exploration of alternative interpretations of the nexus between religion, ethnicity, and the nation.

I have called this necessary exploration the *hermeneutics of citizenship*. Amounting to an examination of the political theology undergirding the nation and its institutions, it draws on notions of nationalism as a theory of political legitimacy and underscores the "elective affinity" between interpretations of ethnicity, religion, and nation.[2] This view, in turn, is grounded in Max Weber's understanding of national identity as constituting a "subjective belief in common descent" and of political legitimacy as involving "a 'belief' in the existence of a valid and justified political order."[3] The key here is the emphasis on the "subjectivity" of both the national identity and the "nation" itself, which represents a "subjective" set of core beliefs rather than "objective" attributes. While acknowledging the nation's authenticity, Weber's view also acknowledges its elasticity and insinuates the possibility of rethinking and reevaluating the nation's core beliefs and the precise contours of its interrelation or "elective affinity" with ethnicity and religion. To grant the nation's subjectivity is thus to admit that it functions as a heterodox religion, open to reassessment and introspection.

This process of reinterpretation may be defined as a *hermeneutics* because it entails not only revisiting the religious and theological resources of the community through recognizing the "ambivalence of the sacred," but also scrutinizing the modes by which the community has drawn on these resources in legitimizing its authority, actions, and account of "who we are." This is the reason why the hermeneutics of citizenship cannot take place in a historical vacuum, asking abstractly whether the selective retrieval from "religion X" to legitimate the claims of "nation Y" is just or justifiable.

Rather, the hermeneutics of citizenship demonstrates a high degree of attentiveness to the narratives of the subaltern and their experiences of injustice. It is the overarching argument of this book that, when contextualized through the counternarratives and memories of subaltern groups (with great consideration of power dynamics) and when evaluated in relation to a dynamic interpretation of universal conventions of justice (one that does not entail a predetermined telos and thus allows for multidirectionality in interpreting justpeace as opposed to formulaic unidirectional dictation of oughts), such a scrutiny or hermeneutics is effective in envisioning peacebuilding. This is particularly relevant in zones of conflict defined by ethnoreligious claims and modes of justification. Along with normative political theory, peace studies, and cultural theory, this hermeneutical process brings insights to bear from the secularism debates that deconstructed and historicized simplistic dichotomizing between the categories of the "religious" and the "secular."

In *Why I Am Not a Secularist*, political theorist William Connolly offers such effective insights. Of secular-liberal claims to impartiality, he writes: "The historical *modus vivendi* of secularism, while seeking to chasten religious dogmatism, embodies unacknowledged elements of immodesty in itself. The very intensity of the struggle it wages against religious intolerance may induce blind spots with respect to itself."[4] In order to correct this "immodest conception," Connolly argues for a polycentric "public ethos of engagement."[5] This vision directly challenges the philosophical abstraction embodied in the Eurocentric idea of the liberal and democratic "nation."[6] In arguing for a "post-secular secularism," Connolly concludes that "today the challenge is to explore distinctive pluralities of political identity, allegiance and communication irreducible to liberal, secular, communitarian, or chauvinistic images of the nation."[7]

The reason for evaluating the Israeli peace camp and for engaging in a hermeneutics of citizenship is not to eliminate but to refashion secularism by challenging its basic blind spots as they come to light through the discussion of justpeace. But my analysis also critically moves beyond the post-secularism debates in thinking about religion not solely in terms of "rights" but also in terms of negotiable symbolic boundaries of national identities. The hermeneutics of citizenship recognizes that a polycentric "public ethos of engagement" requires a reimagining of symbolic boundaries and collective passions rather than their mere diffusion and structural decentering. Overcoming the majoritarianism inherent in the Westphalian construct necessitates more than a respatialization of geopolitical boundaries. My claim that radical structural change involves an equally radical reimagining of collective passions therefore moves beyond the merely agonistic and necessary questioning of the naturalness of the supposed prepolitical "we" and the boundaries of the political to interrogating and reimagining religion qua national identity.

Indeed, critical to this discussion is the notion of civil society, for it suggests a multiplicity of resources for reimagining the interrelation between religion and nationality. One distinct feature of modernity is the diversification of religious authority, a characteristic that—as I show in this work— may prove destructive when deployed toward violent or chauvinistic ends, yet constructive when retrieved for the purpose of conflict transformation through the hermeneutics of citizenship. Hence, I have argued, the critical integration between the ethical traditions that valorize the diasporic experience of nonbelonging (Butler) and the radical Mizrahi discourse and its reimagining of Jewish Israeliness through a reclaiming of belonging; the prophetic and humanistic traditions (RHR, Leibowitz); and the interpretations of "return" as an opportunity to renew and reimagine the covenantal relations and the meanings of Jewish political self-rule (Hartman) or as an opportunity to think of Jewish political self-determination in nonmessianic terms (Leibowitz, Ravitzsky)—all are necessary to critique and rethink Judaism qua Israeli nationalism and thus to encourage peacebuilding.

The book also situates discussions of the definition of Israel as Jewish within broader Jewish conversations concerning modernity, nationalism, and secularism—conversations dating back to the time of the German-Jewish Haskalah philosopher Moses Mendelssohn. Highlighting a relationship of continuity with, rather than a radical break from, such conversations intimates recognition of the possibility, on the part of the Jewish diasporas, to provincialize Israel or to reimagine modes of being Jewish in the contemporary world outside of, and irreducible to, the frames of Zionist teleology or narratives of "redemption and return." Such a process of provincialization does not eradicate but rather entails the rethinking of the substantive parameters of Jewish Israeli identity.

While the Zionist peace paradigms are based on ambivalent interpretations of Israel's political theology and while non-Zionist formulas rely on unrevised liberal notions of secularism, the case of the Mizrahim or the Arab Jews significantly challenges both. In an effort to imagine the possibility of postsecular secularity in Israel/Palestine, I therefore explored the case of the Mizrahim (the primary Jewish victims of Zionism) through an investigation of the Keshet and its proposals for multiculturalism as well as its understanding of religiosity and the colonial and Eurocentric legacies associated with political Zionism.

By "postsecular secularity" I mean a shift away from a conception of the liberal, secular nation-state as culturally or religiously neutral. Instead, postsecular secularity entails a multiperspectival scrutiny of the nation's underlying political theology and/or recognition of the persistent role of religion or culture in imagining and reimagining the parameters of belonging or membership. Israel presents an instructive case study because, despite its commitment to civil liberties and rights, even the liberal peace camp holds onto an ethnonational agenda reflected in its general commitment to the continuous cultivation of the idea of a Jewish and democratic nation-state. The self-perception of the Zionist peace camp as secular and liberal neutralizes and naturalizes the relevance of the ethnonational agenda to the conflict with the Palestinians, thus obscuring the root cause of the conflict. The "liberalism" of the Israeli Zionist left is defective because it is unreflective or even unaware of its illiberal assumptions and how they corrupt its conceptualization of peace and justice.

Because of its reliance on the paradigms of modernism and (unrevised) secularism, the peace camp reinterprets Judaism as national "culture" or "history" without considering the intricate dependency of such categories on religious and metahistorical themes and without acknowledging the relevance of these complexities to the logic of the Zionist settlement project in Palestine. This conceptual confusion is evident in the tendency of the secular Zionist peace camp to consider Israel as the representative of the whole, standing in for the irreducible multiplicity and complexity of the Jewish diasporas. It surfaces, as well, in the effort to sustain the concept of a Jewish nation-state as a redemptive imperative mandated by the Torah (read as Jewish history) and vindicated by the Holocaust and a history of periodical pogroms and persecutions. Six decades after the establishment of the state and with successive generations of Israel-born Jewish citizens, the centrality of the ethos of the Torah is receding because the "rootedness" of now third- and fourth-generation Jewish Israelis seems self-evident. What is increasingly stressed, however, is the Jewish ethos of perpetual near extinction.

In addition, the secular Zionist peace movement has reinforced the status quo because it failed to connect the occupation of the territories of 1967, which it resists, to the conquests and displacements of 1948 and domestic questions of social justice. This lack of self-reflexivity constrains the movement's ability to analyze deep-seated issues like structural and cultural violence and the persistence of Eurocentric discourses of colonialism and orientalism. This cultural and political myopia thus limits the vistas of peace and justice within a Euro-Zionist paradigm.

By "Euro-Zionist," to reiterate, I refer to the location of Zionism as initially a nineteenth-century European nationalist movement. As such, Zionism has relied on the discourses of secular nationalism, colonialism, romanticism, and anti-Semitism. Zionism has similarly relied on Eurocentric interpretations of Jewish history in which the experiences of European Jews became generalized and universalized, assimilating the non-European Jewish community into a particular story of pogroms and anti-Semitism. Likewise, Zionism has internalized orientalist lenses. As Hannah Arendt pointed out in her seminal work *Eichmann in Jerusalem*, the human landscape of Jews was defined by a topography that highlighted the superiority of western Jews over Eastern European Jews. This gradation continues systemically in Israel, where Oriental Jews are ranked below Eastern European Jews.[8] Zionism understands itself as a secular, European movement. It is this self-perception that the hermeneutics of citizenship seeks to engage through a multiperspectival approach to justice. The point of departure for a hermeneutics of citizenship is that the Zionist frame can be explained through the prisms of the aforementioned discourses without being reduced to them.

Dispelling Myopia

The myopia of the peace camp regarding its own exclusivist assumptions causes it to attribute the relentlessness of the Israeli-Palestinian conflict primarily to religious radicalism and other explicitly illiberal militant forces within Israeli society. While such forces as the messianic settlers certainly present radically exclusivist conceptions of membership in Israel, Israeli liberalism also presupposes the legitimacy of an ethnonational project. As I pointed out, the peace platforms advanced by the secular liberal camp are limited precisely because of its refusal to acknowledge Zionism as a root cause of the conflict (a critique that applies to the religious Zionist peace camp as well). An engagement with the hermeneutics of citizenship, therefore, may be viewed as a form of a holistic, cultural therapy in that it would address the roots, rather than merely assuage the symptoms, of the problem.

To achieve this goal, it is critical to dissipate national myopia through a multiperspectival remembering of the tragedies and sufferings generated as a result of instituting the national project. This remembering is captured in the voices and embodied experiences of Palestinian Israelis and Mizrahim. Moving beyond remembering, a hermeneutical reimagining involves denaturalizing the meanings of *who we are* as a community. This amounts to challenging a homogenizing construal of Jewish political identity through an embrace of self-estrangement or nonbelonging. This self-estrangement amounts to reclaiming and appropriating Jewish religious, ethical, and historical resources in reframing Jewish Israeliness and Jewish identity more broadly, beyond the Zionist monopoly over history and identity. This empowering self-estrangement characterizes both the cohabitation model and Mizrahi polycentrism. However, while both models advance, in an agonistic fashion, a radical restructuring of the geopolitical space (beyond the confining and persistently bifurcated categories informing the Zionist peace camp), only Mizrahi polycentrism moves constructively toward reimagining belonging. In contrast, the cohabitation model informing Judith Butler's account can afford the reimagining of Jewish-Israeli identity only as individuated and private—a move that prevents the reimagining of collective passions enabled within the Mizrahi discourse. Reconceiving the meanings and boundaries of the community is pivotal for authorizing radical geopolitical restructuring.

The argument runs as follows: in order to engage in the hermeneutics of citizenship, it is crucial to come to terms with the view of secular Zionism as representing a political theology, which deploys and appropriates the resources of the tradition selectively. Such a realization opens a path for a reinterpretation of secular Zionism's core motifs and an exposition of its liberal myopia. This process entails context-sensitive reinterpretation from within and without the sources of Judaism and Jewish history. By sensitivity to context, I mean that reimagining the interrelation between Judaism and Israeliness cannot be divorced from a careful consideration of the experiences of the Palestinians (as well as the other victims of Euro-Zionism). Unfortunately, Israeli Zionist secularism as epitomized by the liberal peace camp has reframed its theological underpinnings as historical and cultural modes of justification. Accordingly, Jewish "return" is interpreted as a historical rather than a religious, metahistorical entitlement, and the Jewish character of the state of Israel as a "cultural" attribute and imperative. This secularization or purification of the motifs of return and redemption as "historical" or "cultural" does not sever them from their roots in the theological sources and the religious imagination, however.[9]

Likewise, I argued that the religious Zionist peace camp, while presenting a challenge to the ambivalent treatment of religion by mainstream Israeli or Zionist secularism, has actually reinforced the general contours of the latter's underlying political theology. My study of RHR demonstrated an ahistorical and axiomatic interpretation of the right of Jewish return to the land of Palestine. This interpretation is ahistorical or metahistorical because it overlooks how historical details, such as the presence of another group of people in the land, may (and even should) constrain the motivation to act upon messianic impulses. A historically contextualized analysis of this movement of return may categorize it as colonialist. This would be possible, despite the special place Zion and the concept of return have occupied in the Jewish imagination over millennia of diasporic life. Second, the return to Zion is perceived as a redemptive moment in Jewish history. Here too religious Zionism has internalized secular Zionism's emphasis on return as physical redemption in the land and history, rather than as metahistorical and metaphysical.

Religious Zionists, however, view physical redemption as either the footsteps of the messianic moment (as in Kook's dialectic theology) or as an opportunity for spiritual growth and fulfillment of Jewish life (Hartman). The religious peace camp falls into the latter category. In the case of RHR, it was shown that the spatial differentiation between pre-1967 Israel and the occupied territories of 1967 also enabled a conceptual separation between the problem posed by the character of Israel as a Jewish nation-state and the problem of the occupation of the territories. While the Jewish character of the pre-1967 war is considered a given, the occupation is criticized as immoral and as corrupting the Jewish ethical fabric of Israel.

Because RHR does not question the automatic right of Jewish return (even if it articulates the "promise of the land" as conditional upon just behavior), thereby accepting the basic claims set forth by the decontextualized and ahistoric political theology of secular Zionism, it overlooks a significant source of the conflict and it further subscribes to the normative differentiation denoted by the Green Line. Similarly, the Gavison-Medan Covenant provides another example of how the liberal discourse of multiculturalism glosses over the underlying exclusive thresholds of citizenship in Israel.

While the religious Zionist camp has called upon the resources of religion in order to articulate its resistance to the occupation and in order to develop an ethics of engagement with the minorities within Israel, its overarching framework attributes an axiomatic status to the basic claims of Zionist political theology. This assumption limits its ability to contextualize and challenge Zionist interpretations of Jewish motifs such as return, redemption, and the ingathering of the exiles. On the other hand, the Mizrahim and the Palestinian citizens of Israel confront and contextualize the basic premises of Zionist teleology. Yet they too evade a hermeneutical reimagining of the interrelation between "religion" and "nation." This evasion indicates a persistent reliance on an unrevised approach to secularism and on a modernist understanding of the secular nation-state (even when radically reconfigured as a polycentric political entity).

The reliance upon what I call "unrevised secularism" manifests in (1) the reluctance of the radical Mizrahi discourse to engage the resources of Judaism in order to cultivate distinctly localized and contextualized interpretations of a Jewish Israeli identity and, similarly, (2) the acceptance of the liberal framework of multiculturalism in the Vision of the Palestinian Israeli citizens of Israel. Hence, both the liberal and the polycentric models of multiculturalism offer only limited frameworks for conflict transformation in zones of ethnoreligious national conflicts. Further, even reclaiming the ethical traditions represented by thinkers such as Hannah Arendt and Walter Benjamin, and articulating the "diasporic" as a defining feature of Jewish experience and history, still does not offer a constructive or contextual framework for reimagining Jewish Israeli identity. This may be indicative of how reclaiming alterity and nonbelonging within the model of cohabitation amounts to an aspiration to imagine Israeli history out of existence because of its apparent inconsistency with nonnationalistic Jewish ethical traditions and because of the injustices remembered through the process of historicist self-estrangement. Hence, the reclaiming of alterity—the multiperspectival insight of the cohabitation model—needs to be supplemented by reclaiming and rearticulating indigeneity. Rearticulating indigeneity through the deeply historical multiperspectival prism of dispelling myopias is categorically different from the self-referential Zionist reclaiming of nativity as a process of national rebirth, rebuilding, and survival. To rearticulate indigeneity denotes a deep historical and cultural engagement with what it might mean to belong to, rather than be estranged from, Israel/Palestine, specifically, and the Middle East, generally. The Palestinian Israeli and Mizrahi discourses begin to move in this direction.

Recognizing the insights as well as the excesses of cultural theory and critique more broadly, my examination of the Palestinian Israelis and the Mizrahim suggested that two key objectives of the hermeneutics of citizenship are, first, to contextualize identities and interrogate the power dynamics that define their relationships and, second, to develop a nuanced "postsecular secularism" that acknowledges the enduring relevance of religion to public life and identity and to a definition of citizenship reimagined along more inclusivist and polycentric lines. Neither the Keshet nor the Vision, however, moves beyond the modernist presuppositions enfolded into the compartmentalization of religion primarily as a human rights issue. This compartmentalization of religion qua faith, afforded by individualist and cognitive biases, prevents these critics from reassessing and reimagining the relation between Judaism, Israeliness, and the dynamics of citizenship. Hence, neither the liberal framework as deployed in the Vision documents nor the polycentrism of the Keshet offers sufficiently elastic and imaginative frameworks for conflict transformation.

Indeed, my scrutiny of the Keshet and the Vision suggested one central obstacle to extrapolating from their models a comprehensive framework for peacebuilding and conflict transformation in ethnoreligious national contexts: their evasion of the role of religion in reimagining the Israeli "nation" and the meanings and parameters of belonging to the Israeli "state." While it focuses on exposing and undoing the orientalist, colonialist, and Eurocentric dimensions of Zionist ideology by reclaiming the Mizrahi past, the Mizrahi discourse represented in the Keshet stops short of asking what might be the Jewish significance of a radically restructured Israel. It also fails to explore what resources might be available for reimagining the political theology of secular Zionism as articulated and perpetuated by the Israeli state and the broader Zionist discourse.

The Vision, on the other hand, renders the interrelation between Judaism and Zionism problematic and contradictory to human rights norms. Thus, the Vision stresses the need to overcome this conflation of religion and nation by relegating religion to a private or autonomous sphere and by ending public manifestations of symbolic, socioeconomic, and political Jewish superiority. This objective, however, cannot be attained solely by citing and dictating international legal norms but rather requires intra-Jewish and intra-Israeli conversations about the appropriate relation between religion and nation, an undertaking that is most taxing and urgent for the Jewish population of Israel and the diasporas.

The Hermeneutics of Citizenship as a Peacebuilding Process

Without a hermeneutics of citizenship, both the Vision and the Keshet will remain paradoxically trapped within the very paradigms they set out to deconstruct. For the Palestinian Israeli sector, this translates into political, cultural, religious, and national empowerment within the constraints of majority-minority relations. At the same time that they conceptualize a shift away from Zionist hegemony, the very framing of Palestinian Israeli demands in terms of minority rights reinforces the "naturalness" of the Jewish nation-state and its underlying ideological formations. On the other hand, Mizrahi reluctance to tackle how religion may fit into the reframing of the Israeli ethos beyond its interiorization and privatization suggests the incompleteness of their critique. While focusing on deconstructing the orientalist and Eurocentrist dimensions of the Zionist narrative, the Mizrahi discourse reproduces Zionist secularism. This offers a degree of irony because Zionist secularism is discursively embedded in its orientalist and Eurocentric background. The Mizrahi critique and constructive agenda could be deepened if the Mizrahim considered the resources of marginalized Jewish ethical traditions, including Middle Eastern and North African ones, relevant to reimagining membership in the Israeli nation-state. As in the case of the Palestinian Israelis, the Mizrahi proposal will move from critique to creative reimagining of Israeliness only through opening an intra-Jewish contestation of the Jewish meanings of Israel.

Therefore, while the Vision, Mizrahi polycentrism, and the cohabitation model identify political theology as a root cause of their predicament and as an obstacle to justpeace, their various modes of reconceiving the geopolitical space offer only limited models of "critical caretaking" and truncated resources for reimagining sociopolitical solidarities. Reimagining solidarities through a hermeneutical engagement with the interface between religion, ethnicity, and conceptions of the nation is pivotal not only for exposing underlying misframing and meta-injustices but also for reframing and transforming the justice discourse. However, the proposals for radical geopolitical reconfigurations—despite their critique of Israeli liberalism—still echo the liberal presumption that multicultural and multinational arrangements can rely solely on an adherence to abstracted constitutional principles. This is where these proposals are limited as frameworks for conflict transformation. To dispel the myopic 1967 paradigm dominating the "peace process," it is necessary to look beyond the interrelation among disparate sites of injustice and how they can all be traced back to Euro-Zionism. Moving beyond denaturalizing the axiomatic building blocks of a national myopia to constructive reimagining *who we are* is an interpretive process, dynamically drawing on lived and historical experiences as the Mizrahi discourse does but also on religious, cultural, and ethical resources as RHR, Butler, Hartman, Leibowitz, and other individuals and groups profiled earlier in this book do.

The study of the Israeli peace camp in this book therefore illuminates why a multidisciplinary approach to conflict transformation that puts peace studies literature and peacebuilding methods in conversation with political theory, cultural theory, and religious studies enriches both the analysis of conflicts (especially those involving identity claims and entitlements) and the design of strategic frameworks for peacebuilding. The peacebuilding literature is correct to focus on the need to transform underlying relational patterns in an effort to move beyond a mere reactionary response to violent conflicts toward a dynamic and holistic understanding of justpeace. This approach, however, should also employ the critical analytic tools available in postcolonial theory that enable one to both listen to and deconstruct the often irreconcilable narratives of victimhood and justifications of violent praxis.

This deconstructive turn that does not accept identity claims and national historiographies at face value also does not entail a paternalistic approach to peacebuilding but rather intends to enrich the scope of conflict analysis, thereby broadening the possible horizons of peacebuilding. Likewise, the focus of political theory on multiculturalism as a model for thinking about ethnocultural justice needs to be supplemented with substantive reinterpretation of identity and belonging. This insight opens the door to new venues of peacebuilding. This book focused on the subaltern as a hybrid terrain where such constructive reframing can take place.[10]

But what is the practical import of this analysis for political platforms and programs? This may be the nagging question for the policy-oriented readers of this book. Is it possible to politically campaign with the hermeneutics of citizenship as a political slogan? Indeed, in arguments about national entitlements and historiographies, the invocation of such a slogan would most likely amount to political irrelevance at best. But the point of the hermeneutics of citizenship is to deconstruct what may appear axiomatic about "who we are" by posing challenges from the sociopolitical, religious, and cultural margins. A skillful politician should be capable of introducing this possibility, and outlining its eventual economic and security advantages, without exploiting the marginalized for expedient but short-sighted political gains.

The nineteenth-century French philosopher Ernest Renan famously talked about the "nation" as "a daily plebiscite."[11] He meant that the perception of national homogeneity and unity would work only as long as people believed in it and enabled its cultivation. Unlike Renan's fundamentally subjectivist and cognitive interpretation of the nation, the hermeneutics of citizenship recognizes the nation as embedded, embodied, and engrained in daily practice and enshrined in memory. Hence, "undoing" it must involve something more than merely telling those that constitute a nation that that figment of the imagination of which they are made should cease to exist. In fact, the hermeneutics of citizenship seeks not to undo but rather to reimagine belonging through estrangement.

The hermeneutics of citizenship, with its focus on the potential resources afforded by marginalized voices and spaces of hybridity, including the vast reservoirs of religious and cultural traditions, provides analytic tools for rethinking "who we are" and "who we ought to be." This process, I contend, is thoroughly polycentric, transhistorical, and multifaceted. It is "polycentric" because the *hermeneutics of citizenship* entails engaging counternarratives and embodied experiences from within (Palestinian Israelis and Mizrahim) and without (diasporas, displaced Palestinians). It is "transhistorical" because it retrieves voices, counterhistories, and traditions from within Judaism that have been eclipsed by prevailing Zionist readings of Jewish history and destiny. Finally, this process is "multifaceted" because it involves more than a mere theoretical reframing; rather, it necessitates actual processes and programs that will engender attitudinal changes, enabling the reimagining of the subjective and normative boundaries of the "nation." Here, more work remains to be done to translate the new vistas opened up by the hermeneutics of citizenship into designs for conflict transformation. Still, the call to challenge homogenizing perceptions of the "national self" through a thick analysis of countervoices assumes the possibility of reconceiving the "we" in a way that would facilitate redressing structural and cultural violence and the effects of past injustices.

The practical import of the hermeneutics of citizenship, therefore, is not an immediate but rather a long-term reframing of the perceptions, attitudes, and narratives that inform and reimagine conceptions of peace and justice. But this is not merely an obscure, theoretical exercise. Rather, this approach carries important practical implications for conflict transformation, a process that begins before "peace" through an interpretative engagement with the meanings of identity and the recognition that peace, in and of itself, "is not enough."

NOTES

INTRODUCTION

1. Francis Deng, *War of Visions: Conflicts of Identities in the Sudan* (Washington, DC: Brookings Institution Press, 1991), 387–88.
2. Rohan Edrisinha, "Constitutionalism, Pluralism, Ethnic Conflict: The Need for a New Initiative," in *Creating Peace in Sri Lanka: Civil War and Reconciliation*, ed. Robert I. Rotberg (Washington, DC: Brookings Institution Press, 1999), 171.
3. The Oslo Accords are officially known as the "Declaration of Principles on Interim Self-Government Arrangements" or the "Declaration of Principles" (DOP), signed on September 13, 1993, between Palestinians and Israelis, under the facilitation of President Clinton of the United States.
4. Oren Yiftachel, *Ethnocracy: Land and Identity Politics in Israel/Palestine* (Philadelphia: University of Pennsylvania Press, 2006), 15.
5. Ibid., 16.
6. This process is "creeping" "because it is undeclared, and is being amplified by a sequence of incremental decisions about practices, such as the ongoing settlement of Jews in the occupied territories and the increasingly heavy-handed policies toward Arabs and non-Jewish immigrants in Israel" (Yiftachel, *Ethnocracy*, 126).
7. Baruch Kimmerling, *Politicide: Ariel Sharon's War against the Palestinians* (London: Verso, 2003).
8. Ilan Pappé, *A History of Modern Palestine: One Land, Two Peoples* (Cambridge: Cambridge University Press, 2004), 255.
9. Nadim Rouhana, *Palestinian Citizens in an Ethnic Jewish State: Identities in Conflict* (New Haven: Yale University Press, 1997), 209.
10. An extensive discussion of peacebuilding appears in chapter 2.
11. Christine Bell, *Peace Agreements and Human Rights*, rev. ed. (2000; Oxford: Oxford University Press, 2003), 205.
12. This understanding of the term "ethnorepublicanism" draws on the analysis in Yossi Yonah, *In Virtue of Difference: The Multicultural Project in Israel*, rev. ed. (2005; Jerusalem: Van Leer Jerusalem Institute, 2007) [in Hebrew]. For further discussion of Yonah's definition as it applies to the analysis in this book, see chapter 7 (especially 227).
13. Dimi Reider and Aziz Abu Sarah, "In Israel, the Rent Is Too Damn High," *New York Times*, August 3, 2011, http://www.nytimes.com/2011/08/04/opinion/in-israel-the -rent-is-too-damn-high.

14. See, for example, Reuven Pedazthur, "The Necessary Cut," *Haaretz*, August 7, 2011, http://www.haaretz.co.il/hasite/spages/1237325.html.
15. For a mapping and critique of the subfield of religious peacebuilding, see Atalia Omer, "Religious Peacebuilding: The Exotic, the Good, and the Theatrical," *Practical Matters*, no. 5, Spring 2012, http://practicalmattersjournal.org/issue/5/centerpieces/religious-peacebuilding (accessed April 24, 2012).
16. While predominantly focused on issues of race, class, and gender demarcations, this genre that explores symbolic and social boundaries as well as the related research of "borders" becomes an interlocutor with this work. Examples of works in cultural sociology that study social and symbolic boundaries include Michèle Lamont, "Symbolic Boundaries and Status," in *Cultural Sociology*, ed. Lynette P. Spillman (Malden, MA: Blackwell, 2002), 98–119; Lamont, *The Dignity of Working Men: Morality and the Boundaries of Race, Class, and Immigration* (Cambridge: Harvard University Press and New York Russell Sage Foundation, 2002); and Alon Lazar, "Cultural Trauma as a Potential Symbolic Boundary," *International Journal of Politics, Culture and Society* 22, no. 2 (June 2009): 183–90.
17. Michèle Lamont and Virág Molnár, "The Study of Boundaries in the Social Sciences," *Annual Review of Sociology* 28 (2002): 168.
18. Ibid., 169.
19. Ibid., 187.
20. See Pierre Bourdieu, *Distinction: A Social Critique of the Judgment of Taste*, trans. Richard Nice, rev. ed. (1979; Cambridge: Harvard University Press, 1984).
21. See also Pierre Bourdieu and Jean-Claude Passeron, *Reproduction in Education, Society, and Culture*, trans. Richard Nice, rev. ed. (1972; Beverly Hills, CA: Sage, 1977); Cynthia Fuchs Epstein, *Deceptive Distinctions: Sex, Gender, and Social Order* (New Haven: Yale University Press, 1988); and Steven Peter Vallas, "Symbolic Boundaries and the New Division of Labor: Engineers, Workers and the Restructuring of Factory Life," *Research in Social Stratification and Mobility* 18 (2001): 3–37.
22. For the earliest articulation of *habitus*, see Pierre Bourdieu, "Intellectual Field and Creative Project," *Social Science Information* 8 (April 1969): 89–119. See also Bourdieu, *Distinction*. For an intellectual review of Bourdieu that illustrates how the concept of habitus enables the articulation of elastic interpretations of agency and the possibility of the transformation of social structures, refer to Omar Lizardo, "The Cognitive Origins of Bourdieu's *Habitus*," *Theory of Social Behaviour* 34, no. 4 (2004): 375–401.
23. See Lamont and Molnár, "Study of Boundaries in the Social Sciences," 184–88; Akhil Gupta and James Ferguson, "Space, Identity, and the Politics of Difference," *Cultural Anthropology* 7, no. 1 (1992): 6–24; Robert R. Alvarez, "The Mexican-US Border: The Making of an Anthropology of Borderlands," *Annual Review of Anthropology* 24 (1995): 447–70; and David Gutiérrez, "Migration, Emergent Ethnicity, and the 'Third Space': The Shifting Politics of Nationalism in Greater Mexico," *Journal of American History* 86, no. 2 (1999): 481–518.
24. For an explication of this idea, see also Atalia Omer, "The Hermeneutics of Citizenship as a Peacebuilding Process: A Multiperspectival Approach to Justice," *Journal of Political Theology* 11, no. 5 (October 2010): 650–73.
25. As I show in chapter 1, the case of Israeli secular nationalism illustrates this argument because, even when framing its claim to the land as "historical and cultural," it relies on biblical themes like "return" and the "ingathering of the exiles."

26. See, for example, Judith Butler, "Is Judaism Zionism?," in *The Power of Religion in the Public Sphere*, ed. Eduardo Mendieta and Jonathan VanAntwerpen (New York: Columbia University Press/SSRC Books, 2011), 70–91, and Judith Butler, *Parting Ways: Jewishness and the Critique of Zionism* (New York: Columbia University Press, 2012).

27. For a defining example of these conversations in religious studies, see Talal Asad, *Formation of the Secular: Christianity, Islam, Modernity* (Stanford: Stanford University Press, 2003).

28. I characterize the works of David Little and R. Scott Appleby as the primary examples of this constructive approach to the study of religion, conflict, and peacebuilding. See, for a succinct articulation of the constructive orientation, Little and Appleby, "A Moment of Opportunity? The Promise of Religious Peacebuilding in an Era of Religious and Ethnic Conflict," in *Religion and Peacebuilding*, ed. Harold Coward and Gordon S. Smith (Albany: State University of New York Press, 2004), 1–26.

29. By the designation "land theology," I refer here to the religious Zionist settlement movement that emerged in the 1970s and has viewed the commandment to settle the entirety of the land as one that overrides the other 612 commandments. This focus on settling the land is grounded in a particular perception of the events that led to the establishment of the state of Israel and the victory of 1967 as denoting the dawn of the messianic era. This messianic orientation and interpretation of historical events was born out of the teachings of Rabbi Kook (the first chief rabbi of Palestine appointed by the British during the time of the mandate), his son who succeeded him as the leader of the yeshiva that Kook the elder had established in Jerusalem, and the religious youth that sought guidance that would enable them to find a degree of consistency between their religiosity, their desire to fully embrace an Israeli identity, and their resentment of the secularist and often antireligious policies and attitudes of the Israeli mainstream. For an excellent overview of the settlement movement in Israel, see Gideon Aran, "Jewish Zionist Fundamentalism: The Bloc of the Faithful in Israel (Gush Emunim)," in *Fundamentalism Observed*, ed. Martin E. Marty and R. Scott Appleby (Chicago: University of Chicago Press, 1991). See also Idith Zertal and Akiva Eldar, *Lords of the Land: The War over Israel's Settlements in the Occupied Territories, 1967–2007* (Or Yehouda: Dvir, 2005) [in Hebrew]. For an account of the ideological clashes between settlers and mainline Israelis within the Green Line, see Gadi Taub, *The Settlers* (New Haven; Yale University Press, 2010). For a radically different account that illuminates the ideological continuities between secular and religious Zionists within and without the Green Line, see Joyce Dalsheim, *Unsettling Gaza: Secular Liberalism, Radical Religion, and the Israeli Settlement Project* (Oxford: Oxford University Press, 2011).

30. By "polycentric," I refer here to critiques that focus on the conservative underpinnings of liberal frameworks of multiculturalism, which, while broadening and diversifying conceptions of membership and participation in the polity, nonetheless maintain the underlying power dynamics (especially while presupposing the presence of a clear "majority" culture). The polycentric approach, in contrast, aims to diversify and push the centers of power and political engagements. See also chapter 2.

31. Butler, *Parting Ways*, 5

32. Ibid., 7

33. Throughout the book, I distinguish between the Palestinian citizens of Israel and the Palestinians of the occupied territories of 1967 as well as the various refugees beyond those geopolitical borders. The Palestinians who became citizens of the Israeli state

remained within the 1949 armistice lines known as the "Green Line," and their experiences and struggles are distinctly different from those of non-Israeli Palestinians.

34. Homi Bhabha, *The Location of Culture* (London: Routledge, 1994), 37.

35. Currently, only a few academically rigorous treatments of post-Zionism are available. See, for example, Ephraim Nimni, ed., *The Challenge of Post-Zionism: Alternatives to Israeli Fundamentalist Politics* (New York: Zed Books, 2003); Laurence Silberstein, *The Postzionism Debates: Knowledge and Power in Israeli Culture* (New York: Routledge, 1999); and Gabriel Piterberg, *The Returns of Zionism: Myths, Politics and Scholarship in Israel* (London: Verso, 2008).

36. For some of the most prominent examples of the work of revisionist Israeli historians, see Benny Morris, *The Birth of the Palestinian Refugee Problem* (Cambridge: Cambridge University Press, 1987), and Ilan Pappé, *The Making of the Arab-Israeli Conflict: 1947–1951* (London: I. B. Tauris, 1992).

37. Uri Ram, "The Colonization Perspective in Israeli Sociology: Internal and External Comparisons," *Journal of Historical Sociology* 6, no. 3 (1993): 327–50.

38. See Amnon Raz-Krakotzin, "Exile in the Midst of Sovereignty: A Critique of 'Shelilat HaGalut' in Israeli Culture II," *Theory and Criticism* 5 (Fall 1994): 113–32 [in Hebrew], and Gabi Piterberg, "The Nation and Its Raconteurs: Orientalism and Nationalist Historiography," *Theory and Criticism* 6 (Spring 1996): 81–103 [in Hebrew]. These Israeli scholars employ postmodern lenses influenced by Michel Foucault, Edward Said, Hayden White, and others to analyze and critique Zionist interpretations of history. To this end, they move beyond the arguments of the revisionist historians.

39. Prominent Israeli sociologist Baruch Kimmerling, for instance, observes that the breakdown since the 1970s of the hegemonic Zionism that consolidated Israeli nation-statehood resulted in the emergence of distinct subcultures. Indeed, this phenomenon may be classified by some standards as multiculturalism. However, far from engendering possibilities for a just reconciliation with the non-Jewish Palestinian citizens and subjects, this phenomenon enabled two metacultural narratives to dominate in amplified form: an Israeli brand of "Jewishness" and militarism. Kimmerling consequently attributes the realization of an ethnocentric chauvinistic political alliance to the lack of an alternative for the hegemonic Zionism of the first three decades of Israeliness. This condition of multiculturalism Kimmerling describes has been detrimental to the Christian or Muslim Palestinians because it is indicative of the persistence of the ethnocentric logic of citizenship. See Kimmerling, *The Invention and Decline of Israeli-ness: State, Society, and the Military* (Berkeley: University of California Press, 2001), 173–228. Instead of this form of multiculturalism within the confines of ethnocracy, Yonah insists on overturning the ethnocratic logic by advancing other polycentric (as distinct from ethnocentric) modalities of multicultural citizenship; see Yonah, *In Virtue of Difference*, 222.

40. This theoretical approach is in conversation with debates concerning multicultural citizenship based primarily in North American and European contexts. See, for example, Iris Marion Young, *Inclusion and Democracy* (Oxford: Oxford University Press, 2002); Nancy Frazer and Axel Honneth, *Redistribution or Recognition?: A Political-Philosophical Exchange* (New York: Verso, 2003); Will Kymlicka and Wayne Norman, *Citizenship in Diverse Societies* (Oxford: Oxford University Press, 2000); and Kymlicka, *Multicultural Odysseys: Navigating the New International Politics of Diversity* (New York: Oxford University Press, 2007).

41. Israeli political theorist Uri Ram helpfully differentiates between four interrelated yet distinctive post-Zionist attitudes: postideological, postmodern, post-Marxist, and postcolonial. See Ram, *The Time of the "Post": Nationalism and the Politics of Knowledge in Israel* (Tel Aviv: Resling, 2006) [in Hebrew], especially 174–85. According to the postideological stance, Zionism is a phase in a teleological progression toward the normalization of Jewish national existence—a progression that consists in a move from collectivist to individualist ethos. Examples of this trend can be found in A. B. Yehoshua, *In Praise of Modernity: Five Essays on Zionism* (Jerusalem: Schocken, 1984) [in Hebrew]; Menachem Brinker, "After Zionism," *Siman Kria* 19 (1986): 21–29 [in Hebrew]; and Charles Liebman and Eliezer Don Yehiya, *Civil Religion in Israel* (Berkeley: University of California Press, 1983). Next, because the point of departure of the postmodern Foucauldian orientation is the perception of nationalism as an oppressive discourse, post-Zionism, which is in fact an instance of postnationalism, is viewed as a liberating concept. It is liberating because instead of denoting a historical phase of fruition, as in the postideological paradigm, the post-Zionist moment involves a disintegration into previously marginalized and eclipsed narratives. To this extent, postnationalism represents one instance in the general postmodern attempt to deconstruct the grand narratives of modernity. For examples, refer to Ariella Azulai and Adi Ofir, "One Hundred Years of a Jewish State," *Tikkun* 13, no. 2 (1998): 68–71. While this Foucauldian strand highlights the need to challenge the hegemonic Zionist narrative, the Habermasian orientation of the postmodern approach underscores the question of Israeli citizenship as a crucial component of a postnational political arrangement. The emphasis here is on the need to move away from the modernist monocultural conception of the nation-state in an effort to redefine Israel as a democratic and secular state for all its citizens. For a prominent example of this genre, see Gershon Shafir, and Yoav Peled, *Being Israeli: The Dynamics of Multiple Citizenship* (Cambridge: Cambridge University Press, 2002). Some scholars in this camp, however, draw on the theoretical discussion of multiculturalism and the politics of recognition in an attempt to uphold cultural specificities despite the decoupling of culture from state (see discussion in chapter 2). Third, the post-Marxist position emphasizes structural and socioeconomic causes (including globalization) of the emergence of post-Zionist attitudes. For a prominent example, see Ram, *The Changing Agenda of Israeli Sociology: Theory, Ideology, and Identity* (New York: SUNY Press, 1995), and Ram, *The Globalization of Israel: McWorld in Tel Aviv, Jihad in Jerusalem* (London: Routledge, 2008). The post-Marxist framework identifies how globalization generated a dialectical relation between the neoliberal, civic, and cosmopolitan pole, on the one hand, and the neo-ethnic, communitarian, and fundamentalist pole, on the other—explaining each attitude epiphenomenally in materialist terms as a function of class. Finally, the postcolonial attitude applies Edward Said's critique of orientalism to the case of Israel. It focuses on subaltern narratives of identity and especially on the Jewish Mizrahi identity as Zionism's domestic "other." Thus, post-Zionism here consists in the new Mizrahi articulation of Zionism as an Ashkenazi-colonialist project. I provide a detailed exploration of this subgenre in chapter 7.

42. Yonah, *In Virtue of Difference*, 220–28.

43. Other critiques of multiculturalism are grounded in the argument that multiculturalism glosses over and enables sociocultural and economic inequalities. See, for instance, Brian Barry, *Culture and Equality: An Egalitarian Critique of Multiculturalism* (Cambridge: Harvard University Press, 2001). Another line of critique of liberal

multiculturalism comes from theorists who observe a tension between the striving toward ethnocultural justice within a multicultural framework and the persistence of a territorial model of ethnic hegemony. See, for instance, Brian Walker, "Plural Cultures, Contested Territories: A Critique of Kymlicka," *Canadian Journal of Political Science* 30, no. 2 (June 1997): 211–36.

44. Nadav G. Shelef, *Evolving Nationalism: Homeland, Identity, and Religion in Israel, 1925– 2005* (Ithaca: Cornell University Press, 2010).

CHAPTER ONE

1. In a work that portrays Israel as a landscape of intersecting and competing discourses of citizenship, Gershon Shafir and Yoav Peled posit the "liberal" discourse of secular Israelis in opposition to the ethnocentric discourse of the settlers. The liberal paradigm, they conclude, is conducive to peace, whereas the ethnocentric one presents the primary obstacle for the peace process. See Shafir and Peled, *Being Israeli: The Dynamics of Multiple Citizenship* (Cambridge: Cambridge University Press, 2002). This rendering of secular and religious interpretations of Zionism as antithetical is also echoed in Gadi Taub, *The Settlers and the Struggle over the Meaning of Zionism* (New Haven: Yale University Press, 2010). A less bifurcated account of the interrelations between secular and religious interpretations of Zionism and one that highlights the important relations of continuity between mainline secular conceptions of Israeli identity and the ideology of the settlers can be found in the work of Joyce Dalsheim, *Unsettling Gaza: Secular Liberalism, Radical Religion, and the Israeli Settlement Project* (Oxford: Oxford University Press, 2011).

2. The title of this chapter uses the more minimalist concept of "peacemaking" rather than the more comprehensive notion of "peacebuilding" to characterize the work and orientation of the Israeli secular peace movement. This is because the peace movement focuses on the cessation of violence without probing into questions of structural and cultural violence. A secularist reinterpretation of Judaism as ethnicity, nationality, and/or culture enables the peace camp to bypass engaging with the root causes of the Israel-Palestine conflict.

3. The groups considered under this "consensus" heading are as diverse as the secular Shalom Achshav (Peace Now), Twenty-First Year, Yesh Gvul (There Is a Border/ Limit), Dai La'kibush (Enough of the Occupation), Gush Shalom (Block of Peace), and a whole host of other organizations to be discussed in the present chapter, as well as the religious Rabbis for Human Rights, Oz veShalom (Courage and Peace), and Netivot Shalom (Paths of Peace), to be analyzed in chapters 4 and 5.

4. Yehouda Shenhav, *The Time of the Green Line: Towards a Jewish Political Thought* (Tel Aviv: Am Oved, 2010) [in Hebrew]. This is a book Shenhav published a couple of years after he served as an external reader of my dissertation, which constitutes the kernel of this book, at Harvard University. I am indebted to Shenhav's work on the Mizrahim in Israel. This later critique of the Israeli left is indeed highly consistent with the conceptual foundations he explicates in his earlier works, which will be discussed throughout the book. Shenhav's thesis typifies a small but growing line of scholarship that treats Israel/Palestine as one unitary geopolitical and analytic space. More on this below in this chapter.

5. In order to examine how perceptions of Israeli citizenship vis-à-vis Judaism and Jewish history relate to resolutions of the Palestinian predicament that might be interpreted as just, this chapter primarily highlights the ideological rather than the organizational and strategic dimensions of the Zionist peace camp. The mechanisms

of social protest, mobilization, and consensus building employed by the peace camp, though an equally important topic of research, have already been addressed in a few pioneering sociological and historical explorations of the Israeli movement for peace as a subset of the growing literature on social movements. For examples of such works, please see David Hall-Cathala, *The Peace Movement in Israel, 1967–87* (Brighton, UK: Macmillan, 1990); Reuven Kaminer, *The Politics of Protest: The Israeli Peace Movement and the Palestinian Intifada* (Brighton, UK: Sussex Academic Press, 1996); Mordechai Bar-On, *In Pursuit of Peace: A History of the Israeli Peace Movement* (Washington, DC: U.S. Institute of Peace Press, 1996); and Tamar Hermann, *The Israeli Peace Movement: A Shattered Dream* (Cambridge: Cambridge University Press, 2009). For a work that focuses on nonviolent activism in the Palestinian and Israeli landscapes in a post-Oslo era—widely considered as a moment of decline of the Israeli peace camp—see Maia Carter Hallward, *Struggling for a Just Peace: Israeli and Palestinian Activism in the Second Intifada* (Gainesville: University Press of Florida, 2011).

6. Walter Laqueur, *A History of Zionism* (New York: Schocken Books, 2003), 545–49. For an account of how the Biltmore summit also marked the inauguration of the dominance of the United States as a party involved in Zionist and later Israeli agendas, see Monty Noam Penkower, "American Jewry and the Holocaust: From Biltmore to the American Jewish Conference," *Jewish Social Studies* 47, no. 2 (1985): 95–114.

7. Ilan Pappé, *A History of Modern Palestine: One Land, Two Peoples* (Cambridge: Cambridge University Press, 2004), 72–116.

8. Laqueur, *History of Zionism*, 493.

9. The text of the Biltmore Declaration can be found in *The Israel-Arab Reader*, ed. Walter Laqueur (New York: Citadel Press, 1969), 77–79, or in *The Jew in the Modern World*, ed. Paul R. Mendes-Flohr and Jehuda Reinhartz (New York: Oxford University Press, 1980), 470–71.

10. Hall-Cathala, *Peace Movement in Israel*, 24. For examples of revisionist historical scholarship and its engagement with the mythos of Zionism, refer to Simha Flapan, *The Birth of Israel: Myth and Realities* (New York: Pantheon Books, 1987); Baruch Kimmerling, *Zionism and Territory: The Socio-Territorial Dimensions of Zionist Politics* (Berkeley: University of California Press, 1983); Benny Morris, *1948 and After: Israel and the Palestinians* (Oxford: Oxford University Press, 1990); Morris, *The Birth of the Palestinian Refugee Problem, 1947–1949* (Cambridge: Cambridge University Press, 1987); Morris, *The Birth of the Palestinian Refugee Problem Revisited* (Cambridge: Cambridge University Press, 2004); Pappé, *Britain and the Arab-Israeli Conflict, 1948–1951* (New York: St. Martin's Press, 1988); Uri Ram, *The Changing Agenda of Israeli Sociology: Theory, Ideology, and Identity* (Albany: State University of New York Press, 1995); Tom Segev, *1949: The First Israelis* (New York: Free Press, 1986); Itamar Rabinovich, *The Road Not Taken: Early Arab-Israeli Negotiations* (New York: Oxford University Press, 1991); and Anita Shapira and Derek Jonathan Penslar, eds., *Israeli Historical Revisionism: From Left to Right* (London: Frank Cass, 2003).

11. Indeed, other Zionist thinkers like Ze'ev Jabotinsky—the ideological father of the later Likud Party—challenged the naïve slogan that presupposed the land of Palestine as empty and available to grab. But that critique led him to articulate more militant and expansionist settlement and defense strategies. See Joseph B. Schechtman, *The Vladimir Jabotinsky Story*, 2 vols. (New York: Thomas Yoseloff, 1956–61). For classical accounts of the Yishuv period and its social, cultural, and political landscape, as well as early reflections and scholarship concerning Jewish-Palestinian

relations, consult Alex Bein, *The Return to the Soil: A History of Jewish Settlement in Israel* (Jerusalem: Youth and Hechalutz Department of the Zionist Organisation, 1952); Shlomo Bardin, *Pioneer Youth in Palestine* (New York: Bloch, 1932); Moshe Burstein, *Self-Government of the Jews in Palestine since 1900* (Tel Aviv: Hyperion Press, 1934); Walter Laqueur and Barry Rubin, eds., *The Arab-Israeli Reader: A Documentary History of the Middle East Conflict* (New York: Penguin Books, 1984); Dan V. Segre, *Israel: A Society in Transition* (London: Oxford University Press, 1971); Jacob C. Hurewitz, *The Struggle for Palestine* (New York: Norton, 1950); John Marlowe, *The Seat of Pilate: An Account of the Palestine Mandate* (London: Cresset Press, 1959); Christopher Skyes, *Crossroads to Israel, 1917–1948* (Bloomington: Indiana University Press, 1973); Yehoshua Porath, *The Emergence of the Palestinian-Arab National Movement, 1918–1929* (Tel Aviv: AM Oved, 1976) [in Hebrew]; and Neville J. Mandel, *The Arabs and Zionism before World War I* (Berkeley: University of California Press, 1976).

12. Hall-Cathala, *Peace Movement in Israel*, 24–25. For a critical rethinking of the Zionists' encounters with the indigenous Palestinians and the long-term implications of these encounters, through the prism of postcolonial realities and theories, see the classical work by Maxime Rodinson, *Israel and the Arabs* (Harmondsworth: Penguin, 1968); Rodinson, *Israel: A Colonial-Settler State?* (New York: Monad, 1963); Noam Chomsky, *Peace in the Middle East? Reflections on Justice and Nationhood* (New York: Vintage Books, 1974); Michael Selzer, ed., *Zionism Reconsidered: The Rejection of Jewish Normalcy* (London: Macmillan, 1970); Amos Elon, *The Israelis: Founders and Sons* (New York: Holt, Reinhart & Winston, 1971); Shmuel Almog, ed., *Zionism and the Arabs: Essays* (Jerusalem: Zalman Shazar Center, 1983); Gershon Shafir, *Land, Labor and the Origins of the Israeli-Palestinian Conflict, 1882–1914* (Berkeley: University of California Press, 1996); Georges Friedmann, *The End of the Jewish People?* (Garden City, NY: Doubleday, 1967); Neil Caplan, *Palestine Jewry and the Arab Question, 1917–1925* (London: F. Cass, 1978); Shlomo Avineri, *The Making of Modern Zionism: Intellectual Origins of the Jewish State* (New York: Basic Books, 1981); Amnon Rubinstein, *The Zionist Dream Revisited: From Herzl to Gush Emunim and Back* (New York: Schocken Books, 1984); Laurence Silberstein, *New Perspectives on Israeli History: The Early Years of the State* (New York: New York University Press, 1991); Dan Horowitz and Moshe Lissak, *Trouble in Utopia: The Overburdened Polity of Israel* (Albany: State University of New York Press, 1989); Yael Zerubavel, *Recovered Roots: Collective Memory and the Making of Israeli National Tradition* (Chicago: University of Chicago Press, 1995); David Vital, *The Future of the Jews* (Cambridge: Harvard University Press, 1990); Nahla Abdo and Nira Yuval-Davis, "Palestine, Israel and Zionist Settler Project," in *Unsettling Settler Societies*, ed. Davia Stasiulis and Nira Yuval-Davis (London: Sage, 1995); Scott Atran, "The Surrogate Colonization of Palestine, 1917–1939," *American Ethnologist* 16 (1989): 719–44; Dalsheim, *Unsettling Gaza*; Eugene Rogan and Avi Shlaim, eds., *The War for Palestine: Rewriting the History of 1948* (Cambridge: Cambridge University Press, 2001); Silberstein, *The Postzionism Debates: Knowledge and Power in Israeli Culture* (New York: Routledge, 1999); Oren Yiftachel, *Ethnocracy: Land and Identity Politics in Israel/Palestine* (Philadelphia: University of Pennsylvania Press, 2005); and Ilan Pappé, *The Israel/Palestine Question* (London: Routledge, 1999).

13. See also Itzhak Galnoor, *The Partition of Palestine: Decision Crossroads in the Zionist Movement* (Albany: State University of New York Press, 1995).

14. Ahad Ha'am was the pen name of Asher Grinzberg.

15. See Ahad Ha'am, "This Is Not The Way," available on http://www.zionism-israel .com/hdoc/Achad_haam_not_the_way.htm#1 (accessed January 14, 2012).

16. Hall-Cathala, *Peace Movement in Israel*, 26.
17. Laqueur, *History of Zionism*, 252.
18. See, for example, Alvin Rosenfeld, "'Progressive' Jewish Thought and the New Anti-Semitism," American Jewish Committee, December 2006, http://www.ajc.org/atf/cf/%7B42D75369-D582-4380-8395-D25925B85EAF%7D/PROGRESSIVE_JEWISH_THOUGHT.PDF. For further works exploring Magnes's positions, see Arthur Goren, ed., *Dissenter in Zion: From the Writing of Judah Magnes* (Cambridge: Harvard University Press, 1982), and William M. Brinner and Moses Rischin, eds., *Like All the Nations?: The Life and Legacy of Judah L. Magnes* (Albany: State University of New York Press, 1987).
19. Tamar Hermann discusses the rationales, motivations, and struggles with the mainstream Zionist leadership of this proto-peace movement and its call for relinquishing the aspiration for Jewish majoritarianism in *Israeli Peace Movement*, especially 74–77.
20. Hall-Cathala, *Peace Movement in Israel*, 26, and Silberstein, *Postzionism Debates*, 48–50.
21. Laqueur, *History of Zionism*, 252–53.
22. Despite exerting profound influence on Brit Shalom, neither Buber nor Magnes was an official member. They would assume leadership positions in the later prototypical peace movement Ihud, founded in the midst of World War II (more about it later in the chapter).
23. Paul Mendes-Flohr, editor's prefatory note, in *A Land of Two People: Martin Buber on Jews and Arabs*, ed. Mendes-Flohr (Chicago: University of Chicago Press, 2005), 72.
24. "Brith Shalom (The Peace Association) Statutes" (Jerusalem: Hamadpis Press, 1925), reprinted in Mendes-Flohr, *Land of Two People*, 74.
25. This quotation provided the opening lines for "Towards Union in Palestine," a booklet edited by Buber, Magnes, and Ernst Simon under the auspices of the Ihud Party (see below)—a later manifestation of Brit Shalom. Cited in "The History of the Original Brit Shalom, founded 1925," http://www.britshalom.org/background.htm (accessed October 27, 2011).
26. Tamar Hermann, "The Bi-national Idea in Israel/Palestine: Past and Present," *Nations and Nationalism* 11, no. 3 (2005): 385.
27. Cited in "The History of the Original Brith Shalom, founded 1925," http://www.britshalom.org/background.htm (accessed October 27, 2011).
28. Laqueur, *History of Zionism*, 253. Labeling the Brit as assimilationist situates the debate over the nature of Zionism in the broader context of intra-Jewish conversations concerning Judaism's response to modernity. In many respects, political Zionism gained momentum owing to recognition that despite the assimilation into European culture, anti-Semitism persisted.
29. Hermann, "Bi-national Idea in Israel/Palestine," 385, and Laqueur, *History of Zionism*, 253. Magnes and Chaim Kalvarisky worked tirelessly to bring about a dialogue with the Arab Palestinians and with regional Arab leaders like Mussa Alalmi. But Arabs at the time could not accept the parity formula ("neither people should dominate or be dominated by the other"), as they constituted a majority (Laqueur, *History of Zionism*, 253–54). In one instance in 1946, Fawazi Darwish Hussaini (the cousin of the mufti) agreed to the premises of the parity model and managed to arrange for additional signatories. However, this effort was promptly nullified with the assassination of Hussaini by an Arab militant. This rapprochement effort too was subsequently abandoned (Laqueur, 267).

30. Hall-Cathala, *Peace Movement in Israel,* 26–27.
31. Laqueur, *History of Zionism,* 265–66.
32. *The Case for a Bi-national Palestine* (Bentov Report) (New York: Executive Committee of the Hashomer Hatzair Workers' Party, 1946), 129 (cited in Laqueur, *History of Zionism,* 266).
33. Reprinted in Mendes-Flohr, *Land of Two People,* 149.
34. Buber writes, "Just as the Jewish people need the land to live a full life, so the land needs the Jewish people to be complete." This quotation provides a striking illustration of why even the prestate proposal of binationalism does not fall outside the Zionist imagination. See Buber, *Bein Am Le-Artzo* [Between a People and Their Land] (Tel Aviv: Schocken, 1948), 12.
35. The "admission" by the Palestinian president Mahmoud Abbas, in an interview with Israeli TV, that "it was our mistake. It was an Arab mistake as a whole" to reject the United Nations partition plan of 1947 does not address "justice" issues pertaining to displacement and colonization. It does possibly address questions pertaining to peace in its negative sense as the termination of violence (including the occupation of the territories taken in 1967). For an account of the interview with Abbas, refer to "Arab Rejection of '47 Partition Plan Was Error, Palestinian Leader Says," Associated Press, October 28, 2011, http://www.nytimes.com/2011/10/29/world /middleeast/Arab-Rejection-of-1947-Partition-Plan-Was-Error-Mahmoud-Abbas -Says.html?_r=1&ref=mahmoudabbas.
36. Laqueur, *History of Zionism,* 266. Nonetheless, as will be described in great detail in chapter 4, the cause of binationalism continued to be advanced by critics of official Zionism, ranging from Jewish Israelis like Haim Hanegbi and Meron Benvenisti to Palestinian thinkers like Sari Nusseibah and Edward Said to external observers such as Tony Judt and Helena Cobban (see Hermann, "Bi-national Idea in Israel/Palestine," 387–95).
37. Silberstein, *Postzionism Debates,* 21.
38. Ibid., 22.
39. The representation of a universal Jewish experience and a teleological interpretation of Jewish history will be discussed in greater detail in chapter 7, which elaborates on the case of the Mizrahim and how they challenge the Eurocentrism of the dominant Zionist historiography.
40. Nurith Gertz, *Myths in Israeli Culture: Captives of a Dream* (Portland, OR: Vallentine Mitchell, 2000), 30.
41. Ibid., 31.
42. Gertz poignantly explains this transposition: "The reaction to the image of the passive Jew of the Exile is strengthened when this image, negated and rejected by the new Israeli Jew, is applied to the Arab. The Arabs are the ones who fail to fight, who have no roots in this land, and who are not a people 'like all other peoples.' The Israelis, by contrast, are active, fighting and firmly rooted—integral members of the world community of nations" (33).
43. Ibid., 36–41. See also Zerubavel, *Recovered Roots,* and Anita Shapira, "The Bible and Israeli Identity," *Association for Jewish Studies Review* 28, no. 1 (2004): 11–42.
44. For a relevant exposition of the construction of Zionist periodization and meta-narratives that situates it within literature on collective memory's relation to history, see Zerubavel, *Recovered Roots.*
45. Michèle Lamont and Virág Molnár, "The Study of Boundaries in the Social Sciences," *Annual Review of Sociology* 28 (2002): 168. They contend that one area that needs

further development in the subfield of cultural sociology is the relationship between symbolic and social boundaries. This insight becomes even more critical when we recognize the potentially important ramifications of this research for conflict zones such as the one profiled in this study.

46. Bar-On, *In Pursuit of Peace*, 95–97.
47. Ibid., 30–33.
48. Ibid., 34–35.
49. Yael Yishai, *Land or Peace: Whither Israel?* (Stanford, CA: Hoover Institution Press, 1987), 20–23.
50. Bar-On, *In Pursuit of Peace*, 41.
51. Yishai, *Land or Peace*, 1–27.
52. Bar-On, *In Pursuit of Peace*, 42.
53. Quoted in ibid., 44.
54. For a defense of this approach as the most "pragmatic" option and one that ultimately is the most "just," see Yossi Beilin, "Just Peace: A Dangerous Objective," in *What Is a Just Peace?*, ed. Pierre Allan and Alexis Keller (Oxford: Oxford University Press, 2006), 130–48. Beilin rehearses the Zionist narrative of Jewish history as one of inescapable anti-Semitism and a series of pogroms as the background to the story of return to the "homeland." He argues that deploying the concept of "just peace" is not only redundant, but also dangerous because it could encourage an argument against peace. Beilin tells the story of a series of supposedly missed opportunities for peace in Palestine/Israel, underscoring that the implications of these missed opportunities were more casualties.
55. For an account of the transformation of biblical archeology in the 1970s, refer to Israel Finkelstein and Neil Asher Silberman, *The Bible Unearthed: Archeology's New Vision of Ancient Israel and the Origin of Its Sacred Texts* (New York: Free Press, 2002).
56. Arieh Lova Eliav, *Land of the Hart: Israelis, Arabs, the Territories, and a Vision of the Future* (Philadelphia: Jewish Publication Society of America, 1974).
57. Cited in Bar-On, *In Pursuit of Peace*, 65.
58. See Shapira, "Bible and Israeli Identity."
59. The council's charter reads accordingly: "The country is the home of two peoples—the people of Israel and the Palestinian people. The historic conflict between these two peoples over this land, which is dear to both, lies at the bottom of the Arab-Jewish conflict. The only road to peace is in the coexistence of two sovereign states, each one with a distinct national identity: the State of Israel for the Jewish people and a state for the Arab-Palestinian people which will serve as an expression of their right of self-determination in the political framework of their choosing." Cited in Bar-On (from Avnery's private archive), *In Pursuit of Peace*, 86.
60. Bar-On, *In Pursuit of Peace*, 88.
61. Idith Zertal and Akiva Eldar, *Lords of the Land: The Settlers and the State of Israel, 1967–2004* (Kinneret: Zmora-Bitan, 2004) [in Hebrew].
62. Yishai, *Land or Peace*, 145.
63. Bar-On, *In Pursuit of Peace*, 52–58.
64. Yishai, *Land or Peace*, 145–46.
65. See Yiftachel, *Ethnocracy*; Dalsheim, *Unsettling Gaza*; and Shenhav, *Time of the Green Line*.
66. For an account of this complicity, refer to Zertal and Eldar, *Lords of the Land*, especially chapter 6.
67. This begins a long Israeli tradition of antiwar and anti-occupation protest led by

military heroes. Most recently, the movement of "refuseniks" refused the draft to serve in Gaza during the event of December/January 2009.

68. Bar-On, *In Pursuit of Peace*, 97–98, and Jimmy Carter, *Palestine: Peace not Apartheid* (New York: Simon & Schuster, 2006), 106–7.

69. Hermann, *Israeli Peace Movement*, 10.

70. Hermann (ibid., 189–266) cites a few exceptions to the broad pessimism of the Israeli peace camp, including Galia Golan, *Israel and Palestine: Peace Plans from Oslo to Disengagement* (Princeton, NJ: Markus Weiner, 2007), and Arie Arnon and Saeb Banya, eds., *Economic Dimensions of a Two-State Agreement between Israel and Palestine* (Marseilles: Aix Group, 2007). These works focus on a realist framework for thinking optimistically about the possibility of peace. Hermann also profiles the emergence in the 1990s and 2000s of feminist and women peace activism as well as cross-sectoral (Jewish-Palestinian) activism (see especially 165–213).

71. Michael Feige, *One Place, Two Places: Gush Emunim, Peace Now and the Construction of Israeli Space* (Jerusalem: Magnes Press, 2002), 191–203 [in Hebrew].

72. Hall-Cathala, *Peace Movement in Israel*, 44–46.

73. Cited in Bar-On, *In Pursuit of Peace*, 106.

74. Ibid., 141–46, and Hall-Cathala, *Peace Movement in Israel*, 58–59 and 163–66.

75. Kaminer, *Politics of Protest*, 31–34, and Hall-Cathala, *Peace Movement in Israel*, 163–66. Representing an unprecedented degree of Jewish-Palestinian cooperation, the CSBZU demonstrated against the arbitrary and collective punishment practiced by the IDF in the territories and specifically against the decision to temporarily close Bir Zeit University due to the lack of Palestinian compliance with the new Civilian Administration. In the months leading up to the invasion of Lebanon in 1982, the CSBZU, which supported the two-state formula, gained a certain amount of prestige among Israeli doves who resented the occupation and its detrimental implications. This more radical component of the peace camp also invigorated the activities of PN against the annexationist policy of the Israeli government and the brutality of the occupation.

76. Kaminer, *Politics of Protest*, 35.

77. Hall-Cathala, *Peace Movement in Israel*, 166.

78. Ibid., 171–78.

79. Ibid., 166–71.

80. Hall-Cathala, *Peace Movement in Israel*, 165, and Kaminer, *Politics of Protest*, 34–36.

81. For a fascinating account of the paradox of the commemoration of Gruenzweig's murder by PN, see Feige, *One Place, Two Places*, 204–18.

82. Hall-Cathala, *Peace Movement in Israel*, 83.

83. Ibid., 65–82.

84. Similarly, section 5 (1) of the Political Parties Law, 1992, prohibits the registration of political parties if any aspect of their platforms may be interpreted as implying "the denial of the existence of the State of Israel as a Jewish and democratic state."

85. Chief Justice Aharon Barak, cited in Yousef Jabareen, "An Equal Constitution for All? On a Constitution and Collective Rights for Arab Citizens in Israel," www.mossawa center.org (accessed January 8, 2012)

86. Jack Khoury, "Israeli Arabs Warn against Dangers of 'Racist Legislation,'" *Haaretz*, May 30, 2009, http://www.haaretz.com/hasen/spages/1089021.html.

87. For a coverage of this development and a link to the report in Hebrew, see Noam Sheizaf, "Panel Appointed by Netanyahu Conclude: There Is No Occupation," July 9,

2012 http://972mag.com/judiciary-panel-appointed-by-netanyahu-concludes-there
-is-no-occupation/50451/.

88. Kaminer, *Politics of Protest*, 53.
89. Ibid., 49–51.
90. Ibid., 54.
91. Cited in ibid., 56.
92. For a fascinating comparison between the protest practices of Gush Emunim and PN, refer to Feige, *One Place, Two Places*, 163–90.
93. Excerpts from the *Covenant* cited in Kaminer, *Politics of Protest*, 56.
94. Certainly, as Kaminer, a researcher of the Israeli peace movement, notes, the Twenty-First Year posed a significant challenge to the Zionist left, in general, and to PN, in particular. By exposing the pervasive nature of the occupation through a systematic study of the educational and judicial systems, the group demonstrated the complicity of all facets of Israeli life with the occupation. It articulated the dreadful details of what PN had previously referred to with a rather sanitized slogan: "the occupation corrupts the occupier" (*Politics of Protest*, 55–65).
95. Ibid., 63–65.
96. Ibid., 131.
97. Ibid., 127.
98. The Twenty-First Year focused on the humanitarian crisis in the occupied territories, the brutality of the IDF, and the critical question of complicity. To this extent this movement is akin to the earlier committees (CSBZU and CAWL), Women in Black (and other women's peace groups that emerged after the eruption of the First Intifada), as well as newly formed human rights organizations like Rabbis for Human Rights and B'tselem (In the Image [of God]), a host of parents' groups protesting their children's service in the war against the Intifada, and Yesh Gvul (There Is a Border)—all those groups and organizations (and many more that sprang up in Israel/Palestine) are in some ideological proximity with or overlap with one another.
99. Kaminer, *Politics of Protest*, 78–81.
100. Ibid., 100.
101. Ibid., 100–104, and Bar-On, *In Pursuit of Peace*, 232–34.
102. Kaminer, *Politics of Protest*, 105–13, and Bar-On, *In Pursuit of Peace*, 251–56.
103. Bar-On, *In Pursuit of Peace*, 245–46.
104. Kaminer, *Politics of Protest*, 116–20.
105. Ibid., 132.
106. Bar On, *In Pursuit of Peace*, 267–87.
107. Kaminer, *Politics of Protest*, 45.
108. CRM and Shinui, in fact, cannot be classified as "left" at all because they define themselves as militantly liberal, in direct opposition to the diminishing communist legacy of Mapam and certain components within Labor. The ideological differences between the groups composing the Zionist "peace bloc" in the Knesset are indeed significant and worthy of further exploration. They became especially critical to any attempt to analyze the Oslo Processes.
109. In 1992, the Meretz alliance and the peace movement overlapped almost completely, leading to the diminishing role of extraparliamentary spheres of activities, except the meticulous continuation of the movement's Settlement Watch program. By the end of 1992, a few individuals in PN mobilized against Rabin's harsh retaliatory approach to attacks by Hamas (especially the decision of Rabin's cabinet to deport 415

Hamas leaders to southern Lebanon). The consensus in PN was that such acts were not only a clear violation of international law and human rights but also damaging and counterproductive to peace negotiations. The crisis surrounding the deportation of the Hamas leaders demonstrated that the peace movement was still relevant to the ongoing dynamics of the talks as well as a countervoice to incitements from the right wing that had capitalized on the fear of repeated terror attacks. See, for example, Bar-On, *In Pursuit of Peace*, 296–305.

110. Shafir and Peled, *Being Israeli*, 260–307.
111. Michael Shalev, "Liberalization and the Transformation of the Political Economy," in *The New Israel: Peacemaking and Liberalization*, ed. Gershon Shafir and Yoav Peled (Boulder, CO: Westview Press, 2000), 137–51; Lev Grinberg and Gershon Shafir, "Economic Liberalization and Breakup of the Histadrut's Domain," in *New Israel*, 103–27; Uri Ram, *The Globalization of Israel: McWorld in Tel Aviv, Jihad in Jerusalem* (London: Routledge, 2008).
112. Equally problematic is the effort of the social justice mass protest of summer 2011 (which spilled over to the following summer of 2012) to differentiate its anti-neoliberalism agenda from the Palestinian-Israeli conflict and the peace process. This differentiation is viewed strategically as a mechanism to generate a broad coalition of forces, but failure to probe the Jewish meanings of Israel leaves the discussion concerning the "common good" called for by the mass movement for social justice incomplete at best and myopic at worst.
113. Principles of the Meretz Platform, May 1, 1996, http://www.mfa.gov.il/MFA/Templates/Hasava.aspx?NRMODE=Published&NRNODEGUID={EA4CFCAD-F351-4568-AF2E-728B09535AE4}&NRORIGINALURL=%2fMFA%2fMFAArchive%2f1990_1999%2f1998%2f7%2fPrinciples%2520of%2520the%2520Meretz%2520Platform%25201996&NRCACHEHINT=Guest.
114. See also Shenhav, *Time of the Green Line*.
115. Amnon Raz-Krakotzkin, interview by Youssef Hijazi, February 28, 2005, Berlin: Institute for Advanced Studies, http://peacepalestine.blogspot.com/2005/02/amnon-raz-krakotzkin-i-feel.html.
116. Beilin, "A New Covenant on Religion and State" (1997), http://www.beilin.org.il/item_eng.asp?id=3 (accessed May 23, 2008).
117. Beilin, "Just Peace," 141.
118. Ibid., 144.
119. Ibid., 142.
120. Pappé, transcript of "Two States or One State" (a debate between Avnery and Pappé, 2007), http://www.inminds.com/article.php?id=10155 (accessed April 20, 2008).
121. The Geneva Initiative was drafted and endorsed by high-level Israeli and Palestinian peace activists and leaders (including Beilin). Yet it did not constitute an official binding agreement. The initiative was signed in October 2003. It endorsed the two-state formula. The preamble of the document reinforces an underlying approach to this case as involving two equally legitimate nationalisms: "This agreement marks the recognition of the right of the Jewish people to statehood and the recognition of the right of the Palestinian people to statehood . . . The Parties recognize Palestine and Israel as the homeland of their respective peoples." While the agreement underscored the 1967 borders as legitimate and as the basis for working out a comprehensive peace, the signatories suggested that different zones of Jerusalem might constitute the capitals for the two states. The Geneva Initiative also addressed the issue of Palestinian refugees in a more comprehensive manner than the mainstream

Israeli peace camp and the official stance of the Israeli government. The initiative highlighted that a comprehensive and lasting peace between Israelis and Palestinians would depend on recognizing UN resolutions on this matter as a point of departure. Article 7 of the Geneva document calls for compensating all refugees. The agreement specifies a few options for the refugees: they could return to Palestinian territories, they could remain in their host countries, or they could move to a third country. They may also return to the sovereign areas of Israel, but the numbers would depend on Israeli sovereign decisions. This last option ensures, of course, retaining a certain demographic balance and thus suggests what may be the limits of the "justice" envisioned by the Israeli signatories in the document.

122. Neve Gordon, "The Israeli Peace Camp in Dark Times," *Peace Review* 15, no. 1 (2003): 39–45.

123. When PN and Meretz failed to resist in an unequivocal manner the disproportional Israeli offensive on the Hizb'allah in southern Lebanon in 1993 (retaliating in response to an ongoing firing of Katyusha rockets into Israel), veteran activists like Avnery and Michel Warschawski, who had previously been involved in Sheli and the earlier committees of the 1980s, organized a new group they named Gush Shalom. Gush Shalom argued that PN had been coopted by the Labor-Meretz government and thus could not function as an effective voice of protest. A few weeks before the Oslo Declaration of Principles (DoP) was made public, Gush Shalom began its activity with demonstrations against the deportation of 415 Islamists and the 1993 Lebanon offensive, the "Settling Accounts" (Din veHeshbon) Operation. Since then, Gush Shalom has engaged in a wide range of activities, such as political education campaigns, including the issuing of a document listing the "Violations of the Oslo Agreement" (1994) and a manifesto titled "Jerusalem—Capital of Two States" (1995), a manifesto that broke an official taboo. The movement also launched a national campaign to boycott settlements' products (1997), a campaign to expose the myths and realities of "Barak's Generous Offers" (2001), and a campaign against the Separation Wall (2003). Gush Shalom has also rebuilt demolished houses, demonstrated against illegal settlements on Palestinian lands, and harvested olives on behalf of Palestinian villagers who are prohibited from accessing their groves, among other activities of a similar tenor.

124. See Gush Shalom official website: http://www.gush-shalom.org.

125. Uri Avnery, "The Right of Return" (2001), http://zope.gush-shalom.org/home/en/channels/avnery/archives_article127/ (accessed May 20, 2008).

126. Uri Avnery, "80 Theses for a New Peace Camp" (2001), http://gushshalom.org/archives/80points_eng.doc (accessed May 17, 2011).

127. While recognizing some of the landmark developments associated with the Oslo Processes (i.e., the mutual recognition of the Palestinian people and Israel), GS diverges from PN in interpreting Oslo as a breakthrough and "the beginning of the process to end the conflict." Instead, Avnery claims, "The respective Israeli governments regarded it as a way to maintain the occupation in large sections of the West Bank and the Gaza Strip, with the Palestinian self-government filling the role of an auxiliary security agency protecting Israel and the settlements . . . Throughout the period of the 'Oslo Process' Israel continued its vigorous expansion of the settlements . . . building an elaborate network 'bypass' roads, expropriating land, demolishing houses and uprooting plantations etc" (see Avnery, "80 Theses," 13). In his capacity as the primary voice of GS, Avnery also criticized the myth concerning Barak's "generous offer" in the Camp David Summit in 2000. Barak's offer demanded that

the Palestinians forfeit the right of return and sovereignty in East Jerusalem and the Temple Mount and that they consent to an Israeli annexation of the so-called settlement blocs (see Avnery, "80 Theses," 14–15). Because it believed the myth that Barak had "turned every stone," the eruption of the al-Aqsa Intifada, shortly after the utter failure of the Camp David Summit, devastated PN. Avnery offers a penetrating appraisal of this sense of profound disillusionment that led to what many observers and activists marked as "the end of the Israeli left": "A great part of the Israeli 'Peace Camp' collapsed during the al-Aqsa Intifada and it turns out that many of its convictions were shallow. Especially after Barak had 'turned every stone' and made 'more generous offers' than any previous Prime Minister, Palestinian behavior was incomprehensible to this part of the 'Peace Camp,' since it had never performed a thorough revision of the Zionist 'narrative' and did not internalize the fact that there is a Palestinian 'narrative' too. The only remaining explanation was that the Palestinians had deceived the Israeli Peace Camp, that they had never intended to make peace, and that their true purpose was to throw the Jews into the sea, as the Zionist right has always claimed. As a result, the dividing line between the Zionist 'right' and 'left' disappeared. The leaders of the Labor Party joined the Sharon Government and became its most effective apologists (Shimon Peres)" (Avnery, "80 Theses," 16).

128. Yonatan Shapira, interviewed on Israel Social TV, January 11, 2009, http://tv.social .org.il/politics/2009/01/11/stv-aza-refuseniks-8-1-09 (accessed January 8, 2012).

129. See Idith Zertal, *Israel's Holocaust and the Politics of Nationhood*, trans. Chaya Galai (Cambridge: Cambridge University Press, 2005), and Charles S. Liebman and Eliezer Don-Yehiya, *Civil Religion in Israel: Traditional Judaism and Political Culture in the Jewish State* (Berkeley: University of California Press, 1983).

CHAPTER TWO

1. Benedict Anderson, *Imagined Communities: Reflections on the Origin and Spread of Nationalism*, rev. ed. (1983; London: Verso, 1991). This analysis of nationalism is reminiscent also of Ernest Renan, *Qu'est-ce qu'une nation?* (Paris: Ancienne Maison Michel Lévy Frères, 1882), and Hans Kohn, *The Idea of Nationalism: A Study in Its Origins and Background* (New York: Collier Books, 1944). Notably, Anderson distinguishes his notion of *imagining* from Ernest Gellner's functionalist understanding of the nation as an "invented" community. See Anderson, 6, and Gellner, *Nationalism* (New York: New York University Press, 1997).

2. Anderson, *Imagined Communities*, 9–46.

3. Ibid., 5.

4. Partha Chatterjee, "Whose Imagined Community?," in *Mapping the Nation*, ed. Gopal Balakrishnan and Benedict Anderson, rev. ed. (1996; London: Verso, 2000), 214–25.

5. John Paul Lederach, *The Moral Imagination: The Art and Soul of Building Peace* (Oxford: Oxford University Press, 2005), 5 (emphasis mine).

6. Ibid., 175.

7. See, for example, John Paul Lederach, *Building Peace: Sustainable Reconciliation in Divided Societies* (Washington, DC: U.S. Institute of Peace Press, 1997); Larissa Fast, "Frayed Edges: Exploring the Boundaries of Conflict Resolution," *Peace and Change* 27, no. 4 (2002): 528–45; Johannes Botes, "Conflict Transformation: A Debate over Semantics or a Crucial Shift in the Theory and Practice of Peace and Conflict Studies?," *International Journal of Peace Studies* 8, no. 2 (Autumn/Winter 2003): 1–27; and

Lisa Schirch, *Ritual and Symbol in Peacebuilding* (Bloomfield, CT: Kumarian Press, 2004).

8. John Paul Lederach, *Preparing for Peace: Conflict Transformation across Cultures* (Syracuse, NY: Syracuse University Press, 1995), 201. Lederach is careful to distinguish conflict transformation from conflict resolution: "transformation includes, but is not bound by the contributions and approaches proposed by resolution-based language. It goes beyond a focus on the resolution of a particular problem or *episode* of conflict to seek the *epicenter* of conflict." See Lederach, *The Little Book of Conflict Transformation* (Intercourse, PA: Good Books, 2003), 31.

9. Lederach, *Little Book of Conflict Transformation*, 29–32, and Lederach, *Moral Imagination*.

10. Lederach, *Little Book of Conflict Transformation*, 10–11.

11. Chadwick Alger, introduction, in *A Just Peace through Transformation: Cultural, Economic, and Political Foundations for Change*, ed. Alger Stohl and Michael Stohl (Boulder, CO: Westview Press, 1988); Ho-Won Jeong, *Peace and Conflict Studies* (Burlington, VT: Ashgate, 2000); John Paul Lederach, "Journey from Resolution to Transformative Peacebuilding," in *From the Ground Up: Mennonite Contributions to International Peacebuilding*, ed. Cynthia Sampson and Lederach (New York: Oxford University Press, 2000).

12. Johan Galtung, "Violence, Peace and Peace Research," *Journal of Peace Research* 6, no. 3 (1969): 167–91. See also Galtung, "Twenty-Five Years of Peace Research: Ten Challenges and Some Responses," *Journal of Peace Research* 22, no. 2 (1985): 141–58.

13. Galtung outlined, in his seminal editorial for the first issue of the *Journal of Peace Research* (1964), "the integration of human society" and, in a later reflection on the concept (1968), "a pattern of cooperation and integration between major human groups." See Galtung, "An Editorial," *Journal of Peace Research* 1, no. 1 (1964): 1–4, and Galtung, "Peace," in *International Encyclopedia of the Social Sciences*, vol. 11, ed. D. L. Sills (New York: Macmillan and Free Press, 1968), 487–86. The distinction between negative and positive peace was first articulated by Quincy Wright, *A Study of War* (Chicago: University of Chicago Press, 1942). In this work, he argues that the elimination of war does not necessarily amount to justice or positive peace (based on conceptions of international justice). See discussion in Kathleen M. Weigert, "Structural Violence," in *Encyclopedia of Violence, Peace and Conflict*, vol. 3, ed. Lester A. Kurtz (San Diego: Academic Press, 1999), 431–40.

14. See Ofer Aderet, "Pioneer of Global Peace Studies Hints at Link between Norway Massacre and Mossad," *Haaretz*, April, 30, 2012, http://www.haaretz.com/news/diplomacy-defense/pioneer-of-global-peace-studies-hints-at-link-between-norway-massacre-and-mossad-1.427385.

15. To be clear, I have no interest in making apologies for and/or justifying the remarks espoused by Galtung. At the same time, however, they do not negate nor are they direct implications of his contributions to peace research.

16. For a related explication of this issue, see Atalia Omer, "'It's Nothing Personal': The Globalization of Justice, the Transferability of Protest, and the Case of the Palestine Solidarity Movement," *Studies in Ethnicity and Nationalism* 9, no. 3: 497–518. See also Omer, "'Tell Them to Get the Hell Out of Palestine': Solidarities, Diasporas, and Breaking the Cycle of Mutual Silencing," in *Oxford Handbook on Religion, Conflict, and Peacebuilding*, ed. R. Scott Appleby, David Little, and Atalia Omer (Oxford: Oxford University Press, forthcoming).

17. Galtung defines "cultural violence" as "those aspects of culture, the symbolic sphere of our existence—exemplified by religion and ideology, language and art, empirical science and formal science . . . that can be used to justify or legitimize direct or structural violence." See Galtung, "Cultural Violence," *Journal of Peace Research* 27, no. 3 (1990): 291–305. While there are important differences, Galtung's analysis of cultural violence resonates with Pierre Bourdieu's account of symbolic violence (see introduction).

18. These conversations resulted in an edited volume, featuring multiple disciplinary approaches to peacebuilding. See Daniel Philpott and Gerard F. Powers, eds., *Strategies of Peace: Transforming Conflict in a Violent World* (New York: Oxford University Press, 2010).

19. John Paul Lederach and R. Scott Appleby, "Strategic Peacebuilding: An Overview," in Philpott and Powers, *Strategies of Peace*, 22.

20. Ibid., 23. Consistent with Appleby and Lederach's framework for thinking strategically about peace is the explanation of Lisa Schirch, another reflective practitioner who attempts to think strategically about peacebuilding, that "peacebuilding is strategic when resources, actors, and approaches are coordinated to accomplish multiple issues for the long term." See Schirch, *The Little Book of Strategic Peacebuilding: A Vision and Framework for Peace with Justice* (Intercourse, PA: Good Books, 2004), 9. She likewise connects questions of justice to peacebuilding.

21. Lederach and Appleby, "Strategic Peacebuilding," 24. For a similar approach, see also Schirch, *Little Book of Strategic Peacebuilding*, especially 71–79.

22. Pierre Allan and Alexis Keller underscore the analysis of the root causes of conflict as key to meaningful peacebuilding. They advance a "bottom-up" approach to achieve a just peace, which they define as a "process whereby peace and justice are reached together by two or more parties recognizing each other's identities, each renouncing some central demands, and each accepting to abide by common rules jointly developed." See Allan and Keller, "The Concept of a Just Peace, or Achieving Peace through Recognition, Renouncement, and Rule," in *What Is a Just Peace?*, ed. Allan and Keller (Oxford: Oxford University Press, 2006), 195. Allan and Keller's approach is a "process approach" because it emphasizes "justice" as a process of cultural translation and conversation rather than as a top-down deployment of a set of preconceived principles. While critical of universalizing liberal discourse, the authors nonetheless indicate that the first phase in their understanding of just peace as a process would consist in a "thin" minimalist recognition of the "other"—a convention consistent with the liberal tradition.

23. Herbert Kelman, "Reconciliation as Identity Change: A Social Psychological Perspective," in *From Conflict Resolution to Reconciliation*, ed. Yaacov Bar-Siman Tov (Oxford: Oxford University Press, 2004), 111–24.

24. Ibid., 120. Elsewhere, Kelman himself begins to revise the definition of the "core" by calling for a diminishing role of non-Israeli Jews and an increasing influence of non-Jewish Israelis in the affairs of Israel; see Kelman, "Israel in Transition from Zionism to Post-Zionism," *Annals of the American Academy of Political and Social Science* 555 (January 1998): 46–61.

25. Incidentally, Allan and Keller clarify their argument by alluding to the example of Israel and the pivotal importance of defining its identity as a function and tactic of peacebuilding and reconciliation: "That those representing a party need to fully understand the core identity of their own party in order to be able to devise a solution that will be, sometimes only with time, recognized and accepted by their own

people. For example, is Israel to be understood foremost as a nation-state in search of its security, or the Jewish State, the Jewish State on holy lands, or simply a state that welcomes all Jews the world over, or a Jewish democratic state? What are the essential features of its ontology? What constitutes the deeper core characterizing it is the crucial question since other definitions of Israel can be envisioned besides the ones mentioned here" ("Concept of a Just Peace," 200).

26. This synergistic lens could draw on and intervene in the yet unutilized conversations in the cultural sociology of religion that engage the interrelations between symbolic and sociopolitical boundaries and practices. For a stimulating review of the various research trajectories in the subfield of the cultural sociology of religion, see Penny Edgell, "A Cultural Sociology of Religion: New Directions," *Annual Review of Sociology* 38 (2012): 247–65.

27. Cultivating justpeace is a complex objective that requires multileveled, multidisciplinary, and translocal strategic engagements and collaborations. Lederach and Appleby write to this effect: "To succeed in fostering a *justpeace*, peacebuilders must nurture sustainable human relationships at every level of society—between local ethnic and religious groups, political parties and governments, faith-based groups and NGOs . . . and so on. In this context peacebuilding therefore requires, inter alia, various kinds of expertise, including knowledge of international norms and institutions, global politics, economic development, the requirements of vibrant civil societies, the religious and cultural dynamics of deadly conflict, and religiously and culturally nuanced methods of conflict transformation. Accordingly, any comprehensive effort to build sustainable peace must draw on the experiences and writings of reflective practitioners and scholars working in the fields of conflict resolution, security studies, and religion and spirituality . . . This confluence of actors, competencies, and resources underscores our definition of peacebuilding as a set of complementary practices aimed at transforming a society riddled by violent conflict, inequality, and other systemic forms of injustice into a society oriented toward forging a *justpeace*" ("Strategic Peacebuilding," 34–35).

28. Howard Zehr defines restorative justice as "a process to involve, to the extent possible, those who have a stake in a specific offense and to collectively identify and address harms, needs, and obligations, in order to heal and put things as right as possible." See Zehr, *The Little Book of Restorative Justice* (Intercourse, PA: Good Books, 2002), 37.

29. Daniel Philpott, "Beyond Politics as Usual: Is Reconciliation Compatible with Liberalism?," in *The Politics of Past Evil: Religion, Reconciliation, and the Dilemmas of Transitional Justice*, ed. Philpott (Notre Dame, IN: University of Notre Dame Press, 2006), 40, and Philpott, *Just and Unjust Peace: An Ethic of Political Reconciliation* (Oxford: Oxford University Press, 2012).

30. In this work, Kymlicka's analysis of the problems arising from the attempts to globally diffuse the framework of liberal multiculturalism addresses some of the critiques leveled against liberal political theory and his earlier works on liberal multiculturalism. He demonstrates that the preoccupation of international bodies after the cold war with ethnocultural justice for minorities and indigenous populations has placed nation-states increasingly under pressure to demonstrate consistency with such demands. See Will Kymlicka, *Multicultural Odysseys: Navigating the New International Politics of Diversity* (New York: Oxford University Press, 2007).

31. Instead of a restrictive and generic framework, Kymlicka suggests developing "a more complex model of targeted and sequenced minority rights that would attempt to

track important differences across different types of groups and different circumstances." By this Kymlicka means that the generic framework constitutes a mere minimum standard or "a floor from which minority rights should be domestically negotiated, not as a ceiling beyond which minorities must not seek to go." He consequently advances a "sequencing strategy" that would outline "the steps by which states should move from generic to more robust targeted norms" (ibid., 311).

32. Bashir Bashir and Will Kymlicka, "Introduction: Struggles for Inclusion and Reconciliation in Modern Democracies," in *The Politics of Reconciliation in Multicultural Societies*, ed. Kymlicka and Bashir (Oxford: Oxford University Press, 2008), 6.

33. See, for example, works advanced by theorists like William Connolly, *Identity/Difference: Democratic Negotiations of Political Paradox* (Minneapolis: University of Minnesota Press, 2002); Bonnie Honig, *Political Theory and the Displacement of Politics* (Ithaca: Cornell University Press, 1993); Chantal Mouffe, *The Democratic Paradox* (New York: Verso, 2000); and Ernesto Laclau and Mouffe, *Hegemony and Socialist Strategy: Towards a Radical Democratic Politics* (London: Verso, 1985).

34. Bashir and Kymlicka, "Introduction: Struggles for Inclusion," 10. For instance, in a discussion of slavery reparations in the United States, Laurie Balfour draws on the insights of an agonistic model of democracy to articulate a conception of justice as fugitive, "as always susceptible to revision, change, loss, on the one hand, and as explicitly invoking the history of the many thousands gone, on the other." See Balfour, "Act and Fact: Slavery Reparations as a Democratic Politics of Reconciliation," in Kymlicka and Bashir, *Politics of Reconciliation in Multicultural Societies*, 112. Balfour highlights the emphasis of the agonistic model on "revisability, innovation, creativity, and incompleteness" as posing important challenges to the presumed connection between the granting of democratic equality and the aspiration for healing and societal repair (ibid., 96).

35. Balfour, 96.

36. See Mouffe, "Difference, Dilemmas, and the Politics of Home," in *Democracy and Difference: Contesting the Boundaries of the Political*, ed. Seyla Benhabib (Princeton: Princeton University Press, 1996), 257–77.

37. For notable efforts to deploy agonistic insights constructively in analysis of conflict and reconciliation, see Paul Mouldoon, "The Very Basis of Civility: On Agonism, Conquest, and Reconciliation," in Kymlicka and Bashir, *Politics of Reconciliation in Multicultural Societies*, 114–35, and Jason A. Springs, "On Giving Religious Intolerance Its Due: Prospects for Transforming Conflict in a Post-Secular Society," *Journal of Religion* 92, no. 1 (January 2012): 1–30.

38. Bashir and Kymlicka, "Introduction: Struggles for Inclusion," 11.

39. This approach to a "politics of reconciliation" resonates with the intention of deliberative democracy to give voice to everybody who needs to be involved in deliberating on the common good. It also exploits usefully the focus of the agonistic model on "converting enemies to adversaries" (viewing the political arena as a space of agonistic contestation) and exposing the power dynamics underlying deliberative democratic processes. Likewise, theories of political reconciliation in the aftermath of violent conflict and mass atrocities share the inclination of the multicultural approach to "valorize stigmatized identities" (Bashir and Kymlicka, "Introduction: Struggles for Inclusion," 12). For various discussions of approaches to political and societal reconciliation, see Philpott, *Politics of Past Evil*; Daniel Philpott, "What Religion Brings to the Politics of Transitional Justice," *Journal of International Affairs* 61, no. 1 (2007): 93–110; Priscilla Hayner, *Unspeakable Truths: Transitional Justice and*

the Challenge of Truth Commissions (Hoboken, NJ: Taylor & Francis, 2010); Hayner, *Unspeakable Truths: Confronting State Terror and Atrocity* (New York: Routledge, 2001); Paul Mouldoon, "Reconciliation and Political Legitimacy: The Old Australia and the New South Africa," *Australian Journal of Politics and History* 49, no. 2 (2003): 182–97; as well as the debates in Robert Rotberg and Dennis F. Thompson, eds., *Truth vs. Justice: The Morality of Truth Commissions* (Princeton: Princeton University Press, 2000), and Naomi Roht-Arriaza and Javier Mariezcurrena, *Transitional Justice in the Twenty-First Century: Beyond Truth versus Justice* (Cambridge: Cambridge University Press, 2006).

40. Further, critics voice a concern with a presupposed contradiction between justice as *recognition* and justice as *redistribution*, where a focus on recognition is perceived as potentially threatening to individual liberties. See, for example, Susan Moller Okin, *Is Multiculturalism Bad for Women?* (Princeton: Princeton University Press, 1999), and Brian M. Barry, *Culture and Equality: An Egalitarian Critique of Multiculturalism* (Cambridge: Harvard University Press, 2001). Nancy Fraser attempts to reconcile the supposed philosophical contradictions between recognition and redistribution. See Fraser and Axel Honneth, *Redistribution or Recognition?: A Political-Philosophical Exchange* (New York: Verso, 2003). See also Keith G. Banting and Will Kymlicka, eds., *Multiculturalism and the Welfare State: Recognition and Redistribution in Contemporary Democracies* (Oxford: Oxford University Press, 2006), and Charles Taylor, Amy Gutmann, and other contributors in *Multiculturalism: Examining the Politics of Recognition*, ed. Gutmann (Princeton: Princeton University Press, 1994).

41. This involves demonstrating the consistency (despite important divergences) between Rawls's insistence on a set of "constitutional essentials" as a means of mediating between "comprehensive" worldviews and human rights documents' opposition to any form of domination by a single doctrine or culture. David Little, "Human Rights, Public Reason, and the International Protection of Religion or Belief: A Way Forward," delivered in the Conference on Law and Religion at Emory Law School, October 24, 2007; also a revised version of this paper was published as "Religion, Human Rights, and Public Reason: The Role and Limits of a Secular Rationale," in *Religion and Human Rights: An Introduction*, ed. John Witte Jr. and M. Christian Green (Oxford: Oxford University Press, 2012), 135–52. See also Little, "Ground to Stand On: A Philosophical Reappraisal of Human Rights Language," unpublished paper.

42. The parameters for this "thin" conception of the role of government are set in article 29.2 of the UDHR: "In the exercise of his rights and freedoms, everyone shall be subject only to such limitations as are determined by law solely for the purpose of securing due recognition and respect for the rights and freedoms of others and of meeting the just requirements of morality, public order and the general welfare in a democratic society." Articles 3 through 21 of the UDHR specify the basic rights implied by the ideal of the rule of law articulated in article 29.

43. See, for example, Glyn Ford, "Racism and Xenophobia in Europe Stemming the Rising Tide," *UN Chronicle* 41, no. 1 (February 2005): 32–33; editorial, "Xenophobia: Fear-Mongering for American Votes," *New York Times*, August 5, 2010, http://www.nytimes.com/2010/08/06/opinion/06fri1.html.

44. Lisa Schirch stresses the importance of linking the fields of human rights and conflict transformation precisely when programs of transitional and restorative justice are initiated to transform underlying relational patterns. She explains that human rights norms provide standards for evaluating the legitimacy of diplomatic efforts to transform conflict. Further, the documentation of human rights abuses during the

time of conflict offers a tangible and indisputable record to contend with in peace negotiations and settlements. Similarly, the human rights approach supports conflict transformation processes such as a careful consideration of offenders' perceptions of injustice. The inclusion of human rights offenders in peace negotiations is crucial. It is also crucial, however, to deploy human rights standards as an evaluative framework that enables public accountability for offenses and demands for restitution. (See Schirch, *Little Book of Strategic Peacebuilding*, 78–83.) This issue is also central to scholarly conversations about restorative justice and reconciliation. I address this scholarly current later in this chapter. Christine Bell's comparative analysis of peace agreements is consistent with Schirch's. The discussion in Bell's work exemplifies the broader trend in peace research to integrate questions of justice with discussions of peace negotiations and agreements. International conventions of human rights, Bell argues, are key for cultivating a sustainable peace and redressing past injustices. See Bell, *Peace Agreements and Human Rights* (Oxford: Oxford University Press, 2000). Julie Mertus and Jeffery Helsing likewise see human rights and enforceable legal mechanisms as crucial ingredients in conflict prevention and postconflict restructuring. Of particular importance is a careful incorporation of the status of refugees and those displaced by conflict into peace negotiations and agreements as individuals fully possessed of unalienable human rights. See Mertus and Helsing, "Toward a More Integrated Approach," in *Human Rights and Conflict: Exploring the Links between Rights, Law, and Peacebuilding*, ed. Mertus and Helsing (Washington, DC: U.S. Institute of Peace Press, 2006), 513–14. See also Susan Martin and Andrew I. Schoenholtz, "Promoting the Human Rights of Forced Migrants," in Mertus and Helsing, *Human Rights and Conflict*, 405–29.

45. In the words of the preamble to the International Covenant on Economic, Social, and Cultural Rights, "the ideal of free human beings enjoying freedom from fear and want can only be achieved if conditions are created whereby everyone may enjoy his economic, social and cultural rights, as well as his civil and political rights." The text of the preamble can be found online; see the Office of the United Nations High Commissioner for Human Rights, http://www2.ohchr.org/engish/law/cescr.htm (accessed August 28, 2012).

46. The ideal typical liberal nation-state (that is, the Weberian analytical construct) would exhibit great consistency with the norms articulated in the UDHR, and conversely the ideal typical illiberal nation-state would manifest chauvinistic attributes like those exhibited in Nazi Germany. Little further underscores that the treatment of minorities and religious freedom usually provide important indices for assessing the liberality or illiberality of a given nation-state. This thesis was developed under the auspices of the United States Institute of Peace's Intolerance Project; see David Little, "Belief, Ethnicity, and Nationalism," *Nationalism and Ethnic Politics* 1, no. 2 (March–April 1995): 284–301.

47. Ibid.

48. Political theorist Bernard Yack, for instance, considers the civic-ethnic dichotomy to be ambiguous and analytically ineffective. He asserts that the conception of civic nationalism is delusional insofar as it is indicative of the conviction that mutual association is founded solely on consciously chosen principles. He underscores the ethnic and particularistic dimensions underlying the models of civic nationalism. Yack's rendering of the civic-ethnic distinction as incoherent is, however, not inconsistent with Little's conceptual framework. Little underscores the particular cultural, historical, religious, and linguistic specificities as elastically pertinent to the analy-

sis of each case of nationalism. They become especially pertinent when conflicts erupt precisely along these lines of identity. Yet he maintains a normative commitment to liberal civic principles as articulated in the universal conventions of human rights. Therefore, each instance of ethnoreligious national conflict would involve a hermeneutical engagement with embedded rather than abstract notions of identity. Yack writes: "The civic/ethnic dichotomy parallels a series of other contrasts that should set off alarm bells: not only Western/Eastern, but rational/emotive, voluntary/inherited, good/bad, *ours/theirs!* Designed to protect us from the dangers of ethnocentric politics, the civic/ethnic distinction itself reflects a considerable dose of ethnocentrism, as if the political identities *French* and *American* were not also culturally inherited artifacts, no matter how much they develop and change as they pass from generation to generation. The characterization of political community in the so-called civic nations as a rational and freely chosen allegiance to a set of political principles seems untenable to me, a mixture of self-congratulation and wishful thinking." See Yack, "The Myth of the Civic Nation," in *Theorizing Nationalism*, ed. Ronald Beiner (Albany: State University of New York Press, 1999), 105.

49. Little, "Belief, Ethnicity, and Nationalism."
50. Anthony Marx, *Faith in Nation: Exclusionary Origins of Nationalism* (Oxford: Oxford University Press, 2003), 6. Marx persuasively delineates this critical distinction between the "nation" and the "state": "nationalism is the potential basis of popular legitimacy or expression of support for state power, and as such the two are tied by definition. But institutions of power and sentiments about such institutions are not the same, and in practice the relation between nation and state varies" (6). Consistent with Weber's point about the unavoidability of authority in social life, Marx's argument holds that power always must be legitimated (whether or not it is truly legitimate in some absolute normative sense). However, Marx's explication of emergent nationalisms in Western Europe overemphasizes the "state" variable. Moreover, his analysis is teleological or unidirectional in that he views an inevitable movement from exclusion to inclusion—a movement that implies the diminishing role of religion as a social force of identity formation and similarly of the "nation" as a meaningful identity marker. In Marx's framework, the founding exclusionary principle of the "nation" ultimately dissolves through the liberalizing and pluralizing practices of the democratic "state." Marx further draws on this teleological orientation to provide an explanation of non-Western contemporary instances of violent nationalisms, implying that eventually they will "evolve" or develop into the liberal inclusionary model.
51. This approach developed by Anthony Smith highlights the ethnic and symbolic dimensions of "nations."
52. Anthony D. Smith, *Nationalism: Theory, Ideology, History* (Oxford: Blackwell, 2001), 57.
53. Anthony D. Smith, *Chosen Peoples: The Sacred Sources of National Identity* (Oxford: Oxford University Press, 2003), 24.
54. Ibid.
55. The terms "authenticity" and the "authentic," in their simplest forms, mean "possessing a collective proper name and the fact of having this particular name." The national flag and anthem are two necessary forms of the symbolic public display of authentic nationhood. Smith further argues that in their more complex varieties, "authenticity" and the "authentic" have attained auxiliary purist, pristine, unaffected, inner-determined, self-determining, and autochthonous meanings. Ibid., 37–40.

56. For an intriguing analysis of the interrelations between ideologies, religions, and social practices in Northern Ireland, see Claire Mitchell, *Religion, Identity, and Politics in Northern Ireland: Boundaries of Belonging and Belief* (Burlington, VT: Ashgate, 2006).

57. See David R. Smock, "Religious Contributions to Peacemaking: When Religion Brings Peace, Not War," for a discussion of Little's "Intolerance Project," conducted under the auspices of the U.S. Institute of Peace's program on religion, ethics, and human rights in the 1990s. This program engaged in a comparative study of conflict zones around the globe, www.usip.org/publications/religious-contributions-peace making-when-religion-brings-peace-not war (accessed November 11, 2011).

58. Scott Hibbard, *Religious Politics and Secular States: Egypt, India, and the United States* (Baltimore: Johns Hopkins University Press, 2010), 38.

59. See especially ibid., 32–41.

60. The most articulate theoretical framing of what I refer to as the constructive approach to religion and peacebuilding is associated with the works of Appleby and Little. The theoretical framings found especially in R. Scott Appleby, *The Ambivalence of the Sacred: Religion, Violence, and Reconciliation* (Lanham, MD: Rowman & Littlefield, 2000), have informed an extensive subgenre that studies religious peacebuilding.

61. Marx's analysis is revisionist because he pushes back the supposed "onset" of nationalism to the period that is largely classified as "premodern." Modernist accounts view the "nation" as a historically situated construct that could emerge only due to certain developments constitutive of modernity, such as the Protestant Reformation, the Industrial Revolution, the invention of print, and vernacularization. Modernist studies of nationalism share an understanding of the nation as a modern phenomenon, a sociological necessity related to secularization and modernization. For this reason, they tend to classify "religion" as instrumental in the initial phases of nation making but ultimately as having a diminishing force. The following are representative of modernist theories of nationalism. For neo-Marxist accounts, see Tom Nairn, *The Break-up of Britain: Crisis and Neo-nationalism*, 2nd ed. (1977; London: Verso, 1981), and Michael Hechter, *Internal Colonialism: The Celtic Fringe in British National Development, 1536–1966* (London: Routledge & Kegan Paul, 1975). For modernist analyses that focus on transformations in how politics is conducted (i.e., the emergence of the bureaucratic state) as an explanatory framework, see, for example, John Breuilly, *Nationalism and the State*, 2nd ed. (1982; Manchester: Manchester University Press, 1993); Paul Brass, *Ethnicity and Nationalism: Theory and Comparison* (New Delhi: Sage, 1991); Eric Hobsbawm, *Nations and Nationalism since 1780: Programme, Myth, Reality* (Cambridge: Cambridge University Press, 1990); and Hobsbawm and Terence Ranger, eds., *The Invention of Tradition* (Cambridge: Cambridge University Press, 1983). For modernist theories that emphasize social and cultural transformations as an explanatory framework for the rise of nationalism, see Ernest Gellner, *Nations and Nationalism* (Ithaca: Cornell University Press, 1983); Gellner, *Culture, Identity and Politics* (Cambridge: Cambridge University Press, 1987); Gellner, *Nationalism*; and Anderson, *Imagined Communities*. For a general critique of modernist theories of the emergence of nationalism, see Anthony Smith, *Theories of Nationalism*, 2nd ed. (1971; London: Duckworth1983), and Craig Calhoun, *Nationalism* (Minneapolis, MN: Open University Press, 1997).

62. See, for instance, John Rawls: "I assume that the basic structure is that of a closed society; that is, we are to regard it as self-contained and as having no relations with other societies. Its members enter it only by birth and leave it only by death." *Political Liberalism* (New York: Columbia University Press, 1993), 12.

63. Theorist of nationalism Rogers Brubaker captures what is at stake: "Debates about citizenship, in the age of the nation-state, are debates about nationhood—about what it means, and what it ought to mean, to belong to a nation-state". Brubaker, "Immigration, Citizenship, and the Nation-State in France and Germany," in *The Citizenship Debates*, ed. Gershon Shafir (Minneapolis: University of Minnesota Press, 1998), 132.

64. See chapter 1 for an extensive discussion of the secular Israeli peace camp.

65. Judith Butler, *Parting Ways: Jewishness and the Critique of Zionism* (New York: Columbia University Press, 2012), 7.

66. In debates over the limits of multicultural citizenship in Northern American contexts, one of the philosophical problems is whether the claims to entitlement of various groups, taken at face value, have unjust implications. For an example of this kind of critique of liberal multiculturalism, see Brian Walker, "Plural Cultures, Contested Territories: A Critique of Kymlicka," *Canadian Journal of Political Science* 30, no. 2 (June 1997): 211–34.

67. A polycentric orientation challenges the ethnocentrism undergirding the tradition of political liberalism and its universal pretenses. Accordingly, the source for ethnic stratification found in many liberal democracies is Eurocentrism—the self-conception of the West as "modern," "rational," and "civic" and of the East as "backward," "irrational," and "ethnic."

68. See Fraser and Honneth, *Redistribution or Recognition?* Fraser attempts to demonstrate that redistribution and recognition do not constitute mutually exclusive theories of justice. While the prioritization of redistribution is more characteristic of the Anglo-American liberal tradition and associated with Kantian frameworks, the intellectual roots of theorists of recognition like Charles Taylor can be traced back to Hegelian philosophy. Yet Fraser insists that the treatment of these two models as antithetical is false and misleading: "A two-dimensional conception treats distribution and recognition as distinct perspectives on, and dimensions of, justice. Without reducing either dimension to the other, it encompasses both of them within a broader overarching framework" (*Redistribution or Recognition?*, 35). Consequently, in a political strategy for institutionalizing justice, this two-dimensional approach demands a concurrent deliberation of questions of distribution and recognition because they are both, Fraser claims, "fundamental and irreducible dimensions of justice, which runs throughout the entire social field" (86–87).

69. See Yossi Yonah, *In Virtue of Difference: The Multicultural Project in Israel* (Jerusalem: Van Leer Jerusalem Institute, 2005), 48–54 [in Hebrew], and Dipesh Chakrabarty, *Provincializing Europe: Postcolonial Thought and Historical Difference* (Princeton: Princeton University Press, 2000). Likewise, in developing the agonistic orientation in their *Hegemony and Socialist Strategy*, political theorists Laclau and Mouffe wish to distinguish between the principles and values undergirding liberal democracies and the systems of control and domination that rearticulate and delimit their implementation.

70. Fraser and Honneth, *Redistribution or Recognition?*, 6.

71. Bashir and Kymlicka also acknowledge that the framework of liberal multiculturalism is not easily conducive to redressing past injustices ("Introduction: Struggles for Inclusion," 17).

72. Insofar as he engages the question of the structures and patterns of religion's publicity, Philpott dovetails with extended conversations on religion and public life (especially but not exclusively in the North American context). I discuss this genre later in the chapter.

73. Yehouda Shenhav, *The Time of the Green Line: Towards a Jewish Political Thought* (Tel Aviv: Am Oved, 2010) [in Hebrew]. I further discuss Shenhav's thesis throughout the book but especially in the context of the Mizrahim in chapter 7.

74. For a description of an extensive collaborative research project executed by Saba Mahmood and Elizabeth Shakman Hurd, looking at the discourses of "religious freedoms," "minority rights," and their political-ideological functions, see "Politics of Religious Freedom: Contested Norms and Local Practices," http://iiss.berkeley .edu/politics-of-religious-freedom/saba-mahmood/ (accessed January 11, 2012). This project historicizes and offers critique of the domestic and international operational- izing of the discourse of religious freedom and liberty, stressing the colonialist and orientalist underpinnings of this discourse. Grounded in anthropologist Talal Asad's genealogical study of the religious and the secular, this discursive critique is quick to associate the concept of "religion" with the modern liberal state and with a built-in privileging of majority cultures and religions. But, this Asadian line overlooks the complex interfacing between religion and nationalism, which renders such a dis- cursive critique prohibitive of theorizing about religion and social change, within the nexus of the nation-state as well as internationally and globally. Subscribing to the "state" as the most basic unit where questions of "freedoms" and "religions" are debated is myopic and may be faulted as power reductionist and as ironically reliant on a modernist paradigm. This is "ironic" because the hallmark of an Asadian cri- tique is the debunking of this paradigm by deploying the method of genealogy. For a related work that likewise suggests the indispensability yet limits of a deconstructive critique that stresses the "state" as a novel, modernist construct (inattentive to its complex interrelations with the imagining and reproducing of "nations"), see Saba Mahmood, "Religious Freedom, the Minority Question, and Geopolitics in the Mid- dle East," *Comparative Studies in Society and History* 54, no. 2 (2012): 418–46.

75. By "denaturalizing," I mean that the analyses of conflicts need to probe beyond concep- tions of the "we" as essentialized, fixed, natural, and ahistorical. An agonistic reimagin- ing of the "who" can also carry profound ramifications for the question of justice.

76. For examples of analyses that focus on gender as an important lens in peace studies, see Rebecca Barlow, "The First International Conference of the Nobel Women's Ini- tiative: Women Redefining Peace in the Middle East and Beyond," *Journal of Middle East Women's Studies* 4, no. 1 (2008): 125; Robin Whitaker, "Gender and the Politics of Justice in the Northern Ireland Peace Process: Considering Róisín McAliskey," *Identities* 15, no. 1 (2008): 1; Yaacov Boaz Yablon, "Gender Differences in Peace Education Programmes," *Gender and Education* 21, no. 6 (2009): 689–701, Catia Cecilia Confortini, *Intelligent Compassion: Feminist Critical Methodology in the Women's International League for Peace and Freedom* (Oxford: Oxford University Press, 2012), and Cynthia Cockburn, "Gender Relations as Causal in Militarization and War," *International Feminist Journal of Politics* 12, no. 2 (2010): 139–57.

77. Authors who write with a particular emphasis on the question of women and agency in South and Southeast Asia are Alex Argenti-Pillen, *Masking Terror: How Women Con- tain Violence in Southern Sri Lanka* (Philadelphia: University of Pennsylvania Press, 2003); Veena Das, Arthur Kleinman, Mamphela Ramphele, and Pamela Reynolds, eds., *Violence and Subjectivity* (Berkeley: University of California Press, 2000); and Ronit Lentin, ed., *Gender and Catastrophe* (London: Zed Books, 1997).

78. For example, in analyzing the role of religion in articulating women's agency in Sri Lanka, anthropologist Patricia Lawrence concludes that "as a repository of cultural beliefs and values from which the local population in the war zone draws, religion is

a source of solace and recovery for survivors." See Lawrence, "Mothers and Wives of the Disappeared in Southern Sri Lanka: Fragmented Geographies of Moral Discomfort," in *Women and the Contested State: Religion, Violence, and Agency in South and Southeast Asia*, ed. Monique Skidmore and Lawrence (Notre Dame, IN: Notre Dame University Press, 2007), 104.

79. I refer here specifically to Saba Mahmood, *Politics of Piety: The Islamic Revival and the Feminist Subject* (Princeton: Princeton University Press, 2005). The critique I offer is born out of a conversation with my colleague Jason Springs.

80. William Cavanaugh, *The Myth of Religious Violence: Secular Ideology and the Roots of Modern Conflict* (Oxford: Oxford University Press, 2009).

81. Political theorists like Samuel Huntington and Monica Toft hold an unreconstructed conception of the secular and the religious, presupposing the validity of the classical secularist and modernist discourses. This orientation leads them to construe Islam and modernity (i.e., liberal values) as incompatible. See Huntington, *The Clash of Civilizations and the Remaking of World Order* (New York: Touchstone, 1997), and Toft, "Getting Religion? The Puzzling Case of Islam and Civil War," *International Security* 31, no. 4 (Spring 2007): 97–131. For Huntington, the purported incompatibility between "civilizational" identities provides the building blocks for a reductive explanatory framework that analyzes values and religious or civilizational orientations as the primary causes of conflict in a post-cold-war era. While Toft advances a more context-sensitive explanatory framework for what she calls "the puzzling case of Islam and civil war," she—like Huntington—deploys a particular (Western European) hegemonic narrative concerning the supposedly correct place of religion in modern political life and presumes the "secular" to be nonviolent, rational, and tolerant. Accordingly, religion (and specifically Islam) is violent and irrational; thus, when it assumes a position of centrality in a conflict, the likelihood of negotiations decreases. While Toft offers a historical, geopolitical, and structural explanation, she nonetheless substantiates Huntington's provocative claim concerning the "bloody borders of Islam." Toft argues that Islam is involved in many contemporary conflicts in part because Islamic history lacked a development akin to the internecine European wars of religion and in part because of circumstantial factors, like the proximity of Islamic sacred sites to Israel, the petroleum factor, Islam's transnational links, and the principle of jihad. Yet, unlike Huntington, whose explanation of the role of religion in contemporary conflict is reductionist, Toft views religion instrumentally. She proposes a theory of "religious outbidding" (based on Jack Snyder's model of "nationalist outbidding," developed in *From Voting to Violence: Democratization and Nationalist Conflict* [New York: Norton, 2000]), which explains that religion becomes a factor—to varying degrees—in the course of a conflict because different political parties wish to enhance "their religious credentials and thereby gain the support they need to counter an immediate threat" (103). She further argues that the utility of religious outbidding is most pronounced in Islamic contexts and that the greater the likelihood of religious outbidding, the greater the chance religion will come to occupy a central role in conflict. This increased centrality of religion, in turn, constitutes an obstacle for rational negotiations and conflict resolution and vindicates violence against noncombatants. Perhaps the most mainstream and audible treatment of the question of religion and conflict is associated with the work of Mark Juergensmeyer. In his *Global Rebellion: Religious Challenges to the Secular State: From Christian Militias to al Qaeda* (Berkeley: University of California Press, 2008), Juergensmeyer reiterates his earlier theses from *The New Cold War?:*

Religious Nationalism Confronts the Secular State (Berkeley: University of California Press, 1993) and *Terror in the Mind of God: The Global Rise of Religious Violence* (Berkeley: University of California Press, 2003). He explains the so-called resurgence of religion as a function of a fundamental clash between two competing "ideologies of order": religion and secular nationalism. The doctrine of secular modern nationalism is accordingly incompatible with religion because these two ideologies seek different sources to legitimate their sociopolitical authority. While religious ideologies look for divine warrants, secular nationalism legitimates itself by invoking the tradition of natural law or *volkist* myths. Attributing the emergence of "religious nationalism" to the erosion of secular national identities, Juergensmeyer analyzes the phenomenon as a synthetic formation that bridges the two purportedly divergent ideologies of order. Juergensmeyer explains that religion serves as a vehicle and language of protest against the structures of the secular state. In his *Terror in the Mind of God*, he also discusses how religiously vindicated political violence often betrays a conception of a "cosmic war" in which political battles symbolically transform into contemporary manifestations of cosmic-mythic struggles between good and evil. This ritualized, performative violence offers a clear perception of cosmic order that transcends the sense of disorder or displacement introduced by the institution of the modern secular nation-state. To this degree, Juergensmeyer's account of religious violence is thoroughly Girardian because he views it as motivated by the desire to restore and maintain a sense of social order. For expositions and critiques of René Girard's theory of religion and violence, see Girard, "Violence and Religion: Cause or Effect?," *Hedgehog Review* 6, no. 1 (2004): 8, and Mack C. Stirling, "Violent Religion: René Girard's Theory of Culture," in *Destructive Power of Religion*, vol. 2: *Religion, Psychology, and Violence*, ed. J. Harold Ellens (Westport, CT: Praeger, 2004). Not unlike Juergensmeyer in his conceptual differentiation of religious and secular ideologies of order, sociologist Roger Friedland interprets the phenomenon of religious nationalism by exploring how it seeks to displace a "cosmology that placed democracy and capitalism as its institutional ground." See Friedland, "Money, Sex, and God: The Erotic Logic of Religious Nationalism," *Sociological Theory* 20, no. 3 (2002): 381–425. Friedland argues that religious nationalists seek to remake the national space by reconfiguring the patriarchal family (not individuals) as its most basic unit. This amounts to reconfiguring national ontologies through a characteristic preoccupation with controlling the bodies of women. Both in Toft's and in Juergensmeyer's respective analyses as well as in Friedland's account, one identifies a conceptual reliance on the modernist paradigm; accordingly secular nationalism denotes a radical break from traditional political and religious formations. Slavica Jakelić's work (*Collectivistic Religions: Religion, Choice, and Identity in Late Modernity* [Burlington, VT: Ashgate, 2010]) challenges this modernist bias by providing genealogies of what she calls "collectivistic religions."

82. The primarily U.S.-based "religion and public life" debate contains conversations about the modes in which religion can enter and/or participate in public discourses. See Ronald Thiemann, *Religion in Public Life: A Dilemma for Democracy* (Washington, DC: Georgetown University Press, 1996); Nicholas Wolterstorff and Robert Audi, *Religion in the Public Square: The Place of Religious Convictions in Political Debate* (Lanham, MD: Rowman & Littlefield, 1997); and Jeffrey Stout, *Democracy and Tradition* (Princeton: Princeton University Press, 2003). This context-specific debate has received much airtime in the American Academy of Religion in recent years, especially following the publication of Stout's *Democracy and Tradition*. See also Jason A.

Springs, ed., along with Cornel West, Richard Rorty, Stanley Hauerwas, and Jeffrey Stout, in "Pragmatism and Democracy: Assessing Jeffrey Stout's *Democracy and Tradition*," *Journal of the American Academy of Religion* 78, no. 2 (June 2010): 413–48.

83. For instance, Stout's *Democracy and Tradition* retrieves a specifically American tradition, exhibited in the persons and works of John Dewey, Walt Whitman, and Ralph Waldo Emerson, of articulating the proper place and practice of religious reasoning in public debates. Stout attempts to respond and offer correctives to both secularist liberals like Rorty who view religion as a "conversation stopper" and antiliberal, neo-traditionalist thinkers such as John Milbank, Alasdair MacIntyre, and Hauerwas.

84. See Atalia Omer, "The Hermeneutics of Citizenship as a Peacebuilding Process: A Multiperspectival Approach to Justice," *Journal of Political Theology* 11, no. 5 (October 2010): 650–73.

85. To this extent, Hurd's work can be traced to the highly self-reflexive work of the political theorist Roxanne Euben. Her book, *Enemy in the Mirror: Islamic Fundamentalism and the Limits of Modern Rationalism* (Princeton: Princeton University Press, 1999), underscores the importance of analyzing the thought of Sayid Qutb on his own terms rather than as merely reactive to modernist-secularist Western modes of being. Hurd's focus on multiple secularisms and on contesting and parochializing the hold of laicism and Judeo-Christian secularist narratives and presuppositions resonates with José Casanova's study of secularism in global comparative perspective. In his "Public Religions Revisited" (in *Religion beyond the Concept*, ed. Hent de Vries [New York: Fordham University Press, 2008]), Casanova takes into account some of the biases (noted by Talal Asad) inherent in his earlier work, namely, its Western-centrism, its confinement of "public religion" within the bounds of "civil society," and its focus on church-state-civil-society relations—a focus that both overlooks the transnational dimensions of religious communities and accepts the Westphalian paradigm as axiomatic. Casanova's primary intention is to disentangle the normative connection between modernization and secularization and to move away from explanatory frameworks that posit the Western Eurocentric doctrine of secularism as a universal process of social development. For this exchange, see, for example, Casanova, *Public Religions in the Modern World* (Chicago: University of Chicago Press, 1994); Asad, *Formations of the Secular: Christianity, Islam, Modernity* (Stanford: Stanford University Press, 2003); and David Scott and Charles Hirschkind, *Powers of the Secular Modern: Talal Asad and His Interlocutors* (Stanford: Stanford University Press, 2006). Hurd's work has an agenda similar to that of Casanova's project. Yet her audience remains located primarily within the arena of international relations and political science more broadly. She is concerned with how and why new lenses of analysis that denaturalize secularist premises may transform, embolden, and enrich analyses of religion as a factor in international affairs. Along similar lines (with important distinctions relating to the kind of interlocutors and theoretical apparatuses each engages), Daniel H. Nexon pushes theorizing of religion in international relations (IR) beyond a mere replicating of idealist versus materialist explanatory frameworks and their relative efficacy. Instead, he calls for discursive sensitivity. See Nexon, "Religion and International Relations: No Leap of Faith Required," in *Religion and International Relations Theory*, ed. Jack Snyder (New York: Columbia University Press, 2011), 141–67).

86. For an attempt to integrate religion into the existing paradigms in international relations theory, see Jack Snyder, ed., *Religion and International Relations Theory* (New York: Columbia University Press, 2011). Likewise, the work of Abdoullahi Ahmed

314 / Notes to Pages 88–89

An-Na'im, the Sudanese scholar of religion and human rights, reinforces this general point about the conceptual as well as the practical implications of the dominance of the colonial discourse of secularism in Arab and Muslim contexts. See An-Na'im, *Islam and the Secular State: Negotiating the Future of Shari'a* (Cambridge: Harvard University Press, 2008). An-Na'im explains how the premises of colonialism have been integrated into the articulation of identities in the period of anticolonial struggles as well as in the postcolonial period. For instance, in his discussion of India, An-Na'im explains that the colonial strategy of divide and conquer entailed the classification of Indian society according to preconceived notions of religion and culture, which reflected particularly Eurocentric and Christocentric interpretations of "religion." An-Na'im attempts to rescue precolonial conceptions and practices of secularism, highlighting—like Casanova—the multiplicity of secularism.

87. Notably, the challenge to the conventions of international relations theory is echoed by the Task Force Report issued by the Chicago Council on Global Affairs (February 23, 2010). Co-chaired by R. Scott Appleby and Richard Cizik, the task force rethinks how to engage religion on an international level. The Task Force Report recognizes the limiting hold of unreconstructed secularism: "Once considered a 'private' matter by western policymakers, religion is now playing an increasingly influential role—both positive and negative—in the public sphere on many different levels," Task Force Report, 5. In outlining strategic implications of U.S. foreign policy, the task force illuminates the importance of broadening the conversation about religion beyond questions of terrorism and counterterrorism. This expansion necessitates challenging the secularist presuppositions concerning how religion relates to global politics. See chapter 2 of the Task Force Report. Undoubtedly, an unrevised secularism paradigm not only still underlies much of the literature on the role of religion in violent conflict but also continuously informs the practice of conflict resolution and the logic of track 1 (i.e., official) diplomacy. Thinking about religion in international relations thus involves recognizing the influence of globalization on patterns of religious organizing, the increased role played by religious actors especially where governments operate with diminished legitimacy and capacity, and the critical importance of discussions of religious freedoms. Hurd's deconstructive critique and the Task Force Report's constructive attempt to offer policy recommendations that take religion seriously mark an important departure from the normative confinement of religion to the private and nonpolitical spaces. Religion is public and critical for policy concerns.

88. Because of her deconstructive lens, however, Hurd does not sufficiently reflect on how and why pluralizing conceptions of the secular might also decenter the normative values inherent in secularism. Nor does her approach explain whether such decentering, which is prone to cultural relativism, might be desirable.

89. The study of religion and protest has focused primarily on how religious violence challenges rather than reinforces the status quo and the normative presuppositions underlying the social and political order both locally and globally. What has become a worthy topic of exploration is precisely where religious behavior seemed to "deprivatize," as Casanova famously characterized the so-called resurgence of religion. See, for example, Bruce Lincoln, *Holy Terrors: Thinking about Religion after September 11* (Chicago: University of Chicago Press, 2003), and Casanova, *Public Religions in the Modern World*.

90. Here I follow the influential account by Johannes Morsink of the drafting of the UDHR, which shows the underlying cross-cultural negotiations and translations.

Also, subsequent developments and human rights conventions highlight the continuously dynamic character of the human rights tradition. This is not to dismiss the perception of human rights as a code word for another variation and/or mutation of Western-Christian political, economic, and cultural domination. See Morsink, *The Universal Declaration of Human Rights: Origins, Drafting, and Intent* (Philadelphia: University of Pennsylvania Press, 2000).

91. See Michael Ignatieff, *Human Rights as Politics and Idolatry*, ed. Amy Gutmann (Princeton: Princeton University Press, 2001), 95. Clearly, Ignatieff's notion of "the bare human minimum" should itself be subjected to discursive critique.

92. For works addressing the role of constitutionalism in peacebuilding and conflict transformation, see Francis M. Deng and Terrence Lyons, eds., *African Reckoning: A Quest for Good Governance* (Washington, DC: Brookings Institution Press, 2008); David Little, "Peace, Justice, and Religion," in Allan and Keller, *What Is a Just Peace?*; and Bell, *Peace Agreements and Human Rights*. In contexts thoroughly marked by exclusionary conceptions of membership, as in Israel, drawing on the research on comparative secularisms and modernities could provide resources for renegotiating the precise relations between ethnoreligious markers of identity and the thresholds of citizenship. This approach is not inconsistent with Kymlicka's attempt to theorize the diffusion of liberal multiculturalism. It also agrees with Fraser's stress on revealing the meta-injustices underlying the broad misframing of the discourses of justice—a point that becomes acute in my analysis of the conceptual blinders of the Zionist peace camp.

93. While Said does not deploy the neologism *justpeace*, his conceptual framework is consistent with the principles underlying this concept.

94. Edward Said, "A Method for Thinking about Just Peace," in Allan and Keller, *What Is a Just Peace?*, 193.

95. See also Ilan Pappé, "The Bridging Narrative Concept," in *Israeli and Palestinian Narratives of Conflict: History's Double Helix*, ed. Robert Rotberg (Bloomington: Indiana University Press, 2006), 194–204. In reimagining ethical cohabitation in the land, Butler similarly draws on the inextricable interrelatedness of Jewish and Palestinian histories. To this end, she draws substantively on the later work of Said where he illuminates the Jewish and Palestinian experiences and narratives of dispersal as a relational foundation for ethical reframing of cohabitation and justice. See Butler, *Parting Ways*, especially 28–53 and 205–24.

CHAPTER THREE

1. See chapter 2 for an extensive discussion of these points.

2. As I illustrate later (especially chapters 5 through 7), I depart from the kind of relationality proposed by Judith Butler as a basis for justice and cohabitation in Israel/Palestine. Her critical contestation of epistemological and ontological claims as engrained in the Zionist framework is indispensible in its relationality (illuminating the experience of Palestinian dispersal as a fundamental challenge to Zionist historiography, while drawing constructively, through a process of cultural and historical translation, on Jewish resources in an effort to ethically reframe the justice discourse). And yet this critique is an insufficient framework for conflict transformation. For Butler's account, see *Parting Ways: Jewishness and the Critique of Zionism* (New York: Columbia University Press, 2012).

3. See discussion in the introduction and chapter 2 for further explication of the polycentric critique of meta-injustices and misframing of the discourses of justice.

4. Chantal Mouffe, "Difference, Dilemmas, and the Politics of Home," in *Democracy and Difference: Contesting the Boundaries of the Political*, ed. Seyla Benhabib (Princeton: Princeton University Press, 1996), 247.

5. In her *Parting Ways,* Butler develops systematically her conception of relationality along similar lines that problematize an exclusive reliance on Jewish and/or other particularistic sources for reconfiguring ethical relations and approaches for cohabitation. In any case, even the mere retrieval of religious resources involves a process of cultural and historical translation that is, by definition, deeply relational.

6. Ibid., 248.

7. For an important study of the relevance of Leo Strauss's political philosophy in the context of American policy making, see Catherine H. Zuckert and Michael P. Zuckert, *The Truth about Leo Strauss: Political Philosophy and American Democracy* (Chicago: University of Chicago Press, 2006). See also Jim Lobe, "Leo Strauss' Philosophy of Deception," in AlterNet, http://www.alternet.org/story/15935 (posted May 19, 2003). Carl Schmitt's notion of "political theology," however, has been associated with his reactionary critique of modernity and liberalism. See Schmitt, *Political Theology: Four Chapters on the Concept of Sovereignty*, trans. George Schwab, rev. ed. (1922; Chicago: University of Chicago Press, 2005). Accordingly, the liberal state and its constitutional framework have structurally replaced God in his status as the lawgiver. This process signaled the radical restructuring of political legitimacy in the modern nation-state, reflected in the dynamistic form of political legitimization. This transformation, has blocked the possibility for the sovereign to act outside the law in circumstances deemed exceptional. Inhibiting the possibility of the exception became a focus of Schmitt's critique of the liberal modern democratic state as articulated in *Political Theology*. He famously wrote: "All significant concepts of the modern theory of the state are secularized theological concepts not only because of their historical development—in which they were transferred from theology to the theory of the state, whereby, for example, the omnipotent God became the omnipotent lawgiver—but also because of their systematic structure, the recognition of which is necessary for a sociological consideration of these concepts. The exception in jurisprudence is analogous to the miracle in theology" (ibid., 36). Undoubtedly, Schmitt was critical of modernity, classical liberalism, and democracy. His contention was that the emergence of the modern constitutional liberal state signaled the secularization of what were fundamentally theological concepts. Yet the modern state also coincided with the eradication of theistic and transcendental modes of orientation in favor of conceptions of immanence. This juncture also implied the elimination of the monarchical principle of political legitimacy. See Francis Schüssler Fiorenza, "Political Theology and the Critique of Modernity: Facing the Challenges of the Present," *Distinktion* 10 (2005): 87–106. Like Schmitt, Strauss was a detractor of modernity and the Enlightenment ethos. He viewed critically "the scientific culture's faith in technological mastery, the liberal culture's avoidance of public appeals to religion, and the economic culture's reliance on self-interest for the development of policy" (see Fiorenza, 90). Schmitt's emphasis on the power of the sovereign derives from a critique of a demos-based source of political legitimacy. However, as noted by Fiorenza, it overlooks the capacity of the democratic system to "correct defects within democracy" (90).

8. Anthony D. Smith, *Chosen Peoples: The Sacred Sources of National Idenitty* (Oxford: Oxford University Press, 2003). My use of the concept of political theology as a way of deconstructing and reimagining the "nation" may also have affinities with Paul

Kahn's valuable intervention in the study of political theology and especially the applicability of Schmitt's theory to exploring the American political imagination. Kahn effectively underscores: "Whatever Schmitt meant by political theology, it cannot mean today that secular government is secretly doing the work of the church, or that it should . . . The serious claim of political theology today, however, is not that the secular should yield to the church—whatever church that might be—but rather that the state is not the secular arrangement that it purports to be" (Kahn, *Political Theology: Four New Chapters on the Concept of Sovereignty* [New York: Columbia University Press, 2011], 18).

9. See, for example, Anthony Marx, *Faith in Nation: Exclusionary Origins of Nationalism* (Oxford: Oxford University Press, 2003).

10. Benedict Anderson, *Imagined Communities: Reflections on the Origin and Spread of Nationalism*, rev. ed. (1983; London: Verso, 1991).

11. While often contrasted with the modernist paradigm of nationalism, the ethnosymbolist approach likewise employs a modernist implicit theory of religion. For this line of critique, see Slavica Jakelić, *Collectivistic Religions: Religion, Choice, and Identity in Late Modernity* (Burlington, VT: Ashgate, 2010), especially 15–46.

12. For example, Ernest Gellner, *Nations and Nationalism* (Ithaca: Cornell University Press, 1983).

13. For example, John Breuilly, *Nationalism and the State* (New York: St. Martin's Press, 1982).

14. Smith, *Chosen Peoples*, 12.

15. Ibid., 13.

16. Ibid., 13–14.

17. Instrumentalist analysis renders religion a mere epiphenomenon or a form of "false consciousness" and thus is prevalent in social scientific attempts to "explain" or "explain away" religion as it relates to conflict. Monica Toft's work typifies an approach that may provide an explanation of how religion contributes to the escalation of conflict while still failing to explain why religion, and no other "causes," becomes a central variable in the escalation of conflicts. See Toft, "Getting Religion? The Puzzling Case of Islam and Civil War," *International Security* 31, no. 4 (Spring 2007): 97–131. For a further discussion of various approaches to the study of religion and conflict, see chapter 2 as well as note 25 below).

18. Anderson, *Imagined Communities*, 5.

19. Smith, *Chosen Peoples*, 15.

20. Ibid., 15–17.

21. Smith writes, "We must go beneath the official positions, and even the popular practices, of modern nationalisms to discover the deeper cultural resources and sacred foundations of national identities; and that in turn means grasping the significance of the nation as a form of communion that binds its members through ritual and symbolic practices" (ibid., 18).

22. Ibid.

23. For an exposition of the Weberian approach to nationalism, see David Little, "Religion, Nationalism, and Ethnciity," *Ethnic and Racial Studies* 1, no. 2 (1995): 284–301. See also Little, "Religion, Nationalism, and Intolerance," in *Between Terror and Tolerance: Religious Leaders, Conflict, and Peacemaking*, ed. Timothy D. Sisk (Washington, DC: Georgetown University Press, 2011), 9–28.

24. See chapter 2 for an extensive account of these issues. For a "state of the art" overview and critique of the subfield of religious peacebuilding, see also Atalia Omer,

"Religious Peacebuilding: The Exotic, the Good, and the Theatrical," *Practical Matters* Issue 5, Spring 2012, http://practicalmattersjournal.org/issue/5/centerpieces/religious-peacebuilding (accessed April 24, 2012).

25. As observed by theologian William Cavanaugh, whether focusing on the ritualistic (and theatrical) patterns of contemporary religious violence or on the reactionary force and ideology of a so-called religious rebellion (as in the works of Bruce Lincoln and Mark Juergensmeyer), the academic study of religion's treatment of the role of religion in political and ethnoreligious national conflict not only reinforces the secularist narrative concerning the displacement of religion from its former central location as the organizing principle of society but also enables a form of a Girardian functionalism. See Cavanaugh, *The Myth of Religious Violence: Secular Ideology and the Roots of Modern Conflict* (Oxford: Oxford University Press, 2009). See also Cavanaugh, "Does Religion Cause Violence?," *Harvard Divinity Bulletin* 35, nos. 2 and 3 (Spring/Summer 2007). For critiques and reviews of Cavanaugh's argument, see Little, "In Review: Required Reading: A Double-Edged Dilemma," *Harvard Divinity Bulletin* 35, no. 4 (Autumn 2007), found online http://www.hds.harvard.edu/news-events/harvard-divinity-bulletin/articles/a-double-edged-dilemma, and R. Scott Appleby, "Fire and Sword: Does Religion Promote Violence?," *Commonweal* 137, no. 7 (2010): 12–17. For a critique of how scholars of religion have studied questions of religion and conflict, see also Omer, "Can a Critic Be a Caretaker Too? Religion, Conflict, and Conflict Transformation," *Journal of the American Academy of Religion* 79, no. 2 (2011): 459–96.

26. The work most frequently identified with initiating this subgenre of religious peacebuilding is Douglas Johnston and Cynthia Sampson, eds., *Religion: The Missing Dimension of Statecraft* (Oxford: Oxford University Press, 1994). This work highlights that despite the obvious relevance of religion to many conflicts around the world, its potential contribution to diplomacy and peacebuilding is overlooked. The book features a series of case studies in which religious or spiritual factors played a significant role in the prevention and transformation of conflicts. This work initiated a series of conversations concerning "faith-based" diplomacy. My argument, however, goes beyond this preoccupation with "faith-based" diplomacy because it focuses on the more ambiguous spaces where "religion" and/or secularized (selectively retrieved and deployed) theological arguments inform collective identities, which often present themselves as "secular," "national," and "cultural" rather than explicitly "religious." Remaining within the confines of the "religious" betrays an unreconstructed secularist orientation. For further relevant works, see, for example, Lisa Schirch, *Ritual and Symbol in Peacebuilding* (Bloomfield: Kumarian Press, 2005); David Smock, ed., *Interfaith Dialogue and Peacebuilding* (Washington, DC: U.S. Institute of Peace Press, 2002); Mohammed Abu-Nimer, Amal Khoury, and Emily Welty, *Unity in Diversity: Interfaith Dialogue in the Middle East* (Washington, DC: U.S. Institute of Peace Press, 2007); Harold Coward and Gordon S. Smith, eds., *Religion and Peacebuilding* (Albany: State University of New York Press, 2004); Marc Gopin, *Between Eden and Armageddon: The Future of World Religions, Violence, and Peacemaking* (Oxford: Oxford University Press, 2000); and Gopin, *To Make the Earth Whole: The Art of Citizen Diplomacy in an Age of Religious Militancy* (Lanham, MD: Rowman & Littlefield, 2009). For a review of the emerging field of religious peacebuilding, see also Katrien Hertog, *The Complex Reality of Religious Peacebuilding: Conceptual Contributions and Critical Analysis* (Lanham, MD: Lexington Books, 2010).

27. The term "soft power" was coined by Joseph S. Nye in his *Bound to Lead: The Changing Nature of American Power* (New York: Basic Books, 1990) and in his *Soft Power: The Means to Success in World Politics* (New York: Public Affairs, 2004). "Soft power" refers to the power of persuasion and thus calls upon cultural, religious, and other noncoercive means to exercise influence and garner legitimacy.

28. In a study of interfaith dialogue in the Middle East, Abu-Nimer et al. note that "a comprehensive peace based solely on secular values, actors, and frameworks will not be sustainable; peace must involve the religious believers and resonate with their faith" (see Abu-Nimer et al., *Unity in Diversity*, 10). The contributors to this same study further argue that interfaith dialogue (IFD) may contribute significantly to peacebuilding and conflict transformation by highlighting the transformative qualities of its model of confession and forgiveness. The IFD framework may facilitate confession and forgiveness when the interlocutors recognize and acknowledge their moral responsibility for instances of injustice associated with their faith and when they find equal courage to forgive (but not to forget) acts of violence perpetrated against them (see 22–24). Schirch similarly focuses on the power of common rituals practiced by those in dialogue and their capacity symbolically to transform identities and reframe the conflict in a ritualized form. See, for example, Schirch, *Ritual and Symbol in Peacebuilding*, and Abu-Nimer et al., *Unity in Diversity*, 24–26. This mode of analysis of religious peacebuilding resonates strongly with the peace studies subgenre of religion and transitional justice (see chapter 2).

29. This is not to disparage the role of religion and spirituality in motivating and directing the vocation of religious peacebuilders and other individuals involved in peacebuilding as a result of their spiritual proclivities. For examples of reflection on how religion and spirituality have influenced the work of peacebuilders, see John Paul Lederach, *The Journey toward Reconciliation* (Scottdale, PA: Herald Press, 1999). Lederach discusses how his own spirituality and interpretations of biblical narratives have influenced and shaped his vocation as a peacemaker. The profiles of peacemakers represented in David Little, ed., *Peacemakers in Action: Profiles of Religion in Conflict Resolution* (New York: Tenenbaum Center, 2007), also resonate with this theme of the religiously inspired peacemaker. This kind of work is consistent with Philpott's appeal to theological resources and to the role that religious leaders could potentially play in transformative moments such as the event of a truth and reconciliation commission (TRC). Other relevant works include Cynthia Sampson and Lederach, eds., *From the Ground Up: Mennonite Contributions to International Peacebuilding* (Oxford: Oxford University Press, 2000), and Jean Zaru, *Occupied with Nonviolence: A Palestinian Woman Speaks* (Minneapolis: Fortress Press, 2008).

30. Indeed, Schirch's work stresses the symbolic and ritualistic aspects of peacebuilding and conflict transformation by integrating insights from ritual theory into her analysis of peacebuilding. Yet despite drawing on the study of religion for categories of analysis and practice, she does not engage the question of how "religion" relates to the dynamics of ethnonational conflict. Schirch's work focuses on the question of how symbolic acts of socializing and transformative ritual practice may function centrally and instrumentally in the practice of peacebuilding itself. We must ask how religion, by inspiring people to act in a certain (peaceful or peacemaking) way, may further contribute to the transformation of conflicts on a substantive/interpretive level. Schirch's work, therefore, remains a "theory of praxis." For the use of this characterization, see Daniel Philpott, "Religion, Reconciliation, and Transitional Justice:

The State of the Field," *SSRC Working Papers*, October 17, 2007, http://www.global
.ucsb.edu/orfaleacenter/luce/luce08/documents/Philpott_SSRC-working-paper.pdf.
Other scholars and practitioners also reflected on patterns and paradigms of cross-
cultural exchange. See Kevin Avruch, *Culture and Conflict Resolution* (Washington,
DC: U.S. Institute of Peace Press, 1998), for example.

31. In many respects, Gopin's notable work exemplifies the fallacies of the field of re-
    ligious peacebuilding. His work has revolved around the potential contribution of
    religious resources and traditional (rabbinic) reconciliatory conduct to peace and jus-
    tice, rather than on a substantive engagement with how religious resources have been
    selectively appropriated by and assimilated into ethnoreligious national political
    agendas and political identities. Informed primarily by his knowledge of the sources
    of Judaism, Gopin's methodology highlights those verses, practices, stories, and
    concepts that promote peace, justice, and reconciliation. Gopin recognizes the crea-
    tive possibilities inherent in a substantive and content-sensitive as well as conduct-
    sensitive (e.g., symbolic acts, rituals, nonverbal gestures) integration of religious re-
    sources with the processes of peacebuilding. Therefore, his work frames the scope of
    religious peacebuilding as falling outside of the secular political realm of peacemak-
    ing. Religion and the religious, it is argued, can provide an auxiliary path for secular
    (rational) attempts to transform conflicts. Attempts to systematize and conceptualize
    religious peacebuilding as a field of study and practice, such as Hertog's *The Complex
    Reality of Religious Peacebuilding*, replicate the overarching secularist dichotomies and
    discourses, subsequently rendering religion a "soft" power, not one to be dimin-
    ished, nonetheless auxiliary. Strides toward complicating this framework of analysis
    of religious peacebuilding were made in Sisk, *Between Terror and Tolerance*. The theo-
    retical orientation of this volume is elaborated in a contribution by Little ("Religion,
    Nationalism, and Intolerance"), and it points to the complex modes by which reli-
    gion can be understood in the volatile contexts of national politics.

32. Similarly, my critique of religious peacebuilding and other works that bracket the
    resourcefulness of religion shows that the involvement of explicitly religious inter-
    locutors in zones of ethnonational conflict would rarely challenge a construal of a
    "nation" or a collectivity as Christian, Jewish, Buddhist, Muslim, and so forth. In-
    stead, it would show how authentic interpretations of those traditions are consistent
    with humanistic and liberal conceptions of political interactions.

33. I address this critique with further detail in my "Religious Peacebuilding: The Exotic,
    the Good, and the Theatrical." Among other locations where this relevant concep-
    tion of relationality is developed, is Butler's discussion of relationality as a condition
    for justice in her *Parting Ways*. She warns against privileging Judaisms and Jewish re-
    sources as an exclusive currency for reimagining cohabitation in Palestine/Israel be-
    cause such privileging normalizes an underlying meta-injustice that can be outlined
    only through relationality. Butler, however, does not engage the particular subfield
    of religious peacebuilding. I address the indispensability yet insufficiency of Butler's
    notion of relationality (and her retrieving of the notions of alterity and dispersal as
    basically Jewish) in detail later in chapters 5, 6, and 7.

34. Russell McCutcheon, *Critics Not Caretakers: Redescribing the Public Study of Religion*
    (Albany: State University of New York Press, 2001), 129.

35. Ibid., 130.

36. Ibid., 133.

37. Ibid., 134.

38. Ibid., 140–41.

39. It is important to stress that the study of religion and conflict transformation or peacebuilding is primarily engaged in by scholars of conflict resolution, and as such this subfield occupies only a marginalized location in conflict transformation literature (e.g., Avruch, *Culture and Conflict Resolution*; Marc Gopin, *Holy War, Holy Peace: How Religion Can Bring Peace to the Middle East* (Oxford: Oxford University Press, 2002); Schirch, *Ritual and Symbol in Peacebuilding*; and Abu-Nimer et al., *Unity in Diversity*). Only occasionally does it receive a nod of recognition from the academic study of religion. Because of its focus on "problem solving," the religious peacebuilding subfield highlights the constructive rather than the destructive or pathological aspects of religion.

40. See David Little and R. Scott Appleby, "Moment of Opportunity? The Promise of Religious Peacebuilding in an Era of Religious and Ethnic Conflict," in *Religion and Peacebuilding*, ed. Harold Coward and Gordon S. Smith (Albany: State University of New York Press, 2004), 1–26. The insistence on the irreducibility of religion to nation also lends itself to an analysis of transnational and global movements (including religious/ethnic/cultural diasporas) and their influence on the dynamics of specific conflicts. The implications of this argument are outlined in "The Task Force on Religion and the Making of U.S. Foreign Policy" (see chapter 1). Also see Appleby, "Building Peace: The Role of Local and Transnational Religious Actors," in *Religious Pluralism, Globalization and World Politics*, ed. Thomas Banchoff (Oxford: Oxford University Press, 2008), 125–54.

41. It would be imprudent for me here to wade into the murkiness of the debates over whether or not "religion" is purely a scholar's invention and/or inevitably a concept too vacuous and encompassing to have any actual analytical purchase. While these debates have arguably degenerated into self-parody for considerable stretches, they have also raised important cautionary provisions against naïve and unreflective appeals to "religion" or "religions" as such. See William Cavanaugh and the various authors he treats, *The Myth of Religious Violence: Secular Ideologies and the Roots of Modern Conflict* (Oxford: Oxford University Press, 2009), especially chap. 2. David Little pragmatically sidesteps the excesses of these debates by drawing on William Alston's much earlier and Wittgensteinian "family resemblance" account of religion in a way that lends contextual flexibility, thereby avoiding the more essentialist tendencies of the phenomenological approach to religion. See Little, "Religion, Nationalism, and Intolerance," 25 n. 4. In my judgment, such a move coheres with the self-consciously historicist yet "critically realist" approach to the study of "religion" perhaps most lucidly articulated in Kevin Schilbrack, "Religion Are There Any?" *Journal of the American Academy of Religion* 78, no. 4 (2010): 1112–38. Further, while I have no interest in salvaging the widely pummeled phenomenological approach to religion (and, in fact, offer my own critique of an unrevised appeal to it in my "Can a Critic Be a Caretaker Too?"), it is important to keep in mind that the phenomenological study of religion is itself a complex and internally variegated discourse, which in its later phases incorporates crucial hermeneutical dimensions. Perhaps the most helpful and succinct account is provided by Summer B. Twiss and Walter H. Conser Jr. in their introduction to *Experience of the Sacred: Reading in the Phenomenology of Religion*, ed. Twiss and Conser (Hanover, NH: Brown University Press, 1992), 1–74.

42. Research on questions of religion and nonviolence similarly began to interrogate and denaturalize chauvinistic interpretations of religion through a creative engagement

with the resources of various traditions. For an example, refer to Daniel L. Smith-Christopher, *Subverting Hatred: The Challenge of Nonviolence in Religious Traditions* (Maryknoll, NY: Orbis Books, 2007).

43. The constructive approach is analytically aided by the comparative study of conflict zones that may offer tools for thinking more generally about questions of religion, conflict, and peacebuilding. In a work on religion and nationalism in a comparative perspective, Little and Donald Swearer identified four essential themes: the salience of religious and ethnic identity in the cases under consideration (Sri Lanka, the Sudan, Bosnia and Herzegovina, and Iraq); the significance of the history of colonialism and imperialism in each case; the challenges and perils of postindependence self-governing; and, finally, the place of international involvement. Despite the peculiarities of each conflict zone, the comparative angle brings to the fore common motifs. Recognizing those commonalities is not a futile exercise in knowledge accumulation; rather, it enables a multidimensional analysis of the role of religion in conflict. Determining the complex role of religion in conflict would subsequently carry direct implications for conceptualizing the role of religion in conflict transformation. This is the response to the *so what* of the comparative exercise.

44. Little and Appleby, "Moment of Opportunity," 5.

45. For works challenging the hegemony of a unitary conception of "modernity," see Shmuel N. Eisenstadt, *Comparative Civilizations and Multiple Modernities* (Leiden: Brill, 2003); Eisenstadt, ed., *Multiple Modernities* (New Brunswick: NJ: Transaction, 2002); and Sandra Harding, *Silences from Below: Feminisms, Postcolonialities, and Modernity* (Durham: Duke University Press, 2008). For works confronting the relevant topic of "multiple secularisms," see José Casanova, "The Secular and Secularisms," *Social Research* 76, no. 4 (2009): 1049; John Bowen, "Secularism: Conceptual Genealogy or Political Dilemma?," *Comparative Studies in Society and History* 52, no. 3 (2010): 680–94; Mark Redhead, "Alternative Secularisms," *Philosophy and Social Criticism* 32, no. 5 (2006): 639–66; and Philip Gorski and Ates Altinordu, "After Secularization?," *Annual Review of Sociology* 34, no. 1 (2008): 55–85.

46. While offering a critique of liberal political theory and the concomitant conception of "negative" or "liberal" peace, the transitional justice literature that focuses on the role of religion in healing and conflict transformation likewise replicates the phenomenological assignment of "religion" to a distinct social sphere. Most notably, Daniel Philpott wishes to isolate the "religious" or the theological as a distinct ahistorical or transhistorical category that best enables political reconciliation when institutionally differentiated. For Philpott, religions "are communities of belief and practice oriented around claims about the ultimate ground of existence." See Philpott, "Has the Study of Global Politics Found Religion?," *Annual Review of Political Science* 12 (2009): 192. This quotation stands in striking contrast to McCutcheon's response to the question of whether religion is "also" or "only" social, biological, political, economic, and so on (*Critics Not Caretakers*, x). "Only" was McCutcheon's response. Philpott's definition of religion as entailing an orientation toward the "ultimate" locates his account within the familiar longstanding phenomenological tradition of scholarship on religion. In his effort to show the limitations of the tradition of political liberalism (see chapter 2), Philpott depicts an unproblematized interpretation of religion and theology that conforms to and privileges liberal definitions of religion (that are wholly consistent with the phenomenological tradition) but also lacks the same kind of self-reflexivity (informed by conversations in religious studies) we found in the critiques of secularist discourse (see also chapter 2). Such

self-reflexivity begins by interrogating the presumption that religion is a positive force central to the possibility of reconciliation. Philpott's theoretical approach also informs his work with co-authors Monica Toft and Timothy Shah, *God's Century: Resurgent Religion and Global Politics* (New York: Norton, 2011), and his *Just and Unjust Peace* (Oxford: Oxford University Press, 2012), which attempts to develop an ethic of political reconciliation through a comparative exploration of traditions of reconciliation within Judaism, Christianity, and Islam.

47. See Linell E. Cady and Elizabeth Shakman Hurd, eds., *Comparative Secularisms in a Global Age* (New York: Palgrave MacMillan, 2010), and Michael Warner, Jonathan VanAntwerpen, and Craig Calhoun, *Varieties of Secularism in a Secular Age* (Cambridge: Harvard University Press, 2010).

48. A similar case could be made for introducing innovations to the human rights tradition as a result of the dynamic exchange between general and particular conceptions of justice.

49. John Paul Lederach, *Building Peace: Sustainable Reconciliation in Divided Societies* (Washington, DC: U.S. Institute of Peace Press, 1997).

50. For a further critique of McCutcheon's notion of the critic and the caretaker as mutually exclusive categories, see Atalia Omer, "On Professor McCutcheon's (Un)critical-Caretaking," *Journal of the American Academy of Religion*, 80(4), 2012: 1083–97.

51. See McCutcheon, *Critics Not Caretakers*, 141.

52. Homi Bhabha, *The Location of Culture* (London: Routledge, 1994). See also Saba Mahmood, *Politics of Piety: The Islamic Revival and the Feminist Subject* (Princeton: Princeton University Press, 2005). Mahmood's ethnographic study complicates the connection McCutcheon establishes between the privatization of religion and the neutralization of dissent vis-à-vis the status quo. In their embodied practices, the pious Egyptian women Mahmood engages offer alternatives to mainstream interpretations of Egyptian religiosity and social life. Mahmood's notion of multiple modalities of agency therefore sheds light on the limits of McCutcheon's analysis of power as well as suggests the creative and transformative alternatives that may be located under the surfaces of the rhetoric and ethos of social and political elites. Likewise, in his study of the Mizrahim in Israel, Israeli sociologist Yehouda Shenhav explains how their identity as "Arab Jews" occupies a hybrid location that challenges official Zionist rhetorical efforts to construe the "Arab" and the "Jew" as inherently antithetical and antagonistic. Further, the Mizrahi experiences strongly challenge Zionist historiography. Reclaiming and (re)narrating Mizrahi history could have profound ramifications for rethinking the relationship between Judaism and Israeliness, among other issues. See chapter 7 for a detailed discussion of the Mizrahi challenge and contestation of an Israeli identity.

CHAPTER FOUR

1. Judith Plaskow, *Standing Again at Sinai: Judaism from a Feminist Perspective* (San Francisco: Harper & Row, 1990), 6.

2. This is consistent with Anthony Smith's discussion of the "nation" as a "heterodox religion" and of nationalism as a this-worldly movement of redemption (see chapters 2 and 3).

3. The Tal Committee, for instance, looked into the issue of exemptions from military service that the Status Quo granted to yeshiva students. Headed by Judge Tzvi Tal (and commissioned by then prime minister Ehud Barak) in August 1999, the committee concluded by July 2002 that only minor revisions would be introduced,

demanding minimal service of yeshiva students who decided to enter the work force rather than remain in the yeshiva. The issue of exemption from military service granted to yeshiva students, however, is increasingly contentious. In August of 2012, defense minister Ehud Barak revoked the rulings of the Tal Commission, ordering the army to produce a plan for a universal draft of Orthodox Jews. However, at the point of the writing of this book, it is not clear how this drastic departure from the status quo will play out on the legislative level, a landscape propelled by political agendas for securing wide parliamentary coalitions.

4. For helpful overviews of the early stages and origins of Israeli politics, see Myron J. Aronoff, "The Origins of Israeli Political Culture," and Yonathan Shapiro, "The Historical Origins of Israeli Democracy," in *Israeli Democracy under Stress*, ed. Ehud Sprinzak and Larry Diamond (Jerusalem: Israel Democracy Institute, 1993), 47–63 and 65–80, respectively, as well as Shapiro, *Democracy in Israel* (Givatayim: Massada, 1978) [in Hebrew].

5. While gradually in the 1990s and 2000s other Jewish and secular routes for life cycle events opened up (albeit in a limited way), there are financial and other incentives involved in, for instance, sanctioning one's marriage through the rabbinate.

6. Haredim constitute only about 10 percent of Israeli society. But, owing to their high birthrate, they are projected to constitute something between a quarter and 40 percent of the population by the middle of the twenty-first century.

7. For some reports on the Haredi-secular clashes in Israel, see BBC News Middle East, "Beit Shemesh Ultra-Orthodox Jews Clash with Police," December 26, 2011, http://www.bbc.co.uk/news/world-middle-east-16335603; BBC News Middle East, "Israelis Rally against Ultra-Orthodox Extremism," December 27, 2011, http://www.bbc.co.uk/news/world-middle-east-16342327; Huff Post World, "Israel Nazi Comparisons Bill Proposed," January 10, 2012, http://www.huffingtonpost.com/2012/01/10/israel-nazi-comparisons-bill_n_1196103.html; Huff Post World, "In Israel, Spate of Ultra-Orthodox Incidents Rattle the Secular Mainstream," January 9, 2012, http://www.huffingtonpost.com/2012/01/09/israel-orthodox-haredim_n_1190500.html; Anshil Pepper, "One Hundred Female Soldiers Left Simkhat Torah Event in Protest Because Required to Celebrate While Segregated," *Haaretz*, October 23, 2011, http://www.haaretz.co.il/news/education/1.1528402 [in Hebrew]; and Oz Rozenberg, "Due to Separation Barrier: Clashes between Haredim and Social Activists in Mea Shearim," *Haaretz*, October 22, 2011, http://www.haaretz.co.il/misc/article-print-page/1.1528161 [in Hebrew].

8. Haim Levinson, "Benny Kazovar: To Dissolve Democracy and Subordinate It to Judaism," *Haaretz*, January 8, 2012, http://www.haaretz.co.il/news/politics/1.1611387 [in Hebrew].

9. I elaborate on Kookism later in this chapter.

10. Bettina Prato, "Prophetic Justice in a Home Haunted by Strangers: Transgressive Solidarity and Trauma in the Work of an Israeli Rabbis' Group," in *Political Theologies: Public Religions in a Post-Secular World*, ed. Hent de Vries and Lawrence Sullivan (New York: Fordham University Press, 2006), 557–90.

11. "Neturei Karta" means "Guardians of the City" in Aramaic. The choice of the name refers to a rabbinic story that posits the "scribes and the scholars" as the most appropriate guardians of the city (Jerusalem Talmud, Tractate Hagiga, 76c). The Neturei Karta group was founded in Jerusalem in 1938, as a radical splinter of Agudat Yisrael, which they perceived as gradually selling out to the Zionists that they set out to oppose. This group refuses to accept the political authority of the State of Israel

and has engaged in protest against Zionism and Israel ever since its formation. See http://www.nkusa.org/aboutus/index.cfm (accessed January 13, 2012).

12. Satmar Hasidism constitutes a version of ultra-Orthodox Judaism. In its inception, the group's leader was Rabbi Yoel Teitelbaum (1887–1979) who, after World War II, founded a network of yeshivot, first in Palestine/Israel and then, after his relocation to the United States, in Williamsburg, Brooklyn, and upstate New York. Satmar communities also exist in Boro Park, Buenos Aires, Antwerp, Bnei Brak, and Jerusalem. Satmar has voiced its opposition to the State of Israel, rendering it blasphemous because it violates the divine injunction against false messianism. The Satmar also rejects the Israeli state on the basis of its secularity. See http://www.jewsnotzionists .org/satmar.htm (accessed January 13, 2012).

13. Neturei Karta International, "Why Orthodox Jew Are Opposed to a Zionist State," http://www.nkusa.org/AboutUs/Zionism/opposition.cfm (accessed May 5, 2008).

14. For a review of central motifs pivotal to Israeli mythological formations, see the discussion in chapter 1. For a theoretical account, explicating the analytic maneuver of rendering secular modes of nationalism a "political theology," refer to chapters 2 and 3.

15. Notably, the so-called unilateral disengagement from the Gaza Strip in 2005 signaled a fracture in the relationship of symbiosis between the settlement movement and the Israeli state. In *Evolving Nationalism: Homeland, Identity, and Religion in Israel 1925–2005* (Ithaca: Cornell University Press, 2011), Nadav G. Shelef observes the elasticity of religious Zionism's relations to the State of Israel (see, especially, 134–46). He argues that the initial Kookist sanctification of the State and its institutions has given way since the 1970s to a growing inclination to prioritize the imperative to settle the land over the interests of the state. This amounts to an inversion of ideological priorities and a theological elevation of a commitment to the "wholeness" of the land above personal piety and even the actual survival of the Israeli state. Hence the ideological shift that became most acutely evident with intense and public resistance to the evacuation of the settlements in the Gaza Strip in 2005. The ideological reshuffling does not mean that the State is no longer theologically significant within the framework of religious Zionism. Instead, it means that if the State acts against the principle of territorial wholeness, it fails to fulfill its redemptive function. As Shelef explains, "Reversing Israel's hold on the territories became tantamount to the heresy of reversing the process of redemption" (136). The upshot is that the state no longer functions as a hegemonic representation of Jewish collectivity but is transformed, in the eyes of the settlers' leadership, to a mere instrument and a source of material subsidies.

16. For an example of such critics, see Uriel Simon, "Religious Zionism: Religion, Morality and Politics," January 2004, originally published as "Challenges and Choices," *Oz Ve'Shalom Publications*, 1979. Available on the website of the World Zionist Organization, http://www.resources.en.wzo.org.il/home/P102.jsp?arc=243937 (accessed May 17, 2008).

17. Yeshayahu Leibowitz, "The Religious Significance of the State," in *Judaism, Human Values, and the Jewish State*, ed. Eliezer Goldman (Cambridge: Harvard University Press, 1992), 218. Indeed, earlier on, Leibowitz saw the halakhic potential presented by the modern Israeli polity. But he became increasingly disillusioned with and critical of the idolatrous practices of religious Zionists of the Kookist variety and the atheist-clerical modus vivendi enshrined in the mechanisms and practices of the state. This disillusionment caused him to retreat to a strict secularist view of the state.

18. Ibid., 217.

19. Leibowitz, "A Call for the Separation of Religion and State," in Goldman, *Judaism, Human Values, and the Jewish State*, 175.

20. Leibowitz, *Torah and Commandments in Our Time* (Tel Aviv: Schocken, 1954) [in Hebrew], and *Jewish People and the State of Israel* (Tel Aviv: Schocken, 1975) [in Hebrew].

21. Leibowitz, "Jewish Identity and Israeli Silence," in Goldman, *Judaism, Human Values, and the Jewish State*, 193.

22. Ibid., 218.

23. Ibid.

24. For a stimulating and innovative account of this framing of Judaism as a religion, see the historical and philosophical exposition by Leora Batnitzky, *How Judaism Became a Religion: An Introduction to Modern Jewish Thought* (Princeton: Princeton University Press, 2011).

25. David Hartman, *Israelis and the Jewish Tradition: An Ancient People Debating Its Future* (New Haven: Yale University Press, 2000), 21.

26. Ibid., 291.

27. Aviezer Ravitzky, "The Zionist Imperative: On Torah, Zionism and Peace," http://www.doingzionism.org.il/resources/view.asp?id=1663 (accessed May 20, 2008), 1–2.

28. Ravitzky, *Messianism, Zionism, and Jewish Radicalism* (Chicago: University of Chicago Press, 1996) [translated from Hebrew], see for instance 29.

29. Ravitzky, *Messianism, Zionism, and Jewish Radicalism*, especially 79–144.

30. Nurith Gertz, *Myths in Israeli Culture: Captives of a Dream* (London: Valentine Mitchell, 2000). See also chapter 1 for a more detailed discussion of this motif.

31. The Israeli civil religion, as I mention throughout this book, has been a dynamic and elastic construct. In the earlier decades, an emphasis on becoming "normal" like "any other nation" eclipsed a narrative of constant "near annihilation," even in the aftermath of the Holocaust. See, for example, Tom Segev, *The Seventh Million* (New York: Hill and Wang, 1993), and Idith Zertal, *Israel's Holocaust and the Politics of Nationhood* (Cambridge: Cambridge University Press, 2005). Clearly, the Holocaust vindicated Zionism, but the motif of the "negation of exile" was instrumental in creating an ethos of a "new Hebrew," one of physical heroism and self-reliance. The physical redemption associated with political self-determination was also closely associated with a social vision that was socialist in orientation (though there are important variations within the Zionist movement, variations that remain critical in analyzing social transformations within Israeli society and its interpretations of the social contract). The late 1970s signaled a shift away from the hegemony of Labor Zionism and its social ideologies, a shift that came to fruition with the implementation of neoliberal policies in the 1990s and 2000s and the almost total dissolution of social safety nets (with the glaring exception of the governmental subvention to settlement projects in the territories of the 1967 occupation). The early social vision translated into the establishment of the kibbutz as a celebrated social experiment. Celebrating the "normalcy" of the Israeli nation-state, however, turned increasingly into highlighting the "extra-ordinary" character of Israel as the sole defender of Jews and Judaism, replicating and assimilating the ghetto images of a "nation dwelling apart" under a constant existential threat from its surrounding hostile environment. Why did this transformation take place? How else was it possible to legitimate the occupation of the Palestinian territories through the repeated invocation of the "se-

curity imperative"? To respond to these and related questions, it is crucial to ponder the cultural and religious motifs appropriated elastically within the framework of Israeli nationalism or Zionism.

32. See also Joyce Dalsheim, *Unsettling Gaza: Secular Liberalism, Radical Religion, and the Israeli Settlement Project* (Oxford: Oxford University Press, 2011).

33. Tanenbaum Center, "An Open House: Yehezkel Landau," in *Peacemakers in Action: Profiles of Religion in Conflict Resolution*, ed. David Little (Cambridge: Cambridge University Press, 2007), 360.

34. Ibid., 361–62.

35. Gershon Shafir and Yoav Peled, *Being Israeli: The Dynamics of Multiple Citizenship* (Cambridge: Cambridge University Press, 2002).

36. See also Dalsheim, *Unsettling Gaza*.

37. "About the Covenant: Background and Goals," http://www.gavison-medan.org.il /english/about/ (accessed May 10, 2008).

38. "Foundations for a New Covenant among Jews in Matters of Religion and State in Israel," http://www.gavison-medan.org.il/Admin/fileserver/2%20The%20Spirit% 20of%20the%20Covenant.pdf?file=31 (accessed January 14, 2012), 13. For an extensive discussion of the principle of Jewish return and the rationales of the authors in expanding it, see http://www.gavison-medan.org.il/Admin/fileserver /4%20Chapter%20One%20-%20%20Return,%20Citizenship,%20Population,% 20%20Registry%20and%20Conversion.pdf?file=40 (accessed January 13, 2012), 22–41.

39. The use of the Christian category of "church" is rhetorical to denote that the institution of an "official rabbinate" is foreign to antecedent Jewish traditions (prior to the establishment of the modern state of Israel). This is very much in line with the antecedent colonial policies of the British mandate that sought to divide and conquer the various "subjects" by consolidating religious, ethnic, and cultural authority in offices such as "chief rabbi" and/or "chief mufti."

40. "Foundations for a New Covenant," 13. For an extensive discussion of personal status with a focus on the marriage regulation in Israel, see http://www.gavison-medan .org.il/Admin/fileserver/5%20Chapter%20Two%20-%20%20Personal%20Status, %20Marriage%20and%20the%20Dissolution%20of%20Marriage.pdf?file=34 (accessed January 14, 2012), 42–54.

41. For an extensive account of the "Sabbath," see chapter 3 of the Gavison-Medan Covenant, "The Sabbath," http://www.gavison-medan.org.il/Admin/fileserver /6%20Chapter%20Three%20-%20The%20Sabbath.pdf?file=35 (accessed January 14, 2012), 55–62.

42. For an account of the principle of noncoercion and specific deliberations and issues related to dietary laws, organ transplant, prayers at the western wall, IDF recruitment and service, and equality and integration of women, see chapter 4 of the Gavison-Medan Covenant, "Other Issues," http://www.gavison-medan.org.il /Admin/fileserver/7%20Chapter%20Four%20-%20Other%20Issues.pdf?file=36 (accessed January 14, 2012), 63–77.

43. Similar blinders may be identified in the mass social protest that emerged in the summer of 2011.

44. http://www.gavison-medan.org.il/Admin/fileserver/English_9%20ekronot% 20medan.pdf?file=28 (accessed January 14, 2012), 84.

45. Ibid., 84–85.

46. Ibid., 85.

47. Ibid.
48. Ibid., 92.
49. Ibid.
50. For an English translation of the central writings of Kook, refer to *Abraham Isaac Kook: The Lights of Penitence, the Lights of Holiness, the Moral Principles, Essays, Letters, and Poems*, trans. Ben Zion Bokser (Mahwah, NJ: Paulist Press, 1978).
51. Gavison-Medan Covenant, 93–94.
52. Ibid., 88–89.
53. Ibid., 90.
54. Ibid., 87.
55. "The Gavison-Medan Covenant: Main Points and Principles," http://www.gavison-medan.org.il/Admin/fileserver/English_10%20ekronot%20gavison.pdf?file=29 (accessed January 14, 2012).
56. See John Rawls, *A Theory of Justice* (Cambridge: Harvard University Press, 1971), 3–168, and *Political Liberalism*, rev. ed. (1993; New York: Columbia University Press, 1996), 1–88 and 131–254.
57. Gavison-Medan Covenant, 101.
58. For examples of what came to be classified as "communitarian" formulations, see Alasdair McIntyre, "Is Patriotism a Virtue?," in *Theorizing Citizenship*, ed. Ronald Beiner (Albany: State University of New York Press, 1995), 209–28; Michael Sandel, "Freedom of Conscience or Freedom of Choice?," in *Articles of Faith Articles of Peace: The Religious Liberty Clauses and the American Public Philosophy*, ed. James Davison Hunter and Os Guinness (Washington, DC: Brookings Institution Press, 1990), 74–92; and Adrian Oldfield, "Citizenship and Community," in *The Citizenship Debates*, ed. Gershon Shafir (Minneapolis: University of Minnesota Press, 1998), 75–89.
59. For a particularly powerful argument along these lines, see Michael Sandel, "Review of Political Liberalism," *Harvard Law Review* 107 (1994): 1765–95.
60. For a relevant critique of Jürgen Habermas's notion of "constitutional patriotism," see Perry Anderson, "Nation-States and National Identity," *London Review of Books*, May 9, 1991, 7–8. Habermas understands liberal nationalism to mean an allegiance to a set of abstracted and generalized principles, or in Habermas's words, "constitutional patriotism." This notion of constitutional patriotism denotes what Habermas perceives as the need in our "post-national" era to generalize political cultures by decoupling them from majority cultures. He thus asserts: "The level of the shared political culture must be strictly separated from the level of subcultures and prepolitical identities . . . On such a basis, nationalism can be replaced by what one might call constitutional patriotism." Habermas, "The European Nation-State—Its Achievements and Its Limits. On the Past and Future of Sovereignty and Citizenship," in *Mapping the Nation*, ed. Gopal Balakrishnan and Benedict Anderson (London: Verso, 1996), 289. Recent attempts to think about citizenship in a supposed "postnational" European context follow Habermas's concept of "constitutional patriotism" that proposes shared principles of justice and democracy as the foundation of postnational citizenship. For example, André Berten, "Identité européenne, une ou multiple?," in *L'Europe au soir du siècle: Identité et démocratie*, ed. Jacques Lenoble and Nicole Dewandre (Paris: Éditions Esprit, 1992), 81–97. See also the introduction for a discussion of applications of a Habermasian frame within post-Zionist scholarship.
61. While Habermas calls for the cultivation of an abstracted constitutional patriotism, advocates of the liberal variety of multiculturalism, like Kymlicka and Taylor, have highlighted the relevance of specific interpretations of cultures or religions to the

construction and maintenance of meaningful citizenship, thus understood as the expression of belonging to a particular political community. Liberal analysts of multiculturalism combine a critical recognition of the legitimate public expression of group membership with normative liberal conceptions of individual rights and liberties whereby the right to public expression of one's culture is acutely important for the well-being of the individual in a pluralistic context. For Taylor, the recognition of a person by another subject is a critical human need and thus a matter of self-realization and identity formation. Charles Taylor, "The Politics of Recognition," in *Multiculturalism: Examining the Politics of Recognition*, ed. Amy Gutmann (Princeton: Princeton University Press, 1994), 25. Taylor draws a distinction between two types of liberalism. The first type is strictly dedicated to upholding individual rights and thus corresponds to a culturally and religiously neutral nation-state. The second type of liberalism enables particular states to advance collective aims, such as the preservation and cultivation of a certain culture or religion, provided that the basic rights of the citizens are secured. In his critique of Taylor, Michael Walzer highlights how the political implications of each type of liberalism ought to be analyzed contextually. See Walzer, "Comment," in Gutmann, *Multiculturalism*, 99–103. Thus, the first type is suitable for the Canadian experiment with multiculturalism, but is it conceivable for the Israeli circumstance? Can Israel become a state for its citizens without transforming its defining characteristics? Gavison, grounding her theoretical liberalism, would render such a political model an abrogation of a basic human right (the right to national self-determination). Kymlicka finds no contradiction between the demands of ethnic and national groups to assert and express their identities and liberal principles of social justice and individual freedom. Like Sandel and other critics of liberalism, he underscores the requirement to respect the demand of cultural groups to preserve their cultural idiosyncrasies. But, unlike communitarian commentators, he considers culture as a matter of individual choice. Yael Tamir offers a cultural definition of the "nation." She argues that nationalism constitutes a "right to culture," which she subsequently understands as "the rights to a public sphere in which individuals can share a language, memorise their past, cherish their heroes, live a fulfilling national life." See Tamir, *Liberal Nationalism* (Princeton: Princeton University Press, 1995), 8. Interestingly, by defining nationalism as a right, Tamir disputes the liberal aversion to particularity and communality, because this hermeneutical maneuver resituates the question of nationalism in a human rights framework as a subset of the right to self-determination. Tamir's formulation constitutes, nonetheless, a clear example of the inability of theorists of liberal nationalism to overcome the modernist attachment to the close connection between culture and state in their attempt to demonstrate the right (and need) of the individual for a public representation of his or her culture. Ernest Gellner's theory of nationalism is a key example of the modernist/functionalist assumption of the imperative of attaining a degree of congruence or synonymy between nation and state. See Gellner, *Nations and Nationalism* (Ithaca, NY: Cornell University Press, 1983), 1. See also E. J. Hobsbawm, *Nations and Nationalism since 1780*, 2nd ed. (Cambridge: Cambridge University Press, 1992), 9, and Ronald Beiner, "Introduction: Nationalism's Challenge to Political Philosophy," in *Theorizing Nationalism*, ed. Beiner (Albany: State University of New York Press, 1999), 7. Gellner's theory also does not provide tools for assessing which claims for recognition may be justifiable or unjustifiable.

62. Gavison-Medan Covenant, 103.
63. Ibid.

64. Ibid., 106.
65. Ibid., 104.
66. Ibid., 103.
67. Ibid., 105.
68. Ibid., 104.
69. Will Kymlicka, *Multicultural Citizenship: A Liberal Theory of Minority Rights* (Oxford: Oxford University Press, 1995), 173–74.
70. Kymlicka's proposal is thus predicated both on a static Rawlsian prescriptive formulation of "constitutional essentials" and on what appears to be an extension of T. H. Marshall's notion of a dynamic progression of rights from civil, political, and social to a fourth generation of cultural citizenship rights. This critique of Rawls's static formulation is greatly indebted to Ronald Thiemann, *Religion in Public Life: A Dilemma for Democracy* (Washington, DC: Georgetown University Press, 1996), especially 80–90, and Jeffrey Stout, *Democracy and Tradition* (Princeton: Princeton University Press, 2004), especially 68–76. See also Marshall, *Class, Citizenship and Social Development* (New York: Anchor, 1965). Marshall's dominant definition of citizenship primarily in terms of civil, political, and social rights to be realized gradually by traditionally excluded groups in the framework of a liberal-democratic welfare state was deemed insufficient on its own because exclusion is also expressed in sociocultural terms. This process will allegedly result in abandoning the communitarian formula of a monocultural nation-state with a unified conception of citizenship in favor of "citizenship as identity" in an explicitly multinational context. See Kymlicka, "Multicultural Citizenship," in Shafir, *Citizenship Debates*, 167–88.
71. In his early works, Kymlicka distinguishes among three types of group-differentiated communal rights: special group representation within political institutions, self-government pertaining primarily to education and family law, and polyethnic rights intended to guard religious and cultural practices—all of which are designed to protect minority groups from the dictates and encroachment of the "larger society." Kymlicka, "Multicultural Citizenship." I further elaborate on Kymlicka's analysis of group-differentiated citizenship in chapter 5 as a part of my discussion of the consociational proposal of Palestinian Israelis.
72. Iris Marion Young, "Polity and Group Difference: A Critique of the Ideal of Universal Citizenship," in Shafir, *Citizenship Debates*, 263–90. Young states: "The attempt to realize an ideal of universal citizenship that finds the public embodying generality as opposed to particularity, commonness versus difference, will tend to exclude or to put at a disadvantage some groups, even when they have formally equal citizenship status" (269).
73. Iris Marion Young, "A Multicultural Continuum: A Critique of Will Kymlicka's Ethnic-Nation Dichotomy," *Constellation* 4, no. 1 (1997): 48–53. For a critique of Young, see Chandran Kukathas, "Multiculturalism and the Idea of an Australian Identity," in *Multicultural Citizens: The Philosophy and Politics of Identity*, ed. Kukathas (St. Leonard's, Australia: Centre for Independent Studies, 1993), 145–57. See also Kymlicka and Wayne Norman, "Return of the Citizen," in Beiner, *Theorizing Citizenship*, 285–300.
74. For example, refer to Susan Moller Okin, *Is Multiculturalism Bad for Women?* (Princeton: Princeton University Press, 1999). Also see chapter 2 for further explication of Kymlicka's framework.
75. Amy Gutmann, "The Challenge of Multiculturalism in Political Studies," *Philosophy and Public Affairs* 22, no. 3 (1993): 171–206, and Yael Tamir, "Against Collective

Rights," in *Multicultural Questions*, ed. Christian Joppke and Steven Lukes (Oxford: Oxford University Press, 1999), 158–82.

76. Todd Gitlin, *The Twilight of Common Dreams: Why America Is Wracked by Culture Wars* (New York: Metropolitan Books, 1995), and Brian Barry, *Culture and Equality: An Egalitarian Critique of Multiculturalism* (Cambridge: Harvard University Press, 2001).

77. Homi Bhabha, "DissemiNation: Time, Narrative, and the Margins of the Modern Nation," *Nation and Narration* (London: Routledge, 1990), 291–322.

78. The later work by Kymlicka as discussed in chapter 2 begins to struggle with the challenges of the diffusion of the liberal multicultural discourse by international organizations like the EU and UN. While upholding the desirability of the liberal model, Kymlicka recognizes its parochial location and its possible misuse and manipulation, usually to the detriment of the most vulnerable within various communities. Subsequently, in his *Multicultural Odysseys*, Kymlicka advocates a "targeted" rather than a "generic" approach to minority rights, whereby different norms apply to different types of minorities (immigrant, indigenous, and so forth). Moreover, he promotes sequencing strategies in addressing questions of multicultural justice in contexts stricken by ethnoreligious national conflicts. Here, the point is to distinguish between "long-term ideals and short-term pragmatic recommendations." Still another complication for the global diffusion of multiculturalism, Kymlicka observes, is the possible tensions and contradictions between multicultural justice and security considerations. See Will Kymlicka, *Multicultural Odysseys: Navigating the New International Politics of Diversity* (New York: Oxford University Press, 2007), 9.

79. See, for example, Gavison-Medan Covenant, 108.

80. See also chapter 1 for a discussion of Shenhav's proposal and a critique of the "Israeli left."

CHAPTER FIVE

1. http://www.shatil.org.il/english/ (accessed June 20, 2010).

2. http://www.shatil.org.il/english/change/religious-pluralism/ (accessed June 20, 2010).

3. http://www.shatil.org.il/english/change/social-justice/ (accessed June 10, 2010).

4. http://www.shatil.org.il/english/change/shared-society/ (accessed June 10 2010).

5. http://rhr.israel.net/who-we-are (accessed May 22, 2008).

6. David J. Forman, "On 'rhr'" (the official website of Rabbis for Human Rights), http://www.rhr.israel.net/press/rabbisforhumanrights.html (accessed May 22, 2008).

7. http://rhr.israel.net/who-we-are (accessed May 20, 2008).

8. This text may be found at http://rhr.israel.net/speech-by-rabbi-ma%e2%80%ayan-turner-rhr-chairperson-at-the-niwano-peace-prize-award-ceremony (accessed May 5, 2008).

9. Yoel Finkelman, "Religion and Public Life: Exile and State in the Thought of Joseph Dov Soloveitchik, Abraham Joshua Heschel, and Mordecai Kaplan," in *Religion and State in Twentieth-Century Jewish Thought*, ed. Aviezer Ravitzky (Jerusalem: Israel Democracy Institute, 2005), 367–70.

10. Ibid., 380–87.

11. Mordechai Kaplan, *The Future of the American Jew* (New York: Macmillan, 1948), chaps. 7 and 17; Kaplan, *The Religion of Ethical Nationhood*, (New York: Macmillan, 1970), chap. 6; Kaplan, *A New Zionism* (New York: Theodor Herzl Foundation, 1955); and Jack J. Cohen, "Reflections on Kaplan's Zionism," in *The American Judaism of Mordecai M. Kaplan*, ed. Emanuel S. Goldsmith, Mel Scult, and Robert Seltzer (New York: New York University Press, 1990).

12. Finkelman, "Religion and Public Life," 396–97.
13. David Hartman explains that "Soloveitchik and Heschel were existentialists who attempted to provide authenticity for the individual Jew. Leibowitz was an existentialist who strove to provide authenticity for the community." *A Heart of Many Rooms: Celebrating the Many Voices within Judaism* (Woodstock, VT: Jewish Lights, 1999), 277.
14. The Israel Policies Task Force Report may be found at http://www.jrf.org/israel/israel-taskforce.html (accessed March 3, 2008).
15. Israel Policies Task Force Report, 12.
16. "Zionism and Communal Covenant; A Reconstructionist Approach to Essential Jewish Principles," http://jrf.org/resources/files/Zionism%20and%20Communal%20 Covenant.pdf (accessed January 15, 2012), 1 (emphasis in text).
17. Ibid., 2.
18. Ibid., 3.
19. The ads were taken off the air as a result of the outcry. For a coverage of this story, see, for instance, Jonathan S. Tobin, "Israel Ad Campaign Targeting Expats Raises Troubling Questions of Identity," *Commentary*, November 29, 2011, http://jrf.org/resources/files/Zionism%20and%20Communal%20Covenant.pdf.
20. "Zionism and Communal Covenant," 5.
21. Ibid., 5.
22. "Israel Policies Task Force Report," 15.
23. See chapter 2.
24. Eliezer Schweid, "Religion and State in the Thoughts of Spinoza, Mendelssohn and Leo Straus," in Ravitzky, *Religion and State in Twentieth-Century Jewish Thought*, 158.
25. Bettina Prato, "Prophetic Justice in a Home Haunted by Strangers: Transgressive Solidarity and Trauma in the Work of Israeli Rabbis' Group," in *Political Theologies: Public Religions in a Post-secular World*, ed. Hent de Vries and Lawrence E. Sullivan (New York: Fordham University Press, 2006), 565.
26. Ibid., 567–68.
27. Ibid., 568–69.
28. Please refer to chapter 2 for an extensive discussion of Marx's theory of nationalism.
29. For instance, this amnesia is evident in Rawls's notion of the "society" as a "closed" and "fixed" variable. See his *Political Liberalism*, rev. ed. (1993; New York: Columbia University Press, 1996), 12.
30. For an analysis of the ban of the veil in France and how it relates not only to *laïcité* as a sacred principle of France's nationalism that is perceived to be under attack by Muslim girls and their hijabs, but also to a reopening of the orientalism undergirding French colonialism in North Africa (where most Muslim citizens and immigrants in France came from), see Joan Scott, *The Politics of the Veil* (Princeton: Princeton University Press, 2007). For a review of why the framing of U.S. foreign policy with respect to the Muslim and Arab contexts is informed by enduring orientalism, see Elizabeth Shakman Hurd, *The Politics of Secularism in International Relations* (Princeton: Princeton University Press, 2008).
31. See chapter 2 for further discussion of the typology of nationalism.
32. See chapter 2 for further explication of this metric.
33. See chapter 2 for a discussion of approaches to political reconciliation.
34. Examples of such deconstructive works include Joyce Dalsheim, *Unsettling Gaza: Secular Liberalism, Radical Religion, and the Israeli Settlement Project* (Oxford: Oxford University Press, 2011); Oren Yiftachel, *Ethnocracy: Land and Identity Politics in Is-*

rael/Palestine (Philadelphia: University of Pennsylvania Press, 2006); and Yehouda Shenhav, *The Time of the Green Line: Towards a Jewish Political Thought* (Tel Aviv: Am Oved, 2010) [in Hebrew].

35. See Shenhav, *Time of the Green Line*. See also Yotam Feldman, "Professor Yehouda Shenhav Thinks That We Have More Than One Conflict to Solve, Before It Will Be Quiet around Here," *Haaretz*, February 19, 2010, http://g.watap.net/haaretz/main?ref =mredir2&go=misc/1.1189833 [in Hebrew], and Shenhav, "A Skeleton in the Closet," *Haaretz*, July 6, 2011, http://www.haokets.org/2011/07/06/%D7%A9%D7%9C% D7%93-%D7%91%D7%90%D7%A8%D7%95%D7%9F-%D7%AA%D7%94% D7%9C%D7%99%D7%9A-%D7%94%D7%A9%D7%9C%D7%95%D7%9D/# .TxO-L43SgUA.mailto.

36. An interview conducted on March 15, 2007, Jerusalem.

37. This positing of the conditionality of the "promise" of the land situates RHR within a long Jewish tradition dating back conceptually (and self-consciously) to the biblical prophets and their explanations of exile, destruction, and dispersal.

38. See also Atalia Omer, "Can a Critic Be a Caretaker Too? Religion, Conflict, and Conflict Transformation," *Journal of the American Academy of Religion* 79, no. 2 (2011), 459–96, and Omer, "On Professor McCutcheon's (Un)Critical-Caretaking," *Journal of the American Academy of Religion* 80 no. 4 (2012): 1083–97.

39. Representative works of this new field are the following: R. Scott Appleby, *The Ambivalence of the Sacred: Religion, Violence, and Reconciliation* (Lanham, MD: Rowman & Littlefield, 2000); Douglas Johnston, *Faith-Based Diplomacy: Trumping Realpolitik* (Oxford: Oxford University Press, 2003); Cynthia Sampson, *Religion: The Missing Dimension of Statecraft* (Oxford: Oxford University Press, 1994); Marc Gopin, *Holy War, Holy Peace: How Religion Can Bring Peace to the Middle East* (Oxford: Oxford University Press, 2002); and David Smock, ed., *Interfaith Dialogue and Peacebuilding* (Washington, DC: U.S. Institute of Peace, 2002). See also chapter 3 in this book for a further explication of the subgenre of religious peacebuilding.

40. Gopin, "The Use of the Word and Its Limits: A Critical Evaluation of Religious Dialogue as Peacemaking," in Smock, *Interfaith Dialogue*, 33–46.

41. John Paul Lederach, *Building Peace: Sustainable Reconciliation in Divided Societies* (Washington, DC: U.S. Institute of Peace Press, 1997), 41–61. In his comprehensive approach to conflict transformation and peacebuilding, Lederach judges the middle-range approach to be the most fitting method for establishing a sustainable infrastructure of peace. This method highlights the role of middle-range leadership, consisting of credible and respected leaders in ethnic and religious sectors, academia, and humanitarian organizations, among others. The middle-range leadership is hence in a position to cultivate a broad and popularized infrastructure of peace by challenging perceptions of conflicting identity groups and biases of policymakers, engaging in localized conflict resolution trainings, and creating collaborative networks and institutions that could play an important reconciliatory role. Applying scholar of conflict resolution Maire Dugan's notion of the "nested paradigm," Lederach distinguishes between interpersonal, subsystemic, and systemic dimensions of conflict and peacebuilding. The middle-range approach enables devoting attention to practical problem-solving concurrently on the interpersonal and subsystemic level and on the macro level of systemic transformation.

42. This commitment explains why RHR (as well as other social justice activists from across the spectrum) resisted the governmental decision in 2012 to deport refugees from southern Sudan, many of whom made a home in Israel (despite widespread

racist attitudes toward them). In mid-August 2012, Eli Yishai, the Israeli minister of the interior, issued an order (scheduled to come into effect by October 15, 2012) authorizing the detention and deportation of southern Sudanese and Eritrean migrants. In explaining his rationale for pushing the deportation drive, Yishai told a reporter from an Israeli newspaper that "the infiltrator threat is just as severe as the Iranian threat." See Omri Efraim, "Yishai: Next Phase—Arresting Eritrean, Sudanese Migrants," *Ynet*, August 16, 2012, http://www.ynetnews.com/articles/0,7340,L -4269540,00.html. Yishai is also reported as saying that "those who want to keep talking and find themselves in the future facing the committee of inquiry over the loss of Israel can keep talking. Those who want to work to ensure a Jewish and Zionist state for our children should act. I chose to act." See Omri Efraim, "Rights Groups Slam 'Cruel' Plan to Detain Sudanese," *Ynet*, August 30, 2012, http://www.ynetnews .com/articles/0,7340,L-4274804,00.html. The tragic irony of this deportation drive of asylum seekers did not escape many of those activists protesting the deportation and its xenophobic and chauvinistic impetus. For an example of RHR's engagement with the decision to deport southern Sudanese refugees (including children who grew up in Israel and are fluent in Hebrew), see Rabbi Avi Novis, "To Integrate the Stranger and Honor His Rights: Dvar Torah Parashat 'Ki Tetze,'" August 28, 2012, http://rhr .org.il/eng/index.php/2012/08/to-integrate-the-stranger-and-honor-his-rights-dvar -torah-for-parashat-ki-tetze/.

43. Prato, "Prophetic Justice in a Home Haunted by Strangers," 574.

44. Nancy Fraser, as I explained in chapter 2, illuminates how the post-Westphalian condition of globalization has transformed the boundaries of justice discourses. She argues that the contemporary reality of globalization suggests the inherent transterritoriality of many issues ranging from environmental pollution to immigration, and thus this condition challenges some of the basic assumptions of the Westphalian constellation of nation-states.

45. See chapter 1 for a discussion of the Geneva Initiative. For another example that typifies a disentangling and differentiation between American Jews and the question of Israel, see Peter Beinart, "The Failure of the American Jewish Establishment," *New York Review of Books*, June 10, 2010, http://www.nybooks.com/articles /archives/2010/jun/10/failure-american-jewish-establishment/?pagination=false. This article generated a heated conversation among American Jews concerning their commitment to the Israeli-Zionist project. This internal questioning and problematizing of the nature of the commitment to Israel and how might it be related to the status of American Jews in the United States also signaled the emergence in 2008 and rapid spread of J Street, an American-Jewish peace movement that offers a counter to the American Israel Public Affairs Committee's (AIPAC) uncompromising attitudes with respect to the Israeli-Palestinian peace process and Israeli objectives specifically. Much of this internal critique of what AIPAC frames as "Jewish interests" nonetheless remains within the bounds of acceptable Zionist debate, devoting primary attention to the 1967 question.

46. Michael Lerner, "There Is No New Anti-Semitism," *Baltimore Chronicle*, February 2, 2007, http://baltimorechronicle.com/2007/020207LERNER.shtml.

47. Michael Lerner, "It Breaks My Heart to See Israel's Stupidity," *Times* (London), January 5, 2009, http://www.timesonline.co.uk/tol/comment/columnists/guest_contributors /article5446519.ece.

48. Jewish Voice for Peace, "JVP Mission Statement," http://jewishvoiceforpeace.org /content/jvp-mission-statement (accessed September 4, 2012).

49. Judith Butler, "Is Judaism Zionism?," in *The Power of Religion in the Public Sphere*, ed. Eduardo Mendieta and Jonathan VanAntwerpen (New York: Columbia University Press, 2011), 73. See also Butler, "The Charge of Anti-Semitism: Jews, Israel, and the Risks of Public Critique," *Precarious Life: The Power of Mourning and Violence* (London: Verso, 2004), 101–27. These earlier essays are also reworked into Butler, *Parting Ways: Jewishness and the Critique of Zionism* (New York: Columbia University Press, 2012).
50. Butler, "Is Judaism Zionism?," 73.
51. Ibid., 74.
52. Ibid.
53. Butler, *Parting Ways*, 214.
54. Ibid. Butler does not engage RHR explicitly, but rather her account challenges, on a theoretical level, the limits of what I call an intratraditional caretaking.
55. I similarly address how I diverge from Edward Said's conceptualization of a method for thinking about just peace in chapter 2, where I concur with his emphasis on the intricacies of relationality and the indispensability of discursive critique but likewise suggest that deploying the paradigm of secularism as potentially liberating one from embeddedness in the racism and xenophobic characteristics of ethnonationalism relies on an unreconstructed view of the "secular" and a problematic assumption that people can develop allegiance to a set of abstract constitutional principles solely on the basis of the persuasive force of such principles, themselves subjected to historicist critique. This point is relevant to the discussion of Butler's critique and reframing of the ethical discourse because her own intervention in the debate so centrally relies on Said's later work and theorizing of justice vis-à-vis the Israeli-Palestinian conflict.
56. Butler, "Is Judaism Zionism?," especially 76–90.
57. Ibid., 77.
58. See also Butler, *Parting Ways*, 74–76.
59. Butler, "Is Judaism Zionism?," 77–78, and Butler, *Parting Ways*, especially 205–24.
60. Butler, "Is Judaism Zionism?," 83.
61. Richard Bernstein, *Hannah Arendt and the Jewish Question* (Cambridge: MIT Press, 1996), 105.
62. Hannah Arendt, *The Origins of Totalitarianism* (New York: Harcourt Brace Jovanovich, 1973).
63. See Butler's discussion of Arendt in "Is Judaism Zionism?," 78.
64. Ibid., 85.
65. In extrapolating these ideas from Arendt, Butler suggests a consistency with the much later concept of "pluralization" theorized by William Connolly in his *The Ethos of Pluralization* (Minneapolis: University of Minnesota Press, 2005). See also Butler, *Parting Ways*, 114–50.
66. See chapter 1 for an extensive discussion of these earlier calls for binationalism.
67. Butler, "Is Judaism Zionism?," 80.
68. Walter Benjamin, ed., *Illuminations*, trans. Harry Zohn (New York: Schocken Books, 1969).
69. Butler, "Is Judaism Zionism?," 83.
70. See, for instance, ibid., 90.
71. Ibid., 88.
72. Arendt, *The Portable Hannah Arendt*, ed. Peter Baehr, rev. ed. (2000; New York: Penguin, 2003), 392.

336 / Notes to Page 170

73. Arendt's "Zionism Reconsidered" serves as the most pronounced context where she articulates her position concerning Zionism. In this article, Arendt expresses her rejection of the decision made at the convention of the World Zionist Organization in Atlantic City (1944). The convention concluded with a demand for a "free and democratic Jewish commonwealth . . . [which] shall embrace the whole of Palestine, undivided and undiminished." Arendt writes in reaction: "The Atlantic City Resolution goes even a step further than the Biltmore Program (1942), in which the Jewish minority had granted minority rights to the Arab majority. This time the Arabs were simply not mentioned in the resolution, which obviously leaves them the choice between voluntary emigration or second-class citizenship" (cited in Bernstein, *Hannah Arendt and the Jewish Question*, 107).

74. It is important to note that during the time of the Holocaust, Arendt did establish some affiliations with Zionist organizations. In describing those years to political theorist Hans Morgenthau, Arendt famously said: "I don't belong to any group. You know the only group I ever belonged to were the Zionists. This was only because of Hitler, of course. And this was from '33 to '43. And after that I broke. The only possibility to fight back *as a Jew* and not as a human being—which I thought was a great mistake, because if you are attacked as a Jew, you have got to fight back as a Jew, you cannot say, 'Excuse me, I am not a Jew; I am a human being.' This is silly. And I was surrounded by this kind of silliness." See *Hannah Arendt: The Recovery of the Public World*, ed. Melvyn A. Hill (New York: St Martin's Press, 1979), cited in Bernstein, *Hannah Arendt and the Jewish Question*, 101.

75. Butler, "Is Judaism Zionism?," 86.

76. Ibid., 88.

77. Notably, in her critique of Zionism and her proposal to denaturalize the Zionist interpretation of Jewish identity, Butler echoes a current of Israeli scholarship most closely associated with the journal *Theory and Criticism* published by the Van Leer Institute in Jerusalem. The work of Amnon Raz-Krakotzkin provides a prominent example of the type of scholarly engagement with the truisms of Zionism found in this venue. In his "Exile within Sovereignty: A Critique of 'the Negation of Exile' in Israeli Culture," part 1, *Theory and Criticism* [Hebrew] 4 (Autumn 1993): 23–56; part 2, *Theory and Criticism* 5 (1994): 113–32, Raz-Krakotzkin draws on Benjamin's insights in "Theses on the Philosophy of History" to reread Zionist ideology and Israeli politics. He also argues that the *galut* (exile/diaspora) concept is definitional and constitutive of Jewish identity. This approach enables a move beyond the Zionist construal of Jewish history in unitary and ahistorical strokes. In *The Returns of Zionism: Myths, Politics and Scholarship in Israel* (London: Verso, 2008), Gabriel Piterberg highlights that the Benjaminian orientation leads Raz-Krakotzkin beyond the mere reclaiming of an exilic identity: "by redeploying exile . . . against the myth that negates it (the negation of exile), what Raz-Krakotzkin aims to salvage is not just the memory and perspective of the suppressed exilic Jew of the past but, crucially, the memory and perspective of the dispossessed and excluded Palestinian of the present." Raz-Krakotzkin underscores "the ineluctable presence and remembrance of the dispossessed Palestinians vis-à-vis any collective definition of Israeli Jews" (Piterberg 116). Drawing on Benjamin's work, Raz-Krakotzkin argues that "remembrance" "is simultaneously directed to the denied Jewish past and to the denied Palestinian past. The Jew who, with a sense of identification and responsibility, turns towards the consciousness of the defeated Palestinians reclaims the principles that are immanent in the theological conceiving of *galut*, and opens up to them" (Piterberg, 122).

78. Other Jewish thinkers who are often associated with a nonnationalist ethical tradition include Gillian Rose (see "Athens and Jerusalem: A Tale of Three Cities," in *Mourning Becomes the Law* [Cambridge: Cambridge University Press, 1996], and "Is there a Jewish Philosophy?," in *Judaism and Modernity: Philosophical Essays* [Oxford: Blackwell, 1993]). Emmanuel Levinas (see his *In the Time of the Nations*, trans. M. B. Smith [Bloomington: Indiana University Press, 1994]) is often also mentioned because his call for "ethical messianism" is in line with Martin Buber's call for ethical treatment of the Palestinians without critically reflecting on why and how they transformed from "indigenous" to "strangers," toward whom one has certain ethical obligations.

79. Butler, "Is Judaism Zionism?," 89.

80. For instance, Emmanuel Levinas, *Otherwise Than Being, or Beyond Essence*, trans. A. Lingis (Dordrecht: Kluwer, 1978).

81. Hannah Arendt, *The Human Condition* (Chicago: University of Chicago Press, 1958), 243.

82. Similar decentering also takes place in theories of diaspora more broadly, with a claim that such theories may have been influenced by the supposedly paradigmatic cases of Jewish and Armenian diasporas. A current within this field of study began to challenge the hold of a centered model of diaspora, viewing "diasporas" as tentacles of a "homeland." A theorist closely associated with a hierarchical conceptualization of the relationship between homeland and diasporas is William Safran (see, for instance, his "Diasporas in Modern Societies: Myths of Homeland and Return," *Diaspora* 1, no. 1 [1991]: 83–89). Critical challenges to Safran's model can be found, for instance, in Arjun Appadurai, "Disjuncture and Difference in the Global Cultural Economy," *Public Culture* 2, no. 2 (1990): 1–24, and Paul Gilroy, "The Black Atlantic as a Counterculture of Modernity," in *The Black Atlantic: Modernity and Double Consciousness* (Cambridge: Harvard University Press, 1993), 1–40. Rogers Brubaker in "The 'Diaspora' Diaspora," *Ethnic and Racial Studies* 28, no. 1 (2005): 1–19, explains that there is also a need to resist the kind of cosmopolitanism presumed in theoretical conceptualizations of diasporas as sites that enable liberation from ethnic boundaries. Instead, Brubaker wants to recognize the conceptual tension between boundary maintenance and erosion. The "nation state," Brubaker insists, continues to function as the conceptual "other" against which "diaspora" is defined (10). See also Atalia Omer, "Rethinking 'Home' Abroad: Religion and the Reinterpretation of National Boundaries in the Indian and Jewish Diasporas in the U.S," *International Journal of Peace Studies* 16, no. 1 (Spring/Summer 2011): 23–51.

83. Caryn Aviv and David Shneer, *New Jews: The End of the Jewish Diaspora* (New York: New York University Press, 2005), 9.

84. Ibid., 15.

85. Danny Ben-Moshe and Zohar Segev, "World Jewry, Identity and Israel," in *Israel, the Diaspora and Jewish Identity*, ed. Ben-Moshe and Segev, rev. ed. (2007; Portland, OR: Sussex Academic Press, 2010), 1–6.

86. See also Leonard Grob, "Forgetting the Holocaust: Ethical Dimensions of the Israeli-Palestinian Conflict," in *Anguished Hope: Holocaust Scholars Confront the Palestinian-Israeli Conflict*, ed. Grob and J. K. Roth (Grand Rapids, MI: Eerdmans Press, 2008). Challenges to the reliance on the motif of "rescue" as a central pillar of Jewish-Israeli identity also come, perhaps unexpectedly, from Jewish-Israeli religious Zionists. A notable example is the work by Avraham Burg, *Victory over Hitler* (Tel Aviv: Yediot Ahronot, 2007). Burg, a political actor associated with the national religious camp,

argues that a captivity to fear and rhetoric about near annihilation amounts to a victory of the Nazi agenda. He calls for resisting it and reframing the meanings of Jewish Israeli identity (albeit still within the frames of acceptable Zionist discourse).

87. Gabriel Sheffer, "Israel in Diaspora Jewish Identity: A Perspective from Israel," in Ben-Moshe and Segev, *Israel, the Diaspora and Jewish Identity*, 306.

88. For an account of Israel and the American popular imagination, see Melani McAlister, *Epic Encounters: Culture, Media, and U.S. Interests in the Middle East since 1945* (Berkeley: University of California Press, 2005).

89. Ofira Seliktar, "The Changing Identity of American Jews, Israel and the Peace Process," in Ben-Moshe and Segev, *Israel, the Diaspora and Jewish Identity*, 125.

90. Ibid., 125.

91. Chaim Waxman, "Israel in Orthodox Identity: The American Experience," in Ben-Moshe and Segev, *Israel, the Diaspora and Jewish Identity*, 52–61.

92. Steven Bayme, "A Perspective from Israel," in Ben-Moshe and Segev, *Israel, the Diaspora and Jewish Identity*, 312.

93. Seliktar, "Changing Identity of American Jews," 124–25.

94. Ibid., 125.

95. There are important divergences and varieties among the various locations of Jewish life. In this work, I provide references mostly to the American Jewish community, but similar developments occur in Anglo-Saxon and other contexts (including Great Britain and Australia), demonstrating the most pronounced patterns of polarization.

96. Aviv and Shneer, *New Jews*, 16.

97. A brief perusal of university courses in the United States illustrates that Yiddish is offered in institutions as diverse as Columbia, Harvard, Berkeley, Princeton, Hebrew Union College, Brandeis University, American University, Bard College, and Arizona State University, among others. See "Academic Jewish Studies Internet Directory," http://www.jewish-studies.com/Jewish_Studies_at_Universities/USA/ (accessed January 6, 2012).

98. Aviv and Shneer, *New Jews*, 16.

99. Ibid.

100. Roni Baum-Banai, "A Haredi-Zionist Movement?," in *Shas: The Challenge of Israeliness*, ed. Yoav Peled (Tel Aviv: Yedioth Ahronot Books, 2001), 111–14 [in Hebrew].

101. Tvi Zohar, "'Lehazir Atara LeYoshna'—Hazono shel HaRav Ovadiah," in Peled, *Shas*, 191.

102. Ibid., 194.

103. Baum-Banai, "Haredi-Zionist Movement?," 116–17.

104. Ibid., 106–7.

105. For an intricate sociological analysis of the transformative and hybrid characteristics of Shas, through a comparative prism grounded in the study of social movements, see David Lehmann and Batia Siebzehner, *Remaking Israeli Judaism: The Challenge of Shas* (Oxford: Oxford University Press, 2006).

106. Homi K. Bhabha, "Introduction: Narrating the Nation," in *Nation and Narration*, ed. Bhabha, rev. ed. (1990; London: Routledge, 2000), 1–7.

107. Tamar Harmann and Ephraim Yaar, "Shas' Doviness: Image and Reality," in Peled, *Shas*, 343–71.

108. Ibid., 344–47. The kind of ethnoreligious centrism enfolded into this "revulsion" also relates to the kind of xenophobia informing the above-mentioned campaign against southern Sudanese and Eritrean asylum seekers, a campaign that centrally involved in the summer of 2012 the upper echelon of Shas (see n. 42 above).

109. Yehouda Shenhav, *The Arab Jews: A Postcolonial Reading of Nationalism, Religion, and Ethnicity* (Stanford: Stanford University Press, 2006).

110. See, for instance, Daniel Boyarin and Jonathan Boyarin, "Diaspora: Generation and the Ground of Jewish Diaspora," in *Theorizing Diaspora*, ed. Jana Evans Braziel and Anita Mannur (Malden, MA: Blackwell, 2003), 85–118.

CHAPTER SIX

1. This reality may change with the introduction (in the summer of 2010) of a pilot program that requires compulsory Arabic studies starting in the fifth grade. The rationale behind this new policy is, says Shlomo Alon, the head of Arabic and Islam education in the Ministry of Education, "to promote tolerance and convey a message of acceptance." See Alon, "Arabic Studies to Become Compulsory in Israeli Schools," *Haaretz*, August 24, 2010, http://www.haaretz.com/news/national/arabic-studies-to -become-compulsory-in-israeli-schools-1.309941.

2. For a powerful critique of the "loyalty oath," see Ahmad Tibi, "The Other Citizens of Israel," *New York Times*, October 21, 2010, http://www.nytimes.com/2010/10/22 /opinion/22iht-edtibi.html?_r=1&scp=1&sq=tibi&st=Search. See also editorial, "Down the Slope of Apartheid," *Haaretz*, January 13, 2012, http://www.haaretz .co.il/opinions/editorial-articles/1.1616388.

3. CBCNEWS, "Arab-Israeli Director Refuses to Represent Israel at Oscars," March 7, 2010, http://www.cbc.ca/news/arts/film/story/2010/03/07/israeli-film-oscars.html.

4. Marwan Dwairy—the chairman of the board of directors of Adalah (the Legal Center for Arab Minority Rights in Israel)—prefaces the "Democratic Constitution" (2007) by underscoring the intention of the writers to clarify that any effort to draft a constitution will have to involve a preoccupation not only with the question "who is a Jew?" but also with the question "who is a citizen?" See Adalah, "The Democratic Constitution," 2007, http://www.adalah.org/eng/democratic_constitution-e.pdf, 3. The question "who is a Jew?" has been central to efforts of Jewish Israelis (see, for example, the Gavison-Medan Covenant) to articulate a constitutional framework. But, as the "Democratic Constitution" states, there is a need to focus the discussion on the meanings of citizenship instead.

5. The "Democratic Constitution" of Adalah likewise addresses these issues enumerated in the Future Vision of the Palestinian Arabs in Israel. The "Democratic Constitution" is grounded in a human rights approach and primarily deploys the language of international law. For example, in explaining the sources for imagining the state of Israel as a multicultural state, the document cites article 27 of the International Covenant on Civil and Political Rights. The document also uses concepts such as distributive and restorative justice to elaborate on how a reframed Israeli state would deal with issues concerning the right to property and the restitution of private property, as well as the issue of internally displaced persons and "unrecognized Arab villages."

6. Mada al-Carmel, "The Haifa Declaration," http://www.mada-research.org/UserFiles /file/haifaenglish.pdf, 14 (accessed July 15, 2010).

7. The story begins prior to 1948, but the Naqba (disaster) is the watershed event that marked subsequent developments in a fundamental way. The "Haifa Declaration" reads as follows: "In concert with world imperialism and with the collusion of the Arab reactionary powers, [the Zionist colonial-settler project] succeeded in carrying out its project, which aimed at occupying our homeland and transforming it into a state for the Jews. In 1948, the year of the *Nakba* of the Palestinian people, the Zionist movement committed massacres against our people, turned most of us into refugees,

totally erased hundreds of our villages, and drove out most inhabitants out of our cities. Later, the State of Israel prevented the return of the Palestinian refugees to their homeland in defiance of United Nations General Assembly Resolution 194, and the UN's successive resolutions in this same regard. Although we were made citizens of the State of Israel, the state nevertheless continued to pursue its uprooting and evacuation operations after its establishment, with the result that many of us were displaced from our towns and villages, becoming refugees in our homeland. Against us, Israel has pursued policies of repression, which at times reached the level of killing, as in the case of the massacre of Kufr Qassem in October 1956. Upon us, it imposed a military regime, which remained in place until 1966. It has prevented the return of the internal refugees (internally displaced persons) to their towns and villages, and to this very day it refuses to recognize dozens of Arab villages in the Naqab, where it follows policies of land dispossession. The State of Israel enacted racist land, immigration, and citizenship laws, and other laws that have allowed for the confiscation of our land and the property of the refugees and internally displaced persons. Israel further sought to distort the identity of our sons and daughters through educational curricula that aim at educating them in accordance with the Zionist narrative and leaving them ignorant of their own national narrative. It has spread an atmosphere of fear through the Arab educational system, which is supervised by the security services. The state has exercised against us institutional discrimination in various fields of life such as housing, employment, education, development, and allocation of resources. See al-Carmel, "The Haifa Declaration," http://www.mada-research.org/UserFiles/file/haifaenglish .pdf, 12–13. Certainly, there are various educational efforts and initiatives to combat the monoperspectival approach to history articulated in the "Haifa Declaration." See, for instance, Neve Shalom/Waah-at-salaam, or Oasis of Peace, which is a village deriving its name from Isaiah 32:18, cofounded by Jewish and Palestinian-Israeli citizens in order to meaningfully engage peace education and to cultivate equality and mutual understanding between Palestinian and Israelis. Another initiative is the Open House of Ramle; see http://www.friendsofopenhouse.co.il/story-of-the-house/ (accessed January 20, 2012). There have been other educational initiatives to present Palestinian and Jewish Israeli perceptions side by side in various experimental textbooks and actual social and educational encounters. However, while encouraging valuable social interaction in a context of extreme segregation, this tends to caricature each side and reduce internal pluralities as well as lead to the presupposition that each side of this history has "equal" standing and value. In other words, it may preclude the kind of ethical reflection and reframing called for by the cohabitation model articulated in chapter 5. See, for a notable example of efforts to cultivate deep links and understanding among the groups, Givat Haviva Face-to-Face: Jewish-Arab Teen Encounters, http://givathaviva.homestead.com/ (accessed January 20, 2012).

8. Al-Carmel, "The Haifa Declaration," http://www.mada-research.org/UserFiles/file /haifaenglish.pdf, 14–15.

9. Ibid., 15–16. As the memory of the Holocaust becomes increasingly indirect, the commemoration of the Holocaust (Shoah) also transforms, with trends toward a universalistic rather than a particularist message. However, this transformation in the representation of the Holocaust in various museums is highly contested. For an overview of the changing character of remembering, see Edward Rothstein, "Holocaust Museums in Israel Evolve," *New York Times*, September 4, 2012, http://www .nytimes.com/2012/09/05/arts/design/israels-holocaust-museums-evolve-in -message-and-methods.html?pagewanted=1&tntemail1=y&emc=tnt.

10. See chapters 1, 4, and 5.
11. As'ad Ghanem, *The Palestinian-Arab Minority in Israel, 1948–2000: A Political Study* (Albany: State University of New York Press, 2001), 31–35. Ghanem is thus critical of the analytical frameworks deployed by scholars such as Yitzhak Reiter ("The Ideological and Political Structure," in *Jews and Arabs in Israel*, ed. Rami Hochman [Jerusalem: Hebrew University, 1989] [in Hebrew]); Elie Rekhess (*The Arab Minority in Israel between Communism and Arab Nationalism* [Tel Aviv: Hakibbutz Hameuchad, 1993] [in Hebrew]); and Sammy Smooha (*Arabs and Jews in Israel*, vol. 1 [Boulder, CO: Westview Press, 1989]).
12. Ghanem, *Palestinian-Arab Minority in Israel*, 35–36.
13. Ibid., 36–135.
14. Ibid., 62–63. This stream encompasses Palestinian citizens of Israel who have operated politically either through direct participation in Zionist political parties such as Mapam (the United Workers Party) or through satellite lists. The latter constituted an instrument of mobilization and control of the Palestinian vote deployed by Zionist political parties that had initially refused to accept Palestinian candidates directly in their ranks. Those lists allied with Zionist political parties and facilitated their influence and control over the Palestinian vote. The satellite lists (relevant from 1949 until 1977) that had managed to cross the electoral threshold were primarily those affiliated with Mapai (the Eretz Israel Workers' Party), the party of David Ben-Gurion, which later became the Labor Party. In 1973, the Labor Party opened its ranks to Palestinian Israelis, thereby signaling the decline of the satellite political lists and encouraging Palestinian citizens to cast their ballots directly for the Zionist political parties. For a careful study of issues relevant to the electoral behavior of the Palestinian citizens of Israel, see ibid., 40–42; Yaakov Landau, *The Arabs in Israel: Political Studies* (Tel Aviv: Maarachot, 1971) [in Hebrew].
15. Ghanem, *Palestinian-Arab Minority in Israel*, 53.
16. Nadim N. Rouhana, *Palestinian Citizens in an Ethnic Jewish State: Identities in Conflict* (New Haven: Yale University Press, 1997), 104–5.
17. Rouhana observes: "The dilemma the ADP faces is that in order to achieve material gains for the Arabs, including participation in future government coalitions, the party will have to submit to structural subordination to and the ideological exclusivity of the state. Its failure to achieve the status of even a potential coalition partner, however, merely highlighted the problem of effective parliamentary participation by Arab-dominated parties in a Jewish state" (ibid., 105–6).
18. Ghanem, *Palestinian-Arab Minority in Israel*, 50–53.
19. Ibid., 49–50.
20. Ibid., 54–61.
21. Ibid., 55–58.
22. For an example of this thesis, see Ilan Peleg and Dov Waxman, *Israel's Palestinians: The Conflict Within* (Cambridge: Cambridge University Press, 2011).
23. Ghanem, *Palestinian-Arab Minority in Israel*, 76–94.
24. The history of the Communist Party in Palestine/Israel predates the establishment of the State of Israel. For extensive accounts of the history of the Communist Party, see Ilana Kaufman, *Arab National Communism in the Jewish State* (Gainesville: University Press of Florida, 1997), and Ori Stendel, *The Arabs in Israel* (Brighton, UK: Sussex Academic Press, 1996).
25. Ghanem, *Palestinian-Arab Minority in Israel*, 66–67.
26. Kaufman, *Arab National Communism in the Jewish State*, 29.

27. Ibid.
28. Ghanem, *Palestinian-Arab Minority in Israel*, 68. Ghanem further elucidates that one key to Rakah's success was its establishment of local committees confronting a variety of concerns pertinent to the Palestinian community in Israel.
29. Rouhana, *Palestinian Citizens in an Ethnic Jewish State*, 97.
30. Ghanem, *Palestinian-Arab Minority in Israel*, 71–75.
31. Kaufman, *Arab National Communism in the Jewish State*, 112. The PLP combined the Arab Progressive Movement for Peace and the Jewish Alternative groups, advancing a single-issue ticket: self-determination for the Palestinians in the occupied territories. As for the Palestinian citizens of Israel, the PLP called essentially for binationalism or national equality.
32. Ibid., 109.
33. Ghanem, *Palestinian-Arab Minority in Israel*, 94.
34. DFPE Platform 1993, quoted in ibid., 69.
35. The DFPE and ICP have emphasized the principle of equality not only as a vision for the status of the Palestinian citizens of Israel, but also as a key organizational principle. Hence, the ICP rejected organization on an Arab national (or secessionist) basis, subsequently encouraging an egalitarian organizational framework based on Jewish-Arab/Palestinian coexistence (see Ghanem, *Palestinian-Arab Minority in Israel*, 76).
36. http://www.hadash.org.il/matzahadash.html#1 (accessed April 15, 2008).
37. See the official website of the political party: http://www.hadash.org.il/matzahadash .html#1 (accessed April 15, 2008).
38. Ibid.
39. I further discuss the legislative trend below.
40. For an attempt to illuminate the connections between the Jewish identity of Israel and its implications for the Palestinian citizens of the state and the Palestinian-Israeli conflict more broadly, see Peleg and Waxman, *Israel's Palestinians*. The authors call for the deepening of Israeli democracy through the granting of individual and collective rights to Palestinian Israelis while respecting and ensuring the right of Israel to exist as a Jewish nation-state. Hence, their thesis does not go into the possibility of reimagining Jewish Israeliness through an intra-Jewish and intra-Israeli contestation as suggested by the hermeneutics of citizenship.
41. Ghanem, *Palestinian-Arab Minority in Israel*, 120–22.
42. The first two attempts to organize on a national basis are those of the Arab Front and the al-Ard Movement. Led by Yani Yani, the Arab Front (established in 1958) focused primarily on discrimination, the return of the refugees of 1948, and the expropriation of Arab land. The movement was disbanded shortly after its inception because of what the military government perceived as subversive and unauthorized activities. Also short-lived, the al-Ard Movement was in operation in the early 1960s. It derived its ideological orientation from pan-Arab Nasserism and was subsequently squashed by the Israeli authorities, who blocked its registration as a political party (see Ghanem, *Palestinian-Arab Minority in Israel*, 95–100). The al-Ard Movement expressed an anti-Zionist agenda. It also targeted the traditional Arab political forces as obsolete and considered them puppets of the Israeli infrastructure. Its struggle was framed as a Palestinian struggle for the liberation of Palestine and the establishment of one secular and democratic state (see Stendel, *Arabs in Israel*, 109–17).
43. Ghanem, *Palestinian-Arab Minority in Israel*, 100–102.

44. Ibid., 113–16. The Sons of the Village has also focused on internal issues relevant to Arab society. It has rejected the traditional domination of the unit of the clan as well as the monopoly of local leaders who had collaborated with the Jewish Zionist infrastructure. It has additionally focused on other internal issues such as women's status and rights in Arab society. The Sons of the Village was able to generate considerable support among students and on university campuses as well as in local councils. In the 1990s, the movement disintegrated and merged into a larger political alliance—the National Democratic Alliance (NDA).

45. See the NDA's official website: http://www.crwflags.com/fotw/Flags/il%7Dbalad .html (accessed January 20, 2012).

46. Ghanem, *Palestinian-Arab Minority in Israel,* 111.

47. Azmi Bishara resigned from the Knesset in April 2007 owing to an ongoing accusation of treason during the Second Lebanon War; see Bishara, "Why Israel Is After Me," *Los Angeles Times,* March 5, 2007, http://www.latimes.com/news/opinion /commentary/la-oe-bishara3may03,0,5123721.story.

48. Michael Warschawski, "A Return to the 1950s? The Bishara Affair," Znet, June 19, 2007, http://www.zmag.org/content/showarticle.cfm?ItemID=13116.

49. Bishara, "Why Israel Is After Me."

50. Edward W. Said, "A Method for Thinking about Just Peace," in *What Is a Just Peace?,* ed. Pierre Allan and Alexis Keller (Oxford: Oxford University Press, 2006), 193. See also chapter 2, especially p. 91.

51. Ibid.

52. Ibid., 194.

53. The emergence of the Islamic Movement in Israel may be linked to the broader Islamic wave that swept the Middle East in the 1970s and reached particular fruition with the success of the Iranian Revolution in 1979; see Nachman Tal, "The Islamic Movement in Israel," *Strategic Assessment* 2, no. 4 (February 2000): 1–10. For a critical differentiation between Palestinian Israeli Islamism and a supposed broader Islamist agenda, see Peleg and Waxman, *Israel's Palestinians,* 81–102.

54. The decision to enter national politics also brought about a split within the Islamic Movement; see Raphael Israeli, "The Islamic Movement in Israel," October 15, 1999, http://www.jcpa.org/jl/jl416.htm (accessed March 22, 2007). The radical wing, headed by Ra'id Salah and Kamel Hatib, calls for separatism and refuses to recognize the right of Israel to exist; see Tal, "Islamic Movement in Israel."

55. Ghanem, *Palestinian-Arab Minority in Israel,* 126–28.

56. Shany Payes, *Palestinian NGOs in Israel: The Politics of Civil Society* (New York: I. B. Tauris, 2005), 59.

57. The designation "radical" is, of course, context dependent. As pointed out by Peleg and Waxman, from the point of view of Zionist Israelis, any critique of this framework is understood as "radical," and hence the general trends and convergences of the various threads of Palestinian Israelis are all viewed as denoting the radicalization of a minority population. See Peleg and Waxman, *Israel's Palestinians,* 78–102.

58. The National Committee for the Heads of the Arab Local Authorities in Israel, "The Future Vision of the Palestinian Arabs in Israel" (2006), 5. An English translation can be accessed at http://www.adalah.org/newsletter/eng/dec06/tasawor-mostaqbali.pdf, 6.

59. Ibid.

60. Meron Benvenisti, "Threats of the Future Vision," *Haaretz,* December 16, 2006, cited in http://www.dayan.org/kapjac/future_vision_2007_update_eng.pdf, 16.

61. Oren Yiftachel, "Take Slovakia for Example," *Haaretz*, December 21, 2006, cited in http://www.dayan.org/kapjac/future_vision_2007_update_eng.pdf, 16.

62. Yossef (Tommy) Lapid, "A State within a State," *Maariv*, December 6, 2006, cited in http://www.dayan.org/kapjac/future_vision_2007_update_eng.pdf, 17.

63. Alexander Jacobson, "How Many of These Does the World Really Have?," *Haaretz*, December 12, 2006, cited in http://www.dayan.org/kapjac/future_vision_2007_update _eng.pdf, 17–18.

64. Elie Rekhess, "The Arabs in Israel—Vision and Reality," http://www.dayan.org/kapjac /future_vision_2007_update_eng.pdf, 5.

65. Yossi Alper, "An Israeli View: A Profoundly Disturbing Document," in *Four Views on the "Future Vision of the Palestinian Arabs in Israel*," http://72.14.205.104/search?q=cache: Wbk1P65tESOJ:www.ziopedia.org/index2.php%3F, 3 (accessed January 13, 2007).

66. The Or Investigative Commission was appointed in 2002 to investigate the tragic events of October 2000 (the use of deadly force on Palestinian Israelis who had protested Israeli policies in reaction to the emergence of the Second Intifada). The commission's report articulated for the first time the systemic discriminatory practices of the Israeli state against its Palestinian citizens. However, while it condemned the violence instigated by the police, it refrained from recommending indictment of the police personnel involved. Indeed, the Or Commission addressed questions of institutional and social inequities and misguided state violence against minorities. Lapid (at the time the justice minister), who was entrusted with the implementation of the report, failed to address the commission's points. See Oren Yiftachel, *Ethnocracy: Land and Identity Politics in Israel/Palestine* (Philadelphia: University of Pennsylvania Press, 2006), 179.

67. Shimon Shamir, "An Open Letter to the Authors of the Future Vision," *Al-Sinara*, January 5, 2007, cited in http://www.dayan.org/kapjac/future_vision_2007_update _eng.pdf, 17.

68. Ibid.

69. Reuven Kaminer, "The Future Vision of the Palestinian Arabs in Israel," http://political affairs.net/article/view/4628/1/44, 1 (accessed April 13, 2008).

70. Ibid., 2. One of the drafters of the Vision, Yousef Jabareen concurs with this critique. He explains that the connection between the status of the Palestinian citizens of Israel and the Palestinian-Israeli conflict and the problem of the occupation should have been underscored in the Vision (phone interview with author, February 15, 2008).

71. Jamal Zahalka, http://www.dayan.org/kapjac/future_vision_2007_update_eng.pdf, 15 (accessed February 12, 2007).

72. Amal Helow, "View of a Palestinian Citizen of Israel," *Four Views on the "Future Vision of the Palestinian Arabs in Israel*," http://72.14.205.104/search?q=cache: Wbk1P65tESOJ:www.ziopedia.org/index2.php%3F, 3–4 (accessed March 14, 2008).

73. See also Amal Helow, "Challenging Israel to Become Democratic," January 29, 2007, http://www.bitterlemons.org/previous/bl290107ed4.html#pal2.

74. Working from the perspective of a political geographer, Yiftachel subsequently identifies a process (especially in operation since the late 1970s) that he terms "creeping apartheid." This process is "creeping" because it "is undeclared, and is being amplified by a sequence of incremental decisions about practices, such as the ongoing settlement of Jews in the occupied territories and the increasingly heavy-handed policies toward Arabs and non-Jewish immigrants in Israel" (*Ethnocracy*, 126). Yiftachel's analysis of Israel as a system of "creeping apartheid" profoundly challenges the spatial bias that delineates a clear territorial and conceptual boundary between Israel

and the territories occupied in 1967. In his study of the Israeli ethnocratic state, Yiftachel stresses the importance of looking at the entire land as one contiguous analytical unit. Yehouda Shenhav, *The Time of the Green Line: Towards a Jewish Political Thought* (Tel Aviv: Am Oved, 2010) reinforces this analysis (see relevant discussions throughout the book, especially chapters 1, 4, and 7).

75. See Yiftachel, *Ethnocracy*, especially 104–30, for an overview of the making of an ethnocracy. Some scholars argue for the diminishing hold of the colonizing project as a result of the forces of globalization, the liberalization of the Israeli economy, and the developments on the front of the Israeli-Palestinian conflict. See Uri Ram, *The Globalization of Israel: McWorld in Tel Aviv, Jihad in Jerusalem* (London: Routledge, 2008); Gershon Shafir and Yoav Peled, eds., *The New Israel: Peacemaking and Liberalization* (Boulder, CO: Westview Press, 2000); and Shafir and Peled, *Being Israeli: The Dynamics of Multiple Citizenship* (Cambridge: Cambridge University Press, 2002).

76. The National Committee for the Heads of the Arab Local Authorities in Israel, "The Future Vision of the Palestinian Arabs in Israel" (2006), 5.

77. This approach, which challenges the ethnocratic logic of the Israeli state while aspiring to balance and synthesize the ethnonational and civic aspects of a Palestinian Israeli identity, highlights Yiftachel's point about a burgeoning ethnoregionalism. See note 121 below.

78. The underlying logic of the proposed consensual democratic system is highly similar to what is known as the "consociational model of democracy," which is based on a perceived contradiction or incompatibility between the principles of democracy and majority rule. According to Arend Lijphart, the two principal characteristics of consocialism are executive power-sharing and governments composed of broad coalitions. The model of consocialism, he notes, may be especially appropriate for plural societies defined by cross-cutting social cleavages and a potential for overarching loyalties. This model is then designed to ensure the meaningful participation of minorities in policy designs and deliberations through the cultivation of segmental autonomy and political systems based on proportional representation with the possibility of decentralization (i.e., instituting territorial and nonterritorial federalism) and through securing the right of minorities to exercise veto power (even over constitutional matters). The usefulness of the consociational model to the struggle of Palestinians in Israel notwithstanding, critics of this model have pointed out that the reliance on grand cross-cutting coalitions and the exercise of the veto right yields a counterproductive, cumbersome, and slow political system. Further, this model is viewed as privileging elites as the primary agents in the formation of political coalitions and groups over individuals. For extensive work on consociational democracy, see Lijphart, *Democracy in Plural Societies* (New Haven: Yale University Press, 1984) and *Democracies: Patterns of Majoritarian and Consensus Government in Twenty-One Countries* (New Haven: Yale University Press, 1977).

79. The drafters of the document write to this effect: "The Palestinian Arabs in Israel are in need of changing their status. While they are preserving their Arab Palestinian identity, they need to obtain their full citizenship in the State and its institutions. They also aspire to attain institutional self-rule in the field of education, culture and religion that is in fact part of fulfilling their rights as citizens and as part of the Israeli state. They also seek to obtain full equality with the Jewish majority. Such self-rule within the State poses a system based on Consensual Democracy." See National Committee for the Heads of the Arab Local Authorities in Israel, "Future Vision of the Palestinian Arabs in Israel," 10.

80. The model instituted in Belgium is itself not immune to various forms of symbolic and cultural violence that could also result in direct explosiveness as in the case, in February of 2012, of the detention of young children for speaking French in the contexts of Flemish schools.
81. Jabareen is currently a law lecturer at Tel Aviv University and the University of Haifa.
82. Jabareen, "An Equal Constitution for All?," 7, available online at http://www.mossawa .org/files/files/File/An%20Equal%20Constitution%20For%20All.pdf (accessed January 20, 2012).
83. Ibid., 12.
84. Ibid.
85. See chapter 4 in this work.
86. Jabareen, "Equal Constitution for All?," 11–12.
87. Ibid., 13.
88. In their reimagining of the Israeli state, the authors of the Vision underscore: "[The] official discrimination on a national basis is the core of all forms of discrimination against the Palestinian Arabs in Israel. It is the root cause from which Palestinians in Israel suffer, individually and collectively. Thus, the official definition of Israel as a Jewish state created a fortified ideological barrier in the face of the possibility of obtaining full equality for the Palestinian Arab citizens of Israel" (National Committee for the Heads of the Arab Local Authorities in Israel, "Future Vision of the Palestinian Arabs in Israel," 13).
89. See Jabareen, "Equal Constitution for All?," 28.
90. Ibid., 25–34.
91. Ibid., 58–59.
92. Jabareen writes: "The question of the legal-formal definition of the State is central to any discussion of the legal status of the Arab minority in Israel, and it is doubly important today, in light of the debates concerning the wording of the future constitution in Israel. The dominant approach today in the public Jewish-liberal dialogue on the subject of the constitution appears to be the one that seeks to establish the definition of the State as 'Jewish and democratic' and to improve in parallel the socio-political status of the Arab citizens by securing their collective rights in one way or another. This approach might have improved the present status of the Arab minority in Israel to some extent, but it cannot achieve full equality between Jews and Arabs in Israel" (ibid., 61). Notably, when I asked Jabareen about the prospect of reimagining the basic narrative and self-perception of the Israeli state, he expressed the need to tackle first more tangible targets such as education reform. In his view, it is important to continue to operate on the level of civil society (primarily through the activities of various NGOs) to bring about incremental change. A radical reconceptualization is, accordingly, still unattainable (phone interview with the author, February 15, 2008).
93. Jabareen claims: "From the point of view of the Arab-Palestinian minority in Israel, formulating a constitution by social consent can constitute a turning point in the attitude of the State to that community. Will the State relate to the Arab minority as a full partner in the vision of Israeli society or as a junior partner, if at all? Will the Arab minority have an equal place around the decision-making table, or will it again be requested to settle for leftovers? Will the constitutional vision include all Israeli citizens, or will it exclude an entire public? These questions also make one ponder

the definition of the State in the constitution . . . The question is whether the definition of the State will describe an inclusive universal-democratic entity, encompassing all its citizens and residents, or an exclusive one, which does not include an integral part of them" ("Equal Constitution for All?," 22–23).

94. Ibid., 41. He also states: "The Jewish national institutions, as per their definition, operate for the benefit of Jews only, and therefore the legislation dealing with them grants clear advantages to the Jewish majority, the sole beneficiary of their services. For Arab citizens there are no national institutions in Israel which enjoy a legal status similar to that of the Jewish national institutions. On the contrary: popular-voluntary institutions established in the past by the Arab population in order to promote its interests in the matter of land and residential accommodation, such as the Committee for the Protection of Arab Lands, encountered a hostile attitude on the part of the State authorities" (44).

95. Ibid., 29–30.

96. Ibid., 65.

97. Ibid., 45. For a discussion of section 7A of the Basic Law, see chapter 1, 48–49.

98. Ibid., 45–46.

99. For examples of works analyzing the Zionist project using the broader lens of "settler society," see Nahla Abdo and Nira Yuval-Davis, "Palestine, Israel and the Zionist Settler Project," in *Unsettling Settler Societies: Articulations of Gender, Race, Ethnicity and Class*, ed. Daiva K. Stasiulis and Nira Yuval-Davis (London: Sage, 1995), 291–322; Scott Atran, "The Surrogate Colonization of Palestine: 1917–1939," *American Ethnologist* 16 (1989): 719–44; Ian Lustick, *Arabs in the Jewish State: Israel's Control of a National Minority* (Austin: University of Texas Press, 1980); and Joyce Dalsheim, *Unsettling Gaza: Secular Liberalism, Radical Religion, and the Israeli Settlement Project* (Oxford: Oxford University Press, 2011).

100. National Committee for the Heads of the Arab Local Authorities in Israel, "Future Vision of the Palestinian Arabs in Israel," 9.

101. Ibid., 10.

102. Ibid.

103. Ibid., 10–11. Jabareen concurs and reinforces this position when he insists that the only way to bridge the socioeconomic gaps is through the implementation of a policy of affirmative action (see "Equal Constitution for All?," 58–59).

104. National Committee for the Heads of the Arab Local Authorities in Israel, "Future Vision of the Palestinian Arabs in Israel," 14.

105. See Dorit Shippin, "The Future Vision of the Palestinian Arabs in Israel: A Meeting in NS/WAS with Prof. Aziz Haidar," March 29, 2007, http://nswas.org/spip.php?article733.

106. Helow, "View of a Palestinian Citizen of Israel," 3.

107. National Committee for the Heads of the Arab Local Authorities in Israel, "Future Vision of the Palestinian Arabs in Israel," 12.

108. Ibid., 9.

109. Ibid., 11.

110. Ibid. See also note 78 in this chapter.

111. Jabareen, "Equal Constitution for All?," 19–20.

112. Ibid., 17.

113. See Will Kymlicka, *Multicultural Citizenship: A Liberal Theory of Minority Rights* (Oxford: Oxford University Press, 1995), 26–33. Also see chapter 2 in this work.

114. Kymlicka, *Multicultural Citizenship*, 35.
115. Brian M. Barry, *Culture and Equality: An Egalitarian Critique of Multiculturalism* (Cambridge: Harvard University Press, 2001), 165.
116. Ibid., 8.
117. See chapter 2 for a more detailed exposition of these kinds of critiques.
118. In deconstructing the discourse of religious freedom, illuminating how in the early decades of the twenty-first century this discourse as it is deployed globally is but a new manifestation of colonialist and orientalist discourses and teleologies, anthropologist Saba Mahmood correctly calls into question the emergence of the judicial categories of majority and minority rights as embedded within the modernist history of state making. For Mahmood's historicist debunking of the discourse of religious freedom and liberty, see, for example, "Religious Freedom, the Minority Question, and Geopolitics in the Middle East," *Comparative Studies in Society and History* 54, no. 2 (2012): 418–46. Mahmood, like other theorists working within the genealogical tradition of Talal Asad, relies (despite her critique of modernist epistemological and ontological hegemonies) on a modernist paradigm to the analysis of modern nationalism. This introduces a form of power reductionism that then precludes the possibility of moving creatively beyond critique to a constructive hermeneutics of citizenship that may contribute to reimagining symbolic boundaries and sociopolitical structures.
119. Integrating a consideration of the status of Palestinian Israelis as a litmus test for evaluating the justness of peace platforms is in agreement with Christine Bell's insistence that peace cannot be separated from justice and should thus always be evaluated in a comprehensive manner based on universal conventions of human rights. In her comparative study of peace agreements, Bell argues that human rights protections should be incorporated centrally into the negotiation and implementation of peace agreements. By underscoring a comprehensive consideration of human rights conventions, Bell's interpretation of conflicts for self-determination shifts from "concern over who are 'the people' and what is 'the territory' to concerns around what the people are substantively entitled to." Christine Bell, *Peace Agreements and Human Rights* (Oxford: Oxford University Press, 2000), 198. But this human rights focus can once again risk ignoring lived sentiments of solidarity by completely individuating the subjects of justice, and by overlooking the relevance of a dialectic elasticity between particularistic and universalist interpretative frameworks of the standards of justice (which are also deeply particularistic; see also p. 90 in this volume).
120. Yiftachel, *Ethnocracy*, 164.
121. Ibid., 159–87. Yiftachel defines ethnoregionalism as "the mobilization of collective ethnic struggle within a state, aiming to channel resources to specific spaces; attain collective rights; preserve or build a collective identity; and challenge the state's ethnonational structure" (160). Notably, an ethnoregional agendum, Yiftachel contends, often emerges out of contexts of ethnonational domination as a reaction against such policies of ethnicization and discrimination. The Catalonians in Spain and the Flemish in Belgium represent other examples of this dynamic. Unlike separatist movements, however, ethnoregionalism is inclined to struggle for change from within state infrastructures through a synthesis of ethnonational and civil objectives.
122. This point resonates with critiques of Mahmood's work that charge it with potential cultural relativism. See, for instance, Sindre Bangstad, "Saba Mahmood and Anthropological Feminism after Virtue," *Theory, Culture and Society* 28, no. 3 (May 2011): 28–54.
123. See chapter 3.

124. One of the drafters of the Vision, Hussan Abu Baker, highlights the value of the document along similar lines: "The Jewish public should see this document as an invitation to a significant, focused public debate among equals, a debate that requires more than a small degree of tolerance and ideological pluralism." Abu Baker, *Haaretz*, December 28, 2006, cited in Rekhess, "Arabs in Israel—Vision and Reality," 14.

CHAPTER SEVEN

1. Yossi Yonah, *In Virtue of Difference: The Multicultural Project in Israel* (Jerusalem: Van Leer Jerusalem Institute, 2005), 30–31 [in Hebrew]. The term "ethno-republicanism" was coined by Yoav Peled. The latter, however, focused primarily on how this principle contributed to the exclusion of the non-Jewish Arab population from the Israeli framework. See Peled, "Strangers in Utopia: The Civic Status of Palestinians in Israel," *Theory and Critique* 3 (1993): 21–38 [in Hebrew]. Yonah applies the notion of ethnorepublicanism to suggest the limits of the definition of ethnonationalism for describing the case of Israeli nationalism. He argues that while the ethnonational argument draws the outer boundaries of the collective, thereby excluding non-Jewish Arabs, the republican argument draws internal boundaries that contribute to the marginalization of Jewish groups. In legitimating such marginalization, this republican discourse replicates orientalist and colonialist imageries and practices.

2. Ella Shohat, "The Invention of the Mizrahim," *Journal of Palestine Studies* 29, no. 1 (Autumn 1999): 7.

3. Rogers Brubaker articulates a similar critique of diaspora studies and its enduring metaphysical and essentialist view of the "nation," despite its embrace of processes of global deterritorialization of nationalisms. See Brubaker, "The 'Diaspora' Diaspora," *Ethnic and Racial Studies* 28, no. 1 (2005): 1–19.

4. Sami Shalom Chetrit, "The New Mizrahim: The New Mizrahi Radical Mizrahi Discourse and the Mizrahi Democratic Rainbow," in *Mizrahi Voices: Toward a New Discourse on Israeli Society and Culture*, ed. Gai Abutbul, Lev Grinberg, and Pnina Mutfi-Haler (Tel Aviv: Masada, 2005), 131 [in Hebrew].

5. I wish to thank my colleague Asher Kaufman for his insistence on clarifying this point.

6. Sami Shalom Chetrit, "Mizrahi Politics in Israel: Between Integration and Alternative," *Journal of Palestine Studies* 21, no. 4 (2000): 60.

7. In their analysis of competing citizenship discourses in Israel after the erosion of the republican citizenship claims characteristic of the early decades of the state, Gershon Shafir and Yoav Peled, for example, juxtapose the civic worldview of the liberal secularist and peace-seeking camp primarily held by Ashkenazim with an ethnonational view of citizenship held primarily by the religious and Mizrahi sectors. In my view, such an analysis portrays both religious and ethnic forms of protest epiphenomenally as being *really* about economic- or class-related frustrations. Shafir and Peled write: "For Mizrachim, the (Jewish) state, which has traditionally treated them as secondary to Ashkenazim, is assuming ever-growing importance now, as the republican discourse continues to decline. They seek in the state protection against the adverse effects of economic liberalization and an affirmation of their privileged status as Jews. They cling ever more strongly to the ethno-national discourse of citizenship, increasingly infusing it with religious content and, somewhat inconsistently, with demands for the protection and extension of social citizenship rights . . . it is quite obvious that the fulfillment of social rights through membership in religious institutions, in a manner similar to Islamic fundamentalism, does not allow class interests

to be properly expressed or defended. This has been strikingly attested to in the parliamentary voting record of Shas, a party that sublimated Mizrachi identity and grievances into a religious world-view." Shafir and Peled, *Being Israeli: The Dynamics of Multiple Citizenship* [Cambridge: Cambridge University Press, 2002], 341. For further critique of the kind of presuppositions that go into this analysis, see Ella Shohat, "Sephardim in Israel: Zionism from the Perspective of its Jewish Victims," *Social Text 7*, nos. 19/20 (Autumn 1988): 26–29.

8. Shohat, "Sephardim in Israel," 25.

9. W. E. B Du Bois, *The Souls of Black Folk*, ed. Brent Hayes Edwards, rev. ed. (1903; Oxford: Oxford University Press, 2007).

10. See chapter 5.

11. Shohat, "Sephardim in Israel," 27.

12. Part 3 of this chapter further explores Yehouda Shenhav's conceptual argument concerning the necessity of differentiating among the three interrelated and symbiotic identity markers—religion, nationalism, and ethnicity—in constituting and reproducing the "Zionist subject" and the ethos of Zionism.

13. Yehouda Shenhav, *The Arab Jews: A Postcolonial Reading of Nationalism, Religion, and Ethnicity* (Stanford: Stanford University Press, 2006), 173.

14. See Benny Morris, *The Birth of the Palestinian Refugee Problem* (Cambridge: Cambridge University Press, 1987).

15. Yehouda Shenhav, "The Bond of Silence," http://www.ha-keshet.org.il/english/bond_yehouda.htm, appeared originally in *Ha'aretz*, November 27, 1999 (accessed; April 20, 2008), and Shenhav, *Arab Jews*, 172–73.

16. Shenhav, *Arab Jews*, 173.

17. Yehouda Shenhav, *The Time of the Green Line: Towards a Jewish Political Thought* (Tel Aviv: Am Oved, 2010).

18. See chapters 3, 4, and 5.

19. Shohat, "Sephardim in Israel," 13–14.

20. Ibid., 14. Other scholars looking at the dynamics of Mizrahi identities in Israel reach similar conclusions. For instance, David Mahlev underscores that Mizrahi identity emerged in Israel out of the common experiences undergone by the Arab Jews in the processes of state- and nation-building—processes that relegated them to a distinct socioeconomic and culturally marginalized position, situated between Ashkenazi Israeli Jews and Arab Palestinians ("Arabs"). See Mahlev, "Reflections on Identity," in Abutbul et al., *Mizrahi Voices*, 303–8.

21. See Shafir and Peled, *Being Israeli*, 74–79. See also Shenhav, *Arab Jews*, especially 26–48.

22. The various currents of political Zionism all stressed the need to rectify the "sickly," passive diasporic existence with a physical auto-emancipation grounded on Hebrew labor of one's own soil.

23. Shohat, "Sephardim in Israel," 13–16; Joseph Massad, "Zionism's Internal Others: Israel and the Oriental Jews," *Journal of Palestine Studies* 25, no. 4 (1996): 54–55; and Sami Shalom Chetrit, *The Mizrahi Struggle in Israel: Between Oppression and Liberation, Identification and Alternative, 1948–2003* (Tel Aviv: Am Oved, 2006), 52–55.

24. For historical accounts of the immigration or transfer of Jews from Arab and Islamic lands to Israel, see, for example, Malka Hillel Shulewitz, ed., *The Forgotten Millions: The Modern Jewish Exodus from Arab Lands* (New York: Cassell, 1999), and Jiladi Jada, *Discord in Zion: Conflict between Ashkenazi and Sephardi Jews in Israel* (London: Scorpion, 1990).

25. Chetrit, *Mizrahi Struggle in Israel*, 61.
26. Shenhav, *Arab Jews*, especially 77–109.
27. Ibid., 78.
28. The moshav (pl. moshavim) is a type of cooperative agricultural settlement with an emphasis on communal work similar to that in the kibbutz. However, it differs from the kibbutz in that its members do have private property. Like the kibbutz, the moshav type of a community was initiated during Mandatory Palestine by Labor Zionism.
29. Shohat, "Sephardim in Israel," 18–22.
30. See also Chetrit, *Mizrahi Struggle in Israel*, 63–67.
31. For an interesting account of this point, see Melani McAlister, *Epic Encounters: Culture, Media, and U.S. Interests in the Middle East since 1945* (Berkeley: University of California Press, 2001).
32. Shenhav, *Arab Jews*, 110–35. Also see Moshe Krif, "Don't Touch the Property," *Haaretz*, July 1999, reprinted in Krif, *Hamizrahit: The Story of the Keshet HaDemokrati HaMizrahit veHamavak Hahevrati BeYisrael, 1995–2005* (Tel Aviv: Globes, 2005), 378–79 [in Hebrew].
33. Israeli prime minister Golda Meir is known for her infamous statement: "There is no Palestinian people."
34. Shenhav, *Arab Jews*, 132.
35. Ibid., 136–83.
36. Ammiel Alcalay, *After Jews and Arabs: Remaking Levantine Culture* (Minneapolis: University of Minnesota Press, 1993), 1.
37. Ibid., 269.
38. Ibid., 266.
39. See Laurence Silberstein, *The Postzionism Debates: Knowledge and Power in Israeli Culture* (New York: Routledge, 1999), 67. For an interesting treatment of this movement's relation to Zionism, see Boaz Evron, *A National Reckoning* (Tel Aviv: Devir, 1988) [in Hebrew]. Other accounts of interest are Elliott Rabin, "'Hebrew' Culture: The Shared Foundations of Yonatan Ratosh's Ideology and Poetry," *Modern Judaism* 19, no. 2 (May 1999): 119–32, and Yoram Bronovsky, "Ratosh, Yonathan—Poet and Ideologist," *Modern Hebrew Literature* 9, nos. 3–4 (1984): 5–12.
40. Analysts have attributed the parliamentary victory of the Likud Party in 1977 under the leadership of Menachem Begin—a victory that ended the continuous control of the Labor Party (or its predecessor Mapai)—to the protest vote of the Mizrahim. The 1977 victory was viewed as the Mizrahi "ballots' rebellion."
41. Chetrit, *Mizrahi Struggle in Israel*, 199–201.
42. As was indicated in chapters 1 and 6, since the 1970s, Israel has undergone a process of economic liberalization. This process entailed the diminishing space of social services and the decline of the hegemony of Labor Zionism and its institutional infrastructure. For interesting discussions of those processes, see Shafir and Peled, *Being Israeli*, especially 213–348; Lev Luis Grinberg, "Are Dualism and Corporatism Compatible Patterns of Political Economy? Some Implications of the Israel Case," *International Sociology* 6 (1991): 211–25; and Yoav Peled, "The Evolution of Israeli Citizenship: An Overview," *Citizenship Studies* 12, no. 3 (2008): 335–45.
43. Chetrit, "Mizrahi Politics in Israel," 54–57.
44. Chetrit, *Mizrahi Struggle in Israel*, 210–15.
45. Chetrit, "Mizrahi Politics in Israel," 57–58. For more discussion of Shas's campaign to reclaim the glory of old, see also David Lehmann and Batia Siebzehner, *Remaking*

Israeli Judaism: The Challenge of Shas (Oxford: Oxford University Press, 2006), especially 90–97. For further discussion of Shas, see also chapter 5.

46. For an analysis of the interesting dynamic between Shas "the religious movement" and its capitalization on the social cause, see Ricky Tesler, *In the Name of God: Shas and the Religious Revolution* (Jerusalem: Keter , 2003), especially 187–210 [in Hebrew].

47. Chetrit, "Mizrahi Politics in Israel," 59.

48. Shohat, "Sephardim in Israel," 26.

49. Chetrit, "New Mizrahim," 139. For more accounts of the Black Panthers, see Philip Foner, ed., *The Black Panthers Speak* (Philadelphia: Lippincott, 1970), and Deborah Bernstein, "The Black Panthers of Israel, 1971–1972: Contradictions and Protest in the Process of Nation-building," Ph.D. diss., University of Sussex, UK, 1976.

50. Matzpen, or the Socialist Organization in Israel, was established in 1962 by a group of political activists who had been expelled from the Israeli Communist Party as a result of questioning the latter's internal undemocratic practices as well as its unreflective allegiance to the Soviet Union. The group advanced a Marxist, anticapitalist, and anti-Zionist platform. As cited on the Matzpen website: "Matzpen's principal sphere of activity is the struggle against the present regime in Israel. This struggle reflects the historical interest of the working class and all others who labour and are exploited in Israel. An integral part of the struggle for socialism is the struggle for defending and improving the workers' standard of living and work conditions. As a vital means of this struggle, Matzpen works for creating independent and militant trade unions of the wage workers. These unions—unlike the *Histadrut*, which subordinates the interest of the workers to that of the Zionist state—will not be led by professional bureaucrats but by direct representatives of the workers, elected at the workplace. The struggle against the regime goes together and merges with the struggle of members of the Mizrahi communities—who for the most part belong to the exploited social strata—against economic, social and cultural discrimination; and with that of members of the Palestinian people in Israel—who for the most part constitute the most exploited stratum—against racist discrimination and national oppression by the present regime." See http://www.matzpen.org/index.asp?p=principles (accessed May 20, 2008). SIAH (the Hebrew acronym for "Israeli New Left") was established in 1968 by—among others—former members of the Communist Party. The movement focused primarily on the moral question posed by the occupation of the West Bank and the Gaza Strip as well as the gradual annexation of significant parts of those conquered territories. The movement dissolved in 1973 and had a mixed constituency, ranging from Zionists to anti-Zionists.

51. Indeed, the Mizrahi protest did not start with the BP. Other instances of protest predate the appearance of the Panthers. The Wadi Salib Uprising is routinely identified as the first instance of Mizrahi (predominantly North African) mass protest against the discriminating policies of the Israeli state. By the end of the 1950s, the formerly Arab neighborhood in downtown Haifa had transformed into a Mizrahi slum. What sparked the Wadi Salib protest in 1959 was the recognition on the part of Mizrahim of preferential treatment to new immigrants from Poland. The uprising, however, was short-lived and did not result in the emergence of a sustained mass protest, partly owing to official efforts to discredit and delegitimize the grievances. In contrast, after the Mizrahim had proved their loyalty to Israel by participating in the 1967 war, the BP was able to generate considerable momentum. But it too was short-lived. See Massad, "Zionism's Internal Others," 60–61. For an account of

individual acts of resistance to state practices vis-à-vis the Mizrahi immigrants, see Adriana Kamp, "'The Migration of Peoples' or 'The Great Fire': State Control and Resistance in the Israeli Frontier," in *Mizrahim in Israel: A Critical Observation into Israel's Ethnicity*, ed. Hannan Hever, Yehouda Shenhav, and Motzafi-Haller (Jerusalem: Van Leer Jerusalem Institute, 2002), 36–67 [in Hebrew].

52. Massad, "Zionism's Internal Others," 61–62.

53. Chetrit explains that the ability of the system to placate the resistance dates back to patterns that had been established already during the recruitment of the Mizrahim from their countries of origin. The Zionist leadership coopted certain individuals within the communities as their agents. A variety of coopted "ethnic leaders" enabled the government to generally neutralize and contain subversive winds. Chetrit argues that this pattern may explain why Mizrahi protest till the 1980s tended to come in short bursts. See Chetrit, "Mizrahi Politics in Israel," 52–53.

54. Joseph Massad, *The Persistence of the Palestinian Question: Essays on Zionism and the Palestinians* (New York: Routledge, 2006), 72.

55. Matityahu Shmuelof, "Viewing the Movie 'The Black Panthers Speak' from a Wide Angle," 2, http://www.e-mago.co.il/e-magazine/blackpanthers.html (accessed March 27, 2008).

56. With the decline of the BP, the Ohalim Movement emerged in 1973 as a theater group in one of the Jerusalemite slums (*HaKatamonim*). It presented plays with penetrating social critique. Gradually, theater "tents" sprouted in other neighborhoods. In 1977, the movement underwent a process of politicization and radicalization that resulted in the expansion of its spheres of activity. Despite its localized focus on the neighborhood, the movement appealed to and drew upon a universal rhetoric of class struggle. Hence, Chetrit terms the Ohalim "the Movement of the Universal Mizrahi Neighborhood" to express the global and universal nature of an interconnected global struggle of which the Mizrahi neighborhood constitutes only one instance. The Ohalim's primary accomplishments included building a model for autonomous management of community life, initiating public dismay and disillusionment with the Likud regime that had instigated (under the advisement of Milton Friedman) the privatization of the economy, and maintaining the radical tone of the post-BP Mizrahi struggle. Furthermore, because the Ohalim, unlike the BP, did not associate with anti-Zionist groups, it was harder for the authorities to dismiss its social and economic protest. (This also led, however, to the eventual cooptation of the group and its leaders into the "establishment.") Similar to the Ohalim, HILA may be situated in the tradition of protest dating back to the BP. The impetus for the struggle of HILA (founded in 1987) is an acknowledgment of equal access to education and equal educational services as a basic civil right. Yet HILA's official website states: "Although this right is guaranteed by law in Israel, in practice certain communities . . . do not receive the educational resources and opportunities to which they are entitled. These poor educational standards have led to high drop-out rates, increased crime and unemployment and the fragmentation of social networks, thus perpetuating the vicious cycle of poverty and discrimination which these communities experience." See the official HILA website http://www.hila-equal-edu.org.il/index.asp (accessed March 20, 2008). HILA has subsequently focused its work in development towns, Arab villages, and urban slums and has directed its advocacy at policymakers. Chetrit describes this organization as the most important agent in promoting radical political consciousness in the Mizrahi as well as Arab communities during the 1980s and 1990s because it introduced and incorporated parents into the radical Mizrahi

discourse. The work of HILA thus has contributed to deepening awareness and has empowered Mizrahi activists to engage in other radical forms of organizing. One example is the establishment of three alternative schools of Kedma in 1993, whose primary objectives revolved around developing a model for equal and undiscriminating education. These schools were designed to depart from the official Eurocentric curriculum by integrating Mizrahi, Palestinian, feminist, Muslim, and Christian narratives. Although two of the Kedma schools, which had been branded by the authorities as divisive and subversive, were forced to close, Kedma, like HILA, was able to continue in the radical tradition of the BP by offering a critique of the profound inequality between Mizrahim and Ashkenazim in Israel. For a discussion of the complexities of these social movements, see Massad, "Zionism's Internal Others," 63–64, as well as Chetrit, *Mizrahi Struggle in Israel*, especially 186–97 and 280–90.

57. Chetrit, "Mizrahi Politics in Israel," 53. Also see Chetrit, *Mizrahi Struggle in Israel*, 181–86.
58. Shmuelof, "Viewing the Movie 'The Black Panthers Speak,'" 2.
59. Chetrit, "Mizrahi Politics in Israel," 54.
60. Shohat, "Sephardim in Israel," 19.
61. Massad, "Zionism's Internal Others," 64–65.
62. Krif, *Hamizrahit*, 12.
63. See the movement's official website: http://www.ha-keshet.org.il.
64. "Main Projects of Hakeshet-2004-2005," http://www.ha-keshet.org.il/english/Main_projects.htm (accessed March 22, 2008).
65. Krif, *Hamizrahit*, 80–81 and 374–76.
66. For a poignant critique of the educational system in Israel with a focus on the role of vocational education in deepening the socioeconomic gaps between Ashkenazim and Mizrahim, see Yossi Yonah and Yitzhak Sparta, "Vocational Education and the Creation of the Proletariat Class in Israel," in Hever et al., *Mizrahim in Israel*, 68–104. The authors provide an alternative argument to the dominant frameworks offered by theorists of education to explain the disproportionate representation of Mizrahim in the vocational, nonacademic educational track. They consider the Mizrahim as captives of the modernist paradigm; accordingly, the vocational track was developed in order to accommodate the special needs of Mizrahi youth and out of recognition of their inferior capacity for academic work. Ostensibly, the vocational track was developed in the 1950s in order to absorb the masses of Mizrahim into the society. In contrast, Yonah and Sparta argue that the decision to develop vocational education was a calculated one and has had the profound systemic effect of preserving the marginality of the Mizrahim in Israeli society. It was designed to enable the development of the Israeli economy through the creation of a working class. For conventional status quo accounts of vocational education in Israel, see, for example, Reuven Kahane and Liora Star, *Education and Labor: Processes of Vocational Socialization* (Jerusalem: Magnes, 1984).
67. For example, it participated in a coalition with the Ahoti and Mossawa organizations to protest what it has termed the "Apartheid in Israeli Anthropology." In response to the 2005 annual meeting of the Israeli Anthropological Association, the coalition concluded that a recent effort to incorporate Mizrahi and Palestinian scholars into the conference was a mere cosmetic alteration rather than a paradigm shift. Hiring practices are still grossly skewed toward Ashkenazim (see Smadar Lavie, "Our Response to the 2005 Annual Meeting of the Israeli Anthropological Association,"

http://www.ha-keshet.org.il/english/Our_Response.htm [accessed May 20, 2008]). The Mossawa Center (established in 1997), or the Advocacy Center for Arab Citizens in Israel, is a not-for-profit, nongovernmental organization devoted to advancing equal status for the Palestinian citizens in Israel. Very much along the lines of the "Vision," the Mossawa Center promotes the struggle for equal social, economic, and political rights for the Palestinian citizens of the state while preserving their Palestinian culture and history. The Ahoti Movement was established in 1999 by Mizrahi feminist activists. The movement has focused on projects that promote the self-empowerment of marginalized women.

68. The Keshet website, "Education," http://www.ha-keshet.org.il/english/Education.htm (accessed April 12, 2008).

69. Yehouda Shenhav, "The History Books of Israel," http://www.ha-keshet.org.il (accessed March 12, 2008).

70. Most beholden to the modernization paradigm and to a version of American structural functionalism was the influential sociologist Shmuel Eisenstadt. See, for example, Eisenstadt, "The Oriental Jews in Israel (A Report on a Preliminary Study in Culture-Contacts)," *Jewish Social Studies* 12, no. 3 (1950): 199–222. The modernization thesis as an explanatory framework to analyze the "ethnic problem" was first challenged in the 1970s by Shlomo Swirski, who underscored the connection between the power differential between Mizrahim and Ashkenazim in Israel and Mizrahi economic and cultural dependency. Swirski, *Israel: The Oriental Majority* (London: Zed Books, 1989). In the 1980s, Shohat analyzes the Mizrahi as a victim of Euro-Zionism and thus introduces postcolonial lenses of analysis to the discussion.

71. Chetrit, "Mizrahi Politics in Israel," 62.

72. Indeed, Shohat explains the oppressive as well as misleading nature of Zionist teleology as a function of its Eurocentrism. She writes: "The notion of the unique, common victimization of all Jews everywhere and at all times, a crucial underpinning of official Israeli discourse, precludes historical analogies and cultural metonymies, thus producing a Eurocentric reading of 'Jewish History,' one that hijacks the Jews of Islam from their own geography and subsumes them into the history of the European-Ashkenazi shtetl" ("Invention of the Mizrahim," 6).

73. For a fascinating exposition of the use of the Holocaust and World War II in the construction and reconstruction of Israeli nationalism, see Idith Zertal, *Israel's Holocaust and the Politics of Nationhood*, trans. Chaya Galai (Cambridge: Cambridge University Press, 2005). See also chapter 1 of this work for a discussion of the assimilation of the indigenous Palestinians into a long list of prototypical enemies of the Jewish people.

74. Shohat, "Invention of the Mizrahim," 8.

75. See Yehouda Shenhav, "Jews from Arab Lands in Israel: An 'Ethnic' Community in the Realms of 'National' Memory," in Hever et al., *Mizrahim in Israel*, 108. See also Shenhav, *Arab Jews*, 139.

76. Shenhav, *Arab Jews*, 139.

77. See also chapters 1 and 4.

78. Shenhav, *Arab Jews*, 139.

79. Ibid., 110–11.

80. See also chapter 1.

81. Yossi Yonah and Yehouda Shenhav, *What Is Multiculturalism? The Politics of Difference in Israel* (Tel Aviv: Babvel, 2005), especially, 147–76 [in Hebrew].

82. See chapter 2.
83. Ibid.
84. See chapter 1 for an extensive review of this point.
85. Yonah and Shenhav, *What Is Multiculturalism?*, 157–58.
86. Ibid., 162–71.
87. Ibid., 173–76.
88. Shenhav, *Time of the Green Line*.
89. Yonah and Shenhav, *What Is Multiculturalism?*, 147–55. Aware of the critiques of multiculturalism, the authors nonetheless embrace multiculturalism as an emancipatory project. They recognize the possibility that subaltern identity struggles may perpetuate internal discrimination of further disenfranchised subgroups like Mizrahi women.
90. The Forum for the Study of Society and Culture, Van Leer Jerusalem Institute, "Epistemology of Mizrahiness in Israel," 20–27.
91. Pierre Allan and Alexis Keller, "The Concept of a Just Peace, or Achieving Peace through Recognition, Renouncement, and Rule," in *What is Just Peace?*, ed. Allan and Keller (Oxford: Oxford University Press, 2006), 200.
92. See also chapters 2 and 4.
93. This more integrative scheme may approximate the normative lessons derived from peace studies approaches that consider human rights provisions as the primary criteria for the evaluation of peace agreements. See Christine Bell, *Peace Agreements and Human Rights* (Oxford: Oxford University Press, 2000).
94. Shenhav, *Time of the Green Line*, 122.
95. Shenhav discusses how different religious groups and even the settlers themselves could become coalition partners for various initiatives that seem to challenge the official premises of the peace process. For instance, he discusses a Jewish-Islamic interfaith initiative in the summer of 2009 that protested the rather ironic establishment of the Museum of Tolerance in Jerusalem on the site of an ancient Muslim cemetery. The protest generated a coalition of Muslim organizations, leftist Israeli political activists, Shas leadership, and a variety of religious Jewish organizations (see *Time of the Green Line*, 158–59).
96. Umut Özkirimli, *Theories of Nationalism: A Critical Introduction* (New York: St. Martin's Press, 2000), 64. Özkirimli (see 66–84) identifies three types of primordialist analysis of the phenomenon of nationalism: "naturalist," "sociobiological" (see also Pierre van den Berghe, *Man in Society: A Biosocial View* [New York: Elsevier, 1978]), and "culturalist" (see, for example, Edward Shils, "Primordial, Personal, Sacred and Civil Ties: Some Particular Observations on the Relationships of Sociological Research and Theory, *British Journal of Sociology* 8, no. 2 [1957], 130–45, and Clifford Geertz, *The Interpretation of Cultures* [New York: Basic Books, 1973]).
97. Yonah and Shenhav, *What Is Multiculturalism?*, 70–74.
98. Ibid., 87–115.
99. The reductionist position, in effect, betrays a certain degree of affinity with that of interpreters such as John Breuilly, a modernist theorist of nationalism. Breuilly considers the nation primarily as a product and a form of politics. In the introduction to his influential book *Nationalism and the State* (Chicago: University of Chicago Press, 1994), Breuilly says accordingly: "To focus upon culture, ideology, identity, class or modernisation is to neglect the fundamental point that nationalism is, above and beyond all else, about politics and that politics is about power. Power, in the

modern world, is principally about control of the state. The central task is to relate nationalism to the objectives of obtaining and using state power" (1). This approach is reminiscent of the work of Eric Hobsbawm and Ernest Gellner, which betrays a functionalist-Marxist modernist understanding of the "nation" as an invention engineered to facilitate social homogenization, standardization, and control. For modernist theories of nationalism, see the works cited in chapter 2, note 61.

100. Anderson's famous definition of the nation as an "imagined community" already poses a challenge to the interpretation of the nation as an invention ex nihilo. Anderson writes that Gellner's insistence that nationalisms "*invent* nations where they do not exist" is flawed because "Gellner is so anxious to show that nationalism masquerades under false pretenses that he assimilates 'invention' to 'fabrication' and 'falsity,' rather than to 'imagining' and 'creation.'" Unlike Gellner's, Anderson's view of the nation as an imagined community recognizes an active and selective engagement with antecedent cultural and religious roots. See Anderson, "Imagined Communities," 9–36. See Ernest Gellner, *Nations and Nationalism* (Oxford: Blackwell, 1983); Gellner, *Culture, Identity and Politics* (Cambridge: Cambridge University Press, 1987); Gellner, *Nationalism* (New York: New York University Press, 1997); and Benedict Anderson, *Imagined Communities: Reflections on the Origins and Spread of Nationalism*, rev. ed. (1983; London: Verso, 1991).

101. See my discussion in chapter 5.

102. See, for example, Nadav Shelef, *Evolving Nationalism: Homeland, Identity, and Religion in Israel, 1925–2005* (Ithaca: Cornell University Press, 2010).

103. See chapter 2.

104. For an interesting discussion of the emergence of the movement and the deliberations involved in framing its Mizrahi and universal character, see, for example, Krif, *Hamizrahit*, 17–30.

105. Ibid., 36 (my translation).

106. Ibid. (my translation).

107. Ibid., 37–38.

108. Quoted in ibid., 38.

109. See also chapter 1.

110. Shenhav, *Arab Jews*, 13.

111. Shenhav contends: "Zionism . . . hybridizes the secular with the religious, while at the same time obscuring this hybridization, thus purifying nationalism (the very product of hybridization) and treating nationalism and religion as two separate spheres. Through the simultaneous processes of hybridization and purification, the religious is relegated to the premodern (and to the Arab Jews), while the secular is consigned to the modern sphere (and to European Jews)" (*Arab Jews*, 80). Shenhav adds that despite the symbiotic relation between those three identity markers, Zionism has attained a hegemonic status precisely because it was able to construe them as if they were distinct from one another. In effect, the logic of Zionism has relied on the basic dichotomizing of, for example, religion versus secular and ethnicity versus nationality. This dichotomizing enabled the cultivation of the system of stratified citizenship that defines Israeli ethnocracy. For further discussion, see Bruno Latour, *We Have Never Been Modern* (Cambridge: Harvard University Press, 1993), and Shenhav, *Arab Jews*, 13, 80, and 87–88.

112. Shenhav, *Arab Jews*, 183.

113. Ibid., 196–97.

CONCLUSION

1. The ethnorepublican ethos has continuously defined Israeli nationalism, despite arguments to the contrary, which have suggested that the collapse of the hegemonic control of the Labor Party in the late 1970s signaled the emergence of two dichotomous discourses of citizenship—liberal and ethnonational—implying that the liberal discourse is devoid of the ethnonational agenda. See, for example, Gershon Shafir and Yoav Peled, *Being Israeli: The Dynamics of Multiple Citizenship* (Cambridge: Cambridge University Press, 2002).

2. David Little, "Belief, Ethnicity, and Nationalism," *Nationalism and Ethnic Politics* 1, no. 2 (March–April 1995): 284–301. See the website of the U.S. Institute of Peace: http://www.usip.org/religionpeace/rehr/belethnat.html, 5 (accessed May 20, 2008). See also chapter 2 of this book.

3. Max Weber's definition of "ethnicity" as distinct from nationality and as constituting a subjective belief in a common descent is relevant to this discussion because it exposes the complexities of blood-based definitions of belonging by framing them as a matter of belief or perception. According to Weber: "'national' affiliation need not be based upon common blood . . . although a specific common anthropological type is not irrelevant to nationality, it is neither sufficient nor a prerequisite to found a nation. Nevertheless, the idea of the 'nation' is apt to include the notions of common descent and of an essential, though frequently indefinite, homogeneity. The nation has these notions in common with the sentiments of solidarity of ethnic communities . . . But the sentiment of ethnic solidarity does not by itself make a 'nation.'" See Weber, "The Nation," in *From Max Weber: Essays in Sociology*, trans. and ed. H. H. Gerth and C. Wright Mills (London: Routledge & Kegan Paul, 1948), 173.

4. William Connolly, *Why I Am Not a Secularist* (Minneapolis: University of Minnesota Press, 1999), 4.

5. Ibid., 5.

6. Ibid., 91. For another prominent engagement with the conceptual blinders of the secularist tradition with respect to its normative ground, see Rajeev Bhargava, ed., *Secularism and Its Critics* (Oxford: Oxford University Press, 1998).

7. Ibid.

8. Although there are numerous instances of hybridization—the upshot of mixed marriages and of social and political mobility, lifting Mizrahi individuals to positions of political, social, and cultural influence—the stratified social topography of Israeli society endures, and the "Mizrahi," as I explain in chapter 7, remains a critical category for analyses of systemic and cultural violence, with deep connections to the military occupation of Palestinian territories.

9. In their critique of Zionism, the Canaanite movement had this insight concerning the conceptual inconsistencies inherent in the ideology of Zionism. But its articulation of and demand for the establishment of a Hebraic identity entirely divorced from Judaism is problematic, not only owing to its call for instituting Hebraic supremacy in the region through the integration of other non-Arab minorities, but also because it is comparatively unconcerned with the latter's agency and autonomy. Thus, while the Canaanites' call for a *jus soli* principle of citizenship challenges the ethnocentrism of Zionism, it nonetheless advances a chauvinistic conception of membership. See, for instance, Boaz Evron, *A National Reckoning* (Tel Aviv: Devir, 1988) [in Hebrew]. I also discuss the Canaanite movement in relation to my analysis of the motif of reclaiming nativity in chapter 7.

10. Of course there are many more silences that I could not profile here, including those of women across the many cultural, national, religious, and ethnic terrains I touched on. A gender analysis though would only reinforce and further illuminate the normative topography I do outline in this book.

11. Ernest Renan, *Qu'est-ce qu'une nation?* (Paris: Ancienne Maison Michel Lévy Frères, 1882). An English translation is available on the website of *The Nationalism Project*, http://www.nationalismproject.org/what/renan.htm (accessed January 26, 2012).